DATE DUE

JE 11'02			
DE 17 '04			

DEMCO 38-296

THE DISENCHANTMENT OF ART

THE DISENCHANTMENT OF ART

The Philosophy of Walter Benjamin

✳

RAINER ROCHLITZ

Translated by Jane Marie Todd

THE GUILFORD PRESS
New York London

First published in English in 1996 by The Guilford Press
A Division of Guilford Publications, Inc.
72 Spring Street, New York, NY 10012
© 1996 The Guilford Press

Translation has been made possible in part by a generous grant from the
French Ministry of Culture

Originally published in French under the title *Le désenchantement de l'art:
La philosophie de Walter Benjamin* by Editions Gallimard
© 1992 Editions Gallimard

Printed in the United States of America

This book is printed on acid-free paper.

Last digit is print number: 9 8 7 6 5 4 3 2 1

Library of Congress Cataloging-in-Publication Data

Rochlitz, Rainer.
    [Désenchantement de l'art. English]
    The disenchantment of art : the philosophy of Walter Benjamin /
by Rainer Rochlitz ; translated by Jane Marie Todd.
        p. cm.
    Includes bibliographical references and index.
    ISBN 0-89862-408-8
    1. Benjamin, Walter, 1892–1940—Aesthetics.   2. Aesthetics,
Modern—20th century.   3. Art—Philosophy.   I. Title.
B3209.B584R63   1996
111'.85'092—dc20   96–26
                                                         CIP

Contents

✵

Introduction

I

The author of *The Origin of German Tragic Drama* and *Arcades,* of *One-Way Street* and "The Work of Art in the Age of Mechanical Reproduction," is one of the rare thinkers who matter in France, in Germany, in Italy, and, to a certain extent, in the United States as well; he has escaped the petty squabbling and outlived the dominant currents and fashions that have succeeded one another in Western philosophy for the last fifty years. This durability is grounded in the literary qualities of his writings, in his exceptional biography, tragically representative of the destiny of the German–Jewish intelligentsia in the twentieth century, and, finally, in his acute sense of the theoretical issues of the era, whose contemporary character has not yet been belied. Among the authors who did not live long enough to participate significantly in postwar debates, only Ludwig Wittgenstein has had a comparable destiny and remains, like Benjamin, a contemporary through and through.

This book on Walter Benjamin is concerned above all with the conceptual underpinnings of his thought. Its ambition is both to understand the internal logic of his thought and to evaluate his contribution to the disciplines he took on: philosophy of language, aesthetics, historiography. The biographical aspect will move to the background, to the extent that this is possible in the case of a thinker whose life provokes the same passion as his work.[1] Many of Benjamin's texts that deal with different writers or with historical and sociological themes will not be considered in order to focus the analysis more closely on the conceptual structure. In the literature devoted to him thus far, the richness of the Benjaminian universe has been adequately emphasized; in contrast, studies that manage to grasp the logic

1

that assures the coherence of a philosopher's system of thought across the proliferation of his writings have been rare.

Despite my profound admiration for the thinker and the individual, this book is not at all hagiographical. It rests on the principle that only a critical rereading can both link Benjamin's thinking to contemporary inquiries in philosophy and do justice to the critical imperative inherent in his own work. Until now, too many studies of Benjamin have manifested a fascination—often recognizable in a virtually uncritical imitation, encouraged, as it happens, by the seductive, assured, even authoritarian style of Benjamin's writing—that limits any real productivity of the work.

Whatever judgment they make of his thinking, all those who have taken an interest in his work and life have been conscious of the debt that a peaceful Europe with permeable borders owes to this man whom neither Germany nor—during his exile—France was able to offer decent living conditions and work; his suicide at the Spanish border has come to symbolize the situation of the persecuted intellectual. Such a feeling of debt, nevertheless, does not justify renouncing the task of a critical reading: Benjamin himself had good reasons for being wary of any idea of "celebration" or "homage." Not only does this attitude disregard what is refractory in a work, what is opposed to the constitution of a culture of reference, if only in its use of authors reputed to be subversive, but it also fails to recognize the rigorous imperative Benjamin formulated for a knowledge of the contemporary period; for him, a past determined at every instant reveals the present to itself. Benjamin's experience is not necessarily a key that will open up *our* present; his experience could just as easily conceal the issues of our time and lead to false connections. But, regardless of any application of the principles he formulated to his own work, Benjamin does not deserve the claims made on him by the defeatism of a way of thinking that makes his "failure" a model, as though the historical constellation to which he succumbed remained unchanged today, condemning us to meditate endlessly on the apocalyptic thought that the beginning of World War II and the German–Soviet pact inspired in him. In such cases, faithfulness to the memory of the victims turns to morbid imitation and intellectual laziness.

Benjamin's progeny could not be more diverse. Literary criticism and art criticism continue to refer to his writings. Theodor W. Adorno's work is a ceaseless commentary on him. Jacques Derrida and Jean-François Lyotard, even the later Michel Foucault, refer to him as often as do Jürgen Habermas and Paul Ricoeur. Both modernists and postmodernists claim him as one of their own; advocates and detractors of the Enlightenment divide up his inheritance. His most committed exegetes place his thinking on the same level as that of the most discussed living philosophers.[2] The diversity of his heirs itself poses a problem: Are *all* these claims equally legitimate? Some focus on his diagnosis of the age, others on more systematic aspects of his thinking, such as his philosophy of language or his conception of history; most merely cling to particular aspects of his research on art, film, literature, and the modern city. Benjamin's work is a gold mine of suggestive quotations, usable for the most contradictory ends. It would be pointless to try to curb these uses on the pretext that they are unwarranted or superficial; it is perhaps more productive to detail the meaning and ramifications of these expressions and formulas that have been emancipated from their author to serve the most diverse causes.

Through the diversity of forms, themes, and conceptions that overlap or succeed one another in Benjamin's corpus, the reading I propose here will trace a guiding thread. Only such a "systematic" approach will allow us to discover, behind this multifaceted critic, the philosopher who remains faithful to a few guiding ideas. Such a search for unity will not be able to avoid resorting to a certain structured *periodization*. Without such a scheme, we would either have to be satisfied with subsuming Benjamin's thought under a few abstract notions that would not elucidate any of his successive positions, or we would end up dissolving his central ideas in a multiplicity of positions drawn from an infinity of contexts.

From the beginning, Benjamin's thought is a philosophy of *language* that, as such, is linked to efforts by numerous other thinkers of the twentieth century—in particular, by Wittgenstein—to escape the aporias of the philosophy of consciousness, in particular those inherent in the privilege accorded to the cognitive and instrumental relation to reality. Benjamin was also among those seeking to put an end to the "myth of interiority."[3] He shared with Wittgenstein the ambition of bringing about "the elimination of the inexpressible in language" (*Correspondence*, 80, letter of July 1916, translation modified).[4] The "spirit" has no reality for him except in the form of symbols. In his view, language cannot be understood in terms of subject and object. But to the extent that Benjamin takes no interest in most everyday functions of language, concentrating instead on the "Adamic" and poetic function of naming, he cannot radically escape the schema of the subject who names and the object that is named. The theoretical consequences of this incomplete rupture with the philosophy of the subject makes itself felt in particular when Benjamin seeks to give a social function to his theory, that is, a function in which the naming subject endeavors to change the course of history.

Beginning with this conception of language as faculty for naming and absolute expression—as communication not with men but with God—Benjamin attempts to elaborate a theory of art: From the time of man's entry into history (or the expulsion from Paradise, according to the biblical myth), art has conserved in a privileged manner the Adamic power of naming. Benjamin's theory encompasses three periods. In the first, during which Benjamin seeks to correct the aesthetic tradition, the "theological" dominates: reestablishing the unrecognized meaning of romantic criticism, namely, its messianism; restoring the meaning of the work of the later Johann Goethe, its rejection of myth; bringing baroque allegory, the forgotten flip side of classical traditions, back from its unjustified exile.

The second period is that of political commitment and the discovery of the European avant-garde: Dadaism, surrealism, photography, and Russian cinema. Benjamin attempts to place the force of his criticism in the service of social revolution, to the point of sacrificing, in "The Work of Art in the Age of Mechanical Reproduction," the very autonomy of art: its quality of absolute expression. During this period, drawing on surrealism, he also elaborates a series of models for redeeming the integrity of human forces in the face of historical action: creative intoxication and a total presence of mind that could assure humanity mastery over history and control of a technology that, without such a redemption, is in danger of turning against humanity and destroying it through the aesthetic fascination of war.

The third period tends to restore aesthetic autonomy and the theological foundation it has for Benjamin: Beginning with "The Storyteller," Benjamin no longer accepts the liquidation of the traditional element in works of art. Finally, his "Theses on the Philosophy of History" reveals the ethical and political character of his strategy as an art critic: When he brushes history "against the grain" to reestablish concealed or forgotten meanings, he is attempting to save a threatened past, to make heard the stifled voices of history without which there could be no redeemed humanity.

Language, art and literature, history—beginning with romanticism, these philosophical themes, stemming from the Immanuel Kant of the *Third Critique* and from authors such as Giambattista Vico, Johann Georg Hamann, Johann Gottfried Herder, and Wilhelm von Humboldt, belong to the "humanities" and, more especially, to the *hermeneutic* tradition. They define the fields of knowledge that Hans Georg Gadamer's *Truth and Knowledge* in particular will grapple with.[5] Scientific knowledge and morality are characteristically excluded from them; they occupy a place secondary to that of the practice that consists in opening up the horizons of meaning, within which knowledge and norms of action will come to be inscribed. What distinguishes Benjamin from Gadamer is the former's imperative for breaking with a tradition that by privileging continuity overwhelms the decisive moments of history, moments of a liberating interruption in a course of things that, according to Benjamin, has always been in great part catastrophic. If he lays claim to a tradition, it is one that is concealed, oppressed, always threatened, and always to be reconquered. His vision of history is Manichaean. To the mythical continuity of repression that the "victors" have at all times exercised, it opposes the discontinuity of revolts that were immediately repressed and forgotten, difficult to rediscover subsequently but vital for the future destiny of freedom. It is this excluded part of history that carries the messianic hope of a reversal.

This book is less a monograph on Benjamin's thought than an attempt to render his intuitions operative for the theory of language, for the reflection on historical method, and, especially, for the theory of art, a field in which his intuitions seem to have remained productive. His philosophy of language and his conception of history are the premises and extensions of a theory of art and criticism ordered around his concept of *origin*: the actualization of certain figures from the past, crystallized especially by art and waiting to be saved from oblivion, from denial, and from misreading. Through this dedicated rescue operation applied each time to a threatened past and entering into a significant constellation with an obscure present that it can nevertheless elucidate, Benjamin attempts to revise the official history of Western civilization and its reason.

This study must begin by seeking to grasp the logic of Benjamin's writings across their disconcerting diversity. What is unilateral and nevertheless irreplaceable in this logic has to be underscored within the framework of an approach that, I hope, does not betray Benjamin's intuitions, despite the fact that I have different premises.

II

First, and this is perhaps the most critical point, it proves impossible to identify a traditional symbolic model—Judaism—that Benjamin could be linked to. When he affirms that only theological categories allow us to think about truth or history (*Origin*, 28; "Theses on the Philosophy of History," 253; "Program," 5ff.), he is not speaking in the name of a particular symbolic identity but is, rather, claiming the unconditional truth of his assertions. A thinker, whether linked to Judaism or not, should, according to Benjamin, have recourse to "theology." There is no doubt that, within the framework of a German philosophical tradition dominated by Protestantism and by tendencies he considered mythical or pagan, Benjamin attempted to put forth the critical power of Judaism.[6] But he did so not simply to affirm one identity against others but to approach a more comprehensive philosophical truth.

The Jewish identity of Benjamin's thought remained ambiguous, even for his best friend, Gershom Scholem: On the one hand, Scholem sees in Benjamin an authentic representative of the Jewish tradition[7]; on the other, he maintains that Benjamin knew almost nothing about that tradition[8] and that he was not committed enough to Judaism to adjust to the climate of the Palestine of his time.[9] How the Jewish tradition is transmitted through

Benjamin's thought remains to be clarified.[10] The least adventurous hypothesis seems to be that, even though he knew virtually nothing about the Jewish tradition, he nevertheless represented one of its characteristic attitudes, in an environment that tended to deny and conceal it.

The same is roughly true for most of those German–Jewish philosophers of the time who came from extremely assimilated families, particularly Ernst Bloch and Adorno. Others, such as Franz Rosenzweig and Scholem, made an effort to reappropriate the concealed part of Jewish tradition. Rosenzweig, the author of *The Star of Redemption*,[11] was for Benjamin the model for a new questioning of the dominant tradition of Western philosophy from within a mode of concealed thought. Unlike Scholem and Rosenzweig, however, Benjamin did not want merely to reconquer a lost *identity*—a perfectly legitimate undertaking, by the way—but, rather, through the critical and constructive contribution of the Jewish tradition, to transform Western rationalism and irrationalism in its entirety in order to arrive at a less unilateral concept of universality. We have hardly begun to inquire into the success or failure of this attempt.

The status of theology—Jewish or Christian—remains controversial in philosophical debates, even though in France in the early 1990s a "theological turn" of thought seemed to go without saying.[12] After several centuries of criticism both of metaphysics and of the theological content it conveys, a pure and simple return to metaphysical and theological categories is not automatically justified; however noble its intentions, it bears the stigma of regression. The genesis of such a return in Benjamin's thought—and in that of an entire generation of thinkers in Germany—is quite transparent: In 1914–1915, when the young Benjamin was drafting his first essays within a neo-Kantian context, the representatives of that current, which dominated in the universities, had in large part converted to German nationalism. The reference to "theology"—in fact, to an often very personal reinterpretation of the Bible and of certain mystic writings—can then be considered an attempt to safeguard the universal content of Western reason that seemed to be faltering and compromised in its secularized form.

But this safeguarding had a price: By becoming substantial once more, reason, which had become formal and procedural with Kant, could no longer rely on every subject's faculty to account for its acts and words, a faculty the subject cannot demand for itself without recognizing it in others as well. In no longer having recourse to this faculty, the subject finds itself referred back to a collective that is supposed to guarantee the validity of substantial reason.[13] Whether willingly or not, the philosopher-"theologian" is transformed into a mouthpiece for this implicit collective, which is dogmatic to the extent that it is obliged to exempt certain fundamental categories from all discussion. In seeking to save reason from the hazards of immanence, it is the philosopher-"theologian" who prepares the way for reason's subversion.

III

Walter Benjamin's thinking barely distinguishes between diagnosing the historical present and uncovering its normative bases. Several versions of his theory of knowledge exist, each elaborated ad hoc as a function of a particular research project. In each, the urgency of the historical present dictates the principles of his approach. In an essay on Kant's "What Is Enlightenment?" Foucault has distinguished between two great critical traditions stemming from Kant—the "analytic of truth" and the "ontology of contemporary reality"—that, according to Foucault, one must choose between. He himself chooses the second, which G. W. F. Hegel and the Frankfurt School, Friedrich Nietzsche and Max Weber, also embraced.[14] Benjamin also certainly chose the second, except in certain of his earliest writings, which still betray a systematic ambition. Between "On Language as Such and on the Language of Man" or "On the Program of the Coming Philosophy" and the "Theses on the Philosophy of History" the move from the "analytic of truth" to the "ontology of contemporary reality" is accomplished, even as the attempt at a rupture between "universal" and "university" philosophy is carried out.

It remains to be seen whether this opposition is pertinent in the long run, whether the reduction of the theory of knowledge to the simple function of an analysis of the present does not lead to a dissolution of philosophy into literary essays and philosophical journalism. Benjamin has contributed to the discrediting and discouraging of any systematic philosophical inquiry; nonetheless, his "ontology of the present" still had a system in the background. The "ontologists of contemporary reality" have reached the point of ignoring advances in the philosophy of language, in historical methodology, and in the philosophy of art. Such a separation between the two aspects of Kantian thought identified by Foucault seems today to have lost its legitimacy. Neither of the two traditions has emerged intact. In this context, it is useful to recall that Benjamin did not *start from* the "ontology of contemporary reality," that he maintained his contact with the university as long as possible and then his contact with the members of the Frankfurt School, who continued to respect its requirements, and that his thinking remains permeated by the systematic intuitions of these beginnings. Finally, the "Theses on the Philosophy of History," his last important work, makes explicit an ethics of universal solidarity with every creature who has suffered human violence, and the whole of his aesthetic criticism bears the signature of this ethics.

IV

We therefore need to take into account Benjamin's initial normative bases (explicit and implicit), the reasons that led him to modify them, and the risks of dissolution that followed from these modifications. The fragility of these bases lies particularly in the fact that, in Benjamin's early philosophy, the only aspect of language's function that he takes into account is that of revealing the world through the medium of the word. This privilege is in accord with his central interest in literature, but it is also responsible for certain impasses in this theory.

Viewed from the perspective of the revelation of the world through the word and the image, the historical movement of desacralization can only represent an impoverishment, whereas this same evolution appears in a different light if one takes into account the growing importance of the exchange between a proposed image and the interpretations of it that reverberate in the social space. No work of art today can possess the magic and authority of a masterpiece from the Middle Ages or the Renaissance, but a disrespectful collage that twists that masterpiece's meaning can be incomparably valuable as a revelation for *our* age. Benjamin is certainly on the trail of this idea when he situates historical evolution between cult value and exhibition value, but he once more privileges the trajectory of the artistic, or even technical, medium—in this case, film—without placing it in relation to the dynamic proper to social life. Thus, anticipating Marshall McLuhan, he formulates the primacy of the media over political initiative: In encouraging the display of the charisma of dictators, radio, television, and film seem to doom "bourgeois democracy."

By operating his "linguistic" (or "mediatic") turn, Benjamin replaces the spirit with the word, the name, or, in a general way, the medium of communication, according them primacy over the subject. But this substitution leaves intact the dual relation between the medium and the subject. To the extent that Benjamin does not analyze the ways that subjects use meanings, he remains a prisoner of the premises of a philosophy of consciousness. Hence his thinking remains centered on the traditional themes of that philosophy: the awakening from a dream state and the reappropriation of a lost origin.

The move from the spirit to the letter brings together philosophy and literature: The literary work is the quintessential medium where the spirit has no existence independent of the letter. In remaining at this symbolic "materialization" of the spirit, Benjamin has contributed to the effacement of the boundaries that make the philosopher-writer a "creator of concepts."[15]

V

For many readers, in France perhaps more than elsewhere, Walter Benjamin is seen as a *writer* first and a philosopher only second. He himself had the ambition of being "considered the foremost critic of German

literature" (*Correspondence*, 359). In the eyes of Adorno[16] and Scholem (*Correspondence*, 374),[17] however, he was primarily a *philosopher*. The context of recent (but already dated) debates, the assimilation of any conceptual philosophy to a quasi-totalitarian system of thought, and the vogue for a philosophy that would be indistinguishable from literature have favored the more "literary" approaches to Benjamin's work. The reading proposed here is philosophical. It remains suspicious of the belief in a simple reversal of an instrumental conception of language. Benjamin certainly polished all his texts as if they were literary works, and he published—in part to pay the rent, in part to satisfy his taste for writing—texts that without a doubt are literary forms: sonnets, translations of Baudelaire, childhood memories ("A Berlin Chronicle," *Berliner Kindheit um Neunzehnhundert* [A Berlin childhood in the nineteenth century]), novellas (such as "Rastelli Narrates"), travel narratives (*Moscow Diary*), dreams and aphorisms (*Einbahnstrasse* [parts of which were translated as "One-Way Street"]). It is nevertheless easy to show that even in texts of this type he never loses sight of the philosophical questions that are his own.

Undoubtedly, there is no philosophical system of Walter Benjamin. He is, in the most elevated sense of a term that is sometimes used to discredit him, an essayist. But he is not an essayist in the manner of Montaigne; the scientific imperative is not lacking in his essays. He conducts concrete research from a philosophical perspective. He has created or rethought numerous concepts that are part of philosophical debates today: notably, truth content and subject matter, symbol and allegory, aura and mechanical reproduction, cult value and exhibition value, dialectical image and remembrance.

If there is no system in Benjamin, we can nevertheless speak of a fundamental schema in his approach and philosophical conception. In the movement of historical "progress," the succession of catastrophes that moves from a fullness of meaning, impure because of its mythical character, to a poverty of meaning incarnated by abstract "meaning" and by the "reification" of the mechanically reproduced commodity, Benjamin seeks to mark the pauses where the liberating "genius" of humanity has manifested itself while pointing toward a decisive liberation. Here, art occupies a privileged place, but only to the extent that the enchantment of its appearance is dominated by the disenchantment proper to knowledge. Greek tragedy, baroque allegory, Charles Baudelaire's modern poetry, and revolutionary film are among these privileged moments where a loss of meaning is heroically converted into a symbolic form free from all pretense. This schema undergoes several versions, from the first conception of a world of Ideas bringing together authentic forms to the transformation of the critical act into political action, and from the privileging of the actualization or destruction of tradition to the remembrance of a past threatened with

definitive occultation. But the idea of rescuing a liberating act of signification, forgotten or disregarded by the official tradition, remains constant.

What can such a schema signify for a reader formed in other schools—
that of analytic philosophy, for example—who does not share the historical,
philosophical, and aesthetic passions of the European continent? That reader
will have a tendency to think that Benjamin is not a philosopher in the strict
sense of the term. Nevertheless, a rereading of Benjamin today must respond
to these analytic imperatives. By means of criticism and explication, the
rereading at work in this book attempts to identify in Benjamin the element
that can be integrated into theories of art, language, and history and into
ethics and political theory.

✳

Philosophy of Language

THE MAGIC OF LANGUAGE

Walter Benjamin considered himself a "philosopher of language" first of all.[1] Any effort to understand his thought must begin with his first works, "On Language as Such and on the Language of Man" (1916) and "On the Program of the Coming Philosophy" (1918). It is here that the conceptual choices that will determine the totality of his positions and interests are laid out. During World War I, in fact, he formulated his ideas on the particularity of baroque drama ("*Trauerspiel* und Tragödie" [*Trauerspiel* and tragedy] in 1916) and on Friedrich Hölderlin ("Zwei Gedichte von Friedrich Hölderlin" [Two poems by Friedrich Hölderlin] in 1915); he began to translate Baudelaire's *The Flowers of Evil*; and, through his contact with Martin Buber and Gershom Scholem, he defined his particular position in relation to Judaism (which would also be his attitude toward Marxism): faithfulness to an idea and a refusal of allegiance to any organization.

To understand Benjamin's interest both in art theory and in the philosophy of history, we need to begin with his philosophy of language. This philosophy has no scientific status. Rather, it is a myth through which the young philosopher attempted to define his task as a thinker. First of all, for Benjamin, language was not particular to man. *Everything* in Creation is language, and man's language is only a particular, albeit a privileged, form, one mode of "language as such." By this Benjamin means not the different forms of producing signals that exist in the animal kingdom but, rather, a linguistic implication in everything, be it organic or inorganic: "There is no event or thing in either animate or inanimate nature that does not in some way partake of language, for it is in the nature of all to communicate their mental meanings" (*Reflections*, 314). At a time when Ferdinand de

Saussure and others were elaborating a scientific linguistics, Benjamin seems to be returning purely and simply to the premodern—metaphysical and mystical—conception of the Book of the World in which everything speaks to us. But he rapidly reveals the more specific intention that guided him and linked him to a symbolist context (Stéphane Mallarmé, Stefan George); his intention is to rescue language from any instrumentalist conception: "What does language communicate? It communicates the mental being corresponding to it. It is fundamental that this mental being communicates itself *in* language and not *through* language. Languages therefore have no speaker, if this means someone who communicates *through* these languages" (*Reflections,* 315–316). Benjamin insists repeatedly on the fact that "all language communicates itself" (*Reflections,* 316) before it can become—and this is an illusion—an instrument for the communication of a particular content. He speaks of the "immediacy" or the "magical" character of all mental communication, linked to the fact that it is produced *in* and not *through* language. The magic of language lies in the fact that, of itself, it communicates in an absolute way. This magic has to be distinguished from the false magic inherent in the instrumental use of language, from which it must be liberated. Like the language of things and events, human language expresses and communicates before any intentional communication.

There nevertheless exists an important difference between the language of things and that of men:

> The linguistic being of things is their language; this proposition, applied to man, means: the linguistic being of man is his language. Which signifies: man communicates his own mental being *in* his language. However, the language of man speaks in words. Man therefore communicates his own mental being (insofar as it is communicable) by *naming* all other things. . . . *It is therefore the linguistic being of man to name things.* (*Reflections,* 317, emphasis in the original)

The difference between the two types of language lies in the addressee. Things and beings in nature communicate themselves "to man" (*Reflections,* 317). In contrast, "*in naming the mental being of man communicates itself to God*" (*Reflections,* 318). Benjamin needs God to save human language from an instrumental conception that he calls the "bourgeois conception of language":

> Anyone who believes that man communicates his mental being *by* names cannot also assume that it is his mental being that he communicates, for this does not happen through the names of things, that is, through the words by which he denotes a thing. And, equally, the advocate of such a

view can only assume that man is communicating factual subject matter to other men, for that does happen through the word by which he denotes a thing. This view is the bourgeois conception of language, the invalidity and emptiness of which will become increasingly clear in what follows. It holds that the means of communication is the word, its object factual, its addressee a human being. The other conception of language, in contrast, knows no means, no object, and no addressee of communication. (*Reflections*, 318)

God is the witness of this human faculty for naming through which humanity expresses its mental being. In this way, Benjamin short-circuits any theory of language that links human speech to pragmatic functions, which are here called "bourgeois" in a sense that as yet has nothing to do with Marxist criticism. At the time of his interest in dialectical materialism, in fact, Benjamin felt the need to reformulate his theory of language. But what he called at that time the "mimetic faculty" of man was nothing other than that same noninstrumental relationship, the materialist version of a conception of language that excluded any function of "communication" in the usual sense. "Communication" appeared only in the absolute sense of a revelation without addressee. God is here the name for that absolute nonaddressee who liberates language from all instrumental finality but also from all noninstrumental communication in dialogue.

In "On Language as Such and on the Language of Man," the function of naming makes the human being a privileged instance of divine Creation. Creation *is completed* through the linguistic activity of man:

Man is the namer, by this we recognize that through him pure language speaks. All nature, insofar as it communicates itself, communicates itself in language, and so finally in man. Hence he is the lord of nature and can give names to things. Only through the linguistic being of things can he gain knowledge of them from within himself—in name. God's creation is completed when things receive their names from man. (*Reflections*, 318–319)

From these presuppositions, Benjamin deduces a metaphysics, which he himself links to scholastics; it includes a "graduation of all mental beings . . . in degrees of existence or being" (*Reflections*, 320), as a function of the philosophical–religious concept of *revelation*. Benjamin's idea is that

the highest mental region of religion is (in the concept of revelation) at the same time the only one that does not know the inexpressible. For it is addressed in name and expresses itself as revelation. In this, however, notice is given that only the highest mental being, as it appears in religion, rests solely on man and on the language in him, whereas all art, not excluding poetry, does not rest on the ultimate essence of language-mind, but on language-mind confined to things, even if in consummate beauty. . . . Language itself is not perfectly expressed in things themselves. (*Reflections,* 321)

This hierarchy of being, established on the basis of the relation to language, elucidates the internal economy of Benjamin's oeuvre. What it aspires to, without being able to attain it, is a fusion of philosophical and religious discourse in the perfect *doctrine* (*Lehre*) that knows nothing of the inexpressible. Only such a doctrine could rest exclusively on man and language. In contrast, art, including poetry, is situated at a lower level whose language is "impure" and still acquainted with the inexpressible through the thingness of its language. Even lower on the chain of being, the languages of things are "imperfect" and "mute." Just as man in general *saves* things that are in themselves mute by naming them and thus including them in Creation, the philosopher, as Benjamin conceives it, has the task of *saving* the mental being of art and poetry by stripping away their thingness and bringing them back to the bosom of pure language. That is what the infinite work of the critic and translator consists in.

A letter to Martin Buber written in June 1916, a few months before the essay "On Language as Such," illustrates the meaning Benjamin gave both to the *magical* character of language and to the process of eliminating the inexpressible or muteness of the thing from language. Invited to contribute to the journal *Der Jude* [The Jew], Benjamin refused to make his writing a means of "influencing" the moral world and human behavior, in [placing] the motives behind actions at their disposal" (*Correspondence,* 79). He contrasted this to a different relation between word and act:

I can understand writing as such as poetic, prophetic, objective in terms of its effect, but in any case only as *magical,* that is as un-*mediated.* Every salutary effect, indeed every effect not inherently devastating, that any writing may have resides in its (the word's, language's) mystery. In however many forms language may prove to be effective, it will not be so through the transmission of content but rather through the purest disclosure of its dignity and its nature. And if I disregard other effective forms here—aside from poetry and prophecy—it repeatedly seems to me that the crystal-pure elimination of the inexpressible in language is the most obvious form given to us to be effective within language and, to that extent, through it. This elimination of the inexpressible seems to me to coincide precisely with what is actually the objective and dispassionate manner of writing, and to intimate the relationship between knowledge and action precisely within linguistic magic. My concept of objective and, at the same time, highly political style and writing is this:

to awaken interest in what was denied to the word; only where this sphere
of speechlessness reveals itself in unutterable pure power can the magic
spark leap between the word and the motivating deed, where the unity
of these two equally real entities resides. (*Correspondence*, 80, translation
slightly modified)

In his interpretation of the first chapters of Genesis,[2] Benjamin declares
that he is following the Bible in its principle by "presupposing [language]
as an ultimate reality, perceptible only in its manifestation, inexplicable and
mystical" (*Reflections*, 322). The Benjaminian interpretation nevertheless
establishes a hierarchy between the divine word (*verbe*) and the human name
(*nom*),[3] a hierarchy that could be Kantian in its inspiration. He then
comments on the rhythm of Creation in Genesis—"Let there be—And
there was—And he called":

> Therefore, language both creates and is finished creation, it is word and
> name. In God the name creates because it is the word, and God's word
> is knowledge because it is a name. . . . The absolute relation of name to
> knowledge exists only in God, only there is the name inwardly identical
> to the creating word, the pure medium of knowledge. This means that
> God made things knowable in their names. Man, however, names them
> according to knowledge. (*Reflections*, 323, translation modified)

The particularity of man is that he was not created by the word and
that he was not named. Drawing mystical conclusions from the biblical
narrative, Benjamin continues:

> In man God set language, which had served *Him* as medium of creation,
> free. . . . Man is the knower in the same language in which God is creator.
> God created him in his image, he created the knower in the image of the
> creator. . . . In the word creation took place and God's linguistic being
> is the word. All human language is only reflection of the word in name.
> Name is no closer to the word than knowledge to creation. The infinity
> of all human language always remains limited and analytic in nature in
> comparison to the absolutely unlimited and creative infinity of the divine
> word. (*Reflections*, 323)

The "Kantian" character of this distinction between the word and the
name, between a knowledge (of intellectual intuition) that creates and a
finite knowledge with access only to the "reflection" of the divine Word, is
underscored by the introduction of the passive term "receptivity" to characterize human language: "In the name, the word of God no longer creates;
it has become in one part receptive, even receptive to language. Through
this receptivity [or conception, *Empfängnis*], it aims to give birth to the

language of things themselves, from which in turn, soundlessly, in the mute magic of nature, the word of God shines forth" (*Reflections,* 325, translation modified). This passive relation of receptivity will later be found in the theory of the mimetic faculty.

As the limiting case between word and name, man's proper name has no knowledge value; instead, it is "the communion of man with the *creating* word of God" (*Reflections,* 324, translation modified). Hence the high value Benjamin always grants to the proper name: In a form that has, of course, been stripped of meaning, man has at his disposal a piece of the divine Word. Conversely, the name that man gives to things has a value of knowledge and, unlike the Kantian concept, is even directed at the "thing in itself":

> The thing in itself has no word, being created from God's word and known in its name by a human word. This knowledge of the thing, however, is not spontaneous creation, it does not emerge from language in the absolutely unlimited and infinite manner of creation; rather, the name that man gives to the thing depends on how language is communicated to him. (*Reflections,* 324–325, translation modified)

Benjamin sidesteps any cognitive *problem,* which, for him, seems to stem from a false conception of knowledge: To name adequately, one need only understand Creation; from that point on, there is no longer any problem of method. Similarly, he rejects—as he will also do within the framework of this materialist theory—any idea of a conventional character of linguistic signs: "The human word is the name of things. Hence it is no longer conceivable, as the bourgeois view of language maintains, that the word has an accidental relation to its object, that it is a sign for things (or knowledge of them) agreed by some convention. Language never gives *mere* signs" (*Reflections,* 324).

Both spontaneous and receptive, human language is for Benjamin essentially *translation*; at this point, he formulates his first theory of translation: "It is the translation of the language of things into that of man. It is necessary to found the concept of translation at the deepest level of linguistic theory. . . . Translation attains its full meaning in the realization that every evolved language (with the exception of the word of God) can be considered a translation of all the others" (*Reflections,* 325). The translation of the language of things into human language—the very operation of human knowledge—is possible because there exists a kinship between them:

> The objectivity of this translation is, however, guaranteed by God. For God created things; the creating word in them is the germ of the cognizing name, just as God, too, finally named each thing after it was created. But obviously this naming is only an expression of the identity

of the creating word and the cognizing name in God, not the prior solution of the task that God expressly assigns to man himself: that of naming things. In receiving the unspoken nameless language of things and converting it into sounds through the name, man performs this task. It would be insoluble were not the name-language of man and the nameless one of things related in God and issued forth from the same creating word, which in things became the communication of matter in magic communion, and in man the language of knowledge and name in blissful mind. (*Reflections,* 325–326, translation slightly modified)

Through this theological description of language, Benjamin does not account for that which needs explanation and which he is presupposing: namely, the relationship between language, knowledge, and things. How could knowledge progress given these foundations, and how could there have been a modern science of nature? In positing a God who guarantees the objectivity of translation, does not Benjamin avoid asking the arduous question of the functioning of language and the possibility of a translation?

An aphorism in Wittgenstein's *Philosophical Investigations* underscores the aporetic character of Benjamin's approach. By dissociating the human faculty of naming from the everyday practice of language, Benjamin grasps only a "language on holiday." Wittgenstein denounces

the conception of naming as, so to speak, an occult process. Naming appears as a *queer* connexion of a word with an object.—And you really get such a queer connexion when the philosopher tries to bring out *the* relation between name and thing by staring at an object in front of him and repeating a name or even the word "this" innumerable times. For philosophical problems arise when language *goes on holiday.* And *here* we may indeed fancy naming to be some remarkable act of mind, as it were a baptism of an object.[4]

Such questions will be at the center of the reflections of Willard Van Orman Quine (who will deny the very possibility of an objectivity of translation in the absence of God as guarantor) and Gadamer (who attempts to show the paths by which such an objectivity is nevertheless established in the use of language); such reflections are foreign to Benjamin, whose concern lies elsewhere. In "On Language as Such"—which he never published, merely passing it around to several friends, but which helped him see his own ideas more clearly and to which he was still referring in the 1930s—he seeks to ground the task of the philosopher. In a sense, the biblical text plays a role analogous to tragic texts and pre-Socratic thought in Nietzsche's philosophy: It is a primitive wisdom lost by modernity.

It is also in biblical terms that the origin of the "confusion of tongues" is reformulated, with the biblical text in fact "corrected" by the philosophical concept:

> As the unspoken word in the existence of things falls infinitely short of the naming word in the knowledge of man, and as the latter in turn must fall short of the creating word of God, there is reason for the multiplicity of human languages. The language of things can pass into the language of knowledge and names only through translation—as many translations, so many languages—once man has fallen from the paradisiac state that knew only one language. (According to the Bible, this consequence of the expulsion from paradise admittedly came about only later.) The paradisiac language of man must have been one of perfect knowledge; whereas later all knowledge is again infinitely differentiated in the multiplicity of language, was indeed forced to differentiate itself on a lower level as creation in name. (*Reflections*, 326–327, translation slightly modified)

Benjamin interprets original sin and the tree of knowledge in the same spirit. According to him, they put an end to the magic immanent in language, to the immediacy of knowledge through the name, *and* to the concrete and pertinent character of language:

> The knowledge to which the snake seduces, that of good and evil, is nameless. It is vain in the deepest sense, and this very knowledge is itself the only evil known to the paradisiac state. Knowledge of good and evil abandons name, it is a knowledge from outside, the uncreated imitation of the creative word. Name steps outside itself in this knowledge; the Fall marks the birth of the *human word,* in which name no longer lives intact, and which has stepped out of language, the language of knowledge, from what we may call its immanent magic, in order to become expressly, as it were externally, magic. The word must communicate *something* (other than itself). That is really the Fall of language-mind. (*Reflections,* 327)

External communication and the knowledge of good and evil are the same thing: "prattling," to use Søren Kierkegaard's term, which Benjamin borrows and which in this case designates in a derogatory way the necessity, to which finite beings are subject, of understanding one another and resolving their conflicts. Such a "prattling," according to Benjamin, *calls for* the judging word, the legal judgment (*Reflections,* 328). Benjamin takes it literally, going so far as to deduce from it "the mythical origin of law" that will be at issue in "Critique of Violence" and "Goethes *Wahlverwandtschaf-ten*" [Goethe's *Elective Affinities*]:

> But the abstract elements of language—we may perhaps surmise—are rooted in the word of judgment. The immediacy (which however, is the linguistic root) of the communicability of abstractions resides in judgment. This immediacy in the communication of abstraction came into being as judgment, when, in the Fall, man abandoned immediacy in the communication of the concrete, name, and fell into the abyss of the mediateness of all communication, of the word as means, of the empty word, into the abyss of prattle. For . . . the question as to good and evil in the world after creation was empty prattle. The tree of knowledge did not stand in the garden of God in order to dispense information on good and evil, but as an emblem of judgment over the questioner. This immense irony marks the mythical origin of law. (*Reflections,* 328)

The myth of original sin also explains a change in the vision of nature that Benjamin will evoke again in *The Origin of German Tragic Drama:*

> After the Fall, however, when God's word curses the ground, the appearance of nature is deeply changed. Now begins its other muteness, by which we mean the deep sadness of nature. It is a metaphysical fact that all nature would begin to lament if it were endowed with language. . . . She would lament language itself. Speechlessness: that is the great sorrow of nature. . . . Because she is mute, nature mourns. Yet the inversion of this proposition leads even further into the essence of nature; the sadness of nature makes her mute. (*Reflections,* 329, translation slightly modified)

The function of art and philosophy is to *restore* what has been altered in the Fall: the language of names. Just as the language of poetry is "partly, if not solely, founded on the name language of man, it is very conceivable that the language of sculpture or painting is founded on certain kinds of thing languages, that in them we find a translation of the language of things into an infinitely higher language, which may still be of the same sphere" (*Reflections,* 330). Benjamin's entire oeuvre is placed under the sign of this task of reparation. In the late writings, we find it in the definition of the thinker's work as seizing a signifying dimension that presents itself fleetingly and instantaneously: In that case, a "resemblance" signals our mimetic faculty of reading, or, in the words of the early Benjamin, our faculty of knowing through naming.

The Benjaminian conception of language makes the poetic function of revelation absolute, at the expense of any denotative social function. It does not confine itself to isolating and privileging the poetic function, "the aiming of the message as such, the emphasis placed on the message for its own sake."[5] *That* function of language is radically opposed to any form of "degrading" use—that is, an intersubjective and tendentious use—of the noble gift of human language. Benjamin's exegesis of the Bible reveals an idealism that is *purer* than modern idealism. He calls the misunderstanding of the religious nature of language the original sin both of modern philosophy—in the thesis of the "arbitrary sign"—and of modern society, in which "prattle" reigns and an instrumental degradation is combined with the desacralization and rationalization of the word.

In refusing the instrumental function of language and in designating language as the *medium* of all knowledge, prior to all thought and constitutive of all consciousness, Benjamin partakes in the movement of thought that in the twentieth century establishes the "linguistic turn" of philosophy. But the language that he substitutes for the "spirit" of ancient idealism does not include the language of everyday life. It consists only of the privileged and monological forms of expression known as literature and philosophy. In this sense, Benjamin brings about the linguistic turn from within idealist premises. During the same period, on grounds that were totally different but equally marked by mysticism, Wittgenstein also proposes "the elimination of the inexpressible." He opposes the false depth of an interiority beyond words, but he does so in the name of a logico-mathematical ideal of precision.[6] Later, basing himself on Martin Heidegger and the romantics, Gadamer developes a hermeneutics that is also opposed to the instrumentalist conceptions of language.[7] In his view, language is "the medium in which substantive understanding and agreement take place"[8]; hence, unlike Benjamin's conception, his is not a mystical conception that confers a messianic role to man in Creation but, rather, a profane theory of the primacy of the tradition inherent in language over reason and knowledge: "Being that can be understood is language."[9] But through their common inspiration in romanticism, Benjamin and Gadamer meet, each granting a primordial importance to the dimension of language *meaning,* in opposition to its forms of validity. Both confer a grandiloquent meaning on the concept of "truth," which goes beyond the refutable or justifiable validity of a statement: "The certainty achieved by using scientific methods does not suffice to guarantee truth."[10] Benjamin, however, attempts to preserve a minimal agreement between his thinking and the Kantian system.

THE TASK OF THE COMING PHILOSOPHY

The Benjaminian conception of language stems in essence from a German tradition that was itself nourished on mystical and kabbalistic texts (Jakob

Böhme, Hamann, Friedrich Schlegel, Novalis, Humboldt).[11] It is to that tradition—against the neo-Kantian context within which his studies in philosophy were taking place in Berlin and Freiburg—that he refers to valorize the elements of language and knowledge that could not be reduced to scientific rationality and to the concept of experience that is their correlative. Begun in November 1917, one year after "On Language as Such," and written in a rather tortuous style unusual for Benjamin, "On the Program of the Coming Philosophy" formulates the paradoxical project of a thinking founded on a religious experience and on a mystical conception of language; nevertheless, this work seeks to establish links with the Kantian critique in a more coherent way than in the earlier essay: "The central task of the coming philosophy will be to turn the deepest intimations it draws from our times and our expectation of a great future into knowledge by relating them to the Kantian system" ("Program," 1).

This entails preserving certain of Kant's central intuitions while detaching them from the context of the Enlightenment: "The question of the certainty of knowledge that is lasting" must be separated from "the question of the integrity of an experience that is ephemeral" ("Program," 1) but whose historical character Kant did not consciously reflect upon. In Benjamin's view, what is dated is a concept of experience borrowed "from the sciences, especially from mathematical physics" ("Program," 2), an experience that "in a significant sense could be called a *world-view* [and that] was the same as that of the Enlightenment. . . . It was an experience or a view of the world of the lowest order" ("Program," 2); according to him, it was even a kind of nadir of experience. Even though it may have been a condition for Kant's undertaking, that experience "whose best aspect, whose quintessence, was Newtonian physics" ("Program," 2) now had to be considered reductive and an obstacle to the development of science.

Entirely in the sense of Gadamer's conservative hermeneutics, and in fact in the spirit of that same romantic tradition, Benjamin contrasts a notion of *authority* to the concept of experience: "For the Enlightenment there were no authorities, not only in the sense of authorities to whom one would have to submit unconditionally, but also of intellectual forces who might have managed to give a higher content to experience" ("Program," 2). At this point, he is alluding to a well-established view concerning that "state of affairs that has often been mentioned as the religious and historical blindness of the Enlightenment" ("Program," 2). Benjamin does not suggest what the "great content" of experience might consist in; he simply indicates that "this experience, then, also includes religion, as the true experience, in which neither god nor man is object or subject of experience but in which this experience is based on pure knowledge. As the quintessence of philosophy alone can and must think of God . . ." ("Program," 5).

In "On Language as Such," God was the guarantor of the noninstrumental dimension of language, forbidding any relation to language as means or object. In "On the Program of the Coming Philosophy," "the task of future epistemology is to find for knowledge the sphere of total neutrality in regard to the concepts of both subject and object" ("Program," 5). That said, such a knowledge without counterpart can only be mystical if the relation is not made explicit. The linguistic turn of philosophy that Benjamin proposes remains peculiarly indeterminate:

> The great restructuration and correction which must be performed upon the concept of experience, oriented so one-sidedly along mathematical–mechanical lines, can only be attained by relating knowledge to language, such as was attempted by Hamann during Kant's lifetime. For Kant, the consciousness that philosophical knowledge was absolutely certain and *apriori*, the consciousness of that aspect of philosophy in which it is fully the peer of mathematics, caused the fact that all philosophical knowledge has its unique expression in language and not in formulae or numbers to go almost completely untreated. ("Program," 9)

This concept of knowledge, transformed through the reflection on its linguistic being, must include religion, so that

> the demand upon the philosophy of the future can finally be put in these words: to create on the basis of the Kantian system a concept of knowledge to which a concept of experience corresponds, of which the knowledge is the doctrine. Such a philosophy in its universal element would either itself be designated as theology or would be superordinated to theology to the extent that it contains historically philosophical elements. ("Program," 9)

In the addendum to his essay, Benjamin returns to this obscure relation between religion and philosophy. He speaks of a "virtual unity" ("Program," 12) between the two, already anticipated by the term "doctrine." In "On Language as Such," Benjamin did not hesitate to use his philosophical perspective to correct biblical teachings, to make them more coherent. In this addendum, he proposes to integrate knowledge relating to religion into philosophy, following an approach that recalls Hegel. Finally, he wishes to maintain the threefold nature of the Kantian system within a metaphysical "doctrine" reestablished both on the foundation of language and on a conception of experience that would assure it unity and continuity in its diversity. This once more recalls the role of the Hegelian concept of "spirit."

In opposing a concept of experience grounded in language and religion to the Kantian concept of experience grounded in the physical and mathematical sciences, while seeking to maintain the Kantian division into the three fields of logic, ethics, and a third sphere, a kind of hermeneutics destined to include "art, jurisprudence, . . . history . . . and other areas" ("Program," 8–9), Benjamin is aware that he is running into problems of coherence and is far from grasping their solution: He himself fears "that with the discovery of a concept of experience that would provide a logical place for metaphysics the distinction between the realms of nature and freedom would be abolished" ("Program," 7), something he wishes to avoid at all cost. In reality, the synthesis promised in "On the Program of the Coming Philosophy" turns out to be unrealizable, and Benjamin will not delay in abandoning the project for a system.

THEORY OF TRANSLATION

"The Task of the Translator," written in 1921 to introduce his translation of Baudelaire's "Tableaux parisiens" and published in 1923, is the first essay in which Benjamin publicly sets out his philosophy of language, since the essays "On Language as Such" and "On the Program of the Coming Philosophy" remained unpublished during their author's lifetime. In "The Task of the Translator," the theory of language is indissociable both from the theory of art and from a messianic conception of history, topics that had formed the subject matter both of Benjamin's first book, *Der Begriff der Kunstkritik in der deutschen Romantik* (The concept of art criticism in German romanticism, written in 1918–1919 and published in 1920) and of the essays "Fate and Character" and "Critique of Violence" (both published in 1921).

The essay on translation begins by reiterating the idea of the noncommunicational nature of language that was developed in "On Language and Such," this time applying it to art: "In the appreciation of a work of art or an art form, consideration of the receiver never proves fruitful. . . . Art . . . posits man's physical and spiritual existence, but in none of its works is it concerned with his response. No poem is intended for the reader, no picture for the beholder, no symphony for the listener" (*Illuminations,* 69).

In this, Benjamin is merely borrowing for his own use a fundamental credo of artistic modernity dating from the eighteenth century: "If in drawing a picture, one imagines beholders, all is lost," writes Diderot, "and the painter steps out of his canvas in the same way the actor who addresses the pit leaves the stage."[12] Here, Benjamin is drawing support from the modern metaphysics of *l'art pour l'art,* which tends to snatch art away from any social function of representation. Thus, the role of the work of art is not to establish a relation of communication of the type that prevails in everyday life; it is not subject to the constraints of a kind of speech that anticipates and elicits a response and a position for or against in practical contexts. Benjamin had already expressed this idea in "On Language as Such" by saying that language "communicates itself to God." In this essay, he asks whether a translation is "meant for readers who do not understand the original" (*Illuminations*, 69). The fact that a work of art expects from its public not an attitude of immediate "communication" calling for a reaction but a reflective attitude prepared to follow the development of the work before forming a judgment and reacting to the whole is here related to the specific function of translation, which for Benjamin is *not* that of making accessible a work that the barrier of language prohibits us from knowing.

Translation as a particular *form*, as an irreducible and irreplaceable mode of expression, thus stems from that "absolute readability" without addressee that characterizes language in general and the work of art in particular. Benjamin refuses to admit that the elements of a work of art other than those on the order of content or information—connotation, the coherence of an underlying vision of what is said or shown, or even, in Humboldt's expression, the "internal form" of language—enter into a relation between the work and the profane public. He thinks that this dimension of language communicates itself only to God; it signifies or expresses absolutely, in the absence of any "reception." He remains convinced that, at bottom, language has no profane and pragmatic function and that there is no truth in the "bourgeois conception" of language that posits the conventional character of the sign and the communicative function, which Benjamin considers purely instrumental. What is new in relation to "On Language as Such" is simply the detail provided regarding the aspect of language that eludes communication.

Translation—which in "On Language as Such" is the fundamental relation between human language and the language of things—is envisioned in this essay only from the point of view of transposing a literary work:

> What does a literary work "say"? What does it communicate? It "tells" very little to those who understand it. Its essential quality is not statement or the imparting of information. Yet any translation which intends to perform a transmitting function cannot transmit anything but information—hence, something inessential. This is the hallmark of bad translations. But do we not generally regard as the essential substance of a literary work what it contains in addition to information—as even a poor translator will admit—the unfathomable, the mysterious, the "poetic," something that a translator can reproduce only if he is also a poet? This, actually, is the cause of another characteristic of inferior translation, which consequently we may define as the inaccurate transmission of an inessential content. This will be true whenever a translation undertakes to serve the reader. (*Illuminations*, 70)

A *good* translation is as yet defined only negatively: It does not seek to serve the reader; it abandons the task of trying to communicate a meaning; it does not attempt to rival the poet in translating the inexpressible poetic.

In denying any communicative function in the work of art—which must necessarily belittle what is essential in it or what "communicates itself to God"—Benjamin is now aiming at a function of art that stems from the philosophy of history. In language, the German word *Brot* and the French word *pain* (bread) " 'intend' the same object, but the modes of this intention are not the same" (*Illuminations,* 74). In other words, the *connotations* are so different that the two words are not interchangeable:

> While the modes of intention in these two words are in conflict, intention and object of intention complement each of the two languages from which they are derived; there the object is complementary to the intention. In the individual, unsupplemented languages, meaning is never found in relative independence, as in individual words or sentences; rather, it is in a constant state of flux—until it is able to emerge as pure language from the harmony of all the various modes of intention. Until then, it remains hidden in the languages. If, however, these languages continue to grow in this manner until the messianic end of their time, it is translation which catches fire on the eternal life of the works and the perpetual renewal of language. Translation keeps putting the hallowed growth of languages to the test: How far removed is their hidden meaning from revelation, how close can it be brought by the knowledge of this remoteness? (*Illuminations,* 74–75, translation slightly modified)

Translation is thus the measuring rod that in some sense allows us to determine how much time still separates us from the messianic moment when the curse of Babel and original sin will end: "All translation is only a somewhat provisional way of coming to terms with the foreignness of languages. . . . The growth of religions ripens the hidden seed into a higher development of language" (*Illuminations,* 75).

If such a mystical conception is to be correctly preserved within a profane context, an attempt must be made to retranslate it. The differences between languages highlight the gulf of incomprehension existing between the members of a single linguistic community, a gulf due to the fact that the same words can designate "internal forms," totally different visions and meanings. But just as every language includes mechanisms allowing us to overcome such pitfalls, each language is open to the connotations and visions articulated in other languages, through an aspiration to infinitely extend understanding and include new ways of meaning. What leads to this continual pushing back of limits—which Benjamin calls a "growth" of religions and languages—is a process of exchanges and hermeneutic efforts between cultures that leave the differences between languages intact while multiplying the catwalks and seepages that allow each of them to be open to the others.[13] This may be the profane meaning of what Benjamin terms "the harmony of all the various modes of intention," a harmony that does not complete languages to constitute *one* pure language but that adjusts *each* language to another, to an infinitely extensible number of other languages, whose modes of signifying it can welcome and make its own with its own modes.

Benjamin speaks of "growth" because his philosophy of history includes a concept of nature that deals with the "life" of works. It is this life or afterlife that reveals the "translatability" of a work, a quality by which it *demands* translation (*Illuminations*, 72):

> The history of the great works of art tells us about their antecedents, their realization in the age of the artist, their potentially eternal afterlife in succeeding generations. Where this last manifests itself, it is called fame. Translations that are more than transmissions of subject matter come into being when in the course of its survival a work has reached the age of its fame. . . . The life of the original attains in them to its ever-renewed latest and most abundant flowering. (*Illuminations*, 71–72)

Translation allows us to measure the degree of recognition attained by a work whose literary quality and significance radiate beyond one cultural and linguistic sphere. As for the notion of "fame" presupposed by translation, it introduces the criterion of aesthetic value into the religious conception of history, a criterion that Benjamin does not separate from the inherent teleology of languages but that constitutes the nonspeculative kernel of his construction, to which the text constantly refers.

"The Task of the Translator" establishes the link between the life of a work and its messianic finality, based on an idea already set forth in "On Language as Such": The messianic finality of that life is the "expression of its essence," the "presentation of its meaning." "Translation," writes Benjamin, "thus ultimately serves the purpose of expressing the central reciprocal relationship between languages," a relation that is marked by "a distinctive convergence. Languages are not strangers to one another, but are, a priori and apart from all historical relationships, interrelated in what they want to express" (*Illuminations*, 72). The profound meaning of every translation is thus its anticipation, in the form of an attempt or a "germ," of the convergence between languages, a convergence that has nothing to do with the more or less exact "transmission" of a translated content.

On the one hand, then, Benjamin assigns translation a function that goes beyond the translator's aim: The translator is contributing in spite of himself to the afterlife of the work and the revelation of the relation between languages. On the other hand, by setting forth this transcendental finality, Benjamin is nevertheless dispensing advice to translators, inasmuch as he distinguishes between good and bad translations. Yet, there is an ambiguity: A translation can be good or bad *for* the transcendental finality of the growth of languages and religions, and it can be good or bad *in itself,* from an intrinsic, and especially an aesthetic, point of view. These two qualities are not necessarily congruent. But Benjamin's objective is to suggest that transcendent finality and intrinsic criteria coincide inasmuch as the task of the translator is to translate the "noncommunicable."

In the first place, Benjamin underscores the idea that an "exactitude" of translation is immaterial in any case. Works do not remain the same across time: "For just as the tenor and the significance of the great works of literature undergo a complete transformation over the centuries, the mother tongue of the translator is transformed as well. While a poet's words endure in his own language, even the greatest translation is destined to become part of the growth of its own language and eventually to be absorbed by its renewal" (*Illuminations,* 73). The function of translation is to observe this growth of languages and to "watch . . . over the maturing process of the original language and the birth pangs of its own" (*Illuminations,* 73). We can conclude from this that a translation is good to the extent that it is up to the task of this historical process and bad to the extent that it does not take the state of languages into account.

Benjamin then focuses more closely on the noncommunicable, "the primary concern of the genuine translator [which] remains elusive" (*Illuminations,* 75). Instead of determining it positively according to its structure (for example, as connotation or as a component of the particular vision of a work or a language), he defines it negatively as "the element in a translation . . . that does not lend itself to translation" (*Illuminations,* 75). He does not indicate the structural reason for this: the fact that only in exceptional cases can the translated connotation or vision render the rich connotations of the original. Benjamin immediately links this untransmittable element to his philosophy of history: In his view, what cannot be retranslated refers to *another* language, a "higher language" than that incarnated in general by translation. This reference is expressed through the loose relation between "content" (*Gehalt*) and language: "While content and language form a certain unity in the original, like a fruit and its skin, the language of the translation envelops its content like a royal robe with ample folds. For it signifies a more exalted language than its own and thus remains unsuited to its content, overpowering and alien" (*Illuminations,* 75).

The difference between the original and the translation in this relation is therefore that between a natural and an artificial link, between an organic and an inorganic connection. But instead of concluding that a text is problematic when the artificial and inorganic nature of this relation "smells of" translation, Benjamin sees a merit in such a text, inasmuch as the language of translation (which, because of its fragility, cannot be retranslated) is closer to the messianic end of language. Every translation "ironically, transplants the original into a more definitive linguistic realm since it can no longer be displaced by a secondary rendering" (*Illuminations*, 75). Benjamin explains that he is using the word "ironically" in the sense of the romantics, to whom, in fact, he has just devoted his thesis on the concept of art criticism: "They, more than any others, were gifted with an insight into the life of literary works which has its highest testimony in translation. To be sure, they hardly recognized translation in this sense, but devoted their entire attention to criticism, another, if lesser, factor in the continued life of literary works" (*Illuminations*, 76). Criticism and translation are messianic functions in the process of history; they work to restore the purity of the name.

Taking into account the fact that translation is a form apart, a form of autonomous *expression* defined by this relation to the messianic end of languages, Benjamin then formulates what he considers "the task of the translator," a task that until that time translators had not been conscious of: The task of the translator "consists in finding that intended effect [*Intention*] upon the language into which he is translating which produces in it the echo of the original" (*Illuminations*, 76). Unlike literary creation, translation must therefore be directed "at language as such, at its totality," in order to bring about the "reverberation" of the original. "Echo" and "reverberation" indicate the "derivative," "ideational" character of the language of translations; as for the matter of finding in the target language (as a general rule, the translator's mother tongue) the intended effect that awakens the echo of the original, that effort amounts to conferring on one language connotations and a particular vision that are theoretically foreign to it. In other words, it is a question of enriching the rhetorical (metaphorical or metonymic) potential of the language into which one is translating.

But that is not the aspect that interests Benjamin. The aesthetic or rhetorical accuracy of translation is a function of truth. The ideational character of the intentional effect of translation is *philosophical:* It aims at "true language," the "language of truth": "For the great motif of integrating many tongues into one true language is at work" (*Illuminations*, 77). Through this work, languages, supplemented and reconciled in their mode of signification, harmonize. If there is such a thing as a language of truth, the tensionless and even silent depository of the ultimate truth which all thought strives for, then this language of truth is—the true language. And this very language, whose divination and description is the only perfection a philosopher can hope for, is concealed in concentrated fashion in translations. (*Illuminations*, 77)

Translation is situated "midway between poetry and doctrine [*Lehre*]" (*Illuminations*, 77), exactly where, in the essay on baroque drama, criticism is located. Nor, like translation, can criticism anticipate the true doctrine where philosophy and theology intermingle. From the philosophical point of view, therefore, criticism and translation are practiced with an eye toward doctrine. It remains to be seen whether this connection between philosophy and translation is pertinent and beneficial to either of them, whether that theory accounts for what is involved in translation, which may, after all, have something to do with "readers who do not understand the original" and to whom it is necessary to "communicate" more than a simple discursive content.

The difficulty of translation is defined as an exalted task: "ripening the seed of pure language" (*Illuminations*, 77). The task of the translator is to give up restoring meaning in order to "lovingly and in detail incorporate the original's mode of signification, thus making both the original and the translation recognizable as fragments of a greater language, just as fragments are part of a vessel" (*Illuminations*, 78). Benjamin adds that "it is the task of the translator to release in his own language that pure language which is under the spell of another, to liberate the language imprisoned in a work in his re-creation of that work" (*Illuminations*, 80).

Translation would thus consist in aiming not at the singularity of a work but, rather, at the totality of a language, the universality of a way of signifying. Benjamin erects what is a secondary effect of translation into a principal aim: In the interest of pure language, the translator must break through "decayed barriers of his own language. Luther, Voss, Hölderlin, and George have extended the boundaries of the German language" (*Illuminations*, 80). But what Benjamin designates as "pure language" is the always-unique solution to a problem posed by the limits of the target language, and these limits are pushed back using the capacities inherent within that language. As a result, what is at issue is not a "pure" language but a broadening of the possibilities actualized in *each* language treated separately. In a manner characteristic of his entire aesthetic, Benjamin confuses the level of the *imperative* inherent in artistic activity with that of its *function* in the historical process; he confuses "good translation" with what contributes to the "growth of languages" toward their messianic end, the effacement of

Babelian confusion. These two merits can coincide only indirectly, through the growing suppleness of a language that is more and more "welcoming" of foreign ways of signifying.

Through the exercise of translation, every language tends to become more and more universal. We need to distinguish the possibilities of signifying that are thus acquired from "Grecisms," "Germanisms," "Gallicisms," or "Anglicisms," which Benjamin indirectly defends in holding up Hölderlin's translations of Sophocles as a model: "In them the harmony of the languages is so profound that sense is touched by language only the way an aeolian harp is touched by the wind" (*Illuminations,* 81). Benjamin certainly sees the risk of this kind of translation: "The gates of a language thus expanded and modified may slam shut and enclose the translator with silence" (*Illuminations,* 81). But two other passages at the end of the text show that he does not recognize the reasons for this risk. By confusing aesthetic quality and doctrinal truth, which in his view are united by their common refusal of a "meaning" to be communicated, he is no longer able to distinguish the literary value of a highly idiomatic text, which challenges translation as such, from the text's truth value, which hardly poses an obstacle for the translator.

> The lower the quality and distinction of [the original's] language, the larger the extent to which it is information, the less fertile a field is it for translation, until the utter preponderance of content, far from being the lever for a translation of distinctive mode, renders it impossible. The higher the level of a work, the more does it remain translatable even if its meaning is touched upon only fleetingly. (*Illuminations,* 81)

If translation is a fertile field, it is so in view of a "translation of distinctive mode" and hence of a *literary* quality, an *aesthetic* quality in the broad sense. Thus Benjamin's assertion is hardly disputable. In contrast, when he addresses the problem of translating a sacred text, the question of some literary quality able to bring about a figural *intensity* of linguistic creation even in translation no longer arises. Alluding to the disappearance of meaning in Hölderlin's Hellenizing translation, Benjamin writes: "Where a text is identical with truth or dogma, where it is supposed to be 'the true language' in all its literalness and without the mediation of meaning, this text is unconditionally translatable" (*Illuminations,* 82).

According to Benjamin, then, and in conformity with his theory of language as absolute readability independent of any communication of a meaning, a doctrinal text transmits truth through its pure literalness. Such is the logic of the Benjaminian construction, close to Judaic interpretation in general—and the kabbalistic interpretation in particular—of the *letter:* This logic links the *revelation* that the language of the sacred text bears with the more limited revelation that the language of great poetic works offers. But the word "revelation" is ambiguous here: What a literary work reveals to us is not truth in the sense that a doctrine articulates it; otherwise, all works in their infinite diversity would have to converge toward a single doctrinal truth. Because he links the sacred *word* and the poetic *word,* both stemming from Adamic naming, Benjamin can speak grandiloquently of the "truth content" in works of art, thus confusing aesthetic value and cognitive value. But what confers translatability on the great literary works is not their truth value but their literary quality of intensity in the broad sense and of significant coherence, such that even an impoverished translation retains part of the work's connotations. It is this idiomatic intensity, this constitutive metaphoricity, that is difficult to translate, not the discursive truth of the doctrinal text, which is linked to no specific aesthetic quality. The literalness of the sacred text, the sacralization of its *letter* rather than its spirit, does not coincide with aesthetic or tropic literalness, with its "literariness." Benjamin's essay, however, ends by identifying the two, assimilating literary translatability and the literal translatability of the sacred text: "For to some degree all great texts contain their potential translation between the lines; this is true to the highest degree of sacred writings. The interlinear version of the Scriptures is the prototype or ideal of all translation" (*Illuminations,* 82). This claim neglects a difference to which the literary text owes its freedom from any doctrine, from anything sacred, a freedom to which *The Divine Comedy* itself owes its blasphemous character, which is precisely at the origin of the idiomatic singularity of poetic texts, that which in them resists translation.

Benjamin seems to be paying tribute here to the linguistic speculation developed by eighteenth-century thinkers, in particular, Jean-Jacques Rousseau and Hamann. "Figural language was the first to be born," writes Rousseau in his *Essai sur l'origine des langues* (Essay on the origin of languages); "the literal sense came only later. . . . At first, everyone spoke only in poetry; they thought to reason only much later."[14] Here again, the concern is with profane texts, but in this case with autonomous expression stripped of instrumental meaning. It was Hamann who, by introducing kabbalistic themes into the debate of the German Enlightenment, conferred on that original language the status of a sacred text: In his view, "speaking is translating—from an angelic language to a human idiom," and "poetry," sacralized in this way, "is the mother tongue of the human race."[15] In contrast to profane reason, which breaks with the religious and metaphysical tradition in order to accept only what is justified by the pertinence of argument, Benjamin's position seeks to preserve the letter of the tradition, the absolute expression of a way of signifying that must be preserved for the messianic time of the original language's recomposition. In 1938 he said that Kafka "sacrificed truth for the sake of clinging to transmissibility" (*Correspondence*, 565, letter of 12 June). Without going so far as to sacrifice truth, Benjamin seeks to save it by transmitting its literalness.

THEORY OF IDEAS

Ideas and Names

The idea of absolute readability in "The Task of the Translator" shows the close link in Benjamin's thought between a philosophy of language and a theory of art. The language of great literary works gives him a base on which to establish a continuity between language in general, the sacred or doctrinal text, the work of art, and philosophy. *The Origin of German Tragic Drama* is the most explicit, coherent, and comprehensive presentation of this early philosophy of Benjamin's.

In the introduction to this book, he presents his conception of language as a theory of ideas. "Ideas are the object of [philosophical] investigation. If representation is to stake its claim as the real methodology of the philosophical treatise, then it must be the representation of ideas" (*Origin*, 29). Like the name as it was defined in "On Language as Such," the idea is characterized by the fact that it cannot "be taken possession of" (*Origin*, 29). It is not simply an object of knowledge, since "knowledge is possession" (*Origin*, 29). The idea is the correlative of a theory that defines truth as a manifestation or revelation transcending the cognitive dimension of language. This explains the status of truth in "The Task of the Translator": Truth, "bodied forth in the dance of represented ideas, resists being projected, by whatever means, into the realm of knowledge" (*Origin*, 29). As the essay on translation demonstrates, this dance of ideas is constituted by the exemplary works of literature.

Instead of being appropriated by knowledge, truth can only "present itself." Like Heidegger,[16] Benjamin holds that truth originates not in the concept but in being: "As a unity of being rather than a conceptual unity, truth is beyond all question. Whereas the concept is a spontaneous product of the intellect, ideas are simply given to be reflected upon. Ideas are pre-existent. The distinction between truth and coherence provided by knowledge thus defines the idea as being" (*Origin*, 30, translation slightly modified). Benjamin is referring to Plato, but from the beginning of his text, he explains that in his view truth is inconceivable without "theology" (*Origin*, 28). In this case, as in "On Language as Such," "theology" means nonsubjective and nonformal substantiality, the unavailability of truth for human beings and their communication: Truth is what "communicates itself to God." Benjamin attempts to set out the same conception with the classic distinction between concept and idea.

He dissociates knowledge and truth in this way because he is still indebted to the definition of knowledge as a relation of possession between subject and object and as instrumental rationality—an approach current in a conception of knowledge defined by the natural sciences. When one does not distinguish between perceptible objects and described and asserted facts, truth can be conceived as an object of appropriation. This is not, however, the fundamental relation to truth.[17] Truth is a propositional structure—it is a mode of validity in our linguistic utterances—and it is indissociable from the possibility of proof in cases of dispute. Truth cannot be conceived without a commitment toward an interlocutor, a commitment that one must be able to honor. Yet because the intersubjective dimension of a commitment to speak truthfully, of the claim to validity, and of the possibility of proof can hardly be conceived in terms of a relation between subject and object, Benjamin is led to situate truth, insofar as it is a relation between subject and object, in a *transcendental* dimension; that is what he calls the theological character of truth or its ontological status. In fact, he hesitates between a definition in Platonic terms and an approach that conforms to his philosophy of language. Furthermore, for Benjamin, truth means more than cognitive validity. It is a part of the world's intelligibility and readability, the opening of a horizon of meaning, and it is, as in metaphysical thought, a determination that is indissociable from *the true life*. It refers to the *doctrine* anticipated by every truth content in a work of art. Thus, in Benjamin's work, theological inspiration triumphs over Platonism.

In a letter to Scholem, Benjamin describes his methodological introduction to the book on baroque drama as a kind of ruse, claiming that it is "a kind of second stage of my early work on language . . . with which you are familiar, *dressed up as a theory of ideas*" (*Correspondence*, 261, letter of 19 February 1925, my emphasis; let us note in passing that the importance of Benjamin's *Correspondence* lies in, among other things, such explanations, which were not published at the time). No one has yet asked the question of what this dressing up signifies. In an earlier letter to Scholem, it was already an issue:

> It is difficult [to formulate] my philosophical ideas, especially the epistemological ones, in this study, which has to present a *somewhat polished façade*. It will get easier in the course of my presentation, as the subject matter and the philosophical perspective draw closer together; it will remain difficult to do the introduction. I am currently writing it and must give some evidence of my most intimate hidden motives,

without being able to *conceal myself* completely within the confines of the theme. (*Correspondence*, 241–242, letter of 13 June 1924, my emphasis)

The obvious reason for dissimulation is the university framework within which Benjamin planned to present his work in order to obtain his *Habilitation*—which, in fact, was refused him. What he is suggesting is that the university would be unlikely to accept his philosophy, and especially his philosophy of language, unless it was *dressed up* as a theory of ideas, that is, as a Platonism like that in force in university philosophy inspired by neo-Kantianism. According to Benjamin, this philosophy of language would be unacceptable inasmuch as it was inspired by the Hebrew tradition. What Benjamin is *dressing up* into a theory of ideas is his theory of Adamic naming. In *Der Begriff der Kunstkritik*—another book on the idea—he was already dissimulating (*Correspondence*, 135–137, 139–140, letters of 8 November 1918 and 7 April 1919) so as not to speak openly of the subject that primarily interested him, namely, messianism. In a word, in his university writings, Benjamin made an effort not to lay himself open to anti-Semitism.

In another letter, addressed to Florens Christian Rang, Benjamin explains more clearly his true conception of the idea: "Philosophy is meant to name the idea, as Adam named nature, in order to prevail over those *that have returned to their natural state*" (*Correspondence*, 224, letter of 9 December 1923, my emphasis). This conception of the idea as stemming from a pagan nature that remains to be dominated by naming distinguishes Benjamin's thought from Platonism. Between the Hebrew tradition and Greek thought, Benjamin—even as he uses the concept of the idea—institutes a relation that opposes theology and mythic paganism.

In the letter to Rang, which is a first outline of the introduction to *The Origin of German Tragic Drama*, Benjamin introduces the term "idea" to characterize "the relationship of works of art to historical life" (*Correspondence*, 223), a relation that is revealed only through *interpretation:*

For in interpretation, relationships among works of art appear that are timeless yet not without historical relevance. That is to say, the same forces that become explosively and extensively temporal in the world of revelation (and this is what history is) appear concentrated in the silent world [*Verschlossenheit*] (and this is the world of nature and of works of art). (*Correspondence*, 224)

These are the "ideas." They constitute an original form of confrontation between human beings and the universe and as such can be renewed throughout history. They appear in works of art as manifestations of the true language, manifestations that are still obscure and endowed with a thingness from which criticism and interpretation must deliver them. That is the case, in particular, for forms such as allegory or tragic drama, which Benjamin wishes to have accepted among the "ideas" whose totality alone gives us access to truth:

> These ideas are the stars, in contrast to the sun of revelation. They do not shine their light into the day of history, but work within it invisibly. They shine their light only into the night of nature. Works of art are thus defined as models of a nature that does not await the day, and thus does not await judgment day either; they are defined as models of a nature that is neither the staging ground of history nor a human domicile. The night preserved. And in the context of this consideration, *criticism* (where it is identical with *interpretation* and the opposite of all current methods of art appreciation) is the representation of an idea. Ideas' intensive infinitude characterizes them as monads. Allow me to define it: criticism is the mortification of works of art. Not that consciousness is enhanced in them (romantic!), but that knowledge takes up residence in them. Philosophy is meant to name the idea, as Adam named nature. . . . The task of interpreting works of art is to gather creatural life into the idea. (*Correspondence*, 224–225, my emphasis)

More discreetly, the introduction to *The Origin of German Tragic Drama* says the same thing, clearly opposing Plato and Adam:

> In philosophical contemplation, the idea is released from the heart of reality as the word, reclaiming its name-giving rights. Ultimately, however, this is not the attitude of Plato, but the attitude of Adam, the father of the human race and the father of philosophy. Adam's action of naming things is so far removed from play or caprice that it actually confirms the state of paradise as a state in which there is as yet no need to struggle with the communicative significance of words. Ideas are displayed, without intention, in the act of naming, and they have to be renewed in philosophical contemplation. In this renewal the primordial mode of perceiving words is restored. (*Origin*, 37)

Like Heidegger, Benjamin claims a particular *attitude* for the philosopher, that of a "primordial perception" (*Urvernehmen*), through which ideas and words rediscover their ancestral value as names:

> The idea is something linguistic, it is that element of the symbolic in the essence of any word. In empirical perception, in which words have become fragmented, they possess, in addition to their more or less hidden symbolic aspect, an obvious, profane meaning. It is the task of the philosopher to restore, by representation, the primacy of the symbolic character of the word, in which the idea is given self-consciousness, and that is the opposite of all outwardly-directed communication. Since

philosophy may not presume to speak in the tones of revelation, this can only be achieved by recalling in memory the primordial form of perception. (*Origin*, 36)

The most obvious difference from "On Language as Such" lies in the fact that "philosophy may not presume to speak in the tones of revelation" and in the consequences Benjamin draws for his philosophy of language. Yet he never makes explicit just how the philosopher gains access to that "primordial form of perception, in which words possess their own nobility as names, unimpaired by cognitive meaning" (*Origin*, 36). It is hardly satisfying to say that ideas must be renewed in a philosophical contemplation through which the primordial perception of words is restored. How are we to proceed so that, in this contemplation, a primordial perception is restored? How can this restoration be controlled? In employing such expressions, Benjamin is using a magical language that recalls Heidegger's similar pretensions, which were just as ill founded. We would do better to turn toward the exercise of that "philosophical contemplation" in Benjamin's actual work of interpretation. In fact, in the letter of 13 June 1924 already cited, Benjamin himself underscores his difficulty in formulating general philosophical reflections and his greater facility in drawing them out "in the course of my presentation, as the subject matter and the philosophical perspective draw closer together" (*Correspondence*, 241–242).

The change in perspective from "On Language as Such" allows us to understand the status of the work of art and of art theory in Benjamin's thought: It is through the interpretation of works of art and art forms that Benjamin practices the "philosophical contemplation" through which he hopes to rediscover the original force of naming that, in his view, has been lost in abstract meaning, possessive knowledge, and prattling communication.

System, Treatise, Doctrine

In contrast to "On Language as Such," the introduction to *The Origin of German Tragic Drama* homes in on the historical perception of the role of philosophy. "In its finished form, it will, it is true, be doctrine, but it does not lie within the power of mere thought to confer such a form. Philosophical doctrine is based on historical codification" (*Origin*, 27). Like translation, philosophy measures the gap that separates us from doctrine and hence from the messianic end of history. That is why philosophy is essentially the "representation" of truth, in the sense that Benjamin gives to this term: not a systematic justification of arguments but an evocation of things as a function of a primordial perception of language. In relation to inaccessible doctrine and philosophical practice as Benjamin conceives it—founded on the representation of truth through language—the "system" in the nine-teenth-century sense seems to him to be an aberration; he sees it as "a syncretism which weaves a spider's web between kinds of knowledge in an attempt to ensnare truth as if it were something which came flying in from outside. But the universalism acquired by such philosophy falls far short of the didactic authority of doctrine" (*Origin,* 28).

In particular, Benjamin's target is the mathematical model of knowl-edge, characterized by the "total elimination of the problem of repre-sentation" (*Origin,* 27). Drawing support from a work by Emile Meyerson, he is thinking generally of a scientific knowledge grafted onto the model of the exact sciences, a knowledge that believes it can bypass any hermeneu-tic and linguistic consideration:

> Flawless coherence in scientific deduction is not required in order that truth shall be represented in its unity and singularity; and yet this very flawlessness is the only way in which the logic of the system is related to the notion of truth. Such systematic completeness has no more in common with truth than any other form of representation which at-tempts to ascertain the truth in mere cognition and cognitional patterns. The more scrupulously the theory of scientific knowledge investigates the various disciplines, the more unmistakably their methodological inconsistency is revealed. In each single scientific discipline new assump-tions are introduced without any deductive basis, and in each discipline previous problems are declared solved as emphatically as the impossibil-ity of solving them in any other context is asserted. (*Origin,* 33, transla-tion modified)

In contrast to this scientific fluidity, which corresponds to the very principle of modern fallibility, Benjamin's approach is characterized by the wish to solve philosophical problems by abandoning the terrain of controll-able knowledge—deductions, proofs, and argumentation—and replacing it with a hermeneutics of "objective interpretation" as a function of a limited number of idea-forms or monads, an interpretation he identifies with a "representation of truth."

This interpretation takes the form of a *treatise,* a medieval term that Benjamin attempts to resurrect. Faced with the impossibility of attaining doctrine, true philosophy in the sense Benjamin intends it is condemned to express itself in "the esoteric essay," "a propaedeutic, which can be desig-nated by the scholastic term treatise" (*Origin,* 28). Unable to possess doctrinal truth, it seeks its only element of authority in *quotation,* through which the author refers to words whose status is more definitive than his own. Quotation, which was Benjamin's theme in many of his discussions of Karl Kraus, or in the context of the "montage" of quotations that was to be the book *Paris Arcades,* is one of the prototypes for a repetition of the origin in language, an exercise in naming.

For Benjamin, transcendental truth, beyond the grasp of knowledge and inconceivable without "theology," is thus the object not of proofs but of a "representation," that is, an apprehension and an exposition of meaning. As does the phenomenological tradition from Edmund Husserl to Heidegger and beyond[18] (to which Benjamin in fact refers in "On the Program of the Coming Philosophy" [8]), Benjamin links truth and meaning. But for him, this meaning has an aesthetic value in the broad sense: The fact that, as Hegel said, truth must appear or must be represented instead of being directly known through the appropriation of an object justifies the privilege of aesthetic criticism as an approach to truth, as long as doctrine, true truth, is not accessible. In the absence of revelation and doctrine, the representation of truth through criticism is a makeshift solution, in an even more grandiloquent sense than is the "critique" in Kant. It is on the near side of metaphysics, but as a makeshift solution it is superior to any system.

Representation as method is a tireless but discontinuous return to "one single object" (*Origin,* 28): "Tirelessly the process of thinking makes new beginnings, returning in a roundabout way to its original object" (*Origin,* 28). Adorno saw in this approach the fulfillment of promises that were not kept by phenomenology: total abandonment to the richness of experience, an unregulated experience of things.[19] Benjamin's thought is fascinating because it lacks sterile preliminary considerations, because it is able to analyze texts and phenomena concretely in order to draw out profound intuitions and a historical diagnosis: "Truth-content is only to be grasped through immersion in the most minute details of subject-matter" (*Origin,* 29). Like Nietzsche, Benjamin sets aside the "systematic" tradition of Western philosophy with a stroke of the pen, to return to a hidden tradition, in this case, that of the "esoteric essay." But this subversive undertaking does not account for the legitimacy either of its own intuitions, which are insufficiently explained in the reference to a "primordial perception," or of parallel undertakings founded on more explicit and more rational foundations.

In 1911, in the introduction to his book *Soul and Form,* Georg Lukács, who had also broken with neo-Kantian thought, presented a conception of the essay that is quite close to Benjamin's.[20] What Benjamin calls "doctrine" Lukács still calls "system," but the connotations are comparable: The essayist is John the Baptist, "who goes out to preach in the desert about another who is still to come, whose shoelace he is not worthy to untie."[21] "System" therefore also has messianic connotations, which become even more obvious in *Theory of the Novel* (1916), in which Lukács develops a philosophy of history that has many similarities to that of Benjamin. For both thinkers, aesthetic criticism occupies a privileged place in philosophy. In this current born on the eve of and during World

War I, Nietzschean subversion is associated with a philosophy of history that is messianic in its inspiration.

Art and Truth

Although Benjamin "dressed up" his philosophy of language into a theory of ideas, the reference to Plato is still not totally fortuitous. In the biblical tradition, there is no direct link between Adamic naming and the aesthetic sphere. In contrast, the theory of ideas had introduced the concept of the beautiful from its Platonic origin. In Benjamin's thought, the importance of the beautiful and of art is justified by the fact that doctrine is beyond reach: In every age, it is art alone that presents a "definitive" image of the world. In this case, philosophy is a practice analogous to art. On the near side of revelation, it also "represents" truth in the medium of ideas. According to its precedents in Nietzsche and the romantics of Jena, this analogy with art distances the philosopher from science and its concern for proofs and forges links to the artist.

In "On the Program of the Coming Philosophy," Benjamin had already underscored the fact that, for Kant, any depth was to be linked to the rigor of proofs. He asserts in *Origin* that

> the scientist arranges the world with a view to its dispersal in the realm of ideas, by dividing it from within into concepts. He shares the philosopher's interest in the elimination of the merely empirical; while the artist shares with the philosopher the task of representation. There has been a tendency to place the philosopher too close to the scientist, and frequently the lesser kind of scientist; as if representation had nothing to do with the task of the philosopher. (*Origin,* 32)[22]

Falling "far short of the didactic authority of doctrine" (*Origin,* 28), philosophical prose is characterized by its "sobriety" and recognizable in its "style": "The art of the interruption, in contrast to the chain of deduction; the tenacity of the essay in contrast to the single gesture of the fragment; the repetition of themes in contrast to shallow universalism; the fullness of concentrated positivity in contrast to the negation of polemic" (*Origin,* 32). Deduction and universalism are linked to a "scientific" conception of philosophy. Benjamin's early rejection of polemical negativity and his opposition to the fragmentary gesture contrasts with his later views, often associated both with committed writing, which he practiced during the 1930s, and with romantic fragmentism.

Benjamin refers to Plato because in him he finds the link between the true and the beautiful in the idea, which is constitutive of his theory of art. For Benjamin, as for Kant and as in German idealism, the beautiful is the *accessible* face of a transcendent truth. Thus, art criticism is a privileged exercise in approaching truth. Benjamin draws two theses from the *Banquet:* "It presents truth—the realm of ideas—as the essential content of beauty. [And] it declares truth to be beautiful" (*Origin*, 30). First, then, beauty is not independent of truth—something Benjamin had already underscored in "Goethes *Wahlverwandtschaften*"—but, second, truth is not independent of beauty either: "The beautiful remains an appearance, and thus vulnerable, as long as it freely admits to being so" (*Origin*, 31, translation modified). Conversely, "this representational impulse in truth is the refuge of beauty as such" (*Origin*, 31).[23] The first assertion provides aesthetic criticism with the criterion that tends to disappear with the romantics in favor of a religion of art; the second renders the theory of art indispensable to philosophy.

The world of ideas is fundamentally discontinuous. That is what is revealed by the great articulations of "logic, ethics, and aesthetics" (*Origin*, 33), to which Benjamin had already laid claim in "On the Program of the Coming Philosophy." But that is also what characterizes different ideas themselves, which cannot be reduced to one another: "Ideas exist in irreducible multiplicity. As an enumerated—or rather a denominated—multiplicity, ideas are rendered up for contemplation" (*Origin*, 43). This qualitative plurality has consequences for the concept of truth. Instead of stemming from utterances open to criticism and reasoned proofs, truth for Benjamin becomes a "harmony of the spheres," a virtual relation between irreducible signifying structures: "Every idea," he writes, "is a sun and is related to other ideas just as suns are related to each other. The musical [*tönende*] relationship between such beings is what constitutes truth" (*Origin*, 37, translation slightly modified).

A musical relation is difficult to determine; what matters more in Benjamin's view of truth is both that it is absolutely revelational, independent of human knowledge, and that it depends on an irreducible plurality of idea-forms or "monads," which present a complete vision of the world each time. Every "idea"—tragedy, tragic drama, story—presents a "part" of truth that has to be integrated into an enumerable totality. For Benjamin, the world of ideas is a discontinuous set of individual "constellations" or "monads" that escape consciousness in the physico-mathematical sense and are revealed only to contemplation. That is what determines the function of *concepts.*

Concepts have an intermediary status between ideas and empirical phenomena. They divide phenomena into their elements, following an order prescribed to them through the contemplation of ideas:

> Phenomena do not, however, enter into the realm of ideas whole, in their crude empirical state, adulterated by appearances, but only in their basic elements, redeemed. They are divested of their false unity so that, thus

divided, they might partake of the genuine unity of truth. In this their
division, phenomena are subordinate to concepts for it is the latter which
effect the resolution of objects into their constituent elements. Conceptual
distinctions are above all suspicion of destructive sophistry only when their
purpose is the salvation of phenomena in ideas, the Platonic τα φαινμενα
σωξειν. Through their mediating role concepts enable phenomena to
participate in the existence of ideas. It is this same mediating role which
fits them for the other equally basic task of philosophy, the representation
of ideas. . . . For ideas are not represented in themselves, but solely and
exclusively in an arrangement of concrete elements in the concept: as the
configuration of those elements. (*Origin*, 34)

Since concepts have only an auxiliary function, Benjamin confers the
status of archetypes on the great symbolic structures—"ideas":

Ideas are to objects as constellations are to stars. . . . They are neither
their concepts nor their laws. They do not contribute to the knowledge
of phenomena. . . . Ideas are timeless constellations, and by virtue of the
elements' being seen as points in such constellations, phenomena are
subdivided and at the same time redeemed. (*Origin*, 34)

These original ideas that Benjamin calls timeless constellations—the
tripartition of philosophy and artistic forms such as tragedy or *Trauerspiel*—
are not independent of history. "Timelessness" and "history" are not contradictory terms for Benjamin. That is why he can ask "whether the tragic is
a form which can be realized at all at the present time, or whether it is not
a historically limited form" (*Origin*, 39). It is this link between the timelessness of ideas and the historicity of forms that gives meaning to the
Benjaminian concept of *origin:*

Origin [*Ursprung*], although an entirely historical category has, nevertheless, nothing to do with genesis [*Entstehung*]. The term origin is not
intended to describe the process by which the existent came into being,
but rather to describe that which emerges from the process of becoming
and disappearance. Origin is an eddy in the stream of becoming. . . .
There takes place in every original phenomenon a determination of the
form in which an idea will constantly confront the historical world, until
it is revealed fulfilled, in the totality of its history. Origin is not,
therefore, discovered by the examination of actual findings, but it is
related to their history and their subsequent development. (*Origin*,
45–46)

Through the avatars of the idea, the origin is the sign of history's
authenticity. The history of these ideas, even though it is determined by

their "essential being," is nonetheless not "pure history, but natural history. The life of the works and forms which need such protection in order to unfold clearly and unclouded by human life is a natural life" (*Origin,* 47).[24] In this context, as in "The Task of the Translator," "natural life" means the *pure and simple life* of phenomena that have not been delivered by the word; that life, where the "totality" of their history unfolds, must as a result be "consummated" by philosophy, in a sense that once more recalls Hegel. Philosophy brings together phenomena within the perspective of their messianic end. This totality confers the character of "monad" on the idea (*Origin,* 47). This concept of monad guarantees the permanence of Benjamin's speculative idealism up to his last text, "Theses on the Philosophy of History" (*Illuminations,* 263). More precisely, Benjamin applies the concept of "monad" only to "ideas": "The idea is a monad," we read in *The Origin of German Tragic Drama,* "the pre-stabilized representation of phenomena resides within it, as in their objective interpretation" (*Origin,* 47). In his "Theses on the Philosophy of History," he will apply it to the object of history in general, inasmuch as it constitutes a decisive "idea," an "origin" for the historian's present.

The application of this method to historical reality itself and not only to works of art is suggested even in the introduction to the *Origin of German Tragic Drama:* "The real world will constitute a task, in the sense that it would be a question of penetrating so deeply into everything real as to reveal thereby an objective interpretation of the world" (*Origin,* 48). To redeem the historical reality of an entire epoch by constructing this archetypal idea and revealing its value of "origin" for the present will be the unbounded task of the *Paris Arcades* project.

LANGUAGE AS MIMETIC FACULTY

For Benjamin in this overtly theological period, language was characterized by its noninstrumentality; communication to God through the human faculty of naming; the messianism inherent in the order of language, oriented toward a move beyond nature even in the human order; the ontological character of truth, inaccessible to physico-mathematical knowledge; and the cognitive character of the beautiful. In his materialist period, Benjamin reformulates his theory of language without resorting to theological terminology, through the concept of *mimesis:*

> Nature creates similarities. One need only think of mimicry. The highest capacity for producing similarities, however, is man's. His gift of seeing resemblances is nothing other than a rudiment of the powerful compulsion in former times to become and behave like something else. Perhaps

there is none of his higher functions in which mimetic faculty does not play a decisive role. ("On the Mimetic Faculty," in *Reflections*, 333)

Producing resemblances, mimesis, seems to be a faculty close to that of naming, whereas mimicry is merely another name for the language of natural objects. As he does with the power to name in the 1916 essay, Benjamin envisions the mimetic faculty from the outside, as a manifestation of the species, not from the perspective of those practicing mimesis for one another; that perspective would have seemed to him to instrumentalize language. And, as in his first essay, Benjamin once more refuses to consider language as an "agreed system of signs" (*Reflections*, 334). But instead of resorting to the notion of a kinship between words and things by virtue of their common Creator, Benjamin now introduces a theory of the "onomatopoetic" origin of language. If he escapes the criticisms addressed to that conception of language,[25] it is insofar as he uses the concept of a "nonsensuous similarity" to give onomatopoeia—the sensuous imitation of one sound by another—a peculiar sense (*Reflections*, 334).

It is through this concept, a kind of "intellectual intuition," that he attempts to account for the changes that the mimetic faculty has undergone throughout history: "The direction of this change seems determined by the increasing fragility of the mimetic faculty. For clearly the observable world of modern man contains only minimal residues of the magical correspondences and analogies that were familiar to ancient peoples" (*Reflections*, 334, translation modified). Now, the change is no longer attributed to "original sin"; instead of decay, Benjamin observes a transformation of the mimetic faculty. Astrology, the determination of the newborn by a constellation, provides the first example of a "nonsensuous similarity"; but, following a schema already developed in "On Language as Such," the principal "canon" for it is language: "For if words meaning the same thing in different languages are arranged about that thing as their center, we have to inquire how they all—while often possessing not the slightest similarity to one another—are similar to what they signify at their center" (*Reflections*, 335). What is here wrongly termed a similarity—because Benjamin continues to think that the relation between languages reflects a messianic end of history—is in fact a relation of denotation.[26] Benjamin's theory of language remains unilateral because he needs it to ground his work as a critic and historian.

Even in his materialist period, Benjamin gives a mystical sense of resemblance and *correspondence* to *any* signifying relation. But what interests him in this text on the mimetic faculty is the correspondence between script and the memory of semantic content:

Graphology has taught us to recognize in handwriting images that the unconscious of the writer conceals in it. It may be supposed that the mimetic process that expresses itself in this way in the activity of the writer was, in the very distant times in which script originated, of utmost importance for writing. Script has thus become, like language, an archive of nonsensuous similarities, of nonsensuous correspondences. (*Reflections,* 335)

Benjamin imagines an analogy between the unconscious, which is revealed in graphology, and an archaic mimicry of humanity that has passed into writing. Like the graphologist (he was one, by the way) Benjamin thinks he can detect in writing in general a relation of signification that virtually accompanies the semiotic aspect of language, from which it is not independent: "The mimetic element in language can, like a flame, manifest itself only through a kind of bearer. This bearer is the semiotic element. Thus the coherence of words or sentences is the bearer through which, like a flash, similarity appears" (*Reflections,* 335). In this context, similarity is the relation of an unconscious meaning to an explicit meaning; this unconscious meaning is revealed instantaneously, and, according to Benjamin's theory of knowledge, must be seized in a flash, at the risk of disappearing forever.[27] Benjamin practices this type of indirect reading first of all on works of art and then on history.

In his philosophy of language, Benjamin privileges the aspects of language that reveal indirect meaning, detached from communication. He considers neither expressive intentions, nor the semantic dimension (the representation of states of things), nor the functions of appeal (intersubjective relations), to mention the three aspects identified by Karl Bühler.[28] Despite his touted materialism, he is not interested in any pragmatic function of language even though it may establish social ties; these functions, in his view, are attached to a narrowly instrumental conception of language. Here again, what matters to him is the noninstrumental dimension of language, its faculty of revelation, its burden of memory, its quality of conveying the original powers of the human mind, all of which are related to the transmission of symbols. Hence he concludes his 1935 comment on the theories of language with a quotation from Kurt Goldstein, which he turns to his own account: "As soon as man uses language to establish a living relation with himself or his peers, language is no longer an instrument, it is no longer a means; it is a manifestation, a revelation of our most intimate essence and of the psychological link that connects us to ourselves and to our peers" (Quoted in *G.S.,* 3:480).

In "The Work of Art in the Age of Mechanical Reproduction," in which he focuses on the addressee, who was set aside in his early writings on art, Benjamin seems to be breaking with his conception of language as an absolute expression of a "communication with God." But has he in fact done anything but reverse the relation between language and its addressee? In

Benjamin's early work, language communicated itself to God, its true receiver; in "The Work of Art," the profane receiver *is* God—he makes of the work, which is no longer sacred and no longer carries any absolute imperative, whatever he likes. This inversion is possible only because Benjamin does not have access to a concept that is solid enough to anchor the work of art "horizontally" in a relationship of recognition.

In language as in art, he gives precedence to functions of expression that are irreducible to any expressive intention whatever, by emphasizing two aspects: the expression of the nature of man inasmuch as he is the being that names; and archaic, unconscious expression, through which desires, utopias, experiences, and the hidden meanings of humanity are revealed. Since the definitive doctrine is inaccessible, it is first the relationship between the critic or the translator and the work of art, then the relationship between the historian and the symptoms of an epoch, that become the prime sites of revelation, where the human faculty of naming is recognized and raised to a higher level.

Benjamin does not account for the fact that the suspension of the pragmatic functions of language in art and in revelation does not suspend every contract with a receiving subject. When he writes, in "The Task of the Translator," that no poem is addressed to a reader, he merely underscores the suspension of pragmatic communication, not the fact that another relation is instituted—one that is reflective and subject to constraints of coherence and pertinence. In this new relationship the work of art nonetheless depends on a receptive pole of communication, a pole whose imperatives are felt within the creation itself. Benjamin has carved out a theory of language to fit the task of critic that he has assigned himself. But in suspending the "instrumental" functions of language, he does not target a pure and simple immanence of the linguistic or artistic form. He attaches that form to a symbolic history in which the destiny of humanity is played out.

In the same way, he refuses to reduce *criticism* to an activity on the purely aesthetic plane; it intervenes in a process that it is art's function to reveal:

Just as Benedetto Croce opened the way for the concrete and singular work of art by destroying the doctrine of art forms, all my efforts have until now tended to forge a path toward the work of art by destroying the doctrine of art as a specific domain. Their shared programmatic intention is to stimulate the process of the integration of science that more and more makes the rigid cloistering of disciplines—characteristic of the concept of science in the last century—fall away, through an analysis of the work of art that recognizes it as a complete expression of religious, metaphysical, political, and economic tendencies of an age, an analysis that cannot be reduced in any of its aspects to the notion of domain. ("Curriculum vitae" [3], 31)

When he wrote this text, Benjamin had already entered his materialist phase, and theological themes had moved to the background. The religious framework of his philosophy of language, the linking of the creating Word to the poetic word, the symbolist conception of an exclusion of any consideration of the receiver of the work, had all allowed him to preserve aesthetic autonomy to a great extent. Beginning with *Einbahnstrasse,* the sociological context of the literary and ideological "battle" makes the autonomy of the work of art more vulnerable. In all the great philosophical aesthetics, art tends to transcend the definitions that wish to assign it a particular domain. There is a peculiar difficulty in keeping the aesthetic sphere closed upon itself. Through its cognitive, ethical, political, and other stakes, art always refers to *all* dimensions of life. Its imperatives are specific and stem from a logic that solicits a different attention from that claimed by other types of phenomena, but the meaning of an important work of art is never *purely* aesthetic. Our reading of Benjamin's writings on art will show how the undeniable force of his criticism is due to the systematic foundations of his thought and to the way he succeeds in respecting aesthetic logic even while aiming toward a transcendent function for art in the historical process.

CHAPTER II

✳

Theory of Art

Aesthetic criticism as Benjamin conceived it in his early works is subordinated to the framework defined by his philosophy of language. It intervenes in the "natural" process of the afterlives of works by raising their thing language to a higher, purer, and more definitive language in order to bring it closer to doctrine or to true philosophy. But above all, criticism is the principal raison d'être for a philosophy of language that was never developed as such outside a few elementary theses. For Benjamin, the language of art relates most authentically to *truth*, inasmuch as it preserves the human faculty of naming in the historical stage following the Fall, which led to the splitting of the name into image and abstract meaning. That is why, as an art theorist, he is always dependent on "contemporary" art; he is thus led to adapt his theory to the tendencies that seem the most authentic to him at every stage: His Hölderlin or baroque period is followed by a series of theoretic passions for avant-garde movements or authors (for surrealism; for Marcel Proust, Karl Kraus, Franz Kafka, or Bertolt Brecht), which constitute unstable moments within his second phase. The avant-garde phase finds its definitive formulation in "The Work of Art in the Age of Mechanical Reproduction." During this phase, a political theory and then a philosophy of history progressively replace his philosophy of language as the underpinning of his aesthetics. Benjamin's last text, "Theses on the Philosophy of History," is the epistemological equivalent of his early essay on language for his work during the third phase—that is, for *Paris Arcades* and the writings on Baudelaire.

Despite his reflections on the mimetic faculty, Benjamin's philosophy of language is primarily linked to his theological period, whereas his philosophy of history in essence belongs only to his last period. In contrast, Benjamin's theory of art has three quite clearly differentiated periods. The aesthetics of the sublime, the first period, is governed by the messianic disenchantment of the beautiful appearance (1914–1924). This is followed by the second period, a political aesthetics of revolutionary intervention in society. It aims both at reconstituting human forces into a lucid intoxication, a total presence of mind, and at compensating for the decline or sacrifice of the aura, or even of art in the traditional sense (1925–1935). The third period evaluates the irremediable loss without compensation of the auratic element, which is linked to language as revelation, and insists on the vital importance of memory in the context of a disenchanted modernity (1936–1940).

Throughout these three orientations, Benjamin continually oscillates on the fundamental question of post-Kantian aesthetics: How do we define the criterion allowing us to state accurately that a work of art is successful, that it is "beautiful," which is not the same thing as simply saying we like it? Beginning with German idealism, "truth" is one of the classic responses to that question. It has the disadvantage of confusing the general question of truth, to which art supposedly offers privileged access, and the question of the validity of art. In Benjamin's first period, aesthetic validity is indistinguishable from the revelation of theological truth communicated "to God" by the artist; in the second, it is subordinated to political truth, which is communicated to receivers concerned with revolution; in the third and last period, it is viewed through the imperatives of the modern work of art, a message in a bottle thrown into the sea that is addressed neither to God nor to receivers.

1. Aesthetics of the Sublime

The philosophy of language has to seek its proofs in art theory. Although, for Benjamin, art is a manifestation of the human power of naming—or of revealing through language the true nature of things and beings—it does not present the name in its pure form, drawn from the language of things. Criticism and translation have the task of raising the name to a purer and more definitive language.

We will not concern ourselves here with retracing the young philosopher's beginnings in the Free Student Movement, which he broke with when its leaders' nationalistic spirit burst forth with World War I. We need only say that the essays on Hölderlin and on Fyodor Dostoyevsky's *The Idiot,* as well as the essay "On Language as Such" and the book *Der Begriff der Kunstkritik in der deutschen Romantik,* are part of a process of reflection that, in mourning the Free Student Movement, attempts to reconstitute the universal foundations of thought in the face of a current of thought that was drawing on the same sources, a current that had, however, sunk into pan-Germanic ideology. In 1939–1940, when Benjamin laid claim to theological concepts in response to the party Marxism of the time, it was with exactly the same goal of reclaiming a universal normative foundation that seemed to him to have been betrayed by the "progressivist" thinking of the age.

UNDER THE SIGN OF HÖLDERLIN

Like his philosophy of language, Benjamin's aesthetic approach is part of the tradition of Kant's *Critique of Judgment,* especially as it was read by the romantics of Jena. According to this reading, the work of art is the passageway that allows us to transgress the metaphysical prohibitions imposed by critical thought. The poet was thus endowed with the meaning and the destiny of culture as a whole. This is how Hölderlin saw his task. "Zwei Gedichte von Friedrich Hölderlin" (Two poems by Friedrich Hölderlin; 1914–1915) is the first essay in which Benjamin, even before formulating his theory of language, presents both his philosophy of art—of poetry in particular—and his method of "aesthetic commentary" (*G.S.,* 2:105). This method is neither philological nor biographical; nor is it concerned with an author's "vision of the world." It is a kind of extremely rigorous "immanent reading" following the principles inherited from the aesthetics of early German romanticism. What matters is the "internal form" of the poem, "what Goethe defined as its content [*Gehalt*]" (*G.S.,* 2:105). At first glance, this "content"—which will soon become "truth content"—is difficult to distinguish from a "vision of the world"; Benjamin speaks of "the structure, which can be grasped intuitively by the mind, of the world to which the poem is the witness" (*G.S.,* 2:105). But what separates that structure from a vision proper to one creator or another is an objective imperative that is inherent to it and that Benjamin calls the poet's "task": "This task is inferred from the poem itself. We need to understand it as the presupposition of poetry, as the structure, which can be grasped intuitively by the mind, of the world to which the poem is the witness. That task, that presupposition, is what we understand as the ultimate foundation an analysis can reach" (*G.S.,* 2:105).

Through this "task," Benjamin seeks to define the criterion for an immanent analysis toward which his aesthetic is oriented. In the name of a grandiloquent concept of truth, he isolates the particular "sphere" of every poem and designates it the "poetized" (*das Gedichtete*), that which has found objective form in a poem: "In it the proper domain that contains truth and poetry is revealed. This 'truth,' which the most serious writers rightly and insistently attributed to their creation, we understand as the objectified form [*Gegenständlichkeit*] of their creative act, the completed realization of any artistic task" (*G.S.*, 2:105). Benjamin places "truth" in quotation marks, suggesting a metaphorical use of the term; for reasons already indicated, however, he sees it as the most authentic form of truth given to us.

Like Novalis, whom Benjamin will again cite in *Der Begriff der Kunstkritik* (" 'Every work of art possesses in itself an a priori ideal, a necessity for its presence' "), he struggles with a difficulty characteristic of post-Kantian aesthetics: that of defining an imperative or a mode of necessity that is proper to the work of art and that is not to be confused with the truth imperative in the narrow sense. How does a work of art impose itself on us, how does it legitimately demand our recognition? Benjamin attempts to wrench art from the arbitrariness of subjective expression by discovering in it a rigorous *law*. To do this, he has to reconstruct the poem's ideal and thus "bracket certain determinations to shed light on the internal relationships, the functional unity of the other elements" (*G.S.*, 2:106).

This consists in giving to a living configuration the necessity of a natural law. Like the German romantics, Benjamin seeks to grasp that necessity through the term "myth," the equivalent of the poetized. For a work of art to exist, life, which is only the poem's "foundation," must be transposed to a level of coherence and greatness that is equal to that of the elements that constitute the criteria for its evaluation. The "myth" invoked by Benjamin could be a styling in the "poetized"—that is, in the philosophically decipherable content of the poem—of a real life, an exemplary life judged in terms of its specific historical and individual conditions. "Myth" is opposed to "mythology" as the coherence of the form itself is opposed to a borrowed coherence that remains at the level of the subject matter. In his analysis of two poems by Hölderlin,[1] Benjamin makes an effort to show precisely how the poet moves from a "mythological" version, marked by references to Greek mythology, to a "mythic" version, in which he elaborates his own myth, his own poetic coherence: "The dependence on mythology is superseded by the cohesion of the myth itself" (*G.S.*, 2:114).

The task of criticism is to show the *intensity* of the realized coherence and through it the *necessity* of the work of art. Following this method, "the judgment we bring to lyric poetry must be, if not proven, at least well-founded" (*G.S.*, 2:108). Abandoning the rigor of scientific proof in aesthetic criticism, Benjamin nevertheless seeks to establish the bases on which an aesthetic judgment can be grounded. In *Einbahnstrasse*, he speaks of "what we rightly call beautiful" (*G.S.*, 4:116). Contrary to what Kantian aesthetics seems to indicate, the act of calling a work of art beautiful, according to

Benjamin, can be justified. Inasmuch as Benjamin's critical activity relies on this principle, which he formulated in his very first essay, it would be interesting to follow its development throughout his oeuvre and to see how his work as a critic draws its force from this idea.

"What we rightly call beautiful" cannot owe its validity to anything other than *aesthetics*, for example, it cannot be beholden to a *truth* that could be formulated just as well or better in theoretical terms. That is why Benjamin encloses "truth" in quotation marks. "Only since romanticism," he writes in a 1918 letter to Scholem,

> has the following view become predominant: that a *work* of art in and of itself, and without reference to theory or morality, can be understood in contemplation alone, and that the person contemplating it can do it justice. The relative autonomy of the *work* of art vis-à-vis art, or better, its exclusively transcendental dependence on art, has become the prerequisite of romantic art criticism. I would undertake to prove that, in this regard, Kant's aesthetics constitute the underlying premise of romantic art criticism. (*Correspondence*, 119)

The goal, then, would be to confer the rigor of a transcendental foundation in Kant's sense on an aesthetics centered not on the concept of taste but on that of the work of art.

The choice of Hölderlin in this context is not gratuitous, inasmuch as, in his theoretical writings and his poetry, he conducted one of the most rigorous reflections on the consequences of the Kantian aesthetic. At the same time, this choice is symptomatic of the orientation Benjamin considers most valuable among the post-Kantian thinkers. The figure of Hölderlin will predominate in both "The Task of the Translator" and the essay on Goethe's *Elective Affinities*. Hölderlin, like Nietzsche later and to some extent like Benjamin himself, embraced the notion of the beautiful in Kant's *Critique of Judgment*—as the sensible sign of the Idea or as an absolute, inaccessible to rational knowledge—as his personal destiny, which led him to defy death and madness. Through his "genius," the poet is charged with giving form to an ultimate meaning. In the end, God himself must "serve the song" (*G.S.*, 2:121). In that way, the immanence of form and the "truth" of the work of art coincide, precisely because the poet's ambition is philosophical. He is the hero of the world insofar as he guarantees its unity:

> The most intimate identity between the poet and the world, an identity from which all identities between the intuitive and the mental flow into that poetry, such is the foundation where the singularized form is again abolished in the spatio-temporal order, where it is suppressed as if

formless, omniform, process and presence, temporal plasticity and spatial
development. In death, which is its universe, all known relations are
united. (*G.S.,* 2:124)

This is a death that the poet—like Empedocles—accepts, as the hero of
humanity.

This suppression of form, of the limit, is interpreted—as in the essay
on Goethe, which evokes the "caesura" of tragedy[2]—as the irruption of the
"inexpressive" or of infinity, concepts belonging to "Eastern" thought,
perhaps to Judaism as Benjamin conceives it: "It is the Eastern and mystical
principle that transcends borders" and that always "abolishes the Greek
principle of structuration" (*G.S.,* 2:124). The essay on Hölderlin already
refers to this "caesura." Referring to lines that evoke the poet who "brings"
a god, Benjamin writes: "The insistent caesura of these lines shows the
distance the poet has to maintain from any form and from the world,
inasmuch as he is its unity" (*G.S.,* 2:125). As the unity of the world for
which he continually crucifies himself, the poet is separated from it, and
this separation is symbolized by his exemplary death. This caesura is the
mark of the "holy sobriety" the poet lays claim to in the name of a break
with the principle of pagan immanence.

Benjamin thus places his aesthetics under the sign of the *sublime.*
Sobriety

> stands in the sublime beyond any elevation. Is this still the Hellenist
> life? It is so no more than the life of a pure work of art can ever be that
> of a people, no more than it can be that of an individual or anything else
> but that element in itself that we find in the poetized. That life is figured
> in the forms of Greek myth, but—and this is decisive—not only in its
> forms; in fact, in the last version, the Greek element is abolished and
> cedes its place to another, the one called . . . the Eastern element. (*G.S.,*
> 2:125–126)

For Benjamin, Judaism's or monotheism's sublime represents the
antidote par excellence to myth or to any particularist or national ideology.
The essay on romantic aesthetics attempts to make explicit the philosophical background for an art founded on this principle.

THE ROMANTIC MODEL

The link between the early Benjamin's philosophy of language and his
inquiry on *Der Begriff der Kunstkritik in der deutschen Romantik* is assured by
the fact that the philosophy of language is itself inspired by romantic

speculations. And Hölderlin's poetics plays a determining role in both Benjamin's theory of language and translation and his theory of literature.

"Reflection," the central concept of Benjamin's first book, seems at first to move away from the central preoccupations of his philosophy of language, but it very quickly leads back to it. As Benjamin develops the concept, it has a threefold meaning: the *philosophical* concept of reflection as it is developed by Johann Gottlieb Fichte and reinterpreted by the romantics; the *aesthetic* concept of reflection as a principle of romantic criticism; and the *artistic* concept of reflection in the sense of a prosaic sobriety opposed to creative ecstasy, especially in Hölderlin. Finally, in an appendix, Benjamin envisions the limits of romantic criticism founded on the concept of reflection by introducing the Goethean idea of the archetypal content of art, from which he draws his concept of *truth content*.

The Philosophical Foundations

The theme of *Der Begriff der Kunstkritik* was developed through a rather long process. Following his "On the Program for the Coming Philosophy," Benjamin considered writing a study entitled "Kant and History." When he was unable to find enough material in Kant's works, he abandoned that topic. He then envisioned an essay relating the notion of the "eternal task" in Kant to the problematic of "messianism," which was his central preoccupation: what characterized romanticism in Kantian terms was that "it abandoned the idea of a perfect humanity whose ideal would find its realization in the infinite. At present, the preference is given to a 'Kingdom of God' that is called for in earthly time" (*G.S.*, 1:12 n. 3).[3] We already find the rejection of the notion of a continuous "progress" and the imperative for an instantaneous transformation of the world, two ideas that will dominate throughout Benjamin's oeuvre, right through the "Theses on the Philosophy of History." From such a perspective, the work of art occupies a central place as the model for an *immediate* realization of the "eternal task." In the works of Kant himself, the work of art, under the name of the beautiful, is the symbolic anticipation of that perfect humanity that, as the reign of ends, is still to be realized through an infinite process of approximation. Kant had already given the quasi-ontological status of reflection to the sign that nature offers—in the form of the beautiful—to our subjective cognitive faculties. In thus privileging the beautiful, a privilege that is transferred to art, Benjamin rediscovers his own idea that the artist conserves a part of the power of naming inherent in human language. Concerning himself only with "absolute" truth, he brackets the entire Kantian theory of knowledge, which was elaborated to ground science and its concept of objective truth.

The philosophical foundations of romantic aesthetics are thus quite remote from an ontological philosophy of language. They have their source in the theory of self-consciousness developed by German idealism: "Thought reflects itself in self-consciousness—that is the fundamental fact from which all of Friedrich Schlegel's, and also, for the most part, Novalis's, gnoseological considerations stem. The relation of thought to itself as it is presented in reflection is seen as the closest relation of thinking in general, and all the others are only extensions of it" (*G.S.*, 1:18). For Kant, that proximity of thought to itself in *reflection*—a theme developed in Cartesianism—poses the problem, first, of the concrete sensible, which thought has to integrate, and second, of the thing in itself, which it cannot know totally. Reflective thought faces the pitfall of "intuition": the finitude of human experience excludes "intellectual intuition." The romantics, however, did not accept Kant's resignation:

> In the reflective nature of thought, the romantics saw an even greater guarantee of its intuitive character. As soon as, through Kant . . . the history of philosophy had affirmed the possibility of having an intellectual intuition, and at the same time, its impossibility in the field of experience, we see multiple manifestations of an almost feverish effort to restore this concept to philosophy, as the guarantee of its highest claims. This effort came first from Fichte, Schlegel, Novalis, and Schelling. (*G.S.*, 1:19)

In Fichte's *Doctrine of Science,* reflective thought and immediate, intuitive knowledge are given through each other: In thought, we intuitively and immediately reach the thought content. Benjamin writes that "the immediate consciousness of thought is identical to self-consciousness. Because of its immediacy we call it an intuition. In this self-consciousness where intuition and thought, subject and object, coincide, reflection is fixed, captured, and, though not annihilated, stripped of its boundlessness" (*G.S.*, 1:25). The identity of subject and object in thought would leave the world unthought, were it not the world itself that was thinking itself when we think:

> The romantics begin with the simple act of thinking oneself as a phenomenon; that is proper to everything because everything is Itself [*ein Selbst*]. For Fichte, the Itself falls only to the Self [*das Ich*]. . . . For Fichte, consciousness is the "Self," for the romantics it is Itself; or, in other words: in Fichte reflection relates to the Self, in the romantics only to thinking. (*G.S.*, 1:29)

Benjamin has rediscovered an equivalent to his philosophy of language: Generalized reflection—"everything is Itself"—corresponds to the "language of things" "translated" by human language. Any objective knowledge is "subordinated" to the object's self-knowledge; it is in this sense that Novalis writes: "perceptibility is a kind of attentiveness," a formula that Benjamin will again recall in 1939, with reference to Baudelairean *correspondances*, as the experience of the aura (*Illuminations*, 188). The same mystical conception is expressed in the romantic form of a "medium of reflection" and in the Benjaminian form of language as a "medium of communication." In both cases, there is an "expression" without addressee, an absolute readability of the world.

As he indicates in "On the Program of the Coming Philosophy," Benjamin shares with the romantics the goal of a philosophy that no longer seeks to justify the approach of modern science; he aims at a much wider "experience" than that defined by Kant and Fichte: "What can be drawn from the *Doctrine of Science* is nothing but the image of the world of positive science. Yet the romantics, thanks to their method, entirely dissolve that image of the world into the absolute; and, in the absolute, what they are seeking is a content other than that of science" (*G.S.*, 1:33–34). Through reflection, the absolute reaches a higher "power," inasmuch as it returns to its own origin: "It is only with reflection that the thinking about which there is reflection arises" (*G.S.*, 1:39). In fact, within the context of transcendental idealism, any reality independent of thought is only the reification of an original reflective act. Insofar as it attributes the true power of creating the world to language, Benjamin's philosophy of language remains a variant of this kind of idealism.

For Fichte, the central point of reflection, the absolute, is the Self. As does Kant, Fichte seeks a guarantee, a certainty upon which to base both the positive knowledge of science and the relation to others—moral and juridical recognition. In contrast, according to Benjamin, "in the sense that early romanticism understands it, the center of reflection is art, not the Self" (*G.S.*, 1:39). Whereas Fichte interprets the Kantian theory of knowledge as based on the *Critique of Practical Reason*, in other words, on acts and not on the theoretical relation to the world, the romantics immediately interpret it as based on the *Critique of Judgment*, that is, on a nature reflected in the beautiful, which is sending signals to man. Furthermore, the romantics bracket Kant's "reflective judgment," which prevails over the beautiful. What disappears in the romantic "reflection" on art is the "as if" of Kantian reflection: "Nature is represented by means of this concept as if an understanding contained the ground of the unity of the variety of its empirical laws."[4] Romantic reflection is mystical; on the one hand, it is an ontological process; on the other, through reflection on that reflection, it claims to attain absolute truth. It is therefore no longer necessary to elaborate a theory of knowledge for the natural sciences, since "all knowledge is the self-knowledge of a thinking being, which does not have to be a Self. . . . For the romantics, there exists no non-Self from the viewpoint of the absolute, no nature in the sense of a being that would not become Itself" (*G.S.*, 1:55). Romantic nature is brother to humanity, and art is the reflection of that nature on itself, with no abyss separating these two universes. Except for its reservations about the limits of human knowledge, that is what the implicit metaphysics of the *Critique of Judgment* virtually suggests. "A Self-less reflection," writes Benjamin of the romantics, "is a reflection in the absolute of art" (*G.S.*, 1:40). This reflection within the medium of art is none other than aesthetic *criticism* as the romantics conceive it.

Reinvested with a magical significance following Kant's critiques, "criticism," according to the philosophy of the romantics as Benjamin explains it, is itself a mystical concept, "an exemplary case of mystical terminology" (*G.S.*, 1:50). According to Benjamin, Friedrich Schlegel's approach to criticism, ignoring the gap that separates human consciousness from the absolute in Kantian criticism, was not a systematic conception of the absolute but, rather, an absolutist conception of system (*G.S.*, 1:45)—through the practice of the fragment and, even more, through terminology. It sought to reduce all thought to a witticism (*Witz*), "an attempt to name the system with a name, that is, to seize it in an individual, mystical concept" (*G.S.*, 1:48–49). Benjamin recognizes this as mystical thinking about *language*, which is nevertheless different from his own, since he respects the Kantian idea of a limit imposed on our faculty of naming. Although romanticism is "the last movement that kept tradition alive one more time" (*Correspondence*, 89), "its efforts [were] premature for that age and sphere," "the insanely orgiastic disclosure of all secret sources of the tradition that was to overflow without deviation into all of humanity" (*Correspondence*, 89).

In this context, "criticism" does not signify an attitude of mere evaluation. Above all, in matters of aesthetics, this approach means that the critic abandons his position as the "judge" of works of art who issues his sentences in the name of preconceived ideas, "whether written or tacit." At the same time, the romantics of Jena rejected the irrational genius of the preromantics of *Sturm und Drang* and sought to establish—between the dogmatism of the one and the skepticism of the other—a "critical" position for aesthetic theory (*G.S.*, 1:52–53). Nonetheless, with a few reservations, "the modern concept of criticism has developed from the romantic concept" (*Correspondence*, 136) of an "immanent" criticism that, through reflection, draws out the internal potentialities of a work. What is missing from this conception is a criterion of "truth" inherent in a work's content. That is why Benjamin complements his analysis of the romantic concept of criticism with an insight into the Goethean conception of criticism, which imposes a limit to the "insanely orgiastic" speculation of the romantics.

Theory of Criticism

Since, in reflection, knowledge is at bottom the object's self-knowledge, criticism for the romantics is the work of art's own *knowledge* of itself. Knowledge is therefore only an intensification, "the potentialization of the reflection" inherent in the object (*G.S.*, 1:57 n.). According to the romantics, however, unlike nature's knowledge, criticism is the work's *judgment* of itself. The work of art judges itself through its own immanent criteria. Nonetheless, Benjamin adds that

> it is clear that that self-judgment in reflection can only improperly be called judgment. For in it the necessary moment of any judgment, the negative moment, is in a state of complete disintegration. Certainly, with every reflection, the mind rises above all the previous degrees of reflection, and in doing so, negates them—that is precisely what gives reflection its critical coloration from the outset—but the positive moment in this intensification of consciousness dominates by far its negative moment. (*G.S.*, 1:66)

This is what distinguishes the romantic concept of criticism from its modern concept, "which views in it a negative judgment" (*G.S.*, 1:67).

When, in *The Origin of German Tragic Drama*, Benjamin defines *his* conception of criticism, he underscores that negative aspect: "Criticism means the mortification of the works. . . . not the—as the romantics have it—awakening of the consciousness in living works, but the settlement of knowledge in dead ones" (*Origins*, 182). In both cases, the reason for the dominant style of criticism, positivity or mortification—the actualization of the work's self-reflection or the contemplation of the work as ruins in the interest of its truth content—seems to be attached to a vision of the determinate world rather than to an imperative inherent in criticism. In both cases, nevertheless, criticism rests on criteria immanent to the work of art—internal "judgment" or "truth content"—whose concept will be made explicit in Benjamin's essay on Goethe's *Elective Affinities*. That is what allows us to understand the very possibility of the romantic theory of reflection: A criticism calling for a certain degree of objectivity would hardly be possible if the work itself did not claim a certain type of validity, if, therefore, there existed no rationality in the process leading from creation to the work of art and from the work of art to the critic-receiver.

This rationality that is *inherent* in the work of art, that is created in the name of criteria that are, consciously or not, established by the object, confers on the work of art a privileged status in the theory of reflection: Here is an "object"—a "non-Self," in Fichtean terms—that presents the characteristics of a "Self," in particular that of producing imperatives and justifying itself through its intrinsic rationality. In his *System of Ethics,* Fichte writes that art *"converts the transcendental viewpoint into a common viewpoint. . . .* From the transcendental viewpoint, the world is made, from the common viewpoint, it is given; from the aesthetic viewpoint, it is given, but nonetheless in a way that shows how it is made."[5] Thus, art responds to the aporia of the philosophy of reflection—the fact that a subject "posits" or "makes" an object that is taken to be a subject—without resolving it. But the subject that posits itself and that becomes a subject only in positing itself must *already* be a subject before "positing" itself[6]; hence there is a circularity that only the work of art escapes, in presenting a "nature" entirely fashioned by "freedom." In making the work of art the medium for reflection par excellence, romantic thinkers avoid the problems inherent in the idealist theory of self-consciousness, but they do not solve them; the problems of objective knowledge and intersubjectivity disappear as if with the wave of a magic wand. The only gain is the idea of an imperative for validity inherent in the work of art that must be demonstrated, interpreted, and examined by criticism.

Through criticism, the reflection immanent in a finite work of art is both related to the infinite of art and transposed to its domain. The central operation of the romanticism of Jena is what Novalis calls "romanticizing": "In giving the finite an appearance of the infinite, I romanticize it. The true reader must be an extension of the author. He is the higher court that contemplates the thing already prepared by the lower court" (quoted in *G.S.,* 1:67–68). Benjamin adds that "that amounts to saying that the particular work of art must be dissolved into the medium of art" (*G.S.,* 1:68). This dissolution brought about by criticism amounts to "transcending the work, making it absolute,"

> in the meaning of the work itself, that is, in its reflection. . . . For the romantics, criticism is much less the judgment of a work than the method for completing it. It is in this sense that they required a poetic criticism, that they suspended the difference between criticism and poetry, affirming that "poetry cannot be criticized except by poetry. A judgment on art that is not itself a work of art . . . has no civil rights in the kingdom of art." (*G.S.,* 1:69)

According to this conception, criticism prolongs and amplifies artistic activity itself. As a result, the reflection or "rationality" immanent within works, as translated by the criticism of the romantics, rather than serving as a mediation between the work of art and ordinary language in order to allow readers to share in the meaning proposed in a figural or narrative form, remains beyond the reach of ordinary reason: Criticism accentuates the gap that separates the language of art and ordinary language. Moreover, it claims to call into question and surpass reason. It is not concerned with communicating a meaning or with recognizing a value, but rather with completing an absolute reflection.

From the point of view of romantic criticism, the work of art is thus "incomplete in terms of its own absolute Idea" (*G.S.,* 1:70). In thus completing the work of art and amplifying its claim to sovereignty, the critic avoids two pitfalls of traditional criticism: first, the rationalist dogmatism that judges in the name of preconceived criteria; and second, "skeptical tolerance, which, in the end, stems from an immoderate worship of the creative faculty reduced to the mere faculty of the creator's expression. . . . [Schlegel] magically captured in the work itself the laws of the mind instead of treating it as a mere by-product of subjectivity" (*G.S.,* 1:71). In that way, Schlegel established "the cardinal principle of any critical activity since romanticism—the judgment of works according to immanent criteria" (*G.S.,* 1:71). In terms of the object—or the artistic configuration—he assures "the autonomy that Kant conferred on the faculty of judgment in his *Critique*" (*G.S.,* 1:72). By autonomy, Benjamin does not mean only the proper legalities that govern both the aesthetic sphere in general and each work of art in particular; he is aiming not only at a purist conception of aesthetic particularity but at the sovereignty of art itself,[7] the fact that the meaning of the work cannot be drawn out except through a form of criticism that poetically finishes it instead of translating it into rational language, whether that of philosophy or that of ordinary consciousness. Through the criticism of the work, an irreducible viewpoint on the world is affirmed, as Schlegel wrote: "To find formulae for individual works that alone allow us to understand them in the most literal sense: that is the substance of art criticism" (quoted in *G.S.,* 1:71).

For the romantics, what has to be grasped in the work is the *form.* For Benjamin, who reveals his reasons in the appendix to *Der Begriff* on Goethe and romanticism, what must ultimately be grasped is, rather, the truth content, but for him, this content is not dissociable from form. The concept of form stems from Fichte's *Doctrine of Science,* which sees "reflection manifesting itself in the simple form of knowledge" (*G.S.,* 1:72); form is both the "transcendental" structure of knowledge, its condition of possibility, and what still limits reflection, which must then become the object of a second-level reflection. Hence, "the pure essence of reflection is revealed for the romantics in the purely formal appearance of the work of art. As a result, form is the objective expression of the reflection proper to the work. . . . It is through its form that the work of art is a center of living reflection" (*G.S.,* 1:73). But because of the particularity of form, it "remains tainted by a moment of contingency" (*G.S.,* 1:73), which is the reason for the work's incompletion: "For criticism to be . . . the removal of all limitations, the work must rest on limitation" (*G.S.,* 1:73); such is the "self-limitation of reflection." In other words, meaning and validity, which in criticism acquire a virtually universal value, are tied in the work of art to the particularity of the figures or the narrative structure. In recognizing an intrinsic reflection in the work, Schlegel, according to Benjamin, resolves the paradox of immanent criticism:

> In fact, it is difficult to see how a work of art could be criticized in terms of its own tendencies, since those tendencies, inasmuch as they can be established indisputably, are realized, and inasmuch as they are not, are impossible to establish indisputably. . . . The immanent tendency of the work, and as a result, the criterion for immanent criticism, is reflection, which is at its formation, and of which its form is the imprint. In truth, however, this reflection is not so much the criterion for judgment as, first and foremost, the foundation of another kind of criticism which does not have judgment as its vocation and for which the essential does not lie in the evaluation of the particular work of art but in the presentation of its relations to art works as a whole, and in the end, to the Idea of art. (*G.S.*, 1:77–78)

It is because Schlegel seeks not to judge the work of art but, rather, to understand and explain it, to complete and systematize it, and finally, to dissolve it in the absolute of art, that the paradox of immanent criticism is overcome: It excludes "any judgment of the work of art, for which it would be absurd to give an immanent criterion. The criticism of the work of art is rather its reflection, which, of course, can never deploy more than the germ that is immanent to it" (*G.S.*, 1:78).

For early romantic criticism, judgment of the work was limited to establishing its mere "criticizability," the criterion that allowed one to tell whether the work had a reflection worthy of the name. At the same time, in criticizable works, there cannot be a scale of values: All works that bear a reflection within them are equally worthy of consideration, and, in contrast, what is not criticizable is by definition bad. Benjamin underlines the fact that "the validity of the critical judgments of romanticism has been amply confirmed. They have determined until our own time the fundamental evaluation of the historical works of Dante, Boccaccio, Shakespeare, Cervantes, and Calderón, as well as the phenomenon contemporary to them: Goethe" (*G.S.*, 1:80). But in the word "evaluation" he does not distinguish between interpretation and value judgment. Recognizing these authors' value is hardly the same as discovering something new; at most, it is a matter of appreciating them at their true value, legitimating them in the face of the canonical texts of Antiquity. Moreover, the early romantics did not "discover" Hölderlin any more than did Goethe. And Schlegel admits the retrospective character of romantic criticism: " 'Only the classic and the eternal pure and simple' can be the subject of criticism" (*G.S.*, 1:81). What remains is the classic status of works criticized or translated by the romantics.

Romantic Art: Irony, the Novel, and Prose

The same concern for objectivity also characterizes the romantic theory of irony, which has frequently been interpreted as the expression of pure subjectivism. Of course, "the poet's arbitrariness, according to Schlegel, suffers no law that dominates him" (*G.S.*, 1:82), but that simply means that the poet obeys no other law than that of his autonomous form. It is only within the framework of that form, relative to the content of the work, that nothing is forbidden him.

Nevertheless, what characterizes the *art* of German romanticism is, in the end, the fact that arbitrariness is also exercised toward form itself, inasmuch as form is only a medium for reflection and the absolute to be attained is the idea of art itself. Properly romantic art rests on the critical idea of "the indestructibility of the work of art" (*G.S.*, 1:86): "Criticism sacrifices the work of art totally to the love of the cohesion of art itself" (*G.S.*, 1:85). The result, according to Benjamin, is fragmented or disordered works like Ludwig Tieck's plays or Jean Paul's novels. Irony tears the work of art to pieces in the name of art, and thus renders it indestructible. A mystical idea underlies the destructive irony of romanticism:

> The ironization of the form of presentation is in some sense the storm that sweeps open the curtain before the transcendental order of art, revealing it even as it reveals the work of art, which remains immediately within it as a mystery. . . . It represents the paradoxical tendency to build up the work by demolishing it: to demonstrate in the work itself its relation to the Idea. (*G.S.*, 1:86)

It is also in the name of this idea that the romantics require a fusion of different forms, a meeting, in the idea of poetry, of "all the separate genres of poetry" (*G.S.*, 1:188). From this conception, the idea of the one Book is born—a mythical reference of modern literature, especially since Mallarmé: "All the books of accomplished literature," writes Schlegel in *Ideen* (fragment 95), "must be only a single book" (quoted in *G.S.*, 1:90). From this same mystical theory, there stems the idea of criticism as "the poetry of poetry," and the task assigned to "universal progressive poetry" to "present the Idea of art in the total work of art" (*G.S.*, 1:91). This total work of art is primarily the novel, the "most resolute working out of self-limitation and of reflective self-broadening" (*G.S.*, 1:98). It is founded entirely on reflection and brings together all forms, from poetry to dramatic dialogue to epic narration, presenting them as a continuum.

Beginning with this romantic idea, Lukács wrote his *Theory of the Novel*

(1914–1915, published in 1916). He, too, addressed the question of novelistic prose. In his view, in the modern period, when meaning can no longer be apprehended in reality, "only prose can then encompass the suffering and the laurels, the struggle and the crown, with equal power; only its unfettered plasticity and its non-rhythmic rigour can, with equal power, embrace the fetters and the freedom, the given heaviness and the conquered lightness of a world henceforth immanently radiant with found meaning."[8] But, for Benjamin, the idea of prose takes on an even stronger meaning: "The Idea of poetry," he writes, "is prose" (*G.S.,* 1:100–101).

Beyond the fusion of poetic genres in the novel, Benjamin is addressing one meaning of the word "reflection," perceived especially, no doubt, through Hölderlin and his idea of sobriety in art. Benjamin adds that "this principle is the fundamental idea of the romantic philosophy of art—an essentially new idea that has yet to reveal itself fully; the greatest age, perhaps, of the Western philosophy of art bears its mark" (*G.S.,* 1:104). For Benjamin, the link between reflection and prose seems to be based on the use of language that associates prose with sobriety.

Literature is conceived as an exercise of lucidity and even calculation, the obverse of feeling and enthusiasm. Here, Benjamin introduces his own nuance concerning the disenchantment of art:

> Under the light of irony, it is only the illusion that falls apart; the kernel of the work of art remains indestructible because it does not rest on ecstasy, which can dissipate, but on an intangible, sober, prosaic figure. . . . The novel is the prototype for this mystical constitution of the work of art beyond the restricted forms that are beautiful in appearance (the poetic in the narrow sense). It is, in the end, in the place it grants to these "beautiful" forms and to beauty in general that this theory marks a break with the traditional conceptions of the essence of art. . . . Form is no longer the expression of beauty but of art conceived as the Idea itself. At the very end, the concept of beauty generally had to disappear from the romantic philosophy of art . . . because beauty, as an object of "enjoyment," of pleasure, of taste, did not seem to be reconcilable with the strict sobriety that, in the new conception, determined the essence of art. (*G.S.,* 1:106)

According to Benjamin, that is the aesthetic theory of Gustave Flaubert and of modern poetry. Above all, it is his own conception of art, founded on his philosophy of language: The task of criticism is to complete the work by presenting its "prosaic kernel" or the "eternally sober consistency of the work" (*G.S.,* 1:109), that is, to transfer the language of art to the level of a higher, more definitive language detached from all sensible beauty, to the level of the inexpressive and creative word that, according to "The Task of the Translator," is the aim of all language.

This destruction of illusion, of appearance, of emotion, and of beauty in the name of prose, sobriety, the Idea, and reflection is the formulation of an aesthetics of the sublime that sacrifices the beautiful appearance in the name of truth. Its form will change often in Benjamin's works, before undergoing a decisive turning point in the theory of the aura. In its first formulations, it leaves intact, even accentuates, the esoteric character of the work of art. Like criticism and translation, the sobriety of artistic prose performs a function of sublimation in the messianic process of history, more through the action stemming from its mere existence than through any supposed persuasion exercised on the mind.

That said, romantic theory speaks only of the form of works and says nothing of their content. The romantics' concern was not the truth of works but their truly aesthetic completion. The romantics' aestheticism was at the origin of their "insanely orgiastic disclosure of all secret sources of the tradition" (*Correspondence,* 89). In addition, "they did not understand the *moral* dimension with which [Goethe's] *life* struggled" (*Correspondence,* 117). In an appendix to *Der Begriff,* Benjamin underscores the necessity of complementing that theory by relying on Goethe's aesthetics.

The Criticism to Come: Form and Original Phenomenon

In the esoteric appendix to *Der Begriff* discussing "the aesthetic theories of the early romantics and of Goethe," Benjamin formulates for the first time the task of the criticism to come. It stems from the fundamental difference between these two aesthetics. The romantics recognized only the "Idea" of art, as an a priori for their method of critical completion; they did not recognize the "Ideal" of art, as an a priori for the work's content, what it was to be about. The romantics' "aestheticism" lay precisely in their refusal to exclude something from the field of art in the name of any ethical or theoretical norm whatsoever. For Goethe, in contrast, there existed a "limited plurality of pure contents" (*G.S.,* 1:111) that compose the Ideal of art. Through this conception, Goethe "is linked to the Greeks. Beginning with his philosophy of art, he interpreted the idea of the Muses under Apollo's dominion as that of the pure contents of art as a whole. The Greeks allowed for nine such contents" (*G.S.,* 1:111). Unlike the forms relativized by the Idea of art, these contents are discontinuous and are not found in any piece of art as such. Goethe speaks of them as invisible archetypes that are accessible only to "intuition" and that works of art can at best "resemble."[9] In Goethe's view, the works that come closest are Greek works, "relative archetypes, models" (*G.S.,* 1:112).

Archetypes are not created by art; they "dwell, before any production of a work, in that sphere where art is not creation but nature. Goethe's concern in his inquiry into original phenomena was ultimately to grasp the Idea of nature in order to make it an archetype (a pure content)" (*G.S.,* 1:112). This was not nature as an object of science, but "true" nature: "It is in art alone, and not in the nature of the world, that true nature, accessible to intuition, originally phenomenal, is visible through reproduction, whereas in the nature of the world it is certainly present, but hidden (submerged under the brilliance of the manifestation)" (*G.S.,* 1:113). This concept of nature is the object of a critical reflection on Goethe that Benjamin will undertake in his essay on Goethe's *Elective Affinities.*

Benjamin shares Goethe's reservations about the romantics' suppression, in art as medium-of-reflection, of any firm distinction between the contingent real and the absolute: "Art was precisely the area where romanticism made every effort to turn to advantage and with the greatest purity the immediate reconciliation of the contingent and the non-contingent" (*G.S.,* 1:114). For Goethe, such a reconciliation has no raison d'être. Benjamin, who also rejects such exaltation but who acknowledges the gains of the romantic aesthetic—its messianic theory of prose and of modern sobriety, its conception of criticism as a reflection of a reflective kernel immanent in the work—raises the problem in the following manner:

> The [romantic] idea of art is the Idea of its form, as the [Goethean] Ideal of art is the Ideal of its content. The fundamental, systematic question of the philosophy of art can thus also be formulated as the question of the relation between the Idea of art and the Ideal of art. The present inquiry must remain on the threshold of that question. (*G.S.,* 1:117)

And since in 1919 he does not yet have an answer, he continues: "Even today, this state of the German philosophy of art as it presented itself around 1800, in the theories of Goethe and the early romantics, is still legitimate. The romantics were no better at solving—or even posing—this problem than was Goethe" (*G.S.,* 1:117).

Just as the romantics neglected to pose the question of content, Goethe did not have a satisfactory theory of form; "He interprets it as style" (*G.S.,* 1:117), in the sense of some particular historical style, that of the Greeks or his own. In contrast to the early romantics' theory, Goethe's theory poses the question of the "criticizability of the work of art" in terms of a general doubt. Benjamin writes that "in the matter of the philosophy of art, all the work of the romantics can be summed up in this: they sought to demonstrate that, on principle, the work is criticizable. The Goethean theory of art, in contrast, is entirely commanded by its intuition of the uncriticizable character of works" (*G.S.,* 1:110). In Goethe's view, criticism was neither possible nor necessary:

At most, it may be necessary to give an indication of what is good or a warning about what is bad; and, for the artist who has an intuition of the archetype, it is possible to pronounce an apodictic judgment on works. But Goethe challenges "criticizability" as the essential moment of the work of art. From his point of view, a methodical criticism—that is, one necessary for the thing itself—is impossible. On the contrary, in romantic art, criticism is not only possible and necessary, it even contains within its theory the paradox of having more value than the work itself. (*G.S.,* 1:119)

Benjamin wants to maintain, against Goethe, the possibility and necessity of criticism, without forgetting the critic's inferiority in principle to the poet, and, in the critical evaluation of a work, to account for its content by seeking to define an imperative for validity that the romantics associate only with form. What prevents Goethe from grasping the idea of a *criticizable* content is the fact that he identifies it with true nature—the archetypal nature of original phenomena, which the poet intuits—instead of perceiving its historical meaning. What prevents Schlegel and Novalis, in their aesthetic theory, from conceiving of a criticizable *content* is their reduction of the world, of nature, and of history to an artistic process that reduces content to form and, in the end, to the Idea of art. In *The Origin of German Tragic Drama,* Benjamin will replace this single Idea with the plural, irreducible idea-forms, which he himself designates as Goethe's "Ideals" (*Origin,* 35).

The romantic critic casts a "sober light" on the Idea of the as-yet contingent work, which "makes the plurality of works go dark" (*G.S.,* 1:119). Benjamin wants to conserve and name that irreducible plurality by associating it with the normative dimension inherent in the content of works, which can be validated by criticism. That normative dimension rediscovers the problems of truth and justice in the work of art, thus reconsidering the radical differentiation of art accomplished by the romantics: For Benjamin, there is no beauty without truth. The task Benjamin assigns to his work to come is to bring about a synthesis between Goethe's aesthetics and that of the romantics. That is the theoretical program of his essays on Goethe and baroque drama.

AN EXEMPLARY PIECE OF CRITICISM

The Authority and Violence of Criticism

Written between the summer of 1921 and February 1922, two years after *Der Begriff der Kunstkritik in der deutschen Romantik,* the essay "Goethes *Wahlverwandtschaften*" (Goethe's *Elective Affinities*) is, from a philosophical point of view, one of the most ambitious texts that Benjamin ever completed.[10] In a letter to Scholem dated 8 November 1921, he wrote: "I have to complete writing my critique of the *Elective Affinities*. This is just as important to me as an exemplary piece of criticism as it is a prolegomena to certain purely philosophical treatises—what I have to say about Goethe is located somewhere between the two" (*Correspondence,* 194).

Beginning with his thesis on the concept of criticism, Benjamin wrote a certain number of extremely dense texts: "Fate and Character" (September–November 1921), "The Task of the Translator" (March–November 1921), "Theologico-Political Fragment" (1920–1921), and "Ankündigung der Zeitschrift: *Angelus Novus*" (Notice for the journal *Angelus Novus*; December 1921–January 1922).

In the notice for *Angelus Novus,* Benjamin distinguishes between an annihilating criticism and a positive criticism, both of which have essentially the same role: challenging the public's expectations. But the primary characteristic of criticism is sovereign authority. The critic is literally Adam naming and citing the works according to their truth: "We must reconquer the force of critical speech in two ways. We must repeat both the accusation and the verdict" (*G.S.,* 2:242). In the manner of Karl Kraus and André Breton, the secular popes of letters, Benjamin conceives of criticism as a practice of "terrorism" against the "counterfeiters of talent." The critic's role is that of a "guardian at the gate" (*G.S.,* 2:242) who refuses entry to mediocrity. Criticism has both a moral and an aesthetic responsibility to the public of the time:

> The criterion of true actuality is absolutely not found among the public. Any journal like this one must embrace what is truly current, what is forming under the infertile surface of the new, that absolute novelty whose exploitation it must cede to the newspapers. In embracing true actuality, it must be pitiless in its thought, imperturbable in its statements; if necessary it must have total disregard for the public. (*G.S.,* 2:241–242)

The authoritarian violence defended by Benjamin corresponds both to his esoteric idea of "revelation" as the essence of the work of art and to his theory, developed in "The Task of the Translator," that the work of art is not destined for the receiver. How do critics justify their claim to authority? If they were to argue for it, they would be within the public's reach; they can therefore only produce imperatives. Benjamin reclaims for the critic the artist's tyrannical freedom, which is justified only by the work of art, not by argument. This freedom is exercised in two forms. When it destroys, it proceeds collectively, in generalizations: "How would it manage otherwise?" (*G.S.,* 2:242). In contrast, "positive criticism," more than it has done in the past, more than the romantics succeeded in doing, . . . must limit itself to the isolated work of art. In fact, great criticism does not have the task, as is sometimes believed, of instructing through historical representation, or of forming minds through comparisons, but rather of attaining knowledge by sinking into its object. It is incumbent upon criticism to account for that truth of works that art and philosophy require. (*G.S.*, 2:242)

"Goethes *Wahlverwandtschaften*" was written in that spirit.

Truth is, therefore, the criterion to be sought in the content, the complement of the aesthetic criterion of form. But this is not truth as opposed to artistic value. In this case, truth means validity in an undifferentiated sense, absolute validity. Benjamin nevertheless rejects all obscurantist interpretation of such a claim. Concerning the underlying philosophical attitude of any position the journal *Angelus Novus* might take,[11] he pronounces the following rule:

For it, the universal validity of the manifestations of the life of the mind must be linked to the question of knowledge if it is to be able to claim a place within the framework of the religious orders being formed. Not that such orders can already be predicted. But we can predict that, without them, the things that these days—the first of a new era—are struggling with to attain life will not be manifested. (*G.S.*, 2:244)

Such a religious exercise is nevertheless incompatible with "the convenient obscurity of esotericism"; Benjamin requires not only Hölderlinian "sobriety" but also "a rationality without concession" (*G.S.*, 2:244), which in this case can only mean a maximum sobriety or clarity in the exposition of the noncontingent and the ungroundable.

It is this same ungroundable character that, on the moral and legal plane, defies the relation between "divine violence" and legal violence. In "Critique of Violence," Benjamin constructs a theory in which divine violence is defined as the pole opposite to the law, which—as the founding violence of power or simply as conservative violence (military service, for example)—he calls "mythic violence":

Just as in all spheres God opposes myth, mythic violence is opposed to divine violence. And the latter constitutes its antithesis in all respects. If mythic violence is law-making, divine violence is law-destroying; if the former sets boundaries, the latter boundlessly destroys them; if mythic violence brings at once guilt and retribution, divine power only expiates; if the former threatens, the latter strikes; if the former is bloody, the latter is lethal without spilling blood. (*Reflections*, 297, translation modified)

Divine violence expiates even as it destroys because of its innate sense of justice: It is located outside the mythic cycle of life, power, and the illusory "equality" of laws.[12] In the religious tradition, the classic example of divine violence is provided by God's judgment, as manifested in the Bible by punishment without warning; but, adds Benjamin, to underscore its actuality, divine violence

> is also found in present-day life in at least one sanctioned manifestation. Educating violence, which in its perfected form stands outside the law, is one of its manifestations. It is defined, therefore, not by miracles directly performed by God, but by the expiating moment in it that strikes without bloodshed and, finally, by the absence of all lawmaking. (*Reflections*, 297, translation slightly modified)

Benjamin sees very well that such an extension of "educating violence" to the scale of society is not without risks:

> The premise of such an extension of pure or divine violence is sure to provoke, particularly today, the most vehement objections, and to be countered by the argument that, taken to its logical conclusion, it leaves men free to exercise even lethal violence against one another. This, however, cannot be conceded. (*Reflections*, 298, translation modified)

Divine violence leaves intact the commandment "Thou shalt not kill." Nevertheless, this commandment's function is not to serve as a criterion of judgment but rather as a "guideline for actions of persons or communities who have to wrestle with it in solitude and, in exceptional cases, to take on themselves the responsibility of ignoring it" (*Reflections*, 298). That responsibility stems from "divine violence" and its sovereign justice. Like educating violence, it is carried out among minorities prey to mythic violence and cannot, according to Benjamin, be grounded in law. In other words, divine violence is authorized by an ethic that has to account for its decisions only to God, not humanity. This is the violence of the general strike, of revolutionary and anarchist violence, according to Georges Sorel (*Reflections*, 291).[13] Such is also the sovereignty of the innovative artist who breaks with an accepted definition of the work of art, and the ethic of the critic who challenges the public's judgment by anticipating aesthetic criteria that have not yet been established. Their violence is a pure manifestation and release of the genius of humanity in its opposition to the forces of myth. For

Benjamin, society has no potential for rationality that the critic could rely on and invoke in addressing the public.

This concept of genius, borrowed from Hölderlin (*G.S.*, 2:116), designates the prophetic, divine faculty of humanity, by virtue of which it escapes destiny and attains freedom. This faculty is intimately linked to poetic creativity. Art and poetry are the privileged locus of a salutary interruption in the fatal course of things:

> It was not in law but in tragedy that the head of genius lifted itself for the first time from the mist of guilt, for in tragedy demonic fate is breached. . . . In tragedy pagan man becomes aware that he is better than his god, but the realization robs him of speech, remains unspoken. . . . The paradox of the birth of genius in moral speechlessness, moral infantility, is the sublimity of tragedy. It is probably the basis of all sublimity, in which genius, rather than God, appears. ("Fate and Character," in *Reflections*, 307)

In a general way, art and philosophy rise up in opposition to myth, and it is in that negation that, for Benjamin, the common ground of the Greek and biblical traditions lies, even though the biblical tradition is then once more related to the Greek as to a pagan and still mythical heritage:

> For truth to be established, we must first know what myth is: we must know it as a reality indifferent to truth and destructive of truth. That is why the Greeks had to eliminate myth so that—after a theurgical phase, which was art and philosophy only in a mistaken sense of these words— true art and true philosophy were born, for both are founded in truth, exactly to the same degree, no more and no less. ("Goethes *Wahlverwandt- schaften*," in *G.S.*, 1:162)

"Divine violence" is the transposition of the genius's faculty to the realm of practice. Since law has been defined as purely instrumental— mythic, and as a result, without relation to transcendent justice—the just act can intervene only in a manner as unpredictable and yet as pertinent as the emergence of the poetic or critical genius. "This criticism . . . [which] ascertains the moments in which the artistic sensibility puts a stop to fate draped as progress and encodes the utopian experience,"[14] is wrongly invested, in Benjamin, with the mark of praxis.

Conversely, Benjamin's aesthetic criticism is always conceived as a practical intervention, an effort to interrupt the blind course of history and bring about an awakening, a raising of consciousness. Although he is opposed to an instrumental writing that intervenes in the name of a cause to convince the public, Benjamin nevertheless aspires to "an objective writing, which for that very reason is highly political." It is in forcing the limits of the inexpressible and of silence, in revealing the unsaid, the forgotten, and the repressed through criticism, that he believes he can have a practical effect.

Criticism and Truth

As an "exemplary piece of criticism," Benjamin's essay on *Elective Affinities* pursues several objectives: It seeks to solve a question left open at the end of the study on the concept of art criticism (the possibility of a criticism of both form and "truth content"); to test a certain number of philosophical ideas (on the Enlightenment and the false emancipation from myth, on redemption, beauty, appearance, truth, and, finally, hope), and to demonstrate the limits of what Goethe was able to say, to submit certain conceptions deeply anchored in the German mentality to a salutary shock. In this sense, it is a theologico-political essay that targets "true actuality" as defined in the notice for *Angelus Novus*. Goethe's novel is interpreted both as the testimony of a culture that remained prey to the obscurity of pagan myth and as a sublime attempt to wrench free of it, and thus as a privileged moment in the break with "destiny." Before the messianic end of history, art alone is capable of making this break, and it is incumbent upon criticism to present the break in order to bring us closer to that end.

The conceptual structure of Benjamin's essay can be outlined as follows: The philosophical problem of the work of art's validity is linked to the idea of truth defined in theological terms. This idea is incarnated in the true work of art, but it is not made conceptually explicit, for it is inaccessible to philosophy; only criticism, in deciphering the work of art, can help philosophy attain it. Within the work of art itself, the subject matter and the truth content have to be distinguished. The artist approaches the subject matter through his technique and receives the truth content in the completed form of the work; the exegete addresses the subject matter in the form of commentary and the truth content in the form of criticism.

The essay is arranged into four schemata. There is, first, a *philosophical* schema grounded in the relation between the idea, intuition, and the concept. It is the task of criticism to relate theological truth both to the inaccessible horizon of philosophical inquiry and to the truth content of the work of art. Art and philosophy relate to each other according to the Kantian complementarity of the concept and intuition, united in the Idea, which is inaccessible to knowledge.

There is, second, a *critical* schema founded in the relation between the components of the work of art and the human subjects—the creator and the receiver—who relate to it. The critic addresses the truth content and the form of the work of art through a commentary on its subject matter; the artist's technique addresses only the subject matter.

There is, third, an *aesthetic* schema of the relation between appearance and essence in beauty. Appearance and essence are united in the work of art but are dissociated through criticism, which grounds beauty in the truth content, whereas the authentic writer corrects the beauty of mere appearance through the sublime caesura of the inexpressive.

Finally, there is a *historical* schema that anchors relations among men in the religious, since criticism's task is, in the modernity of the Enlightenment—a false emancipation placed under the sign of myth and appearance—to assure the continuity of tradition through the truth content contained within the act that gives form to the authentic work of art.

A wall separates modern consciousness from both truth and tradition: Just as the image and the concept do not immediately have access to theological truth, the artist's technique does not immediately have access to the work's form and truth content. And just as modern beauty is dissociated from its anchorage in truth, modern freedom is cut off from its anchorage in tradition and ritual. *Criticism* plays a determinant role in crossing over that wall. It always holds the key to the enigma. Whether they be truth or freedom, art or beauty, criticism is responsible for the founding values of culture. This privilege is tied to the fact that only criticism can act as a link between the image and the concept, the two aspects of a theological truth that has been split in two. The transgressive power of aesthetic criticism is exercised through the deciphering of the absolute in works of art. In the terms of "On Language as Such," the critic, at a time when life is no longer grounded in ritual, is the "Adam" who makes every effort to name in conceptual terms what the artist named imperfectly through the figuration of his work.

In a methodological introduction, Benjamin approaches the question of the work of art's content, which it is incumbent upon the critic to reveal: "In a work of art, the critic is seeking the truth content, the commentator the subject matter" (*G.S.,* 1:125). The commentator, or literary historian, latches on to artistic phenomena in their immediacy and diversity; the philosophical critic is interested in their force of truth and revelation and in their unity.

Seeking to escape the aestheticism of the romantics, Benjamin thus defines the true work of art in terms of its truth content. And yet, he does not move toward a type of thinking associated with Schelling and Hegel. For those two philosophers, the truth of art was the truth of philosophy itself, which translates it into conceptual terms, whereas for Benjamin, as for Kant, "doctrine" is beyond reach. For Benjamin, the authentic exercise of philosophy is limited to criticism, and in particular to aesthetic criticism, inasmuch as the figuration of art, in approximating the meaning of the whole by means of its immanent finality, bears a piece of "doctrine."

From Benjamin's first writings, truth is the correlative of such a philosophical doctrine, which is not distinct from theology; ultimately, theological truth is the aim of all thought, all criticism, all art, and all translation. Despite the discontinuity of forms, there exists a solidarity between the poetic work and the Adamic name given to things as a function of their essence. The essay on *Elective Affinities* reveals its hand only in the third and last part: "All authentic works have their sisters in the field of philosophy. They are precisely the figures in which the ideal of their problem is manifested" (*G.S.*, 1:172). Through the concept of an "ideal of the problem," Benjamin attempts to reformulate the Goethean notion of an ideal of art, which is nothing other than its archetypal content; Benjamin speaks of an ideal *of the problem,* to underscore the link between the truth of art and philosophy. Because of philosophy's inability to possess the ontological character of truth

> there exists no question that embraces in its questioning the unity of philosophy. In philosophy, the ideal of the problem designates the concept of that nonexistent question concerning the unity of philosophy. But the system also is in no sense an object of inquiry. Yet there exist productions that, without being a question, have the deepest affinity to the ideal of the problem. These are works of art. (*G.S.*, 1:172)

Schelling's idea of art as an *organon* of philosophy is thus subject to the restrictions formulated by Kant: Unlike Schelling, Benjamin considers philosophy incapable of formulating the idea of its own unity. In art, the ideal of the problem is buried under the plurality of works,

> and the role of criticism is to extract it from them. In the work of art, criticism shows the ideal of the problem through one of its manifestations. For it finally takes note in them of the possibility for a formulation dealing with the truth content proper to the work of art as the supreme problem of philosophy. In every true work of art, one can detect a manifestation of the ideal of the problem. (*G.S.*, 1:173)

In other words, every true work of art allows the critic to address *the* central problem of philosophy and not just *certain* questions that also, from another point of view, interest philosophers. From the legitimate possibility of approaching a philosophical problem from a work of art (following the

ny, would make criticism a reductive operation. Benjamin's diffi-
ddressing aesthetic validity lies in the fact that he is seeking it at
ial level, in a philosophical message underlying all true works,
f embracing artistic successes whose criteria cannot be established
for all; in the end, he is seeking an evocation of the true life in the
rt that conforms to philosophical doctrine, not an aesthetically
representation of *an* experience that does not allow for existential
phical extrapolation.

quite classic manner, Benjamin thinks that the effort of criticism
truth is aided by the passage of time; over time the truth content
d:

ed in the first moments of the work of art, as time goes on, we see
he subject matter and the truth content become dissociated, since,
ugh the latter remains just as hidden, the former begins to show
gh. The more time passes, the more the exegesis of what is
ishing and bewildering in the work, that is, its subject matter,
nes for the later critic a precondition. (*G.S.*, 1:125)

result, the critic can only begin with commentary (*G.S.*, 1:125).
content remains "hidden" because of a "fundamental law of all
s the truth content takes on more meaning, its link to the subject
comes less apparent and more internal" (*G.S.*, 1:125). In other
more important the work, the more its truth is emancipated from
cal elements as they fade into the past. According to Benjamin,
at defines the fundamental critical question:

he appearance of the truth content lie in the subject matter, or does
e of the subject matter lie in the truth content? For, in becoming
iated in the work, they decide its immortality. In this sense, the
y of works of art prepares for their criticism, whose power is
ented by historical distance. (*G.S.*, 1:125–126)

this mean something more or other than the fact that it is difficult
work of art at the time of its creation, to the extent that its burning
tter dissimulates the source of its force (whether truth or simply
uality)? If so, there is an enormous risk of inferring that the
of posterity is more certain than that of contemporaries, even
Benjamin's thinking is opposed to the falseness inherent in
n: forgeting, repression, deformation, the ideology of progress.
gh he concedes that a true work of art owes its value to its *own*
ent, Benjamin situates the criterion for that value outside the
theological truth that the work of art partakes in. And yet, in

principle of the "essay") Benjamin deduces the claim that criticism is able
to at least evoke "the supreme problem of philosophy," if not to solve it (the
age seems to forbid that).

Or, to set aside Benjamin's systematic claim, criticism is an attempt to
approach a philosophical problem that is vital for the age and to situate it
in history (including the history of thought) through a work of art chosen
because of its universal interest. That is what Benjamin does when he writes
on Goethe, on baroque drama, or on Baudelaire. Yet such an undertaking
does not itself prove that other more systematic approaches, independent of
aesthetic criticism, are not possible in philosophy. Benjamin never sets his
theological and metaphysical concept of truth against other conceptions.
For him, truth means life considered in the light of messianic salvation. It
is not open to polemical justification; rather, it is a quality of the true life.

Whatever we might think of Benjamin's theory, the secularized forms
of such a "truth" are no doubt indissociable from aesthetic "validity." We
need to be able to determine noncircularly what a "true work of art" is.
What makes a work of art "successful" is probably not unrelated to the idea
of a "successful" form of existence, even though art may present its failure
or impossibility. In that case, the work of art tries to compensate for the
absence of a lived realization of that successful existence, or it presents it in
an intense way. As a result, the work of art confers upon that absence, that
impossibility, an imaginary completion. In this sense, every work of art casts
a "messianic" light on the fragment of reality it represents or on the artistic
gesture itself. Whatever is subject to the public gaze is wrenched from the
triviality of the profane and daily world. But what is thus "transfigured"[15]
reaches a nonprofane world only metaphorically; what is lifted from the
quotidian and removed from everyday language does not through this act
alone acquire the status of an ontological truth: Each case is an individual
solution and there is an irreducible plurality of completions that can hardly
claim the cognitive universality implied by the concept of truth.

Benjamin's approach poses the following question: What does grounding an aesthetic judgment as such mean if the work of art must ultimately
be judged as a function of a metaphysical truth to which philosophy has no
direct access[16] but which the work of art represents? In all the great
philosophical aesthetics, art has a tendency to exceed the definitions that
would reduce it to one particular field. That means, in particular, that it is
impossible to account for a work of art by adopting a *purely* aesthetic
viewpoint. A work of art that is satisfying from a formal point of view can
be empty and of little interest from a more general point of view. It therefore
seems that, to judge "beauty"—in other words, the aesthetic quality of a
work of art—one must be aware of criteria that are not purely aesthetic but
that deal with the extra-aesthetic stakes of what is represented. That said,
whatever the interest of the extra-aesthetic stakes of a work of art, they must

be *aesthetically* integrated so that the work can be perceived as a work of art and not as the pretext for a "message" foreign to art.

Benjamin's argument is circular: Having proposed to elucidate works of art by philosophy—"All authentic works have their sisters in the field of philosophy"—he abruptly reverses his inquiry and seeks in works of art a response to the impossible question of philosophy's unity. The problem is no longer one of art, but of philosophy. Kant's critique observes that the human experience imposes limits on our faculty of knowing, whereas there is

> in human reason something that no experience can make us know and yet whose reality and truth are proven by effects that present themselves in experience. . . . That is the concept of *freedom* and the law, which leads to the categorical imperative. . . . Owing to this concept, *Ideas,* which would be totally empty for simply speculative reason . . . become a reality, even though it is only moral-practical; after all, it is a matter of *conducting* ourselves as if their objects (God and immortality), which we can postulate from this (practical) point of view, were given.[17]

According to Kant, the *beautiful* offers an aesthetic Idea for our reflection which, in presenting a subjective finality of nature that is adequate to our faculties of knowing, also exceeds the limits of experience and speculative reason: This is the image of a nature that would be governed by freedom. From his first works, Benjamin sets aside, as a narrow-mindedness characteristic of the Enlightenment, any Kantian effort to establish the foundations of knowledge as a function of a Newtonian vision of nature, and, like the romantics of post-Kantian idealism before him, he seeks to decipher the Ideas in works of art. Leaving aside the function that Kant assigns to Ideas, he indiscriminately rejects the ultimate powerlessness of philosophy and the wise mutism of works of art and instead attributes all the powers of philosophy to aesthetic criticism:

> The totality of philosophy, its system, has more power than the set constituted by all its problems, for unity in the solution of all problems cannot be questioned. In fact, it may even be that, in relation to the question posed, a new question would arise immediately: to know what the unity between the response given to this problem and the response given to all other problems rests on. It follows from this that there exists no question that embraces in its questioning the unity of philosophy. In philosophy, the ideal of the problem designates the concept of that nonexistent question concerning the unity of philosophy. But the system also is in no sense an object of inquiry. Yet there exist productions that, without being a question, have the deepest affinity to the ideal of the problem. These are works of art. (*G.S.,* 1:172)

From the fact that, without infinite reg question that is able to inquire about the unity Benjamin concludes the necessity of turning But art's "affinity" with the problem of phil strated.[18] In a circular argument, Benjami philosophy to art, and art to philosophy, thr on Goethe nonetheless criticizes, that of "af not enter into competition with philosophy most precise relation to it, thanks to its problem" (*G.S.,* 1:172). The supposed "pre nothing more than a postulate, pure and sir

The difficulty is even thornier in that, impossible to speak of *a* truth in *multiple* w

> By virtue of a law that has its foundation general, that ideal of the problem can be But it is not in a plurality of problems t appears. It is rather hidden under the plu role of criticism is to extract it from them shows the ideal of the problem through or finally takes note in them of the possibil with the truth content proper to the work of philosophy. (*G.S.,* 1:173)

What criticism must extract from the the particular work's truth content, but, t art and problems, the *single* ideal of the supreme problem of philosophy. By means the critical essay must aim toward the abs

> In a work, truth, without being an object be recognized as an imperative. If we are that everything that is beautiful refers in and that we can assign it its virtual place that, in any true work of art, we can det of the problem. (*G.S.,* 1:173)

Benjamin's "in one way or another" l a "true" work of art. The relation between t will be treated later in the same essay ar *Tragic Drama*—is no more established tha of art. Furthermore, the plurality of worl the problem, which is supposed to prese principle, he does not have any means for attaining that theological truth other than the "true" works of art that present an affinity with the ideal of the problem. Only the practice of criticism allows him to leave this circle.

The Enlightenment, Myth, and Tradition

The concept of subject matter continues to be somewhat fluid as long as we do not take into account what, for Benjamin, links this term to the theological foundation of the idea of truth content. When he speaks of the subject matter of a historical epoch, that of the German Enlightenment in particular, we rapidly discover that we are dealing with the historical forms of certain eternal constellations such as love, marriage, or death. The poetic technique, which, Benjamin insists, is situated on the borderline between subject matter and truth content, is in this case revealing: "For the writer, the description of subject matter is the enigma that his technique must allow him to solve. . . . But what it signifies, in the end, has to escape the author no less than the spirit of his time" (*G.S.*, 1:146). The meaning, not only of the subject matter but also of the representation that the writer gives it and that itself rests on the truth content, is inaccessible to the creative consciousness; it can appear only through the dual work of time and criticism.

Benjamin considers marriage the central subject matter of *Elective Affinities*, not primarily as a function of the work but, rather, as a consequence of a theological or archetypal definition of marriage. Criticism consists in setting that definition against the Goethean representation: "In completely discerning the subject matter of permanent things, we also discern their truth content. The truth content is revealed as the truth content of the subject matter" (*G.S.*, 1:128). True to his philosophy of language, Benjamin makes every effort to name the subject matter as a function of its truth content and hence to judge the work of art in terms of its force of revelation. But criticism could not be the final authority, in the absence of an ultimate doctrine, if the work of art did not provide it with something to grasp. Through its *representation* of the subject matter, the work of art extends a branch to the critic that allows him or her to anticipate a part of truth, a parcel of definitive doctrine.

Benjamin attributes his own vision—which is moral and not legal—of marriage to Goethe: "In truth, marriage is never justified in law, that is, as an institution, but only inasmuch as it expresses the permanence of love, which would rather seek its expression in death than in life" (*G.S.*, 1:130). If, in Goethe's novel, the law nevertheless intervenes, through the failure of the main character's marriage, it is because Goethe wanted

> to show the force that, in its decline, proceeds from it. And this is assuredly the mythic violence of the law; in it, marriage is only the

fulfillment of a destiny that marriage itself does not dictate. For its
dissolution is only damaging because it is not at all the effect of supreme
powers. . . . It is only in this decline that it becomes the legal relation.
. . . But, however true it may be that Goethe never reached a pure
discernment of the moral consistency of this link, it never occurred to
him to ground marriage in marriage laws. At least he never doubted that
at its deepest foundation, at its most secret, marriage was moral. (*G.S.*,
1:130–131)

It is therefore only indirectly, through premonition and denunciation,
that Goethe "in fact touches on the subject matter of marriage" (*G.S.*,
1:130). He *shows* that "its dissolution transforms all of humanity in appearance, leaving only the mythic to persist as the only essence" (*G.S.*, 1:131).
When the spouses exercise their matrimonial rights toward each other,
primitive violence rears its head.

In underscoring the fact that marriage is not founded in law, Benjamin
pursues ends other than that of establishing the essence of marriage in its
truth. Through the myth of the law—already denounced in "Critique of
Violence"—he attacks modernity, its irreligiosity, and its conception of
freedom. In defending the authenticity of love and marriage and in making
claims for Goethe's premonitions, Benjamin wishes to give the legitimacy
of religious law and of tradition precedence over a modernity whose false
promises of emancipation seem to lead to the return of mythic violence. In
Elective Affinities a pastor removes a tombstone in order to plant his clover;
Benjamin asks in response:

Can we conceive, confronted with tradition, a more characteristic liberation than to lay a hand on one's ancestors' tombs, which, under the
footsteps of the living, form the ground not only of myth but also of
religion? Where does freedom lead those who act in such a manner? Far
from opening new perspectives to them, it makes them blind to what is
real about their fears. And that is because it is inadequate. For those men
to have what they need to defend themselves against the nature within
which they live, they need the rigorous attachment to a ritual that we
cannot call superstitious except when, detached from its true context, it
is only rudimentary survival. Freed from superhuman powers as only
mythical nature can be, it comes into play as a threat. (*G.S.*, 1:132)

With Goethe, Benjamin expresses his strongest reservations about a
carefree break with tradition; he forgets that, although *Faust* describes the
ravages of such a break, it also underscores its heroism and unavoidability.
Benjamin is not sensitive to the subterranean links between Goethe and
Hegel, between the writer and the dialectician of a revolutionary era. Regarding "Goethes *Wahlverwandtschaften*," the least one could say is that Benjamin

does not underscore the ambiguity that modernity had for Goethe. He does not understand that the theme of "elective affinities," the transposition of the romantic philosophy of nature to the field of loving relationships, is a warning against the obscurantism that had reemerged from within the heart of the German Enlightenment. Benjamin—who takes the logic of the work as evidence for his theses—reads it as a controlled demonstration not only of incomplete and irresponsible emancipation held prisoner to superstitions but, in a general way, of the illusions of modern freedom, of the secular values issuing from the French Revolution. Emancipation does not take place, but the chains of tradition, despite the "orgiastic" efforts of the romantics to reactualize them, are disastrously broken.

To fully appreciate Benjamin's appeal to tradition and ritual, we must keep in mind the biographical context of his essay, which is in fact inscribed in the text in its dedication to Jula Cohn. The situation of the central couple in Goethe's novel was, at the time, similar to that of Benjamin and his wife, whose marriage was on the point of breaking up because each was in love with another. The modern person's chimerical freedom, which Benjamin denounced, was something he recognized in himself and against which he mobilized the forces of tradition. Beginning in 1920 when he was writing this essay, one of the leitmotifs of his correspondence was his resolution to learn Hebrew in order to return to the sources. The theology of the first texts, then historical materialism, were doctrines that Benjamin hoped would enable him to rediscover indestructible criteria that were lacking both in his own life and in the modern society in which he lived.

Benjamin's aspiration for "doctrine" through the "treatise" form, for which the essay on Goethe was to act as a model, was motivated by his observation of a link between the decline of tradition and the failure of modern freedom. His gamble was to restore tradition by demonstrating both the disastrous effects of the break with religious ritual and the fact that we remain indebted to tradition. Only such a raising of consciousness seemed capable of neutralizing the return of myth and the perpetuation of cyclical destiny: "Destiny is the set of relations that plunges life into guilt" (*G.S.*, 1:138). For Benjamin, there can be no morality without God; he does not acknowledge the idea of a profane morality, particularly as it developed with the Enlightenment: "When supernatural life disappears in man, even if he commits no immoral act, his natural life is filled with guilt. For it is now prisoner to the simple act of living, which is manifested in man as guilt" (*G.S.*, 1:139). Only the work of art, the act of genius wrenching itself from the context of myth and guilt, allows us to break the fatal shackles.

Above all, that is what Goethe's own relation to nature seems to confirm, as it is manifested in his morphological studies and in his theory of colors. His cult of nature, which includes his theory of art founded on the idea of original phenomena, is opposed to the poetic act that wrenches itself free from mythic forces. Unbeknownst to him, however, the two are closely linked. In *Der Begriff der Kunstkritik in der deutschen Romantik,* Benjamin had underscored both the mythic character of natural archetypes supposedly at the origin of art and the indifference toward the aesthetic criticism that resulted from it:

> Just as [Goethe's] notion of nature itself remained ambiguous, he too often slipped from the original phenomenon as archetype to simple nature in the sense of a model. This way of seeing would never have imposed itself if Goethe had moved away from equivocation, had discerned that the field of art is the only one where, as ideals, original phenomena can be intuitively grasped in an adequate way, whereas, in the scientific order, the idea that represents them, though it may elucidate the object of perception, can never transform it into intuition. Far from preexisting art, original phenomena reside in art. On principle, they must never serve as standards. (*G.S.,* 1:148)

Imprisoned by his concept of nature, Goethe falls prey to the "demonic," to astrology, superstition, and the anxiety attached to them: "Anxiety is the price mythic humanity pays for frequenting demonic forces" (*G.S.,* 1:151). This theme continued to grow in force and extension in Benjamin's thinking.[19] Far from being limited to the Germany of the romantics, it applied to history as a whole, placed under the sign of the mythic eternal return and the phantasmagoria of modern consciousness. It applied in particular to the Paris of the nineteenth century as it was described by Baudelaire and Auguste Blanqui: "Blanqui's cosmic speculation," wrote Benjamin in 1929, "includes this lesson: that humanity will be prey to a mythic anxiety to the extent that the phantasmagoria occupy a place" (*G.S.,* 5:1256). There is no deliverance from this anxiety except "redemption in eternal life" (*G.S.,* 1:154). Benjamin's later dialectical materialism did not change very much in this deep conviction, except that it invested all the qualities of religious eternity in the historical present, the "now" of action.

According to Benjamin's impressive analysis, Goethe dedicated his last works to mythic powers, to "the poet's struggle to escape from the circle where mythology claimed to enclose him" (*G.S.,* 1:164). Like Hölderlin, Goethe became the slave of literature. In his last works, beginning with *Elective Affinities,* he reached the summit of his art. The key is provided in a short novella inserted into the novel that, by way of contrast, reveals the true values that the novel's characters know nothing about. Once more, divine violence attests to authenticity and true love; the characters in the novella are unacquainted with the modern ideas that destroy those in the novel. "In fact," writes Benjamin,

> when the young man chooses to dive in to save the young girl, while far
> from obeying the instructions of destiny, he still does not perform a truly
> free act. In the novel, the chimerical quest for freedom condemns the
> heroes to an evil fate; the characters in the novella are situated beyond
> freedom, beyond destiny; their courageous decision is enough to break
> the circle of a destiny ready to enclose them, enough to unmask a freedom
> that would have led them to the nothingness of choice. (*G.S.*, 1:170)

In short, "in the face of the mythic themes of the novel, the corresponding
motifs of the novella must be considered redemptive themes" (*G.S.*, 1:171).
The life of its characters is real life, in opposition to the confused and
degraded life of the novel's characters.

Such a bias against modernity can hardly be justified. Is it truly the
"chimerical quest for freedom" that destroys the characters and the
"nothingness of choice" that stands in solidarity with the break with
ancestors, ritual, and tradition? Is it not, rather, indecision, half-measures,
and disavowed and cowardly desire over which modernity has no privilege? In opposing tradition and the divine violence of a "courageous
decision" to an ill-conceived freedom applied not to public life but to
one's love life—over which the law in fact loses its power—Benjamin
seems to be hurling abuse at himself, the modern man who knows nothing
of tradition and who has fallen prey to a situation comparable to that of
the characters in the novel. Nevertheless, there is nothing to indicate that
the return to tradition was within his grasp, nor that it is within ours;
there is nothing that allows us to say that the *moral* problem evoked by
Elective Affinities is elucidated in any decisive manner. The "redemption"
that is here the antithesis of myth appears no less irrational than the
behavior of those who, believing they are free, fall prey to myth. The
"decision" reached in response to catastrophe and miracle, through a
gesture of sovereign violence as it is conceived in "Critique of Violence"—
the tragic or irremediable outcome that is barely averted on several
occasions in the novella—could no more be erected into an example or a
rule than can the ambiguity that characterizes the behavior of the novel's
characters; both conditions are part of the same unstable universe and offer
no answer that is valid for all. In presenting redemption as a miracle,
Benjamin deprives it of all moral exemplarity.

The Beautiful, Appearance, the Inexpressive

As he often does when he finds himself confronted with the inextricable
forest of a mythical universe,[20] Benjamin invokes *reason*—an incorruptible
lucidity, a sobriety that resists all seduction—in raising the question of
beauty in relation to *Elective Affinities*: "To confront it, we need a courage

which, from the safety of indestructible reason, can abandon itself to its prodigious, magical beauty" (*G.S.*, 1:180).

According to Benjamin, we must be convinced of the beauty of the character Ottilie—a beauty that moves beyond the framework of the epic form and approaches the field of painting—in order to participate in Goethe's novel (*G.S.*, 1:178–179). "With *Elective Affinities*, the demonic principles of incantatory magic irrupt in the literary work itself. What is evoked is never anything but appearance, that beauty incarnated in Ottilie" (*G.S.*, 1:179). And, according to Benjamin, beauty "in its pure state," appearance evoked by incantation, represents a danger for the work of art, which, in his view, has the role of liberating us from the mythic forces that appearance participates in and of leading us toward truth. There is an opposition between the incantatory "formula" that creates appearances out of chaos and artistic form that, through rational enchantment, momentarily transforms chaos into a universe. No work of art, writes Benjamin, "has the right to elicit a living appearance without conjuring it away; if not, it becomes pure appearance and ceases to be a work of art" (*G.S.*, 1:181).

In reaching that limit where Goethe, fascinated by the powers of myth, almost succumbs and betrays the imperatives of art, Benjamin, as he often does, turns to the philosophy of Hölderlin, the surest guarantor of his philosophy of art. As in *Der Begriff der Kunstkritik*, the *reason* defended by Hölderlin once more bears the name of "Western, Junian sobriety" (*G.S.*, 1:182); here, it is not simply the affirmation of the force of the Idea, but the destruction of the aura that surrounds the beautiful appearance of myth. What Hölderlin—in reference to the "tragic transport" or the movement of the passions that leads to catastrophe for the characters in tragedy—calls "caesura, pure speech, the counter-rhythmic interruption" (*G.S.*, 1:181), Benjamin calls "the inexpressive" (*G.S.*, 1:181), that which in a work of art is without expression and is hence reflective in nature. In other words, it is the moment of mutism in tragedy—or in any work of art—the moment of a virtual raising of consciousness that awaits the critic's explicit explanation. As Benjamin explains: "What suspends appearance, conjures away movement, and interrupts harmony is the inexpressive" (*G.S.*, 1:181). But the *reason* invoked by Benjamin against the beautiful appearance takes on the traits of masculine rigor calling feminine ambiguity back to the moral order. And the role of art, and of criticism, once more evokes a divine violence invested with moral authority:

> By interrupting with an imperative word a woman who is turning to subterfuge, we can wrench the truth from her at the very moment of the interruption; hence, the inexpressive forces the quivering harmony to suspend its movement and, through the protest it emits, confers eternity on this quivering. Thus eternalized, the beautiful is forced to justify

itself, but precisely in that justification, it now seems interrupted, and it owes the eternity of its content to the grace of that protest. The inexpressive is the critical power that can, if not separate appearance and essence in art, then at least prevent them from becoming confused. It is endowed with this power because it is moral speech. It manifests the sublime power of the true as that power defines the language of the real world according to the laws of the moral world. (*G.S.,* 1:181)

This model for the relation between art and life is, not accidently, designated by the term "sublime." For Benjamin, there is no artistic beauty that is not founded on the sublimity of truth. Truth, the ultimate criterion of aesthetic validity, does not seem to be accessible except in an authoritarian and violent way, through an action of breaking and entering. That is the reason Benjamin defines it not in discursive but in theological terms. This truth cannot convince; like the Kantian sublime, it forces one's hand through its energy, through violent emotion, and through its claim to obviousness. Although this kind of truth is conceivable in the realm of the vital illusions that the psychiatrist dissolves by bringing them to light, in the areas where moral, legal, or moral conflicts between adults are decided, where different claims confront one another, claims whose arguments must be weighed against one another, it can only take the form of authoritarian violence.

Beginning with his philosophy of language, Benjamin is led to admit only *one* truth despite the diversity of works of art, a truth that reveals the nature of mythic existence in relation to which art and criticism have a therapeutic role. This truth has a dual status: that of disillusionment and that of radical authenticity. A work of art is aesthetically valid or successful to the extent that it leads the reader toward that truth by destroying the beautiful appearance. For Benjamin, there is no properly aesthetic criterion for the value of art. Nor, as a result, is there any place for a diversity of interpretations. The central truth that has to be recognized also monopolizes meaning. For Benjamin, admitting that there might be many interpretations of a work would entail conferring the status of mythic ambiguity on art; but such an admission is inevitable only to the extent that there exists no access to truth independent of art, and therefore, to the extent that true art must be stripped of all ambiguity.

Nevertheless, Benjamin does not confine himself to a criticism founded on disillusion; he makes an effort to *redeem* the appearance of the beautiful, by linking the beauty of life to the beauty of art:

All that is essentially beautiful is linked to appearance, in a constant and essential way, but at infinitely varied degrees. That link reaches its highest point wherever life is most manifest, and in this case precisely, in the dual aspect of an appearance that triumphs or is snuffed out. For

every living thing escapes the domain of essential beauty in relation to
how advanced its nature is; in its form, essential beauty is thus manifested
more clearly as appearance. (*G.S.*, 1:194)

Hence, according to Benjamin, the living body in its nudity is not
beautiful but, rather, sublime, and in this sense it escapes the domain of
essential beauty.[21] That said—and this is where Benjamin moves from
living beauty to the beauty of art, in the name of an identity based on the
order of the creature—even "in the least living reality, as soon as something
is essentially beautiful, there is something of pure appearance in it. And
that is the case for any work of art—music being the art that is the least
affected" (*G.S.*, 1:194).

Benjamin seeks to provide evidence for the kinship between living
beauty, founded in the sublimity of Creation, and artistic beauty, founded
in the sublimity of truth. In both cases, it is a matter of establishing that
the beautiful cannot be reduced to appearance, even though appearance is
essential to it. The appearance of art does not encompass its essence, which
"refers, much more profoundly, to what in the work of art can be defined as
the very opposite of appearance: the inexpressive, that which, outside that
contrast, can neither have a place in art nor be named without equivocation"
(*G.S.*, 1:194). The fact remains that the inexpressive or the sublime in itself
cannot institute artistic beauty, which is thus indissociable from appearance.
That is why Benjamin—once more for reasons that are ultimately theological[22] and far removed from the motives that lead Nietzsche to give precedence to appearance—makes an effort to redeem the element of appearance
without which there could be no beauty: "The beautiful is essentially
beautiful as long as it maintains an appearance" (*G.S.*, 1:194). For appearance is our access to truth. According to Benjamin, without it there is
neither the revelation of truth nor—as we shall see—hope. As a result,
criticism itself must respect appearances. Appearance is the veil of beauty,
"for its very essence forces beauty to appear only veiled" (*G.S.*, 1:194). This
essence is its theological kernel, which Benjamin terms the mystery inherent
in beauty. Beauty therefore, cannot be unveiled:

Beauty is not an appearance, it is not the veil that would cover another
reality. . . . Beauty is neither the veil nor the veiled, but the object itself
beneath the veil. Unveiled, that object would remain forever lost to
appearance. Hence that very ancient idea that unveiling transforms what
is unveiled, that the veiled thing will not remain "adequate to itself"
except in its veiling. In the case of the beautiful, we must go further and
say that unveiling is itself impossible. That is the guiding idea of any art
criticism. The role of criticism is not to lift the veil, but rather, in
knowing it as such in the most exact manner, to rise to the true intuition

of the beautiful. . . . The intuition of the beautiful is mystery. . . . It is in mystery that the divine ontological foundation of beauty lies. (*G.S.,* 1:195)

This metaphysical conception of the beautiful applies the concept of appearance that is borrowed from the theological conception of human beauty to the work of art, inasmuch as the work of art reveals a sublime ground of truth. In this way, Benjamin believes he is accounting for the non-unveilable character of appearance better than did Nietzsche. Nevertheless, he conserves the Platonic judgment of what is *only* appearance, illusion, make-believe. Artistic appearance is legitimate in Benjamin's view inasmuch as it is the only way that the *essence* of beauty, its divine mystery, can manifest itself. Hegel says nearly the same thing when he asserts that the Idea must appear or that it must attain a sensible manifestation.[23]

Conversely, in defiance of the romantic and Nietzschean subversion of the Hegelian scheme of a beauty founded on transcendental truth, Benjamin remains faithful to the theological ground of his thought, but he abandons the idea of giving an autonomous foundation to the aesthetic sphere, as he had promised in the appendix to *Der Begriff der Kunstkritik.* Through the Goethean concept of the ideal, Benjamin returns to a conception of art and of the beautiful that conforms to metaphysical tradition.

After Benjamin, the question arises of whether it is possible to ground the aesthetic validity of the work of art in a radically nonmetaphysical and atheological way. In other words, can—or, must not—what is "beautiful" or aesthetically valid in a work of art be made explicit independently from "divine mystery"? That formulation implies that it is necessary to dissociate artistic beauty and human or natural beauty, to which the question of "validity" cannot be applied; at most, we can recognize in it a conformity to a canon that is also culturally established. At the same time, we need to distinguish what, in a work of art, is tied to the artist's religious conceptions and what can or must be conceived independent of a metaphysical idea of the beautiful, despite the fact that traditional art, and even modern art to a great extent, rests largely on religious or metaphysical conceptions. What is derived from art itself may be foreign to these conceptions.

The very concept of representation, detached from its metaphysical use as a substitute for the pronouncements of doctrine, might have led Benjamin to abandon the analogy between human beauty and artistic beauty: In the work of art, everything is an act of showing, emphasizing, and demonstrating, just as in criticism everything is interpretation, reconstruction, and completion. What appears in the work of art is the material configuration of the semiotic structure whose signs are to be deciphered and interpreted; what appears in human beauty is not *made* to be interpreted but resides within itself and can at the very most *indicate* the presence of a trait that must nevertheless be proven through actions. There is nothing that allows us to ground an artist's vision in a transcendental power, however sublime the work might be; the sublime is a limiting case of the human faculty for representation, the case where human faculties test their limits.

Even in its inevitable loss, Benjamin, with Goethe, proposes to redeem the being of appearance. *Elective Affinities'* "caesura," the "inexpressive" moment of its truth is, according to Benjamin, "the moment when the lovers, embracing each other, seal their ruin: 'Hope passed over their heads like a star falling from the sky.' Obviously, they do not see it fall, and Goethe could not have indicated more clearly that the ultimate hope is only such for beings for whom one hopes, not for those who themselves hope" (*G.S.,* 1:200). This ingenious interpretation, which also recalls Benjamin's commentary on Baudelaire's *Le jeu (Illuminations,* 180), cannot hide the fact that the falling star is inscribed within the context of Goethe's superstitious beliefs, his myth of nature and destiny, which Benjamin has here transfigured. It is nonetheless in the name of this disinterested sign of hope that Benjamin redeems aesthetic appearance: "Hence, in the end, hope justifies the appearance of reconciliation, and that is the only case where we cannot say, with Plato, that it is absurd to wish for the appearance of the Good. For the appearance of redemption can be, and even must be, wished for; it alone is the dwelling place of hope at its highest degree" (*G.S.,* 1:200). Benjamin recognizes in this "our hope for the redemption of all the dead," adding: "It is the only right of that faith in immortality whose flame could not arise from contact with our own existence" (*G.S.,* 1:200). And he concludes with this expression, which, in its gnomic form, anticipates the "Theses on the Philosophy of History": "Only for the hopeless was hope given to us" (*G.S.,* 1:201). In the "Theses on the Philosophy of History" as well, hope has no raison d'être except to gather together and redeem the memories of the vanquished and of those who failed. It is only in this late text that Benjamin will make explicit the ethic of solidarity that underlies the essay on Goethe.

To judge by the final sentence of his essay, Benjamin sees the "beauty" of *Elective Affinities* as resting on a narration that pushes generosity to the point of an extremely moral disinterest. The narrator, both ironic and moved, painting a situation he knows is desperate, catches a glimpse, beyond the moving illusion of the characters, of the entire meaning that is his to see in this world. The hope that the falling star symbolizes, perceived only by the narrator, has no object: It is self-sufficient. Rejecting the Christian mysticism made explicit at the end of *Elective Affinities,* Benjamin concedes the force of mystery only to the *representation* given of hope in the falling star. According to him, that is where the truth content of literature resides: in what the writer cannot say discursively. Such a redemption of appearance beyond the imperative for sobriety and the destruction of any false aura is nevertheless not indispensable for Benjamin's aesthetics. It has little place in the theory of allegory that is set out in his principal work: *The Origin of German Tragic Drama.*

THEORY OF TRAGIC DRAMA

In his two principal critical early texts, Benjamin undertakes to submit the history of modern literature to a profound revision in the name of a philosophical position. The essay on Goethe seeks to wrench a too-well-known work from the false familiarity surrounding it; the work on tragic drama attempts to restore a forgotten and repressed part of history to the German literary consciousness: "The renewal of the literary heritage of Germany, which began with romanticism, has, even today, hardly touched baroque literature" (*Origin,* 48). This is a radical movement in Benjamin's approach, a new stage in his distancing from the romantic aesthetic. As he writes in a letter to his friend Scholem in 1918—speaking both of his own writings on baroque drama, drafted in 1916, and of a text by his friend on "the lament and . . . mourning" in the Hebrew tradition—it is as a Jew that Benjamin feels his solidarity with the accursed share of literature:

> As a Jew, the inherent code, the "completely autonomous order" of the lament and of mourning, became obvious to me. Without reference to Hebrew literature, which, as I now know, is the proper subject of such an analysis, I applied the following question to the *Trauerspiel* in a short essay entitled "Die Bedeutung der Sprache in Trauerspiel und Tragödie" [The meaning of language in *Trauerspiel* and tragedy]: "How can language as such fulfill itself in mourning and how can it be the expression of mourning?" (*Correspondence,* 120, letter of 30 March 1918 [?])

Mourning for a world that, after the loss of names, has fallen into the confusion of abstract meanings; solidarity with the accursed share of German literature, which, in its cult of mourning, is close to Hebrew lamentation—such are the two principal motivations that led Benjamin to choose the *Trauerspiel* as a subject for his *Habilitation* dissertation.

In the name of a vision of the world that seems to him more comprehensive and more universal, Benjamin opposes a new hierarchy to the privileged status awarded philosophical systems, tragedy, and the artistic symbol in German thought. He contrasts *tragedy* and tragic drama, as two "ideas" opposed in their historical and religious anchorage. The modern tension between Western religions since the Reformation, as he perceives it in studies of the German sociology of religion, serves as an introduction to the particular situation of tragic drama vis-à-vis a disenchanted world. Benjamin explores this backdrop through the concepts of *secularization* and *spatialization,* concepts that he borrowed from Max Weber and Henri Bergson and through which he defines the horizon of modernity within which tragic drama is inscribed. Understood in this way, tragic drama is devoted to the gaze of *melancholia,* as Albrecht Dürer had engraved it a century before the advent of that dramatic form.

Treatise, Tragic Drama, Allegory

The concept of origin that organizes the interpretation requires the restoration of the original force, intensity, and authenticity through which a work or a form imposes an idea, a coherent way of representing the world and setting forth a truth. In every historical constellation that summons it, this idea, always threatened by the inertia of tradition, is waiting to be reactualized in its original force. Aware of the fact that German tragic drama, unlike *Elective Affinities,* does not offer the critic the opportunity to analyze an immortal masterpiece, Benjamin proposes to grasp "the metaphysics of this form" (*Origin,* 48). This entails starting from scratch and constructing what no completed work provides. For, despite an artistic inadequacy, there resides in German tragic drama as *form* a truth that Benjamin seeks to save:

> No sovereign genius imprinted his personality on this form. And yet here is the centre of gravity of every baroque *Trauerspiel.* The individual poet is supremely indebted to it for his achievements within it, and his individual limitation does not detract from its depth. (*Origin,* 49)

Benjamin thus refers only occasionally to a particular baroque tragic drama, embracing instead the notion of constructing its idea, which was never realized yet is still the bearer of a profound "truth content": "The idea of a form . . . is no less alive than any concrete work whatever. Indeed, in comparison with some of the efforts of the baroque, the form of the *Trauerspiel* is much the richer" (*Origin,* 49, translation modified). The mediocre works even reveal the underlying formal structure better than perfect works, which always exceed any determinate genre:

> The life of the form is not identical with that of the works which are determined by it, indeed the clarity with which it is expressed can sometimes be in inverse proportion to the perfection of a literary work; and the form itself becomes evident precisely in the lean body of the inferior work, as its skeleton so to speak. (*Origin,* 58)

Just as Benjamin takes liberties with these historical phenomena, these baroque dramas, in order to draw out an idea or an underlying signifying structure, it must be possible to distinguish between the theological foundations of the Benjaminian philosophy of language and the descriptive contribution of his structural analyses of baroque drama and allegory.

Throughout the three parts of *The Origin of German Tragic Drama*, Benjamin attacks three pillars of nineteenth-century German culture: the idea of a deductive *system,* disparaged in the "epistemo-critical prologue"; the canonical status of *tragedy* (at the top of the poetic hierarchy of German idealism), which is declared unrealizable in the present; and, in romanticism and German idealism, the idea of a reconciliation in the beautiful of the sensible and the suprasensible. Benjamin opposes to these, respectively, the *treatise,* or esoteric essay, as the anticipation of doctrine; tragic drama, or *Trauerspiel*; and *allegory.* These three terms—treatise, *Trauerspiel,* and allegory—as they are opposed to the immanent models of a culture marked by the idealization of Greece, are defined in their relation to transcendence; they are founded in a religious vision, that of medieval Christianity, but Benjamin also recognizes his own Judaism in them. *The Origin of German Tragic Drama* develops as a function of this transcendence, a theory of genre (reflexive and literary genres) and of modes of symbolization (symbol and allegory), a theory that is both normative and historical. It is normative inasmuch as it establishes a hierarchy and historical inasmuch as it rests on a philosophy of history. Despite the complex form of the argument, which continually accelerates in composing a mosaic based on the most diverse aspects, the internal structure of *The Origin of German Tragic Drama* is relatively simple. It relies on schemata elaborated in 1916 in "On Language as Such" and on the conceptions sketched in *Der Begriff der Kunstkritik* and in "Goethes *Wahlverwandtschaften.*" Here again, artistic "beauty," however tenuous and fragile in this case, rest on a truth content that is theological in nature.

Tragedy as Agonal Prophecy

From the end of the eighteenth century until the middle of the twentieth, every self-respecting German aesthetician was required to have at his disposal a theory of the difference between ancient and modern tragedy in order to demonstrate, despite differences in structure, the legitimacy of modern tragedy. Next to the theory of the novel, that was the principal issue in this new *querelle* between Ancients and Moderns. Through the question of tragedy, German culture posed the problem—insoluble on the political plane until the twentieth century—of how to legitimate the Luciferian revolt of those modern individuals who broke with the traditional laws of the community and whose hubris was punished by the immutable order of ancient society. From this perspective, Benjamin's originality is confined to a more radical differentiation, which denies any specifically tragic character to modern drama as it developed from Shakespeare and Pedro Calderón.

Benjamin's attitude toward tragedy is extraordinarily positive; what he rejects is the claim by an epigonic aesthetics that an authentically tragic creation can resurface in the present. Like Hegel and like the early Lukács—whose *Metaphysics of Tragedy* Benjamin cites at length, while neglecting his *Theory of the Novel*, which is even closer to *The Origin of German Tragic Drama*—Benjamin sees artistic forms as part of a "philosophy of history" (*Origin*, 102). To be more precise, for Benjamin—this is also implicit in Lukács—they are part of a "philosophy of religion" (*Origin*, 104). Opposing the vain efforts to "present the tragic as something universally human," he underscores "the simple fact that modern theater has nothing to show which remotely resembles the tragedy of the Greeks" (*Origin*, 101). According to Benjamin, tragedy is linked to a precise moment of history, that of "agonal prophecy."

Against the moralizing interpretation of German idealism, against Nietzsche's aesthetic that, according to Benjamin, does not really engage in criticism but confines itself to sidestepping it, against contemporary epigones, Benjamin erects a theory of tragedy inspired by Lukács, by Rosenzweig, and by the ideas of a friend, Florens Christian Rang (*Correspondence*, 233–234). Benjamin begins by borrowing from Hegel the historical schema claiming that tragedy presents a struggle between the ancient gods and the gods to come, a struggle in which the tragic hero is sacrificed. He introduces his own idea of the prophetic nature of tragedy, as explained in "Fate and Character": Tragedy is the first manifestation of the genius of humanity within a mythical universe. He then draws on Nietzsche, Rosenzweig, and Lukács for evidence of the nature of the tragic hero, his contained mutism, the delimitation of his life by his death. Finally, he develops Rang's ideas on the pragmatic origin of the tragic process, which is linked to the juridical procedure of ancient Greece.

According to Benjamin, tragedy is founded on myth, not on history, which, in contrast, is a determining factor for the *Trauerspiel* (*Origin*, 62). Tragedy is linked to prehistoric heroism. It represents a break in the absence of orientation that still characterizes the epic.[24] In "Fate and Character," Benjamin had already proposed the central idea regarding the nature of the tragic—that of humanity's new consciousness of pagan gods, a consciousness so new that it deprives human beings of speech. It consists in making the tragic hero, through the mere force of his gesture, the mute *"prophet"* of a message that accords with that of the biblical tradition (*Origin*, 118). Such a mutism can be represented only in the register of speech, without which there is no tragedy. This idea is explained by the Hegelian idea of tragic *sacrifice*, which is both beginning and end—the end of the "ancient law of the Olympians," the beginning of the "life of the, as yet unborn, community": "The tragic death . . . offers up the hero to the unknown god as the first fruits of a new harvest of humanity" (*Origin*, 107, translation slightly modified). This is an *agonal* prophecy inasmuch as, arriving at the *akmè*, it is articulated only through the mute struggle of the protagonists who do not know the language of the new god: "In the presence of the suffering hero the community learns reverence and gratitude for the word with which his death endowed it—a word which shone out in another place as a new gift whenever the poet extracted some new meaning from the legend" (*Origin*, 109).

The epigonic theory claims that the tragic is a universal human content. Nietzsche's *The Birth of Tragedy* opposes that idea. Benjamin sees the importance of Nietzsche's book in its underscoring of the incompatibility between the tragic spirit and democratic culture. Nietzsche saw the link that attached tragedy to the hero's myths and age, but he could not take advantage of his discoveries because of his "Schopenhauerian and Wagnerian metaphysics": for Nietzsche, tragic myth "is a purely aesthetic creation" (*Origin*, 102).

Nonetheless, Benjamin does not return to a moralizing criticism. He disputes an "apparently unchallengeable prejudice. . . . This is the assumption that the actions and attitudes encountered in fictional characters may be used in the discussion of moral problems in a similar way to an anatomical model" (*Origin*, 104). Moral phenomena are not reproducible in a work of art, quite simply because "fictional characters exist only in literature" (*Origin*, 105). In other words, "the human figure in literature, indeed in art as such, differs from the human figure in reality" (*Origin*, 105); according to Benjamin, that is one of the implications of the biblical prohibition on making graven images: It "obviates any suggestion that the sphere in which the moral essence of man is perceptible can be reproduced" (*Origin*, 105). That is why the moral content of tragedy must not be grasped "as its last word, but as one aspect of its integral truth: that is to say in terms of the philosophy of history" (*Origin*, 105, translation modified). Benjamin's approach consists in criticizing and commenting on the work of art as a function of its truth content, which stems from a "philosophy of history or of religion."

However convincing this critique of a moralizing or purely aesthetic— a radically amoral—approach to tragedy, the philosophy of history is not the *only* way to avoid a reductive reading. Diderot, for example, indicated the peculiar status of morality in the work of art, but he did *not* have to resort to a philosophy of history or to religious considerations. "There is nothing sacred for the poet," he wrote, "not even virtue, which he ridicules if the person and the moment require it. . . . Has he introduced a villain? This villain is odious to you. . . . Let us judge the poems and leave aside the persons."[25] In this case, aesthetic autonomy changes the status of any moral phenomenon. It is not the philosophy of history that will reveal the truth of the work but, rather, the ever-renewed interpretation of a work as a function of a present horizon, since it is always open to being reactualized in diverse contexts.

In the end, Benjamin owes the elements of an antijuridical interpretation of Greek tragedy in terms of law to his friend Florens Christian Rang.[26] "Here, as always," writes Benjamin, "the most fruitful layer of metaphysical interpretation is to be found on the level of the pragmatic" (*Origin*, 117). The dialogue between the accuser and the accused; the chorus of jurors; the tribunal that prescribes the unity of place, time, and (judicial) action in tragedy—all lie waiting to reveal what escapes the—demonic, according to Benjamin—nature of the law:

> The important and characteristic feature of Athenian law is the Dionysian outburst, the fact that the intoxicated, ecstatic word was able to transcend the regular perimeter of the *agon*, that a higher justice was vouchsafed by the persuasive power of living speech than from the trial of opposed factions, by combat with weapons or prescribed verbal forms. The practice of the trial by ordeal is disrupted by the freedom of the *logos*. This is the ultimate affinity between trial and tragedy in Athens. The hero's word, on those isolated occasions when it breaks through the rigid armour of the self, becomes a cry of protest. . . . But if in the mind of the dramatist the myth constitutes a negotiation, his work is at one and the same time a depiction and a revision of the proceedings. (*Origin*, 116)

There is, in addition, the satyric drama, which, at the end of each cycle of Greek tragedy, is "an expression of the fact that the élan of comedy is the only proper preparation for, or reaction to, the *non liquet* of the represented trial" (*Origin*, 117). Dionysus, the logos, the cry of revolt, poetry, and the comic are so many objections to the autonomy of the law that, as early as "Critique of Violence," Benjamin sees as incapable of dispensing justice.

Reformation, Counter Reformation, and Jewish Messianism

It is on the foundation of this theory of tragedy that Benjamin attempts to bring out the religious structure of baroque tragic drama. In the first place, he rediscovers "the spirit" of the baroque, before specifying the formal peculiarities of theater at that time. In a sense, tragedy is superior to tragic drama, in which no character attains the moral greatness of the tragic hero: whereas the central character of tragedy is a king of the heroic age, that of tragic drama is an absolute tyrant.

Benjamin insistently designates the Counter Reformation as the source for this conception of sovereignty, in which, like Carl Schmitt, he believes he can perceive a particular profundity of political analysis:

This extreme doctrine of princely power had its origins in the counter-reformation, and was more intelligent and more profound than its modern version. Whereas the modern concept of sovereignty amounts to a supreme executive power on the part of the prince, the baroque concept emerges from a discussion of the state of emergency, and makes it the most important function of the prince to avert this. (*Origin*, 65)[27]

The reason for this preference for the doctrine of the Counter Reformation is easy to understand, if we recall the "Critique of Violence." The tyrant's boundless power is the extreme form of absolute evil, which, in Benjamin's view, incarnates the essence of history defined as mythic destiny. The goal of Benjamin's book is to break the spell of this destiny by remembering the origin, to show that the form of tragic drama ultimately represents the subversion of this earthly destiny. Benjamin's intention is thus the opposite of Schmitt's: Schmitt was an ultraconservative jurist who would later place his expertise in the service of National Socialism. But a peculiar complicity unites these two men; Benjamin needs the most cynical theory of the political, understood as the truth of the political in general, to introduce his messianic idea on this foundation: "Nature is Messianic by reason of its eternal and total passing away. To strive after such a passing, even for those stages of man that are nature, is the task of world politics, whose method must be called nihilism" ("Theologico-Political Fragment," in *Reflections*, 313).

It is from this perspective that history is transformed into the "history of nature," the blind process that escapes human actions. Benjamin rediscovers in tragic drama an analogous perspective that explains its immediate affinity with that universe:

The religious man of the baroque era clings so tightly to the world because of the feeling that he is being driven along to a cataract with it. The baroque knows no eschatology; and for that very reason it possesses no mechanism by which all earthly things are gathered in together and exalted before being consigned to their end. The hereafter is emptied of everything which contains the slightest breath of this world, and from it the baroque extracts a profusion of things which customarily escaped the grasp of artistic formulation and, at its high point, brings them violently into the light of day, in order to clear an ultimate heaven, enabling it, as a vacuum, one day to destroy the world with catastrophic violence. (*Origin*, 66)

In this hypothesis, Benjamin rediscovers his own theological nihilism. As the incarnation of the spirit of the Counter Reformation, Schmitt's thought is also "theological"; not messianic, of course, but Catholic. To avoid the state of emergency, the very task of the political according to the baroque conception, is to realize "the ideal of a complete stabilization, an ecclesiastical and political restoration [that] unfolds in all its consequences" (*Origin*, 65). Like Schmitt—and, later, Michel Foucault—Benjamin, extremely skeptical toward the democratic aspirations of modern times, perceives the political sphere through a schema close to that of the absolute power of the baroque age:

> The theological juridical mode of thought, which is so characteristic of the century, is an expression of the retarding effect of the over-strained transcendental impulse, which underlies all the provocatively worldly accents of the baroque. For as an antithesis to the historical ideal of restoration it is haunted by the idea of catastrophe. And it is in response to this antithesis that that theory of the state of emergency is devised. (*Origin*, 65–66)

What is "expressed" here is not the intention but, rather, the profound nature of baroque theory. This vision of history will also determine Benjamin's "Theses on the Philosophy of History," written in 1940; in that text, history is "one single catastrophe" and "it is [the historian's] task to bring about a *real* state of emergency" (*Illuminations*, 257) in order to accelerate the messianic upheaval.

But if, in the last instance, Schmitt and Benjamin find themselves in opposite camps, the messianic Jew knows he is still linked to the counter-reformist Catholic by a shared skepticism, both toward the Protestant ethic and toward the illusion of a progress created by progressive changes in the human condition. Max Weber's studies of Protestantism and its rationality constitute the background for Benjamin's book on baroque drama.[28] Thus, when Benjamin disputes Schmitt's claim by arguing that, "if one wishes to explain how the lively awareness of the significance of the state of emergency, which is dominant in the natural law of the seventeenth century, disappears in the following century, it is not . . . enough simply to refer to the greater political stability of the eighteenth century" (*Origin*, 66), he refers to an argument made by Weber: "If it is true that, 'for Kant . . . emergency law was no longer any law at all,' that is a consequence of his theological rationalism" (*Origin*, 66). That rationalism no longer permits, among the condition for the state of law, the authoritarian break with the law. Weber, however, would not have conceded that Kant's rationalism could be called "theological," whereas when Benjamin makes the claim, it is a term of praise.

For Benjamin, the difference between the baroque drama of Protestant inspiration and that of Catholic inspiration is not fundamental. His view of the religious background of baroque drama is that both Protestant drama and Catholic drama are dealing with the same problem of secularizing the form of the medieval "mystery," a secularization imposed "in both denominations" (*Origin*, 79, translation modified):

> It was just that this century denied them a religious fulfillment, demanding of them, or imposing upon them, a secular solution instead. . . . Of all the profoundly disturbed and divided periods of European history, the baroque is the only one which occurred at a time when the authority of Christianity was unshaken. Heresy, the mediaeval road to revolt, was barred; in part precisely because of the vigour with which Christianity asserted its authority, but primarily because the ardour of a new secular will could not come anywhere near to expressing itself in the heterodox nuances of doctrine and conduct. Since therefore neither rebellion nor submission was practicable in religious terms, all the energy of the age was concentrated on a complete revolution of the content of life, while orthodox ecclesiastic forms were preserved. (*Origin*, 79)

At the beginning of chapter 3, "*Trauerspiel* and Tragedy," Benjamin once more turns to Max Weber's inquiry to introduce the theme of melancholy. The Weberian thesis of secularization and the disenchantment of the world underlies the description of the modern world as the baroque age discovered it.

Secularization and Spatialization

Benjamin tries to deduce the formal language of baroque drama from "the contemplative necessities which are implicit in the contemporary theological situation" (*Origin*, 81). Hence, he alludes to the impossibility of acting creatively in an empty world, a world abandoned by God, which results from the process of *secularization*. In the absence of eschatology, playwrights were led to seek, "in a reversion to the bare state of the creature, consolation for the renunciation of a state of grace" (*Origin*, 81, translation modified). By this, Benjamin means that the baroque spirit, to account for the absence of grace in earthly existence, returns to the state of original sin, which has constituted the human creature ever since the expulsion from Paradise. History brings no notable change to that state; it continually reproduces the same constellations of unhappiness proper to the creature. Contrary to what happens in tragedy, where the hero rises above the state of the creature, the baroque accepts the inevitability of that state as belonging to human nature. At most, it allows itself the utopia or idyll of the pastoral, a reconciliation between the creature and bucolic nature.

By abandoning the soteriological perspective of the Middle Ages—the hope that the stations of the earthly cross would finally lead to salvation—and by secularizing the history of salvation, the baroque transposes the temporal order onto space. On several occasions, Benjamin returns to the Bergsonian theme of a reifying *spatialization* characteristic of modernity: "Here, as in other spheres of baroque life, what is vital is the transposition of the originally temporal data into a figurative spatial simultaneity" (*Origin*, 81). Elsewhere, he underscores the importance of the image of the clock for the baroque:

> The image of the moving hand is, as Bergson has shown, essential to the representation of the non-qualitative, repeatable time of the mathematical sciences. This is the context within which not only the organic life of man is enacted, but also the deeds of the courtier and the action of the sovereign who, in conformity to the occasionalist image of God, is constantly intervening directly in the workings of the state so as to arrange the data of the historical process in a regular and harmonious sequence which is, so to speak, spatially measurable. (*Origin,* 97)

Analogously, "if history is secularized in the setting, this is an expression of the same metaphysical tendency which simultaneously led, in the exact sciences, to the infinitesimal method" (*Origin*, 92). But, unlike Bergson, Benjamin does not object to the process of spatializing time and history; he discovers in it a symptom that confirms his theological vision of humanity at the state of the creature. Nothing could save humanity but a catastrophe of the messianic type that would reverse the course of history.

During the baroque age, time and power were reduced to pure mechanisms, leaving no illusion about the Fall from grace in earthly existence.

> The German *Trauerspiel* is taken up entirely with the hopelessness of the earthly condition. Such redemption as it knows resides in the depth of this destiny itself rather than in the fulfillment of a divine plan of salvation. The rejection of the eschatology of the religious drama is characteristic of the new drama throughout Europe; nevertheless the rash flight into a nature deprived of grace is specifically German. (*Origin,* 81)

In other words, it is specifically Lutheran. It is here that all the ambiguity of Benjamin's relation to German baroque drama appears. German baroque drama pays a high price for its radicality and "moral" superiority, its "less dogmatic" character, and Benjamin continually underscores the *aesthetic* superiority of Calderón's theater: "Nowhere but in Calderón could the perfect form of the baroque *Trauerspiel* be studied" (*Origin*, 81). In

> the drama of Spain, a land of Catholic culture in which the baroque features unfold much more brilliantly, clearly, and successfully, the conflicts of a state of creation without grace are resolved, by a kind of

playful reduction, within the sphere of the court, whose king proves to be a secularized redemptive power. The *stretta* of the third act, with its indirect inclusion of transcendence—as it were mirrored, crystallized, or in marionette form—guarantees the drama of Calderón a conclusion which is superior to that of the German *Trauerspiel*. (*Origin*, 81)

Through its playful aspects, Spanish theater puts all its weight behind the component of play, the *Spiel* of the *Trauerspiel*, a component underappreciated in the German theater of the age but widely appreciated among German romantics, who, for that reason, were not at all attracted to German baroque drama: "To what else did the romantics ultimately aspire than genius, decked out in the gold chains of authority, reflecting without responsibility?" (*Origin*, 84). Their model was Calderón, for whom the prince possessed in miniature the divine power of redemption, the capacity to transform earthly despair—which Lutheran playwrights accepted without reservation—into fairy tales. Despite his aesthetic admiration for the Spaniard, Benjamin must rank German baroque drama more highly, since, in the radicality of its form, it bore a truth content that was essential in his eyes.

Tragic Drama and Melancholy

The images and figures that tragic drama presents, writes Benjamin, "are dedicated to Dürer's genius of winged Melancholy. The intense life of its crude theatre begins in the presence of this genius" (*Origin*, 158). A melancholic gaze on the world emptied of its religious substance constitutes the correlative human subject of tragic drama. This theory of melancholy is broadly developed in Weber's inquiries into the Protestant mind and the ethic of capitalism. Given the relative mediocrity of German baroque dramas, we need to seek Benjamin's interest in that form in the religious radicalism of German Lutherans, which was revealing for the drama of modernity itself.

Protestantism deprived human action of all its meaning. By rejecting "good works as such, and not just their meritorious and penitential character," "human actions were deprived of all value. Something new arose: an empty world. In Calvinism—for all its gloominess—the impossibility of this was comprehended and in some measure corrected. The Lutheran faith viewed this concession with suspicion and opposed it" (*Origin*, 138–139). In reality, Max Weber's analysis does not draw such a hasty conclusion. It observes the birth of a professional ethic within Protestant doctrines, with career being the site of a religious ordeal on earth. But it is only at the end of a long process that the Protestant ethic, without being the cause of this change, contributes toward transforming the medieval world into an empty world of cold calculation and the "iron cage,"[29] that is, into the modern world of work and bureaucracy. Weber does not directly attribute this evolution to Luther; he underscores Luther's mystical attitude, which entailed a rejection of capitalism.[30] In contrast, we find in Luther's thought the idea of

> the fulfilment of duty in worldly affairs as the highest form which the moral activity of the individual could assume. . . . The only way of living acceptably to God was not to surpass worldly morality in monastic asceticism, but solely through the fulfilment of the obligations imposed upon the individual by his position in the world. That was his calling.[31]

Benjamin is not yet interested in the social meaning of the religious upheavals of the baroque age. Lutheranism, he writes, has an antinomic attitude toward everyday life: Even as it rejects "works" or the immediate manifestation of "love of one's neighbor," it teaches a severe morality for the bourgeois conduct of life. In denying "works"

> any special miraculous spiritual effect, making the soul dependent on grace through faith, and making the secular–political sphere a testing ground for a life which was only indirectly religious, being intended for the demonstration of civic virtues, it did, it is true, instil into the people a strict sense of obedience to duty, but in its great men it produced melancholy. (*Origin,* 138)

Melancholy and the way it transforms the world into a spectacle corresponding to his deepest convictions fascinate Benjamin. In melancholy, he sees a revolt of "life" itself against its devaluation by an ascetic faith. Benjamin complacently abandons himself to an erudite history of the theory of temperaments, and especially of melancholy, beginning with the age of Aristotle. Melancholy, a "theological" concept (*Origin,* 155), is linked to one of the deadly sins: "indolence of the heart, or sloth," *acedia,* which consists in turning away from good works "if they are difficult for me" (*Origin,* 155), a gesture characteristic of the modern cult of the earthly world. Like the tyrant, the courtier—attached to the crown, to royal purple, to the scepter—is characterized by this indolence of the heart. But this deadly sin also has a redemptive dimension. The courtier's "unfaithfulness to man is matched by a loyalty to these things to the point of being absorbed in contemplative devotion to them. Only in this hopeless loyalty to the creaturely, and to the law of its life, does the concept of guilt behind this behaviour attain its adequate fulfillment" (*Origin,* 156, translation modified). As does the collector in the universe of *Paris Arcades,* the melancholic contemplates dead objects to redeem them. He "betrays the world for the sake of knowledge" (*Origin,* 157).

Benjamin thus interprets the artistic form of tragic drama as one of the liberating breaks from the context of guilt that characterizes the world of the creature. As in the Goethean universe, the inextricable fabric of guilt is once more rent only through artistic creation. In the baroque era, the aesthetic principle is founded primarily on this creation, and it is radically opposed to the Greek, Renaissance, and modern models of the symbol. This is the allegorical form, to which Benjamin devotes the last part of his book.

THEORY OF ALLEGORY

Allegory, says Benjamin about *The Origin of German Tragic Drama,* is the "entity it was my primary concern to recover" (*Correspondence,* 256). It is thus the aesthetic concept that mattered most to him. From this concept, he undertook to call into question classical aesthetics, in particular that of German idealism. He begins by underscoring the concealed polarity between symbol and allegory. Regarding the relation between language and music in the tragic drama, he develops certain intuitions from his early philosophy of language. Finally, he deploys the theological dialectic of allegory through which the correlative subjectivity of "abstract meaning" is made manifest and hence abolished. Through this reversal, the allegorical form turns out to be a poetic response to the degradation that language undergoes in the instrumental conception that modernity gives to it.

A Concealed Polarity

More than the actualization of the treatise or esoteric essay at the expense of the philosophical "system," more than the reevaluation of the martyr-drama at the expense of tragedy, which is considered unactualizable in the modern era, it is the rehabilitation of the aesthetic concept of allegory that has generally been considered the principal contribution of *The Origin of German Tragic Drama,* and rightly so, since, except for the later theory of the aura, this is Benjamin's most fruitful discovery in art theory and also the one to which he was most attached. The critique of the beautiful appearance, conducted in the name of the early romantics, and the "theological" interpretation of Goethe now take the form of a clearly established polarity between profane symbol and sacred allegory.

Never before had Benjamin so clearly taken a position against the romantic aesthetic, which he had at first attempted to resuscitate. He criticizes it for not being aware of the "theological" foundations of aesthetic concepts:

> For over a hundred years the philosophy of art has been subject to the tyranny of a usurper who came to power in the chaos which followed in the wake of romanticism. The striving on the part of the romantic aestheticians after a resplendent but ultimately non-committal knowledge of an absolute has secured a place in the most elementary theoretical debates about art for a notion of the symbol which has nothing more than the name in common with the genuine notion. This latter, which is in fact the one used in the field of theology, could never have rid itself of the sentimental twilight over the philosophy of beauty which has become more and more impenetrable since the end of early romanticism. (*Origin*, 160)

Unlike the approach adopted in "The Task of the Translator" and "Goethes *Wahlverwandtschaften*," the "theology" of "On Language as Such" is here directly turned against romantic aesthetics. Like the nihilism of the Goethean universe, the catastrophic disarray of the baroque universe seems to call for a theological critique. If Goethe had only an aesthetic premonition of it, the baroque was itself dominated by visions of the world that were religious in their inspiration, but in which the laws of the profane world were beginning to occupy a growing and agonizing place. In his pursuit of a literary universe in consonance with his own, Benjamin discovers a world that was, we might say, predestined for him.

Through its theological conception of the symbol, *The Origin of German Tragic Drama* intends to tear down the speculations of idealism and of German romanticism on "essence" and "appearance," of which the symbol is said to be the unity and reconciliation. Benjamin intends to reestablish the rigor of an aesthetic criticism that abandons the task of linking itself to romantic theory. He now maintains that romanticism was only a kind of screen hiding the term that is truly opposed to classicism, namely, the baroque. In romanticism,

> the unity of the material and the transcendental object, which constitutes the paradox of the theological symbol, is distorted into a relationship between appearance and essence. The introduction of this distorted conception of the symbol into aesthetics was a romantic and destructive extravagance which preceded the desolation of modern art criticism. As a symbolic construct, the beautiful is supposed to merge with the divine in an unbroken whole. The idea of the unlimited immanence of the moral world in the world of beauty is derived from the theosophical aesthetics of the romantics. (*Origin*, 160)

This tendency toward aestheticizing the ethical actually predates romanticism; it dates from the "classical" period of Goethe and Friedrich Schiller. Already, "in classicism the tendency to the apotheosis of existence in the individual who is perfect, in more than an ethical sense, is clear enough. . . . But once the ethical subject has become absorbed in the individual, then no rigorism—not even Kantian rigorism—can save it or preserve its masculine traits. Its heart is lost in the beautiful soul" (*Origin,* 160).

Benjamin opposes the rigor of the concept of allegory, defined in theological terms, to the inconsistencies of classical and romantic thought in Germany around 1800. Allegory is not simply a trope for him, a figure that replaces one idea with another analogous to it[32] and that stands beside other kinds of tropes in the same text. Like romantic irony, which is not simply "the replacement of an idea by another contrary to it,"[33] allegory is not only the formal principle of a certain kind of art—from this perspective, it is opposed to the "symbol" or to an art defined as "symbolic"—but also, more than a rhetorical or even poetic concept, it is an aesthetic concept that alludes to the coherence of a vision of the world.

In reviewing the classical and romantic theories of allegory, Benjamin discovers only the "dark background" (*Origin,* 161) against which the profane concept of the bright symbol can stand out. This concept is announced in Diderot's *Essais sur la peinture* (Essays on painting): "I turn my back on a painter who proposes an emblem to me, a logogryph to be deciphered. If the scene is unified, clear, simple, and coherent, I will grasp the totality at a glance."[34] The "essence" is not dissimulated in such cases but is immediately revealed through the appearance of the work of art. For modern aestheticians since the Enlightenment, allegory—when it is not obscurity pure and simple—is "a mere mode of designation" (*Origin,* 162). In allegory, we seek a particular image to illustrate a universal idea: old age through the image of an old man. In contrast, the symbol, considered more authentically artistic, presents the universal *in* the particular: "Whoever grasps the particular in all its vitality also grasps the universal" (Goethe, cited in *Origin,* 161, translation modified). That, according to Benjamin, is an example of a shallow conception of symbol, contrasted with an allegory that is supposedly "dead" and "abstract."

In Benjamin's view—and in the view of the baroque whose thinking he rediscovers and onto which he projects his own thought—allegory "is not a playful illustrative technique, but a form of expression, just as speech is expression, and, indeed, just as writing is" (*Origin,* 162). Here again, we are dealing with the absolute expression of a language form: Allegory "expresses" absolutely, just as handwriting has an expressive value for the graphologist. In the case of allegory, however, its expression is universal and possesses an aesthetic meaning.

From a "theological" point of view, Benjamin contrasts the expression of the symbol and that of allegory according to their relation to *time.* Time carves out the distance that separates these forms from a shared third term. "The measure of time for the experience of the symbol is the mystical instant in which the symbol assumes the meaning into its hidden and, if one might say so, wooded interior." As for allegory, it "is not free from a corresponding dialectic, and the contemplative calm with which it immerses itself into the depths which separate visual being from meaning, has none of the disinterested self-sufficiency which is present in the apparently related intention of the sign" (*Origin*, 166). Contrary to the sign's intention, Benjamin claims, allegorical intention signifies "as natural history, as the earliest history of signifying or intention" (*Origin*, 166).

Before interpreting one of the most famous passages of the book, a passage that, since Adorno, has become the emblem of an "aesthetics of negativity," we need to acknowledge the presuppositions of the philosophy of language that Benjamin sketched out in his early works and on which his theory of allegory rests. The history of nature, the primitive history of meaning or intention, is that process defined by a theology of history whereby the name deteriorates into a sign, into intention and meaning. Compared to the name, the symbol and allegory are imperfect modes of reference, but compared to the sign pure and simple, they are privileged: Positively or negatively, they reveal the absence of that lasting correlation—that of the name—between a "symbolic form" in the broad sense (in Ernst Cassirer's sense) and a "referent" that would be predestined to it by the divine word.

It is fundamentally a *single* absence, a single nature ravaged by sadness, by mourning for the absent God, that produces the complementary forms of symbol and allegory, which are defined as functions of the category of time:

> Whereas in the symbol destruction is idealized and the transfigured face of nature is fleetingly revealed in the light of redemption, in allegory the observer is confronted with the *facies hippocratica* of history as a petrified, primordial landscape. Everything about history that, from the very beginning, has been untimely, sorrowful, unsuccessful, is expressed in a face—or rather in a death's head. (*Origin*, 166)

In the central emblem of the death's head, allegory presents the failure of history, which, in Benjamin's eyes, is the end of all human life, inasmuch as it amounts to "producing a corpse" (*Origin*, translation modified). Symbolic art conceals this fact by presenting, in the flash of an instant, the transfigured "face" of nature, a face opposed to the death's head. Nonetheless, this flash is the product of the *same* gap that allegorical art melancholically displays: In the abyss between the beautiful appearance and the desolation of the world, the artistic symbol, which produces a "realist" and, at the same time, an idealized image of shimmering nature, loses all its meaning.

Retranslated into "theological" terms, Benjamin's symbol and allegory are principles analogous to those that Nietzsche, following the romantics and Arthur Schopenhauer, called the Apollonian and the Dionysian.[35] Nietzsche opposes the "grace of the beautiful appearance" (similar to the Benjaminian "symbol") and the "horror" of an "ocean of sorrows" (which echoes the *"facies hippocratica"* of history). But whereas the Nietzschean principles *come together* in Greek tragedy, Benjaminian allegory is radically foreign to the "symbolic" principle and cannot in any case be linked to it. Allegory represents a "sublimity" that is unfamiliar with the beautiful appearance.

In terms of his philosophy of language, Benjamin is interested in what distinguishes the written word—in the baroque, typography in particular—from any symbolic conception of art. Baroque typography virtually transforms the Western alphabet into Hebrew or Chinese:

> The written word tends towards the visual. It is not possible to conceive of a starker opposite to the artistic symbol, the plastic symbol, the image of organic totality, than this amorphous fragment which is seen in the form of allegorical script. In it the baroque reveals itself to be the sovereign opposite of classicism, as which hitherto, only romanticism has been acknowledged. (*Origin,* 176)

In a certain kind of baroque—and, to be precise, in the gloomy radicality of the German baroque—Benjamin discovers the formal principle and spirit most clearly opposed to the official culture of the West, which is constituted by Greece, the Renaissance, and German classicism. It is to this antithesis of classicism that he now also links his favorite writers, those heretofore associated with the context of romanticism: "Whatever [allegory] picks up," he writes, "its Midas-touch turns into something endowed with significance. Its element was transformation of every sort. . . . But this passion . . . justifies a more recent linguistic practice, whereby baroque features are recognized in the late Goethe or the late Hölderlin" (*Origin,* 229–230).

Through a radicality that anticipates "The Work of Art in the Age of Mechanical Reproduction," Benjamin pushes this tension to the limit: In romanticism, but especially in the baroque, writers "are concerned not so much with providing a correction to classicism, as to art itself" (*Origin,* 176). In correcting art, allegory does not leave the framework of art but, rather, within that framework itself and by means of immanent disenchantment, corrects the illusory character of any artistic expression. Although it is itself a "symbolic form" in the most general sense, allegory reveals the fragility of the symbol, its always provisional and momentary victory over "the arbitrariness of the sign." From this perspective, the practice of baroque allegory, in Benjamin's view, is a much more powerful critique of classicism than is romantic theory: "Whereas romanticism, inspired by its belief in the infinite, intensified the perfected creation of form and idea in critical terms, at one stroke the profound vision of allegory transforms things and works into stirring writing" (*Origin,* 176). Allegory's expressive writing is destructive: "In the field of allegorical intuition the image is a fragment, a rune. Its beauty as a symbol evaporates when the light of divine learning falls upon it. The false appearance of totality is extinguished" (*Origin,* 176). Not only is allegory "beyond beauty" (*Origin,* 178), but it perceives both the limits of beauty and a certain blindness in the eras of art that cultivated beauty exclusively.

> By its very essence classicism was not permitted to behold the lack of freedom, the imperfection, the collapse of the physical, beautiful, nature. But beneath its extravagant pomp, this is precisely what baroque allegory proclaims, with unprecedented emphasis. A deep-rooted intuition of the problematic character of art—it was by no means only the coyness of a particular social class, it was also a religious scruple which assigned artistic activity to the "leisure hours"—emerges as a reaction to its self-confidence at the time of the Renaissance. (*Origin,* 176)

Nevertheless, it would be wrong to set up allegory as the only true art: Its expressive possibilities are just as limited as those of the symbol. In the overall economy of art, it plays the role of the "inexpressive," which, according to Benjamin's essay on Goethe, prevents appearance from becoming confused with truth. But *without* the beautiful appearance, art would remain desperately fixated on the image of the death's head. Benjamin insistently refers to a normative idea of art, to which German baroque drama does not correspond. That is why "Calderón is essentially the subject of the study" (*Correspondence,* 256), the authentic artist:

> In the *true* work of art pleasure can be fleeting, it can live in the moment, it can vanish, and it can be renewed. The baroque work of art wants only to endure, and clings with all its senses to the eternal. This is the only way of explaining how, in the following century, readers were seduced by the liberating sweetness of the first *Tändeleyen.* (*Origin,* 181)

In Benjamin's view, what counts here is the difference between the baroque and romanticism in their shared opposition to classicism and to the Renaissance. The critique of the baroque work of art gives him the opportunity to redefine aesthetic criticism, this time by setting himself apart from the romantic conception. As in the essay on Goethe, criticism stands alongside time, which annihilates the effect of actuality in the subject matter. Baroque works of art, stripped of their sparkle and secrets,

were [not] intended to spread by growth over a period of time, so much
as to fill up their allotted place here and now. And in many respects this
was their reward. But for this very reason criticism is implied with rare
clarity in the fact of their continued existence. From the very beginning
they are set up for that erosion by criticism which befell them in the
course of time. (*Origin*, 181)

Contrary to his approach in the essay on Goethe, which applies itself
to deciphering the truth content of a secretive work of art, here Benjamin
privileges the aspect of knowledge that encounters no obstacle. Appearance,
sparkle, no longer has any value by itself: "Beauty, which endures, is an
object of knowledge. And if it is questionable whether the beauty which
endures does still deserve the name, it is nevertheless certain that there is
nothing of beauty which does not contain something that is worthy of
knowledge" (*Origin*, 182). Here, Benjamin takes up the methodological idea
that opens the essay on Goethe:

The object of philosophical criticism is to show that the function of
artistic form is as follows: to make historical content, such as provides
the basis of every important work of art, into a philosophical truth. This
transformation of material content into truth content makes the decrease
in effectiveness, whereby the attraction of earlier charms diminishes
decade by decade, into the basis for a rebirth, in which all ephemeral
beauty is completely stripped off, and the work stands as a ruin. In the
allegorical construction of the baroque *Trauerspiel* such ruins have always
stood out clearly as formal elements of the preserved work of art. (*Origin*,
182)

In the end, the critique of baroque drama is no longer necessary. Time
has done the job by reducing the weak attraction of these works to nothing.
Criticism now has only to bring together in the Idea of the *Trauerspiel* the
different themes and structures that constitute it. In spite of the two
sentences that oppose the idea of *true* art to the baroque drama, the work on
the *Trauerspiel* grants little importance to beauty as such; beauty now seems
to be no more than an ornament to knowledge, which is all that counts in
the work of art. The fragile equilibrium of the essay on Goethe is here
disrupted in favor of an annihilation of beauty by criticism and by a
trenchant rejection of romantic criticism: "Criticism means the mortification of the works: not then—as the romantics have it—awakening the
consciousness in living works, but the settlement of knowledge in dead
ones" (*Origin*, 182).

It is no accident that this definition of criticism finds an echo in that
of allegorical exegesis: "It was designed to establish, from a Christian point

of view, the true, demonic nature of the ancient gods, and it also served the pious mortification of the flesh" (*Origin*, 222). In the spirit of religious mortification, Benjamin no longer allows for any force or life belonging to the concrete aspects of works of art, independent of what in them can become the object of knowledge, of what constitutes the truth content, which can be defined once and for all and excludes a plurality of interpretations.[36] "True art" can possess a secret and a sparkle, but they are annihilated by criticism. If Benjamin, starting from romantic and Nietzschean aestheticism, has now fallen into the opposite excess, it is because he expects the key to truth primarily from art. If philosophy were capable of attaining truth *without* the help of art, then investing art with the privileged task of revealing truth to us would no longer be necessary. Similarly, the structure and function of art could be determined in a way that, though no less rigorous, would not overburden it.

Language and Music in the Baroque

As both the devalorization and the sublimation of everything attached to the world of the creature, allegory engenders a violent polarity between speech and writing. The poetry of the German baroque is unacquainted with the liberating lightness of musical language. The profound allegorical meditation produces a series of obscure images that no song can translate. Benjamin speaks once more from the perspective of "true art": "This poetry was in fact incapable of releasing in inspired song the profound meaning which was here confined to the verbal image. Its language was heavy with material display. Never has poetry been less winged" (*Origin*, 200).

Since sound is linked to the sensuality of the creature, meaning has its sole dwelling in the written word:

> The spoken word is only afflicted by meaning, so to speak, as if by an inescapable disease; it breaks off in the middle of the process of resounding, and the damming up of the feeling, which was ready to pour forth, provokes mourning. Here meaning is encountered, and will continue to be encountered as the reason for mournfulness. (*Origin*, 209)

It is this mournfulness that gives its name to the *Trauerspiel*. But it is precisely the erudite and artificial meaning at the furthest remove from nature—the extreme figure for "sentimental poetry"—that translates the baroque nostalgia for nature, as it was expressed in the pastoral of the same era.

Benjamin once more considers themes linked to his early philosophy of language, which, ten years before, had led to his interest in baroque drama: In a letter to Hugo von Hofmannsthal, he speaks of the "the actual but very obscure core of this work: with its literal reminder of a youthful three-page effort called 'Über die Sprache in Trauerspiel und Tragödie' [On language in *Trauerspiel* and tragedy, i.e., "Die Bedeutung der Sprache in Trauerspiel und Tragödie"], my explanation of picture, text, and music is the germ of the project" (*Correspondence*, 309). This conceptual kernel of the book rests on an almost Rousseauian dialectic between nature and culture: "There is a pure affective life of the word," we read in "Die Bedeutung der Sprache," "where the word is decanted by passing from its natural state to the pure sound of feelings. For this word, language is only an intermediate stage in the cycle of its transformation, and it is in this word that the *Trauerspiel* speaks. It describes the trajectory that leads from the natural sound to music by way of the lament" (*G.S.*, 2:138). In this dialectic of nature and culture—the naive and the sentimental—the moment of the lament, which Benjamin associates with Judaism (*Correspondence*, 120), is when "nature is betrayed by language, and it is this formidable inhibition of feeling that becomes mourning" (*G.S.*, 2:138). It is a mourning within nature itself, which, as a result of the Fall, has fallen away from the divine name. For, according to an idea already found in "On Language as Such," "the essence of the *Trauerspiel* is already contained in the ancient wisdom according to which all nature would begin to lament if it were granted speech" (*G.S.*, 2:138).

In "Die Bedeutung der Sprache," music had a redemptive function: "For the *Trauerspiel*, the redemptive mystery is music: the rebirth of feelings in a suprasensible nature" (*G.S.*, 2:139). In *The Origin of German Tragic Drama*, the function of music is more ambiguous. It represents "the opposite of meaning-laden speech" (*Origin*, 211), not as its redemption pure and simple but, rather, as a form of regression and decline toward opera. Undoubtedly, a reflection on Nietzsche's *The Birth of Tragedy* and on his relation to Richard Wagner led Benjamin to shift his position. For Nietzsche, according to Benjamin, it was a matter of "mak[ing] a proper distinction between Wagner's 'tragic' *Gesamt-kunstwerk* and the frivolous opera, which had its preparatory stages in the baroque. He threw down the gauntlet with his condemnation of recitative. And in so doing he proclaimed his adherence to that form which so completely corresponded to the fashionable tendency to re-awaken the primal voice of all creatures" (*Origin*, 212). Nietzsche's target was a Rousseauism "incapable of art" which saw in the recitative the "rediscovered language of . . . primitive man" (Nietzsche, quoted in *Origin*, 212). "Because he does not sense the Dionysian depth of music," continues Nietzsche in reference to the recitative, "he changes his musical taste into an appreciation of the understandable word-and-tone-rhetoric of the passions in the *stilo rappresentativo*" (quoted in *Origin*, 212).[37] Benjamin agrees with Nietzsche only on this one point: On the heels of baroque drama, opera was a form of decadence. As for Nietzsche's ambition to bring back to life the "Dionysian" inspiration of musical drama, Benjamin still has reservations.

Inspired by a romantic thinker, Johann Wilhelm Ritter, Benjamin sketches a theological dialectic of language, music, and writing. According to this theory, speech and writing are intimately linked: If "we write when we speak" or if "the organ of speech itself writes in order to speak," it is because "the whole of creation is language, and so is literally created by the word" (*Origin,* 214). Phonetic language and written language are identified "dialectically as thesis and synthesis" (*Origin,* 214, translation modified), while music, which according to Benjamin is "the last remaining universal language since the tower of Babel," should be the "antithesis," whose "rightful central position" had to be assured "to investigate how written language grows out of music and not directly from the sounds of the spoken word" (*Origin,* 214). In the spirit of "The Task of the Translator," Benjamin envisions a theory of the written word as the absolutely and universally intelligible image that requires no translation. The *allegorical image,* which, like language, is understood by all, is close to the idea of the absolutely translatable literalness of the sacred text. According to Ritter's speculations, all plastic arts stem from writing, from calligraphy. In terms of allegory, Benjamin concludes that "every image is only a form of writing. . . . In the context of allegory the image is only a sign, only the monogram of essence, not the essence itself under its veil" (*Origin,* 214, translation modified); this noninstrumental image is not at the service of any meaning and retains its autonomous value as a universally readable "figure."

This is an aporetic construction that—in the absence of the idea of a daily hermeneutics inherent in the practice of language and in its continual effort at translation—responds to the necessity of situating the transcendence of the confusion of tongues in a tangible reality, an existing and demonstrable form, as a fact, and not in an activity that includes both the particularity of languages and symbols *and* an ever transcendent and universal aspect. To give shape to his messianic project, Benjamin is obliged to imagine an immediately transcendent language, whether the language of criticism, of translation, or of the allegorical image. He cannot be satisfied with a reconstruction of everyday language, of its sensible, finite structure tied to context, and of its transcendental powers. He needs a more precise, more determined sign of salvation from the historical viewpoint.

Manifest Subjectivity

The Origin of German Tragic Drama ends with a theology of history that is fairly ambiguous, because Benjamin, who had first linked the *Trauerspiel* to Hebrew lament, now discovers and assumes the Christian origins of baroque allegory. It is a syncretic theology, constructed entirely by the philosopher. No direct path links it to the allegorical exegesis of the Kabbala that

Scholem studies. Perhaps the allegory of the German baroque, with its radical rejection of any symbolic "reconciliation" as characterized in the dominant inspiration of the Christian tradition, led Benjamin toward those margins of Christianity where he could sense the legacy of Judaism, closer to an experience of history as suffering, lament, and sadness, oriented toward a messianic redemption to come, than to a symbolism of the reconciliation already brought about by Christ. That would explain the book's double ending: It includes both an apotheosis of Calderón's Christianity and a defense of the German *Trauerspiel,* aesthetically "weaker" but closer to the Benjaminian experience of a world in mourning. This double ending mirrors the double ending of his essay on Goethe, in which the hope for the desperate characters of the novel is opposed to the earthly redemption of the characters in the novella. This double ending also corresponds to the ambiguity of the prologue of *The Origin of German Tragic Drama*: a theory of Adamic naming discreetly superimposed on a Platonic theory of ideas.[38]

Thus, only a "theological" perspective is able to "resolve" the limiting form of allegory for Benjamin, since "so long as the approach is an aesthetic one, paradox must have the last word" (*Origin,* 216). This paradox presents scenes of horror and of martyrdom, the accumulation of corpses, which are "the pre-eminent emblematic prop," since the tyrant's task is to "provide the *Trauerspiel* with them" (*Origin,* 218, translation modified). "And the characters of the *Trauerspiel* die, because it is only thus, as corpses, that they can enter into the homeland of allegory. It is not for the sake of immortality that they meet their end, but for the sake of the corpse" (*Origin,* 217–218). Whether it consists of displaying the death mask of history, opposing the death's head to the transfigured face of symbolic art, or pushing the sadism of tyrants and the vicious intelligence of the intriguers to their limits, everything is, in spite of it all, produced with redemption the final goal.

Linked to the Counter Reformation, the Christianity of allegory is anchored in the tension that, beginning with the Middle Ages, opposed the Christian era to the pantheon of ancient gods resuscitated by Renaissance humanism. "There is a threefold material affinity between baroque and mediaeval Christianity. The struggle against the pagan gods, the triumph of allegory, the torment of the flesh, are equally essential to both" (*Origin,* 220). Each time it reappears, allegory bears witness to the vitality of the pagan gods. According to Benjamin, it is "the word which is intended to exorcise a surviving remnant of antique life" (*Origin,* 223). As will also be the case for Baudelaire, "allegory established itself most permanently where transitoriness and eternity confronted each other most closely" (*Origin,* 224).

In addition to the ephemeral, there is the guilt both of the fleshly creature and of an allegorical contemplation "that betrays the world for the love of knowledge": a guilt of meaning and a guilt of theoretical knowledge, symbolized by the prohibition against touching the fruit of the tree of knowledge; a meaning and a knowledge that were in fact cultivated by the

Renaissance and by German idealism. These are the biblical themes of "Die Bedeutung der Sprache," which Benjamin repeats almost word for word: "Because it is mute, fallen nature mourns. But the converse of this statement leads even deeper into the essence of nature: its mournfulness makes it become mute" (*Origin*, 224).

Hence the twofold attitude already observed in relation to the creature: whether to deprive it of all value or to redeem it. Allegory, which undertakes this rescue operation, is always born of the confrontation of the body burdened by sin in Christianity and the exonerated body of the Ancients. "With the revival of paganism in the Renaissance, and Christianity in the Counter-Reformation, allegory, the form of their conflict, also had to be renewed" (*Origin*, 226). Since the Christian Middle Ages, both the beings of flesh (matter) and of knowledge (intelligence emancipated from God) have been demonic, Satanic. Distanced from God, nature and spirit are prey to the sadness or the sardonic laughter of Satan,[39] as it resonates in the throats of Shakespeare's villains. As in his early essay, Benjamin once more indulges, in the spirit of the *Trauerspiel,* in a denunciation of the *knowledge* of good and evil, identified as absolute knowledge. Distanced from God, absolute knowledge is an evil: "Knowledge, not action, is the most characteristic mode of existence of evil" (*Origin*, 230), knowledge such as that deployed by the tyrants and intriguers of baroque drama, at a time when modern science was beginning to prevail. Benjamin is no doubt thinking of Goethe's Faust, that scientist and seducer who links his intelligence to Satan's powers, and of Kant, who limits knowledge by faith. The last lines of *The Origin of German Tragic Drama* return to this conception of the relation between theory and practice.

The weight of theology in Benjamin's works of this era is such that scientific knowledge has no place in his thought. Satan's promises, denounced here as in the essay on Goethe and evoked in a spirit of opposition to the Enlightenment, are "the illusion of freedom—in the exploration of what is forbidden; the illusion of independence—in the secession from the community of the faithful; the illusion of infinity—in the empty abyss of evil" (*Origin*, 130, translation slightly modified).

And yet, according to the schema of the emblem—in which the crown signifies the garland of cypress, the pleasure-chamber the tomb, the throne room the dungeon—evil and the fragility of the creature *signify* something *other* than themselves:

> As those who lose their footing turn somersaults in their fall, so would the allegorical intention fall from emblem to emblem down into the dizziness of the bottomless depths, were it not that, even in the most extreme of them, it had so to turn about that all its darkness, vainglory, and godlessness seems to be nothing but self-delusion. (*Origin*, 232)

Through the theological nature of allegory, death and hell lead to salvation, and the ephemeral character of things is only the allegory of resurrection. "Allegory, of course," admits Benjamin, "thereby loses everything that was most peculiar to it: the secret, privileged knowledge, the arbitrary rule in the realm of dead objects, the supposed infinity of a world without hope. All this vanishes with this *one* about-turn. . . . [Allegory is] left entirely to its own devices" (*Origin*, 232).

The entire movement of allegory, like that of baroque drama, consists in derealizing the pretensions of modern subjectivity. Benjamin establishes his link to the philosophical speculations of mystic traditions, to the romantics of Jena, to Schelling, to the early Lukács of *Theory of the Novel*,[40] and to the Heideggerian critique of modern subjectivity. Irony and allegory are the aesthetic means for subjectivity's relativizing of itself from within the antinomies of the subject–object model. The mystical or "theological" view reveals freedom and evil as the sad or comical illusions of a melancholic subject who has excluded himself from the community of the faithful. In some sense, it is enough to *awaken* from this nightmare—this idea still underlies his analysis of the Paris arcades as a "dream": "By its allegorical form evil as such reveals itself to be a subjective phenomenon. The enormous, anti-artistic subjectivity of the baroque converges here with the theological essence of the subjective" (*Origin*, 233). Benjamin then reiterates the biblical exegesis of his early essay. When God had considered his Creation and found that "it was very good,"

> Knowledge of good, as knowledge, is secondary. It ensues from practice. Knowledge of evil—as knowledge is primary. It ensues from contemplation. Knowledge of good and evil is, then, the opposite of all factual knowledge. Related as it is to the depths of the subjective, it is basically only knowledge of evil. It is "nonsense" [*Geschwätz*] in the profound sense in which Kierkegaard conceived the word. This knowledge, the triumph of subjectivity and the onset of an arbitrary rule over things, is the origin of all allegorical contemplation. . . . For good and evil are unnameable, they are nameless entities, outside the language of names, in which man, in paradise, named things, and which he forsakes in the abyss of that problem. (*Origin*, 234)

According to this religious reading of morality, there is no way to falsify praxis through a knowledge of good and evil.[41] We have always "known" what we must do and what we must not do. In this sense, the categorical imperative, which cannot be disputed or inquired into, is already part of the prohibition on "knowing" good and evil. It may well be that philosophical ethics can only reconstruct our moral intuitions and refute reconstructions that do not take them into account.[42] But Benjamin goes even further.

On the one hand, he does not concede the cognitive character of our normative behaviors and arguments; he denies the possibility of criticizing or justifying them. Like truth, they transcend knowledge. On the other hand, he disputes the idea that modern humanity has emerged from the cocoon of traditions in which one had only to be reminded of the obvious facts shared by all to renew their validity. Through his conception of allegory, he reintegrates modernity—a kind of subjectivist illusion—into the profound continuity of human solidarity founded in God. Through an aesthetico-theological discourse, he has only to demonstrate the illusory character of our subjectivity, which is prey to abstraction, guilt, and a meaning dissociated from the name, to reintegrate the paradisiac universe into art and thought. But is it still a question of allegory? As defined in rhetoric, allegory replaces a thought by another thought that is similar to it.[43] According to that same theory of rhetoric, it is *irony* that is characterized by inversion: It replaces one thought by another that is *opposed* to it; it calls the ugly "beautiful" and the bad "good." Here, Benjamin seems to be interpreting allegory to mean irony. In fact, he calls Jean Paul, one of his favorite authors, "the greatest allegorist in German literature" (*Origin*, 188), and maintains that he demonstrated "that even the fragment, and even irony are variants of the allegorical" (*Origin*, 188).

In this irony, what earthly justice painfully accomplishes through its sanctions is realized fully in heavenly justice, illustrated in works of art, which reveal "the apparent nature of evil."

> Here the manifest subjectivity triumphs over every deceptive objectivity of justice, and is incorporated into divine omnipotence as a "work of supreme wisdom and primial love" [Dante], as hell. It is not appearance, and equally, it is not satiated being, but it is the reflection in reality of empty subjectivity in the good. In evil as such subjectivity grasps what is real in it, and sees it simply as its own reflection in God. In the allegorical image of the world, therefore, the subjective perspective is entirely absorbed in the economy of the whole. (*Origin*, 234, translation slightly modified)

"The display of manifest subjectivity," as it defines the formal principle of baroque art, "proclaims the divine action in itself," in other words, the miracle. That is the sense of the technical tours de force of baroque architecture and the plastic arts, which suggest divine intervention. "Subjectivity," writes Benjamin, "like an angel falling into the depths, is brought back by allegories, and is held fast in heaven, in God, by *ponderación misteriosa*" (*Origin*, 235). That is also the meaning of the apotheosis, the deus ex machina in Calderón: The organization of the stage leads to "that allegorical totality . . . thanks to which one of the images of the sequence stands out, in the image of the apotheosis, as different in kind, and gives mourning at one and the same time the cue for its entry and its exit" (*Origin*, 325). As in baroque music, any sadness on the part of the subject who isolates himself from the community is submerged in a final allegro.

To what might have been the end of his book Benjamin adds a remark on German baroque drama, whose technical "weakness," the inadequacy of plot, does not produce any "allegorical totality" and does not overcome sadness. A "romantic" approach is necessary to save the *Trauerspiel*. In the case of such incompletion, criticism cannot limit itself to "mortifying" through knowledge what is already dead. In the manner of romantic aesthetics, "the powerful design of this form should be thought through to its conclusion; only under this condition is it possible to discuss the idea of the German *Trauerspiel*" (*Origin*, 235). But this incompletion has its own expressive value: Unlike the dramas of Calderón, which "shine resplendently as on the first day," the German *Trauerspiel*, "in the spirit of allegory. . . . is conceived from the outset as a ruin, a fragment" (*Origin*, 235). It pushes as far as possible the allegorical destruction of the beautiful appearance and anticipates a radically negative aesthetics, without the slightest compromise with the world, calling for a final inversion only at the time of the Last Judgment: "This form preserves the image of beauty to the very last" (*Origin*, 235).

Benjamin's grandiose construction opposes a kabalistic and ironic reinscription into tradition to Nietzsche's nihilism and "death of God." Instead of a redemption solely through aesthetic experience—Nietzsche's Dionysian intoxication—Benjamin believes he can outline an intact tradition that has remained untouched by modernity. The criteria for a theological gaze not only seem available to him, they even seem to impose themselves in the theoretical construction of aesthetics, morality, social theory, and history. Benjamin does not envision modernity as such; in his view, it is only a misunderstood avatar of the theological tradition. That is why he does not see the necessity, in a post-traditional society, of profane morality and law inscribed within the grammar of our everyday practices. In contrast, even though the baroque is not the most appropriate aesthetic model in terms of actuality, it represents a model of aesthetic authenticity, beyond the romantics, Nietzsche, and classic German culture. In an "intense" but "probably vain" manner, baroque drama "hopes for the rehabilitation of what is best in it by current dramatic experiments" (*Origin*, 216).

In *Der Begriff der Kunstkritik in der deutschen Romantik*, Benjamin set out a *modern* aesthetics, poetics, and criticism—of reflection, irony, and prose in Schlegel and Hölderlin—that seem to stand in solidarity with a theological (messianic) perspective. Beginning with the essay on Goethe, he turns away from romantic aesthetics; he severely criticizes it in his book on tragic drama. The baroque analysis of the state of the creature seems to be an unsurpassed description of the human condition. Benjamin will try to find in Brecht's work a worthy heir to this form of drama. Through allegory, he is able to conceive of a form of avant-garde art that would not be reducible to aestheticism. Benjamin's attitude toward modernity nevertheless remains ambiguous. When all is said and done, how seriously should we take the reactualization of the baroque and the concept of criticism as mortification, when we read in the *Correspondence* that in February 1925 Benjamin wished "to go back to romanticism" (*Correspondence*, 261)? In reading the "Theses on the Philosophy of History," we realize the permanence of certain theological ideas. It is nevertheless clear that *all* of Benjamin's thought cannot be reduced to this perspective. Inasmuch as they glimpse an immanent possibility of transforming the world, romanticism and, later, surrealism and Brechtian and Marxist political commitment represent the flip side, that of a realization of the possibilities of earthly existence.

In the manuscript of *Paris Arcades*, we find this aphorism: "My thinking is related to theology as the blotter is related to ink: it is totally soaked in it. But if it were up to the blotter, nothing would remain of what is written" (*G.S.*, 5:588). In Benjamin's early work, theology would leave nothing of the profane. The work on baroque drama pushes that sacralization of a profane and fully allegorized world to the extreme. But this radical inversion would be impossible if both options did not obey the same finality: that of a quest for salvation for which the work of art is not an end in itself, but a means of knowledge and, ultimately, the means for a messianic process that rejects it when it has extracted its substance.

2. Art in the Service of Politics

THE STRATEGIST IN THE BATTLE OF LITERATURE

In 1924–1925, even before finishing his book on tragic drama, Benjamin changed his orientation under the influence of the literary and political avant-garde. Since, for him, art was the depository of a truth inaccessible to discursive knowledge, he had to adapt his thinking to the art currently being produced, when that art responded to the imperatives that, until then,

Benjamin had found only in the work of Goethe or in baroque literature. He had not found expressionism significant enough to turn him toward contemporary literature or art.[1] In contrast, with the advent of surrealism and Proust, Kraus and Kafka, Brecht and Russian cinema, he was confronted with a type of contemporary art that he could not honestly call decadent. His entire philosophical perspective was overturned. According to the central idea of his early philosophy, true language communicated itself only to God or expressed human essence through the authentic exercise of the faculty of naming. The avant-garde, on the contrary, was seeking to affect the receiver. For Benjamin, traditional art enclosed truth in its *being* or its *substance*; avant-garde art was related to truth through its *action* on the receiver or through its *function*. Its addressee was no longer God but, rather, the profane public, those who were open to contributing to the transformation of the world. The search for salvation, instead of going through the translation of poetic language into a purer language, now proceeded through revolutionary action and the reconciliation of technology with nature. The cult value or the aura of language without addressee gave way to the exhibition value of a language that was seeking to awaken and motivate.

In principle, then, the early Benjamin's philosophy of language was no longer able to serve as the philosophical background for his new aesthetics. For several years, in fact, he faced the artistic and literary phenomena of the era as a critic, without having at his disposal a fixed epistemology; elements of his philosophy of language coexisted with an opposing orientation toward strategic and instrumental efficacy. It is at first difficult to find a precise common denominator in his essays on surrealism and Kraus, his writings on Brecht, and his reflections on mechanical reproduction, except for the rejection of contemporary society that they all share.

Such a common denominator exists, however, through the central problem of Benjamin's thought: *the work of art,* a term that figures in the title of the most elaborated essay of this second period. It is during this period, in the face of a double subversion, that the concept of a work of art is thematized as such. In surrealism, the work of art foregrounds the force of revelation and action proper to the meaningful *document*; in the tradition of Judaism, it aspires beyond art toward *doctrine.* Nevertheless, contrary to what might have been expected, Benjamin does not purely and simply dismiss the concept of the work of art, precisely because, in the absence of doctrine, the work of art remains the primary support for an interpretation capable of anticipating that doctrine. Thus, in "Karl Kraus" and in *Einbahnstrasse,* Benjamin defends the concept of the work of art against the principle of information and even against the document. The document is legitimate only to the extent that it is used by artists who keep in mind the normative concept of the work of art they are deliberately transgressing.

An encounter and a book were the two determining factors in this change in orientation. In Capri, when he was drafting *The Origin of German Tragic Drama*, Benjamin met Asja Lacis, a Lithuanian woman of the theater and an enthusiast of Brecht and of the revolutionary scene in the U.S.S.R.; he called her the "engineer" who "cut . . . through the author" the new street taken by his thought (*Reflections,* epigraph to "One-Way Street," 61). This encounter coincided with his reading of Lukács's *History and Class Consciousness,* in which Benjamin perceived a bridge between his mystical ethics and the theory of revolution (*Correspondence,* 246–250). He immediately decided that he would no longer "mask the actual and political elements of my ideas in the Old Franconian way I did before, but . . . develop them by experimenting and taking extreme measures" (*Correspondences,* 257, letter of 22 December 1924).

In the same letter, he announced to Scholem a "Plaquette für Freunde" (Booklet for friends), in which he intended to bring together "aphorisms, witticisms, and dreams" (*Correspondence,* 257): This was *Einbahnstrasse.* Soon after, in February 1925, he wrote, regarding *The Origin of German Tragic Drama*: "This project marks an end for me—I would not have it be a beginning for any money in the world" (*Correspondence,* 261). The climate of the book on tragic drama now seemed "too temperate." "The horizon" of his work was no longer the same. In May 1925, he considered joining the Communist Party (*Correspondence,* 268)—a resolve he would never carry out, any more than he would carry out that formulated a few lines later, of learning Hebrew. These two perspectives, that represented by Asja Lacis, Lukács, and Brecht and that incarnated by Scholem, were indissociable in his view and would always remain so, to varying degrees, up to the "Theses on the Philosophy of History," where the "automaton," historical materialism, "enlists the services of theology" (*Illuminations,* 253). "I can attain a view of the totality of my horizon, more or less clearly divined, only in these two experiences," wrote Benjamin in May 1925 (*Correspondence,* 268). In his view, "there are no meaningfully *political* goals" (*Correspondence,* 301); he considered Communist goals "nonsense and nonexistent." But "this does not diminish the value of Communist action one iota, because it is the corrective for its goals" (*Correspondence,* 301). In contrast, the "anarchist methods," stemming from convictions that Benjamin had shared with Scholem in the past, were "useless." Benjamin was thus seeking to reconcile his theological convictions with Communist action and to maintain contact with both Scholem and Brecht.

To understand this turning point in Benjamin's oeuvre and the modification of his aesthetic, we need to take into account the failure of his university career. Despite Benjamin's profound hesitations at the prospect of the constraints imposed by the position of instructor, *The Origin of German Tragic Drama* was conceived as a university thesis. The work was rejected— several professors and associate professors (including Max Horkheimer) judged it obscure—and Benjamin was obliged to imagine a life as a man of letters. In 1925 he accepted proposals for translations (of Balzac and Proust) and a column as a literary critic ("recent French art theory" [*Correspondence*, 267]) in a new review, *Die literarische Welt* (The literary world). Without abandoning the philosophical imperative to justify his approach, Benjamin now felt freed of the academic constraints he had imposed on himself throughout his study of tragic drama. Without ceasing to be a philosopher, he assumed the freedom of the writer. He was not long in realizing the cost of that freedom. Under the pressures of the literary marketplace, the writer made of his subjectivity, his intimate experiences, a commodity in constant search of a buyer. In reference to Baudelaire, Benjamin reflected on that situation, trying to avoid its traps while writing countless book reviews, short pieces, stories, and radio reports to earn his living.

One of the first projects Benjamin proposed after finishing his book on tragic drama was a study, never completed, on the fairy tale form. We find a kind of retrospective summary of it in "The Storyteller," an essay drafted ten years later, in 1936. This passage—concerning a traditional form of art—allows us to understand the change in Benjamin's viewpoint as he was turning from the contemplation of allegory to the universe of the political struggle of the man of letters and the political thinker he had become: "The wisest thing—so the fairy tale taught mankind in olden times, and teaches children to this day—is to meet the forces of the mythical world with cunning and high spirits" (*Illuminations,* 102). In its cunning, Benjamin's new aesthetics included an element of *strategy.* In his view, the critic was "a strategist in the battle of literature" (*Einbahnstrasse,* in *G.S.,* 4:108). Inevitably, his philosophical attitude, which consisted in *not taking the receiver into account* (as formulated in a letter to Buber in 1916), was called into question. Benjamin realized, to a certain extent, that his philosophy of language was untenable. But the new strategic attitude, though the exact opposite of a type of writing that disregarded the receiver, still remained just as authoritarian as the first. In the first case, he subjugated the reader to the law of form; in the second, he led him strategically to act in the manner desired by the author.

Literature and Advertising

The "aura" of a thing is that in it which "communicates itself to God" and not to any receiver targeted by a literary strategy. In *Einbahnstrasse,* completed in 1926, the "decline of the aura," often attributed to Brecht's influence, was clearly foreshadowed in Benjamin's new attitude toward art:

> Criticism is a matter of correct distancing. It was at home in a world where perspectives and prospects counted and where it was still possible

to take a standpoint. Now things press too closely on human society. The "unclouded," "innocent" eye has become a lie, perhaps the whole naive mode of expression sheer incompetence. Today the most real, the mercantile gaze into the heart of things is the advertisement. . . . For the man in the street, however, it is money that . . . brings him into perceived contact with things. And the paid critic, manipulating paintings in the dealer's exhibition room, knows more important if not better things about them than the art lover viewing them in the showroom window. . . . What, in the end, makes advertisements so superior to criticism? Not what the moving red neon sign says—but the fiery pool reflecting it in the asphalt. (*Reflections*, 85–86)

The destruction of distance,[2] the immediate proximity of things, the striking reproduction of the image by *cinema* and *advertising,* such will henceforth be the leitmotifs defining the Benjaminian analysis of actuality; it is in these terms that he will proclaim the decline of the "aura," which, until that time, had determined the entire destiny of art. Even before his encounter with Brecht in 1929, this observation was accompanied by a certain cynicism about the dominant forces of contemporary life: a provocative respect for the power of money; the culture industry; adaptation to the laws of the market; the supposed superiority of the seller's relation to art in comparison to that of aesthetic contemplation— in short, a certain manifest nihilism, even down to the imitation of advertising in the presentation of the text. Only the final "moral" reveals an ulterior motive: What does that fiery pool on the asphalt, which establishes the superiority of advertising in relation to criticism, signify? Even advertising "expresses" more than it says. It betrays the mercantile intention and is transformed into its opposite: The shock is such that the cynical order is in danger of drowning in the fiery pool. The world of advertising is anesthetized; it dreams a sentimental dream. But it produces effects that prepare for the reawakening. Literary writing is now obliged to use the most effective means of the moment: those of advertising. But it is the involuntary effects of advertising—diversion and subversion—that are strategically sought.

Until this point, Benjamin rarely practiced aphoristic writing. The "systematic" or doctrinal ambition is obvious in his first writings. *Der Begriff der Kunstkritik,* however, underscored the fact that aphorism—valorized by Schlegel and Novalis—is in no way incompatible with a systematic intention (*G.S.,* 1:40–41). Certain fragments of *Einbahnstrasse* make clear the functions of aphoristic writing. "Filling Station" (*Tankstelle*), the first text in the book, opposes the power of facts to the "sterility" of "convictions" that, until now, have determined literary life: These facts must be set forth through the writer's practical intervention. *Einbahnstrasse*'s style—pseudo-advertising—seeks to acquire such a factual force.

Literary effectiveness, to be noteworthy, can only come into being in a strict alternation between action and writing; it must nurture the inconspicuous forms that better fit its influence in active communities than does the pretentious, universal gesture of the book—in leaflets, brochures, articles, and placards. Only this prompt language shows itself actively equal to the moment. Opinions are to the vast apparatus of social existence what oil is to machines: one does not go up to a turbine and pour machine oil over it; one applies a little to hidden spindles and joints that one has to know. (*Reflections*, 61, translation slightly modified)

Effectiveness is thus the criterion in whose name Benjamin sacrifices both the old literary style and his own "theological" conception, close to symbolism, that consisted in denying the existence of the receiver. It is not a matter of "convincing" the reader—"To convince is to conquer without conception" (*Überzeugen ist unfruchtbar*), we read in "One-Way Street"[3]—but of acting on his mind through the eloquence of images. Nevertheless, Benjamin attempts to construct a continuity. In another text, he refers to Mallarmé who, in the early period of Benjamin's oeuvre, was one of the guarantors of his philosophy of language. The author of *Coup de dés* (Throw of the dice) now takes on the role of grounding the turning point in Benjamin's thinking. Benjamin goes so far as to associate Mallarmé's "pure art" with advertising, which he has just justified in a half-cynical, half-metaphorical way. The art of the book, at the origin of the diffusion of the Book of Books in its Lutheran translation, seemed to be reaching its end.

Mallarmé, who in the crystalline structure of his certainly traditionalist writing saw the image of what was to come, was in the "*Coup de dés*" the first to incorporate the graphic tensions of the advertisement in the printed page. . . . Printing, having found in the book a refuge in which to lead an autonomous existence, is pitilessly dragged out onto the street by advertisements and subjected to the brutal heteronomies of economic chaos. (*Reflections*, 77)

In *Einbahnstrasse*—a work close in style to a revolutionary tract or lampoon—Benjamin seeks to take the lead by practicing this "picture writing" through which writers "will renew their authority in the life of peoples" (*Reflections*, 78). He feels close to the "traditionalist" (as Benjamin sees him) author Mallarmé when he *constructs* the "graphic tensions of the advertisement" in his work. There is nothing to indicate that this interpretation of Mallarmé's text—writing "pitilessly dragged out onto the street by advertisements"—is legitimate. In any case, it is representative of the type of relation Benjamin conceives between the dynamic of social development and the constructive response of art. This relation is not determinist, not

even in the case of Dadaism's "nervous reactions"—Dadaism is weaker than
Mallarmé's work, according to Benjamin—but is, rather, a privileged
knowledge of the "monadical" artist who, in his "hermetic room" discovers
the laws of actuality (*Reflections,* 77).[4]

More than ever in Benjamin's thought, the construction built by art is
the high seat of reason. Morality amounts to no more than the writer's
professional ethic; science intervenes only in the revolutionary's audacious
calculations.[5] In addition to the advice dispensed to writers and the observations on the mutations of the media, we can distinguish a few recurrent
themes in *Einbahnstrasse*: an ethnography of cities, reflections on love,
childhood memories, transcriptions of dreams, and remarks on the revolutionary crisis of humanity. In each, Benjamin attacks the currently accepted
boundaries between spheres of reality. Metaphorically or literally, he effaces
the opposition between public life and private life, exterior and interior
(furnishings and the soul living among them), the human and the animal,
conscious thought and the dream; in his view, these separations are characteristic of "bourgeois" thought, which is responsible for all abstraction. In
"Imperial Panorama: A Tour of German Inflation," he observes the decline
of all the values that had been taken to be inalienable acquisitions of the
West—freedom, dignity, generosity, dialogue, urbanity—in these difficult
years surrounding 1923, where only the "marvelous" seemed able to bring
salvation (*Reflections,* 70). Nothing in the world revealed its secret, except
through the writer's and philosopher's self-assured deciphering; without
this redemptive intervention, everything would remain myth. As a whole,
Einbahnstrasse is both a sort of hygiene of writing that allowed Benjamin to
escape the everyday myths of bourgeois society, and the "objective interpretation of the world" (*Origin,* 48) that he had announced in *The Origin of
German Tragic Drama*. The philosophy of *Einbahnstrasse* is situated halfway
between that of Nietzsche, who is assuredly one of Benjamin's models, and
that of Adorno's *Minima moralia*. It is an approach that exploits both the
resources of a unique experience and a singular intelligence in order to
counter the intellectual conformity of the environment, and that associates
a sort of historical mission with this subversive status of subjectivity. The
dream and personal experience are instrumentalized in the name of a cause
of general interest and are invested with historical significance.

The introduction to *The Origin of German Tragic Drama* still justified
the essay form for systematic reasons, namely, the impossibility of reaching
doctrine and the impotence of the deductive system. *Einbahnstrasse* adds to
this a new political urgency: "These days," asserts Benjamin, "when no one
should rely unduly on his 'competence,' strength lies in improvisation. All
the decisive blows are struck left-handed" (*Reflections,* 65). Scientific and
philosophical competence are devalued in relation to strategic agility. The
outcast "strikes blows," like Baudelaire, whose talent as a "fencer" Benjamin

will underscore. Having become the model for a generation of intellectuals in revolt, in particular in the 1960s and 1970s, this mode of thinking has revealed its weakness: In believing he could bypass argumentation, Benjamin encouraged the purely strategic attitude of those who believe they are authorized by the corrupt state of the world to use cunning and every possible weapon to realize their intimate conviction of incarnating justice and truth. For Benjamin himself, the antiauthoritarian impulse is already marked by authoritarian aspects. The tone of the short texts in *Einbahnstrasse* is that of the judicial sentence, the imperative that does not suffer contradiction: "Whoever cannot take a position must remain silent" (*G.S.,* *4:108*).

Up to this point, Benjamin has disputed philosophical abstraction as it appeared to him in the neo-Kantian context, by means of theological and literary categories (metaphors), without, however, ceasing to claim a "philosophical" style (*Origin,* 29). *Einbahnstrasse* is resolutely situated not only outside any university context but also outside any philosophical argumentation. The constellation in which Benjamin's texts are inscribed—until his integration into the Frankfurt School when he accepts, for good or ill, the relatively traditional philosophical imperatives associated with the new requirements of a materialist dialectic—is that of literature and politics, under the sign both of a more remote but still present theological reference and of a concept of art that remains its most rigorous element from the philosophical point of view.

Hesitations on the Status of Art

Toward the middle of *Einbahnstrasse,* Benjamin brings together a certain number of rules and bits of advice, humorous or serious, for writers, to which he consigns the essential of his new aesthetics. Three of these texts—"Die Technik des Schreibers in dreizehn Thesen" (The writer's technique in thirteen theses), "Dreizehn Thesen wider Snobisten" (Thirteen theses against snobs), and "Die Technik des Kritikers in dreizehn Thesen" (The critic's technique in thirteen theses) are among the most engaged theoretical formulations of *Einbahnstrasse.* Their goal is to maintain the aesthetic imperative in a strategic context: How does one define a work of art worthy of the name when the principal criterion for creation is the effectiveness of its action on the receiver?

Light in tone, the first series focuses on the author's psychology, on what he or she should or should not do to work successfully: external working conditions, rhythms, techniques for productive delay, how to manage inspiration, discipline, scheduling, material. These recommendations have little normative value and stem from the author's personal preferences or idiosyncrasies. The series ends with a sentence that echoes

The Origin of German Tragic Drama: "The work is the death mask of the conception" (*Reflections,* 81). "Truth," we read in the work on tragic drama, "is the death of intention" (*Origin,* 36). In each case, intention and conception designate subjectivity pure and simple: Its "death" is a gauge of completion; the work of art or truth becomes detached from the person. It is significant—and apparently incoherent from the philosophical point of view—that Benjamin retains the idea of the *work of art,* even though the first text of *Einbahnstrasse* pronounces that treatises, brochures, newspaper articles, and posters are literarily more effective. Perhaps we need to understand that such a subversion is legitimate only to the extent that it is carried out with full consciousness of the traditional requirements of the work of art and in relation to them.

In his "Thirten Theses against Snobs," Benjamin makes a rigorous— and hardly "surrealist"—distinction between the work of art and the document. In fact, we rarely find in his earlier writings a concept of the work of art defined in terms of immanence, independent of any "theological" function. From a profane perspective, Benjamin now conceives the work of art and the document *together.* These theses are heteroclite and establish no hierarchy; they are also not argued. Benjamin limits himself to enumerating the symptoms that permit us to distinguish a work of art from a document. The snob is someone who sets a child's drawing or a primitive fetish against Picasso (and invites Picasso to "pack up all his works of art" [*G.S.,* 4:107]). According to Benjamin, the work of art is opposed to the document in that the former has a legitimate claim to aesthetic appreciation: A document displays these qualities only incidentally. Inversely, "the work of art is a document only incidentally" (*G.S.,* 4:107).

How do we know, when confronted with such an object, that it is only a document? Beginning with the works of Marcel Duchamp, Dadaism, and surrealism, that is precisely one of the questions of modern aesthetics. When Benjamin opposes the artist who "makes a work of art" to the primitive man who "expresses himself in documents" (*G.S.,* 4:107), he seems to be presupposing an a priori distinction that would allow us to distinguish between art and document. But there are documents and there are documents: All fetishes are not equivalent, and prehistoric paintings cannot be reduced to mere historical testimony. "No document," decrees Benjamin, "is as such a work of art" (*G.S.,* 4:107). This is a tautology pure and simple; we would like to know, precisely, how we move from autobiographical writing or the venerated image to the autonomous work of art. Benjamin evokes two types of clues: clues of possible use and analytic clues. When he opposes the "masterpiece" (*Meisterstück*) to "didactic means" (*Lehrstück*), it is more a play on words than a conceptual distinction, since the two terms are heterogeneous: "Masterpiece" designates an aesthetic merit, while "didactic means" is a pedagogical function, whether or not there is an aesthetic aspect. The category "didactic means" also applies to the work of art, since Benjamin adds: "With the work of art, artists learn their craft," while "through documents, the public is educated" (*G.S.,* 4:107). These definitions are not mutually exclusive: Nothing prevents the public from educating itself before works of art, and nothing prevents artists from learning from documents, by drawing inspiration, for example, from the fetish form.

The most instructive distinctions concern the relations between the form, subject matter, and content of the work of art. The document has neither form nor content. "In documents, subject matter has total dominion" (*G.S.,* 4:107) It is linked to the "dream" and opposed to the "experimental" character of the work of art's content; hence, Benjamin opposes the telling characteristics of the document to the necessity of the public's validation of the work of art. This need for validation is translated into the fact that, in the work of art, there exists no "content" independent of its meaningful relationship to form: "Subject matter and form are a single thing: content"—that is, the "truth content" of the essays on Goethe and tragic drama—and subject matter is "ballast" to be jettisoned in considering the work. For "in the work of art the law of form is central" (*G.S.,* 4:108). Everything in the work is subjugated to a principle of unity that is foreign to the document, and it is this formal *coherence* that isolates a work of art from all others, whereas "all documents communicate in the material element" (*G.S.,* 4:107). Owing again to its coherence, "the work of art is synthetic: central power [*Kraftzentrale*]" (*G.S.,* 4:108); a force emerges from it that is amplified upon repeated contemplation. In other words, its coherence establishes ties between the elements that are revealed only through prolonged contemplation. The document, on the other hand, is not even analytical: To realize its fertility, it "requires analysis." From the viewpoint of reception, it "takes only by surprise" due to a surface analogy—which collapses before an insistent gaze—with the work of art.

Finally, the last two theses oppose the "virile" qualities of the work of art and the artist to the passivity, even the "femininity," of the document: Inasmuch as the work of art both submits all matter to form and imposes itself in a lasting way on the receiver, "the virility of works of art is in the attack" (*G.S.,* 4:108). In contrast, "the document's innocence serves as its cover" (*G.S.,* 4:108). In other words, the document means to escape judgment on the pretext of something like an immaculate, irresponsible gestation. Similarly, "the artist goes in conquest of content," while "primitive man conceals himself behind subject matter," which is supposed to speak for itself. Through its "content," the work of art is the bearer of a truth. As a result of the pure materiality of the document or of testimony, it *claims* nothing, neither artistic beauty nor truth.

There is an obvious tension between, on the one hand, this classical distinction between the work of art and the document and, on the other, the demand, in the first piece in *Einbahnstrasse,* for unorthodox forms such as the tract or poster. For a full decade, until after writing "The Work of Art in the Age of Mechanical Reproduction," Benjamin will sacrifice his concept of the work of art, but not without some recurrent reservations. Hence, a short, very critical essay on Philippe Soupault underscores the risks of "automatic writing." If artists have a better chance than dilettantes of escaping stereotypes, if they are freer, they still cannot "win at every stroke," says Benjamin, citing Paul Valéry. "In its deepest strata, the felicitous constellation, the fantastic illumination only appear intermittently and occasionally" ("Philippe Soupault, *Le coeur d'or,*" *G.S.,* 3:73–74). What gives the productions of dilettantes, children, eccentrics, and the mad "the autonomy in banality and freshness in horror that, in spite of everything, are often missing in surrealist productions" is not a technical necessity but a "vital" one. Failure is inevitable when the conscious memory is transposed after the fact into the unconscious. Benjamin prefers the authentic document to the surrealist work of art that claims to be the document of a dream world, an unconscious world; with Valéry, he defends the work of art in the traditional sense against the stylized document.

In contrast, in his essay "Surrealism," published in 1929, Benjamin writes: "The writings of this circle are not literature but something else— demonstration, documents, bluffs, forgeries if you will, but at any rate not literature" (*Reflections,* 179). He no longer defends "the work of art" against the document; he draws the consequences of what he had written in 1925 on surrealism, which he did not clearly assume in *Einbahnstrasse*: "What we used to call art only begins two meters from the body" (*G.S.* 2:622). Between *Einbahnstrasse* and the essay on surrealism, Benjamin had begun to write on the Paris arcades, a study he would pursue until his death and that *broke* with the notion of the work of art. The phenomena analyzed—the architecture of the arcades, ancient curios, aging photographs, advertising—possess the passive eloquence of documents and symptoms, not the "virile" eloquence of works of art that bear a philosophical "content."

Finally, "The Critic's Technique in Thirteen Theses" moves closer to the position defended in the essay on surrealism. In this section, the concept of the work of art appears only once, but in a manner that relativizes its validity in the name of intellectual struggle. The work of art is only an instrument in this struggle, a weapon: "Artistic exaltation is foreign to the critic. The work of art in his hands is the cold steel in the battle of minds" (*G.S.,* 4:109), and "the critic is a strategist in the battle of literature" (*G.S.,* 4:108). Benjamin does not say what is at stake in this battle. Taking the era into consideration, we might think the stakes are political. But Benjamin never uses the term here. He requires only one thing: that one take sides. "Whoever cannot take a position must remain silent" (*G.S.,* 4:108). Such an imperative is far from either the "positive" criticism of the romanticism of Jena, which measured the work of art only against its own Idea, or from criticism as the "mortification" of works of art in the name of their truth content. These two types of criticism, romantic and theological, are not engaged in ideological battle. One of the theses—"The critic has nothing to do with the exegesis of past eras of art" (*G.S.*, 4:108)—could be read as a self-criticism, were the essays on Goethe and tragic drama not conceived as interventions in the process of a literary tradition. Until that point, Benjamin had underscored the necessity for the critic of a temporal distance that allowed him or her to distinguish without possible confusion what, in the interest elicited by the work of art, stemmed from the subject matter and what from the truth content. In a text published in January 1927, after Benjamin's long journey to Moscow in December 1926, he wrote that the criticism opposed to all "tendentious art" belonged to the "heavy artillery drawn from the arsenal of bourgeois aesthetics" ("Erwiderung an Oscar A. H. Schmidtz" [Reply to Oscar A. H. Schmidtz], *G.S.*, 2:751). Such formulations were not yet to be found in *Einbahnstrasse*. But the call to take sides, or to be silent if unable to do so, already stemmed from the "arsenal" of a materialist aesthetic.

This is not necessarily the case for the fifth thesis: " 'Objectivity' must always be sacrificed to the party spirit, if the cause for which one is fighting is worth the trouble" (*G.S.*, 4:108). The qualification that the cause must be worthy introduces an "objective" consideration, since it must be possible to argue in favor of the cause. In this way, Benjamin indicates that the "strategy" he is defending is more than a simple partisan attitude; by taking sides, he is aiming at the universal, as the sixth thesis again underscores: "Criticism is an affair of morality. If Goethe was wrong about Hölderlin and Kleist, Beethoven and Jean Paul, it was not because of his understanding of art but rather because of his morality" (*G.S.*, 4:108). The opposition between morality and understanding is significant. It is not clear why Goethe's lack of understanding for the art of the romantic generation could have been relevant only to his morality, and not to his sense of art. The conceptual bases of the essay on Goethe's *Elective Affinities* would not have allowed such a distinction. By making morality (and implicitly, politics) the ultimate criterion for criticism, Benjamin abandons the *logic proper* to the work of art and its *internal* morality, indissociable from its aesthetic form. Henceforth, the ideas of the work of art are separable from its aesthetic form: "The critic's art *in nuce*: to forge slogans without betraying ideas. The slogans of incompetent criticism sell off the idea to fashion" (*G.S.*, 4:109). The romantic respect for ideas, however, explains why Benjamin's critical essays—whether he is writing on Proust or Kafka—are not as reductive as those of other authors once they embraced Marxism. In spite of his will to conform to the laws of the literary "battle," his attitude toward the work of art remains comprehensive; he continues to seek a "truth content."

The same ambivalence is found again with regard to the public's evaluation. In 1935, Benjamin judges the public competent to evaluate film, which leaves no superiority to the professional critic. In *Einbahnstrasse*, the critic conserves his romantic privilege: "For the critic, his colleagues are the supreme court. Not the public. And a fortiori not posterity" (*G.S.*, 4:108). The public is always wrong: It cannot accept what is innovative in a work of art; it must "nevertheless always feel represented by the critic" (*G.S.*, 4:109). To the extent that the critic's arguments are well-founded, his interpretations judicious, and his judgments convincing, the public can only identify with him. As for posterity, it "forgets or celebrates. Only the critic judges while facing the author" (*G.S.*, 4:108). This face-to-face relation between critic and author contrasts with Benjamin's earlier thoughts on criticism as the "exegesis of past eras of art." Criticism is centered on the present and on contemporary battles. Hence the importance of polemics: "Polemics entails annihilating a book in a few quotations. The less you study it, the better off you are. Once someone can annihilate, he can criticize" (*G.S.*, 4:108). Such is the attitude of Karl Kraus, to whom Benjamin devotes a fairly long text in *Einbahnstrasse* (*G.S.*, 4:121).

Whatever the ambiguity of the relation between the theses on the critic's technique and the theses that distinguish between the work of art and the document, the ambivalence concerning the "law of form" and strategy can be resolved, inasmuch as the strategist's "taking sides" remains faithful to fairly firm criteria such as the "idea," which has to be defended against fashion. And if "objectivity" is sacrificed, the "cause" must be worth the trouble. In contrast, "Space for Rent" articulates theses that are hardly compatible with the aesthetic of the theses against snobs and those on the critic's technique. "Fools lament the decay of criticism. For its day is long past. Criticism is a matter of correct distancing" (*Reflections*, 85). To the "unclouded" and "innocent eye," Benjamin no longer opposes the "side-taking" of the strategist who militates for a cause that is worth the trouble. Rather, he opposes it to "the most real" gaze today, that of advertising. Hence the strategy of an art serving the power of money: It is an *involuntary* strategy, advertising as "absolute expression," as objectively the most advanced medium of the age, turning against its immediate intentions. *Einbahnstrasse* brings together three viewpoints: the aesthetic (the work of art opposed to the document); the political (strategy opposed to a supposed critical objectivity); and the cynical (advertising opposed to all criticism but concealing a subversive ulterior motive). These different viewpoints are also inexplicably intermingled in the *Paris Arcades* project, conceived in 1927, in which "the profane motifs of *One-Way Street* will march past . . . hellishly intensified" (*Correspondence*, 322).

Einbahnstrasse is the heteroclite construction site of different "moments" that constitute Benjamin's thinking in the decade 1926–1935.

Before reaching a relatively firm and well-defined position, in the 1935 Exposé of *Paris Arcades* ("Paris, Capital of the Nineteenth Century") and in "The Work of Art," Benjamin tries out two conceptions represented by contemporary authors, both essential for him and both seeking to actualize a buried past. He does not immediately succeed in synthesizing the two: the first, a Proustian and surrealist conception of a subversive sphere of images; and the second, a conception of Judaism (in Kraus and Kafka) in the process of destroying modern myths, but in the name of a tradition that was itself sick and that made it fall back into the ambiguous sphere of art. If surrealism was in danger of succumbing to the risk of a renewed myth of modernity, modern Judaism did not seem to be reaching a clear awareness of what was at stake in the social sphere. The *Paris Arcades* project must be understood as an attempt to elaborate a theory of modernity that associates the surrealist—nihilist—gaze on the recent past with a moral and political imperative inspired by Judaism.

THE POLITICS OF IMAGES

In *Einbahnstrasse*, a new form of myth begins to forge a path. It is this enchanted mythology of big cities that the *Paris Arcades* project sets forth. Myth as *utopia* is superimposed on myth as *ideology*, that is, as pagan and superstitious belief. The themes of the child and the lover, the dreamer and the animal, the traveler, the collector, and the writer are linked to the utopian myth. These are beings who have an experience of reality situated on the near side of conscious objectification and who thus escape the reality and utility principles. Exposed to the terrors of myth, they are the only ones who still recognize the miraculous: "Stamps are visiting cards that the great States deposit in the bedrooms of children" (*G.S.*, 4:137). Everything in the city possesses the dual characteristic of being a source of anxiety and a promise of happiness. Such is the ambiguity of urban space lived by those who do not have the clouded perception of adults, by those who have conserved the child's keen sensitivity, by those whose gaze reveals the true nature of reality. With reference to educational materials, Benjamin establishes a close relation between the child and the artist, both of whom recognize the miraculous in things diverted from their utilitarian context (*G.S.*, 4:104–105). Other pieces in *Einbahnstrasse* are, in fact, early versions of certain texts in *Berliner Kindheit* ("Vergrösserungen" [Enlargements], *G.S.*, 113–116).

According to a traditional theme of romanticism, the child, in escaping the sole consideration of the useful and the rational, preserves in play the sense of totality. Benjamin seeks to rehabilitate this immediate unity of all human forces in the practical relation between the body and the world. In

"Madame Ariane—Second Courtyard on the Left," he goes so far as to defend telepathy[6] against any *conscious* anticipation of the future, which is suspected of being a source of paralysis. It is through "alert dexterity" that "the man of courage lays hands on the future" (*Reflections,* 89) instead of confining himself to foreseeing it or receiving revelation from it: "For presence of mind is an extract of the future, and precise awareness of the present moment more decisive than foreknowledge of the most distant events. . . . To turn the threatening future into a fulfilled now, the only desirable telepathic miracle, is a work of bodily presence of mind" (*Reflections,* 89).

In abandoning the primacy of the theological reference, Benjamin moves closer to surrealism. He will criticize André Breton's passion for fortune tellers and spiritualism, but he will also say that intoxication—which, according to him, can be "theological"—is an "introductory lesson" of materialist and anthropological inspiration. At a collective level, humanity's relation to technology stems from the same logic: "They alone shall possess the earth who live from the powers of the cosmos" (*Reflections,* 92). Instead of communing with the cosmos in a purely *optical* manner, as modern science does, humanity must commune with it through the intoxication of the entire body, in the fullness of the present instant and with complete presence of mind; otherwise, we risk communing with it through destruction, in spite of ourselves—in the horror of modern wars, for instance. It is here that the philosophical change appears most clearly: Benjamin has moved from a contemplation of origins in the quest for the true name of things to practical intervention in the world as a way of warding off ancient magic with the enlightened magic of technology. Benjamin expects the proletariat to reestablish its tie to the experience of intoxication, which linked the ancients to the cosmos: "The living being conquers the frenzy of destruction only in the intoxication of procreation" (*Reflections,* 94, translation modified). He thus attempts to confer a revolutionary significance on what, in the work of Nietzsche and Ludwig Klages, was conceived as a radical opposition to such a spirit.[7]

Einbahnstrasse already owes a great deal to Paris: In Paris Benjamin found "the form appropriate for this book." There he discovered an affinity between his thinking and the most recent intellectual and literary movements: "I feel that, in Germany, I am completely isolated from those of my generation. . . . In France individual phenomena are engaged in something that also engages me—among authors, Giraudoux and especially Aragon; among movements, surrealism" (*Correspondence,* 315, translation slightly modified). It was also in Paris that, in 1927, he began to draft "the highly remarkable and extremely precarious essay 'Paris Arcades: A Dialectical Fairy Play' " (*Correspondence,* 322), of which he said that he had "never written while risking failure to that point" (*Correspondence,* 333, translation modified). If he were to succeed, "an old and somewhat rebellious, quasi-apocryphal province of my thoughts will really have been subjugated, colonized, managed" (*Correspondence,* 333). It is difficult to say what "province" Benjamin is speaking of; we might suppose these thoughts are linked to certain pieces in *Einbahnstrasse:* notations of experiences or archetypal observations of the city and childhood, where the baroque vision of history as petrified nature and the surrealist vision of the recent past as a primitive, abruptly archaic history come together.

Benjamin would like to "put to the test the extent to which it is possible to be 'concrete' in the context of the philosophy of history" (*Correspondence,* 333). As he wrote in his notes for *Paris Arcades,* he felt that the concreteness of the philosophy of history left something to be desired, both in Hegel and in Marx or Heidegger ("N" 2, 6 and "N" 3, 1, pp. 48, 50–51). He believed he had found in surrealism elements that would allow him to make thinking about history more concrete:

> An all too ostentatious proximity to the surrealist movement might become fatal to the [*Arcades*] project, as understandable and as well-founded as this proximity might be. In order to extricate it from this situation, I have had to expand the ideas of the project more and more. I have thus had to make it so universal within its most particular and minute framework that it will take possession of the *inheritance* of surrealism in purely temporal terms and, indeed, with all the authority of a philosophical Fortinbras. (*Correspondence,* 342)

Benjamin called the essay on surrealism, published in early 1929, "an opaque screen placed before the *Arcades* work" (*Correspondence,* 347). "The issue here," he explains to Scholem, "is precisely what you once touched on after reading *One-Way Street*: to attain the most extreme concreteness for an era, as it occasionally manifested itself in children's games, a building, or a real-life situation" (*Correspondence,* 348). He also indicated the goal of the book in an expression he used for a text written on his trip to Moscow: "In this picture, 'all factuality is already theory,' and therefore it refrains from any deductive abstraction, any prognostication, and, within certain bounds, even any judgment" (*Correspondence,* 313). This philosophy was close to the theoretical ideal of Goethe, who dreamed of a kind of "higher empiricism" grasping "original phenomena" in the most concrete objects and who proposed to "think of science as art if we expect to derive any kind of wholeness from it" (epigraph to *Origin,* 27.) In Benjamin's works, the boundary between theory and literature tends to become effaced along the path of such a science, which affects the consistency of his theoretical constructions: From theory, we continually move toward literary evocations.

In spite of their theoretical nature, most of the writings of that period were in fact characterized by a devaluation of theory. Compared to practice or to the image, theory was judged to be "contemplative" and even false. In that sense, Benjamin was indebted to the tendencies of his age; his aspiration toward concreteness was part of the vast movement of the "detranscendentalization" of thought in which existential ontologies and philosophies, philosophical anthropology, historical materialism, and psychoanalysis all participated. The *image,* according to Benjamin, possessed both an immediate concreteness and the capacity to elicit a practice. He was not yet using the concept "dialectical image," which he would employ during the 1930s; but the concept of the image already occupied a central place, more general than that of "symbol" and "allegory." Benjamin considered himself an expert in images who was placing his knowledge in the service of social transformation. His knowledge was still implicitly supported by his theological conception of language following the loss of the Adamic name: The authentic image overcame the abstraction that characterized conceptual meaning.

From the outset, Benjamin designated surrealist productions not as works of art but as documents (*Reflections,* 179). Contrary to what the "theses against snobs" still suggested, there is nothing pejorative or limiting in the term "document." On the contrary, according to the essay "Surrealism," abandoning art may be a duty of the contemporary artist:

> It is far less a matter of making the artist of bourgeois origin into a master of "proletarian art" than of deploying him, even at the expense of his artistic activity, at important points in this sphere of imagery [that needs to be discovered]. Indeed, might not perhaps the interruption of his "artistic career" be an essential part of his new function? The jokes he tells are the better for it. (*Reflections,* 191)

This is one of Benjamin's most radical texts in terms of favoring the subordination of art to politics. Against the optimism of the bourgeois and the social democratic parties, Benjamin proposes "the organization of pessimism," which will "expel moral metaphor from politics and . . . discover in political action a sphere reserved one hundred percent for images" (*Reflections,* 191)—a sphere inaccessible to contemplation. It will be the sphere of a full integration of the body into political action,[8] which will not allow any gap to remain between knowledge and its object; it will be an instantaneous joining of cognitive, practical, and aesthetic aspects in a profane illumination that incites toward lucid action. In this essay, Benjamin clarifies the idea of a synthesis between Nietzsche and Marx that

he had sketched at the end of *Einbahnstrasse.* In profane illumination, "when
. . . body and image so interpenetrate that all revolutionary tension becomes
bodily collective innervation, and all the bodily innervations of the collective become revolutionary discharge . . . reality [has] transcended itself to
the extent demanded by the *Communist Manifesto*" (*Reflections*, 192).

The surrealists provided the model for such a sphere of images. Their
literary and artistic activity performed an immediately revolutionary function. This was already the program of the romantics of Jena when they
transposed the political issues of the French Revolution onto a purely artistic
terrain. But the move from the work of art to the document was coming
about in a modern situation of the "crisis of the intelligentsia" (*Reflections*,
177), which was precisely "that of the humanistic concept of freedom"
(*Reflections*, 177). A "poetic politics" in the style of romanticism could no
longer be an adequate response (*Reflections*, 190): "Since Bakunin, Europe
has lacked a radical concept of freedom. The Surrealists have one. They are
the first to liquidate the sclerotic liberal–moral–humanistic ideal of freedom" (*Reflections*, 189). They employed the cult of evil, the sulfurous
anti-Catholicism of Arthur Rimbaud, Compt D. Lautréamont, and Guil-
laume Apollinaire, to "disinfect" politics by separating it from any "moralizing dilettantism" (*Reflections*, 187), for that is how Benjamin perceived the
reformist politics of the bourgeois or socialist democrats. Yet he still had
reservations about the surrealists: "Have they bound revolt to revolution?"
he asked, or more precisely, to "the constructive, dictatorial side of revolution[?]" (*Reflections*, 189). Benjamin was expressing a point of view characteristic of the debates on the German extreme left, which was permeated
by the ideas of Lenin.

Like the Leninists and like Carl Schmitt, Benjamin preferred decision
to discussion: The document that was replacing literature had as its goal to
"go beyond the stage of eternal discussion and, at any price, to reach a
decision" (*Reflections*, 177), a decision that, for the surrealists, still oscillated
between revolt and revolution. For them,

> image and language take precedence. Not only before meaning. Also
> before the self. In the world's structure dream loosens individuality like
> a bad tooth. This loosening of the self by intoxication is, at the same
> time, precisely the fruitful, living experience that allowed these people
> to step outside the domain of intoxication. (*Reflection*, 179)

That intoxication, which *Einbahnstrasse* already invited the reader to enjoy
in order to overcome the modern gap between humanity and the cosmos,
was in this case a *"profane illumination,* a materialistic, anthropological
inspiration, to which hashish, opium, or whatever else can give an intro-

ductory lesson. (But a dangerous one; and the religious lesson is stricter)"
(*Reflections,* 179).

This passage indicates how Benjamin intends to integrate the "religious lesson" of his earlier writings into an "anthropological materialism."
He seeks "to win the energies of intoxication for the revolution" (*Reflections,*
189). The *document* of intoxication or of automatic writing, of this fruitful
crossing of the threshold between waking and sleeping, which suspends
both meaning and the self—indexes of the abstract "meaning" of fallen
language—is an image that carries within it profane illumination. Such a
document was thus no longer opposed, as in *Einbahnstrasse,* to the "central
power" of the work of art; it was no longer primitive "entrenchment,"
passivity calling for analysis in order to become productive. If reading and
thought are also forms of illumination and intoxication, if they are also
capable of overcoming the gaps in consciousness, the self, and abstract
meaning, then surrealist irrationalism is no longer justified. Benjamin
wishes to transpose the surrealist experience to a field foreign to it: that of
effective action. Rightly no doubt, Georges Bataille rejected such a fusion[9];
the artistic experience cannot be *instrumentalized* for political action. Neither
art nor politics would benefit: Art would lose its autonomy and politics its
seriousness. Thus Benjamin, without abandoning the principle, would soon
seek another way to place his aptitudes in the service of social transformation.

When he writes that the text on surrealism refers discreetly to his *Paris
Arcades* project, he is alluding to an aspect of his affinity with surrealist
writings that would long remain alive in his thinking. It was the "revolutionary" nihilism of certain individual experiences in the urban space that
allowed Benjamin to actualize certain ideas he had until then associated
with baroque allegory. Surrealism, writes Benjamin in a passage that
perfectly expresses the motivation for his interest in the Paris of the
nineteenth century,

> can boast an extraordinary discovery. [It] was the first to perceive the
> revolutionary energies that appear in the "outmoded," in the first iron
> constructions, the first factory buildings, the earliest photos, the objects
> that have begun to be extinct, grand pianos, the dresses of five years ago,
> fashionable restaurants when the vogue for them has begun to ebb from
> them. The relation of these things to revolution—no one can have a more
> exact concept of it than these authors. . . . They bring the immense forces
> cf "atmosphere" concealed in these things to the point of explosion.
> (*Reflections,* 181–182)

It is the present itself that Benjamin is now able to perceive as a
"petrified, primordial landscape." "Revolutionary nihilism" means convert-

ing what is "prehistoric" and unbreathable about the age into a subversive perception. The surrealist approach, according to him, consists in "the substitution of a political for a historical view of the past" (*Reflections*, 182), an expression that could also apply to the *Paris Arcades* project or to the "Theses on the Philosophy of History." Although those works abandoned the project "to win the energies of intoxication for the revolution" (*Reflections*, 189), like the essay on surrealism they undertook to bring about an awakening by casting a political gaze on the past, as it pressed with all its weight on the present, to make it appear as a petrified, primordial landscape. The method for such a reading consists in applying Adamic naming to a reality prey to abstract meaning, myth, and anxiety. Whatever the sociological concepts that Benjamin would subsequently introduce on the advice of Adorno and Horkheimer, he remained guided by this fundamental intuition.

His essays on Kraus and Kafka show that he could not abandon the critical potential of Judaism; he *links* them to his revolutionary interpretation of French writers, as the positive, messianic face to complement surrealist nihilism. Their lucidity, permeated by tradition, serves as a counterweight to the temptation to "intoxication," which Benjamin rapidly abandoned and which would no longer figure in the sociological *Paris Arcades* project.

Benjamin characterized modern art—in surrealism and in the works of Proust and Kafka—as the emancipation of the image or the represented gesture from any constituted meaning; but, instead of accepting the irreducible character of this status of art, he went on to interpret the emancipated image—in a way he had already experimented with in his work on Goethe—as the supreme form in which truth can appear to us during an age deprived of theological doctrine. Ultimately, he does not admit the open plurality of ever-renewable interpretations because of the philosophico-theological status he grants to the *true* reading, which links the image to doctrine.

Surrealism had shown how the image could fulfill a revolutionary function: by presenting the accelerated aging of modern forms as an incessant production of the archaic, which summed up the true sense of contemporary life. Through the ruins of modernization, it revealed the urgency of a revolutionary turn. Benjamin was then led to animate the static model through which he had identified the contemporary world with a mythical world, in order to oppose to it theological truth. That same operation was now placed in the service of the revolution. In his essay "Franz Kafka," Benjamin for the first time uses the image of progress as a storm blowing from the primitive world—a forgotten world that is present in its very oblivion[10]—a storm to which he opposes the cavalcade of memory and study in quest of the forgotten origin. For such study, gestures—whose significance escapes Kafka himself, but which are most closely linked to truth—are revealing. No longer does the "sphere of images" act immediately on the receiver, as Benjamin still held in the essay on surrealism; rather, a work of memory and interpretation are opposed to the blind action of a historical progress that only reproduces the same catastrophes ad infinitum. The memory work that, in the service of revolution, seizes hold of the forgotten past's liberating force is the *animation* of the projections for which *The Origin of German Tragic Drama* provided the model. Through the *static* interpretation of allegory, modern humanity has been returned to the state of the creature and has seen abstract subjectivity gathered up and abolished in the economy of Creation. Here, the dynamic interpretation of the images of the primitive world, perceived and named in their truth, carries out a revolutionary operation on the oblivion upon which blind progress is founded. But the world of myth is itself animated through the image of the storm. In the same way, the work of projection becomes engaged in history—as active remembrance with a revolutionary function, the reappropriation of the foreign body in which we have been exiled by oblivion.

Stemming from his work translating Proust's *Remembrance of Things Past*, undertaken in 1926 with Franz Hessel, "The Image of Proust" is linked to the conceptions outlined in "Surrealism." Benjamin is totally uninterested in the architectural aims of *Remembrance of Things Past*, the romantic and symbolist metaphysics that make works of art the ultimate aim of human life: "Proust's analysis of snobbery, which is far more important than his apotheosis of art, constitutes the apogee of his criticisms of society" (*Illuminations*, 209–210). Three things interest Benjamin in the Proustian oeuvre: social physiology, the status of the image, and the aspiration for "presence of mind," the authentic form of our relation to time. Benjamin sees in Proust a detective, a spy introduced into the heart of a class "which is everywhere pledged to camouflage its material basis and for this reason must imitate feudalism" (*Illuminations*, 210, translation modified).

The reflection on the status of the image introduces theses that will be developed in "On Some Motifs in Baudelaire": "The image in Proust is the highest physiognomic expression which the irresistibly growing discrepancy between literature and life was able to assume" (*Illuminations*, 202, translation slightly modified). According to Benjamin, the resistance of contemporary forms of existence to a poetic formulation is such that, after Proust, there could never again be a "lifework." More than a work of memory, he sees Proust's work as "a Penelope work of forgetting. . . . Is not the involuntary recollection, Proust's *mémoire involontaire*, much closer to forgetting than what is usually called memory?" (*Illuminations*, 202). Benjamin contrasts the productiveness of such forgetting—a romantic theme to which he had wanted to devote an essay on a novella by Tieck[11]—to the destructive character of everyday rationality: "With our purposeful activity

and, even more, our purposive remembering each day unravels the web and
the ornaments of forgetting. That is why Proust finally turned his days into
nights" (*Illuminations,* 202). Forgetting is associated with dreams and the
resemblance established with the dream world. The object of *Remembrance
of Things Past* is "the image, which satisfied his curiosity—indeed, assuaged
his homesickness. He lay on his bed racked with homesickness, homesick
for the world distorted in the state of resemblance, a world in which the
true surrealist face of existence breaks through" (*Illuminations,* 205). Benjamin confers not merely a literary value but an "ontological" status on
Proust's metaphors. He speaks of surrealism in relation to Proust to indicate
that he has discovered in both a single preoccupation, not merely artistic,
but vital: a quest for happiness and presence of mind, such that they
reconstitute the fragmented human faculties. This integrity of faculties
seems to him to be artists' contribution to social revolution.

The relation Benjamin establishes between the image and time is
linked to that interpretation. For Benjamin, what interests Proust is the
intermingling of time, where memory and aging confront each other:

> It is the world in a state of resemblances, the domain of the *correspondances*;
> the Romanticists were the first to comprehend them and Baudelaire
> embraced them most fervently, but Proust was the only one who
> managed to reveal them in our lived life. This is the work of the *mémoire
> involontaire,* the rejuvenating force which is a match for the inexorable
> process of aging. . . . *A la recherche du temps perdu* is the constant attempt
> to charge an entire lifetime with the utmost presence of mind. Proust's
> method is actualization, not reflection. He is filled with the insight that
> none of us has time to live the true dramas of the life that we are destined
> for. This is what ages us—this and nothing else. The wrinkles and creases
> on our faces are the registration of the great passions, vices, insights that
> called on us; but we, the masters, were not home. (*Illuminations,* 211–
> 212, translation slightly modified)

Voluntary memory, denied access to the best things, and aging due to
forgetting are part of the "poverty" that the surrealists set forth in such a
subversive manner. Like them, Proust—as Benjamin interprets him—
works to create that "sphere reserved one hundred percent for images"
(*Reflections,* 191); like them, he empties "the dummy, his self, at one stroke"
(*Illuminations,* 205); he sets aside the abstract meaning of a language held
prisoner to voluntary memory. This is how Benjamin would like to decipher
the images of the nineteenth century, by wrenching them free from their
mythifying action on our oblivious mind.

The encounter with Brecht in 1929 and the discussions with Horkheimer and Adorno that same year concerning the *Paris Arcades* project led

Benjamin to modify his conception of the relation between literature and revolution. Without renouncing his reflections on the *correspondances* and on the intellectual imperatives of contemporary Judaism, he sought to respond to the exigencies of the most acute social criticism. For a dozen years, the interlacing objections of Brecht, Adorno, and Scholem would be a determining factor in the development of his thought, though he did not manage to make a real theoretical synthesis of these heterogeneous imperatives. "My writings have certainly always conformed to my convictions," he wrote to Scholem in 1934, "but . . . I have only seldom made the attempt—and then only in conversation—to express the whole contradictory grounds from which those convictions arise in the individual manifestations they have taken" (*Correspondence*, 439). The indisputable richness resulting from that unstable situation, which has delighted the literary interpreters of his work, goes hand in hand with a certain philosophical incoherence.

JUDAISM AND SOCIAL CRITICISM: KRAUS AND KAFKA

During the period between *Einbahnstrasse* (1928) and "The Work of Art in the Age of Mechanical Reproduction" (1935), the two most developed texts that Benjamin managed to complete and publish were devoted to Karl Kraus and Franz Kafka. His interest in Kraus dates from about 1916 (*G.S.,* 2:1078),[12] while that in Kafka had manifested itself by 1925 at the latest (*Correspondence*, 279). In 1928–1929, having portrayed Kraus in a fragment in *Einbahnstrasse* ("Kriegerdenkmal" [War memorial], *G.S.,* 4:121), he published four fairly brief texts on Karl Kraus[13] before devoting almost a year's work to him, from March 1930 to February 1931. His first text on Kafka dates from 1927. Until the end of his life, he gathered notes for a book on the author of *The Trial*, even outlining a new interpretation of that work in 1938 (*Correspondence*, 563–566).[14] This speaks to the importance of the two essays, which, in counterpoint to the "nihilist" reflections on surrealism, represented the normative background against which Benjamin assimilated the avant-garde spirit.

We are thus dealing with two texts from the period of radical commitment, which reveal most clearly both the permanence of the theological reference in Benjamin's thinking and the value he accorded Judaism within the framework of that commitment. Benjamin perceived Kraus and Kafka as he perceived himself, as authentic representatives of a great tradition at a time when it was undergoing a deep crisis. All three authors formulated a severe judgment on the age they were living in, which appeared to them to be a return to the most remote stages of civilization, to such a point that myth appeared as a deliverance (*Illuminations*, 117).

In the name of his interpretation of Jewish theology, Benjamin had opposed pagan myth along with its avatars in law, philosophy, and literature. Here he suggests that Kafka's novels "are set in a swamp world. In his works, created things appear at the stage Bachofen has termed the hetaeric. The fact that it is now forgotten does not mean that it does not extend into the present. On the contrary: it is actual by virtue of this very oblivion" (*Illuminations*, 130). Outlined here is Horkheimer and Adorno's *Dialectic of Enlightenment*, which sees modern reason plunging back into prehistoric barbarism. But for Benjamin, it is not a *dialectic* of reason that is responsible for that regression: Law is quite simply not progress away from myth but, rather, a variant of it and a forgetfulness. From the outset, Benjamin relativizes the promise of modern reason; he had never taken it seriously. No progress has yet taken place. Like Kraus and Kafka, he compares the fragility of Western reason to a messianic promise in whose name any progress realized can be reduced to a mere adjustment within a permanent catastrophe. Jewish theology has the task—to use Freud's term—of drying up the swamp of the modern West. "This man," Benjamin writes of Karl Kraus in 1928, "one of a tiny number of those who have a vision of freedom, cannot serve it in any other way than as prosecutor; it is in that way that the power of dialectic peculiar to him appears in its purest form. It is in that way, precisely, that his existence is prayer, the most ardent call for redemption that Jewish lips are uttering today" ("Karl Kraus," *G.S.*, 2:625).

Through the portraits of these two writers and the historical analysis of their literary forms, Benjamin's essays formulate a diagnosis of the age. Their significance for Benjamin's thinking has to do with his philosophy of language and can only be discerned indirectly. At a time when the "empty phrases" of journalism and the loss of tradition had corrupted language, Kraus and Kafka remember the authentic language: that of the Adamic name. But both are fighting an enemy that is assaulting their own minds. Kraus, the editor-in-chief of *Fackel* (Torch)—and Benjamin, a collaborator on *Die literarische Welt*—are nothing but journalists who are more demanding than the others, at a time when "journalism [is] . . . the expression of the changed function of language in the world of high capitalism" (*Reflections*, 242). What is the author of *The Trial* but a writer, whereas—like Benjamin—he would like to illustrate the teaching of doctrine? The introduction to *The Origin of German Tragic Drama* had formulated the thesis that in our time, only *exercises* in view of doctrine are within our reach—and they are better than any philosophy that claims to be systematic. But, for different reasons, neither Kraus nor Kafka can resign himself to a philosophy that so relativizes his era. For Benjamin, they are nevertheless the models of a committed Judaism in an ambivalent process of secularization. In the essay "Surrealism," religious experience appeared only as a lesson in "profane illumination." The texts on Kraus and Kafka show that, as long as the profane models remain as deficient as surrealist projects, the imperatives of Judaism can only change form; they cannot disappear.

Karl Kraus, or the Art of Quotation

The essay on surrealism had substituted the "document" and the political effectiveness of the emancipated image for the work of art: The surrealist artists who had entered politics were capable of crossing both the boundary between art and the document and the threshold between dreaming and waking. As for "The Work of Art," an essay just as radical as "Surrealism," it presents film as a symptom and as the place for a transformation of the concept of the work of art itself, a transformation that—without resorting to intoxication—also effaces the distinction between art and document in the name of a superior, perceptive, and political effectiveness. In contrast, in the domain of the mercantile confusion between art and nonart, the essay "Karl Kraus" maintains the orthodoxy of the "theses against snobs."[15] The essay on Kraus deals both with a form of *art,* namely, satire, which is the form Kraus uses to intervene on the cultural scene, and with the normative concept of art that he defends and that is inscribed within a "theological" poetics with strong moral connotations of the kind defended by the early Benjamin. The term Benjamin opposed to "journalism" could just as easily have been "authentic language," for Kraus's art consists in jealously conserving the sacred character of language even as he sows terror. In this preservation he confuses language, art, and justice, Judaism and the cult of the German language, as does Benjamin.

In his battle, Kraus opposes the "chronic sickness" of inauthenticity. "It is from the unmasking of the inauthentic that [Kraus's] battle against the press arose" (*Reflections,* 241). Like Kraus, Benjamin still has no doubts about this concept of authenticity, which Adorno will find suspect; witness his use of the concepts "origin"[16] and then "aura," which are indissociable from that of authenticity. He is hardly troubled by the authoritarian connotations of that claim to authenticity that is at the foundation of the conservative critique of culture.[17] Benjamin speaks of Kraus's "strange interplay between reactionary theory and revolutionary practice" (*Reflections,* 247), an interplay that is not far from an analogous constellation for the author of *The Origin of German Tragic Drama*—but Benjamin is only partly aware of the ambivalence of his own conceptions. This ambivalence stems from his evaluations of public opinion and of technology in relation to the modern development of the press. Kraus's hatred for the press is not reasoned; it is "more vital than moral" (*Reflections,* 239, translation modified). "The very term 'public opinion' outrages him," writes Benjamin. "Opinions are a private matter" (*Reflections,* 239). As an enemy of discussion, Benjamin mistrusts the contradictory expression of evaluations transmitted by the media. With Kraus, to opinions thus termed "private" he opposes "judgment," an authoritarian evaluation that—he claims—is no longer affected by the private character of "opinion": "It is precisely the purpose of the public opinion generated by the press to make the public incapable of judging, to insinuate into it the attitude of someone irresponsible, uninformed" (*Reflections*, 329). In the name of this critique of public opinion, infantilized by the press, Benjamin defends both Karl Kraus's authoritarian attitude and his refusal to separate private and public life. Just as Kraus "makes his own existence a public issue," he has "opposed the distinction between personal and objective criticism" (*Reflections*, 247). Kraus incarnates "the secret of authority: never to disappoint" (*Reflections*, 248).[18]

Owing to the destructive work of his polemics, Kraus transforms polemics into an instrument of production. Through his technique of quotation, which will inspire Benjamin in his *Paris Arcades*, Kraus's principle is "to dismantle the situation, to discover the true question the situation poses," and then "to present this to his opponent in guise of response" (*Reflections*, 243–244, translation modified). This work of destruction is carried out in the name of Kraus's "tact," which, according to Benjamin, is "moral alertness" (*Reflections*, 244). Such an authoritarian attitude disdains Kantian morality (*Reflections*, 245), the profane and rational morality to which Benjamin opposes "true tact," grounded in a "theological criterion." To present it—and to introduce the figure of Kraus, *the universal man*—Benjamin mobilizes the conceptions of his book on the baroque: "Tact is the capacity to treat social relationships, though not departing from them, as natural, even as paradisiac relationships" (*Reflections*, 244). The conception Kraus has of the creature

> contains the theological inheritance of speculations that last possessed contemporary validity for the whole of Europe in the seventeenth century. At the theological core of this concept, however, a transformation has taken place that has caused it, quite without constraint, to coincide with the cosmopolitan credo of Austrian worldliness. . . . Stifter gave this creed its most authentic stamp, and his echo is heard wherever Kraus concerns himself with animals, plants, children. (*Reflections*, 244)

Kraus—and this is what is at stake in his actions as a dispenser of justice—becomes the protector of the *creature* against the criminal existence of man: "Every day fifty thousand tree trunks are cut down for sixty newspapers" (*Reflections*, 245). Compared to Benjamin's "theology" or that of Horkheimer and Adorno's *Dialectic of Enlightenment*, Kraus's theology, in *Die letzten Tage der Menschheit* (The last days of humanity) is apocalyptic, like a baroque vision: "His defeatism is of a supranational, that is, planetary kind, and history for him is merely the wilderness dividing his race from creation, whose last act is world conflagration. As a deserter to the camp of animal creation—so he measures out his wilderness" (*Reflections,* 246).

Benjamin's deep identification with Kraus, signaled by the reference to the new angel he incarnates, is revealed again through the image of the storm (one of the first formulations of what will become a leitmotif in the Benjaminian oeuvre), in the texts on Kafka and Baudelaire, and also in the "Theses on the Philosophy of History." Through this *image* that no concept could translate without being reductionist, Benjamin determines the situation of the "just man" engaged in the adventure of history. Sometimes— rarely—he is a dialectician for whom it is important to "have the wind of world-history in one's sails" ("Central Park," 44), and sometimes—most often—he is a powerless spectator of the historical catastrophe. Faced with the disaster of his age, Kraus, by a kind of monumental passivity, professes silence: " 'Those who now have nothing to say because it is the turn of deeds to speak, talk on. Let him who has something to say step forward and be silent.' Everything Kraus wrote is like that: a silence turned inside out, a silence that catches the storm of events in its black folds, billows, its livid lining turned outward" (*Reflections,* 243). The political effectiveness of such a gesture of indignant self-styling is uncertain.

The technique of montaging quotations, the art of silence, stems from the same principle. "Kraus," writes Benjamin, "has written articles in which there is not a single word that is his own" (*G.S.,* 2:1093). That will also be Benjamin's project in *Paris Arcades,* as it was in *The Origin of German Tragic Drama,* the "craziest mosaic technique" (*Correspondence,* 256), where quotation was "the only element of authority" (*Origin,* 28, translation modified) available in the absence of true doctrine. Like Adam, the critic originally names things and assigns them their place in Creation:

> To quote a word is to call it by its name. So Kraus's achievement exhausts itself at its highest level by making even the newspaper quotable. He transports it to his own sphere, and the empty phrase is suddenly forced to recognize that even in the deepest dregs of the journals it is not safe from the voice that swoops on the wings of the word to drag it from its darkness. (*Reflections,* 268)

Whether it saves or punishes, the quotation brings together language and justice and confuses them. Quotation "summons the word by its names, wrenches it destructively from its context, but precisely thereby calls it back to its origin" (*Reflections,* 261). Even though Kraus converted to Catholicism, it is this approach that, in Benjamin's view, is his irreducibly Jewish aspect. "To worship the image of divine justice in language—even in the German language—that is the genuinely Jewish somersault by which he tries to break the spell of the demon" (*Reflections,* 254).

This is also a self-portrait of Benjamin and of what ties him to the German language, just as his judgment of Kraus's technique also applies to his own approach: "Kraus knows no system. Each thought has its own cell. But each cell can in an instant, and apparently without a cause, become a chamber, a legal chamber over which language presides" (*Reflections,* 254). Then again, in another form, this is a portrait of Kafka, who is also in a struggle with the "demonism" of that prehistoric world that the contemporary world has never ceased to be: "The dark background from which [Kraus's] image detaches itself is not formed by his contemporaries, but is the primeval world or the world of the demon" (*Reflections,* 250)—the world whose sickness nonetheless affects Kraus.

Benjamin criticizes Kraus's "inadequacies": his demonic vanity as actor and mime, as decadent artist, and as heir to *l'art pour l'art* in which his relation to the law is rooted. "He has seen through law as have few others. If he nevertheless invokes it, he does so precisely because his own demon is drawn so powerfully by the abyss it represents" (*Reflections,* 255). When Kraus latches onto the "trial for sexual offenses," obscene encounters between justice and Venus, he speaks as a "dandy who has his forebear in Baudelaire. Only Baudelaire hated as Kraus did the satiety of healthy common sense, and the compromise that intellectuals made with it in order to find shelter in journalism. Journalism is betrayal of the literary life of mind, of the demon" (*Reflections,* 257–258). The demonic Kraus embraces the alliance between mind and sex. Like Kafka, he falls from a theological role into literature: "The life of letters," writes Benjamin, "is existence under the aegis of mere mind, as prostitution is existence under the aegis of mere sexuality. The demon, however, who leads the whore to the street exiles the man of letters to the courtroom" (*Reflections,* 258). In some sense, he appears in court before being summoned, like Baudelaire or Flaubert.

This critique of Kraus must have seemed strange to Benjamin's friends such as Scholem and Max Rychner, who had not followed the mutation of the philosopher of language into a reader of Marx:

> That to him the fit state of man appears not as destiny and fulfillment of nature liberated through revolutionary change, but as an element of nature per se, of an archaic nature without history, in its primeval, primitive state, throws uncertain, disquieting reflections even on his idea of freedom and of humanity. It is not removed from the realm of guilt that he has traversed from pole to pole: from mind to sexuality. (*Reflections,* 259)

The "nature liberated through revolutionary change" was a new expression, close to Ludwig Feuerbach and the early Marx, in an oeuvre where theology had until then consisted in linking nature to the ephemeral, to death, and to an irremediable nihilism.

In the last part of the essay, Benjamin tries resolutely to place Kraus in the service of political commitment, by making of him a thinker who announces the move from "classical humanism," that of Goethe and Schiller, to "real humanism," that of Marx. Benjamin thus links two critiques of "human rights." The first is that of Karl Kraus, who sees them only as a "toy that grownups like to trample on and so will not give up" (*Reflections,* 261), to which Benjamin adds: "Thus drawing the frontier between the private sphere [that of "man"] and the public sphere [that of the "citizen"], which in 1789 was supposed to inaugurate freedom, became a mockery" (*Reflections,* 261, translation slightly modified). The operetta, which delighted Karl Kraus, presents a jubilant parody of this. The second critique is that of Marx's "The Jewish Question," where we read, in reference to the bourgeois revolution: "The real man is acknowledged only in the form of . . . the abstract *citoyen.* . . . Only when the really individual man takes back into himself the abstract citizen . . . only then is human emancipation complete" (quoted in *Reflections,* 270). By forcing his interpretation and seeking to save Karl Kraus for Marxism, Benjamin makes him the defender of "real humanism" against "classical humanism." The "inhuman" cynic had written a political text in 1920 claiming that communism was a "deranged remedy with a purer ideal purpose—the devil take its practice, but God preserve it as a constant threat over the heads of those who have property and would like to compel all others to preserve it" (quoted in *Reflections,* 272). Kraus, whose Shakespearean model is "Timon, the misanthrope" (*Reflections,* 263), seems to be linked in spite of himself to a theory that, though not philanthropic, is far removed from misanthropy and pessimistic anthropology. Benjamin sees very well the political naiveté that separates Kraus from Marx: "It is his program to reduce the development of bourgeois–capitalist affairs to a condition that was never theirs" (*Reflections,* 269). But he thinks the two are linked through their destructive impulses.

Like Benjamin's thought, Kraus's thinking is centered on language, on the "sanctification of the name" and "Jewish certainty" (*Reflections,* 265). "You have come from the origin—the origin is the goal" (*Reflections,* 265, translation modified): This formula of Karl Kraus's applies both to poetic verse and to history. "Just as blessedness has its origin at the end of time, rhyme has its at the end of the line" (*Reflections,* 266, translation modified). Kraus substitutes, for the demonic relation of mind and sex lying in wait for him, a relation between eros and language: "The more closely you look at a word the more distantly it looks back" (*Reflections,* 267); Benjamin sees in this sentence the very example of a perception of the "aura" of language in what is unapproachable and profoundly traditional about it (*Illuminations,*

200 n. 17). And yet, Kraus is a destroyer because, for Benjamin, the aura is always associated with destruction and decline; it appears to us only in the light of its destruction.

In this second period of his oeuvre, in which writing serves politics, Benjamin continually radicalizes the destructive operation, extending it to the theological traditions that inspired him and that are preserved only in certain artistic or political gestures. It is for this reason that "The Work of Art in the Age of Mechanical Reproduction" approves the liquidation of the aura and of art in the traditional sense. According to the architect Adolf Loos, "human work consists only of destruction" (*Illuminations,* 272), to which Benjamin adds, speaking of Kraus:

> For far too long the accent was placed on creativity. . . . Work as a supervised task—its model: political and technical—is attended by dirt and detritus, intrudes destructively into matter, is abrasive to what is already achieved, critical toward its conditions, and is in all this opposite to that of the dilettante luxuriating in creation. His work is innocent and pure, consuming and purifying masterliness. And therefore the monster stands among us as the messenger of a more real humanism. He is the conquerer of the empty phrase. . . . The average European has not succeeded in uniting his life with technology because he has clung to the fetish of creative existence. (*Illuminations,* 272)[19]

In addition to destruction, there is also the watchword of privation, voluntary poverty. Kraus resembles "Klee's *New Angel,* who preferred to free men by taking from them, rather than make them happy be giving to them" (*Illuminations,* 273). Before becoming a clearly articulated philosophical position, this observation attempts to synthesize the attitude shared by a certain number of literary and artistic works: those of Paul Scheerbart, Karl Kraus, Bertolt Brecht, Adolf Loos, and Paul Klee. All these authors, with the exception of Karl Kraus, will be cited in a 1933 essay entitled "Erfahrung und Armut" (Experience and poverty) in which Benjamin develops the theme of voluntary poverty, even as he introduces certain themes that will be taken up again *in reverse form* in his essay "The Storyteller." According to him, this poverty is linked to the decline both of experience and of its communication in storytelling. "Experience is decreasing, and in a generation that, in 1914–1918, had one of the most momentous experiences of universal history. . . . People came back from the war mute. They were not richer in communicable experience, but poorer" (*G.S.,* 2:214). Modern war introduced a gap between technology and the social order: "This enormous deployment of technology has plunged men into an entirely new poverty" (*G.S.,* 2:214). At the same time, all of traditional culture has been devalorized: "What is the value of all cultural heritage if not that experience attaches us to it?" Thus, a new "barbaric" era has begun. But Benjamin defends it as "a positive barbarism," in the very sense he had defended Kraus's "inhumanity" as a form of "real humanism": "Where does the barbarian's poverty of experience lead him? To begin at zero; to be satisfied with little; to build with few elements, looking neither to the right nor the left. Among the great creators, there have always been the merciless ones who began *tabula rasa*" (*G.S.*, 2:215).

Pell-mell, Benjamin cites René Descartes and Albert Einstein, the cubists and Paul Klee. As in the essay on Kraus, the liquidation of bourgeois private life is part of that poverty. It is symbolized by the idea of the glass house, anticipated by the architecture of arcades in iron and glass and realized by Loos and Le Corbusier. In such a house, the inhabitant leaves almost no trace. It is in this spirit that the initial project of *Paris Arcades* was conceived at that time:

> Glass objects have no "aura." In general, glass is the enemy of the secret. It is also the enemy of property. . . . When a person enters a bourgeois salon from the 1880s, the strongest impression he draws, in spite of any "warmth," is perhaps: "There is no place for you here." There is no place for you here because there is not the slightest space where the person who lives here has not already left his trace. (*G.S.*, 2:217)

In his radical phase of commitment, Benjamin wants to be the joyful barbarian: "Humanity is getting ready, if necessary, to outlive culture. And above all, he does so laughing. This laughter can at time appear barbaric. Let's admit it. It may well be that the individual sometimes gives a bit of humanity to the masses who, one day, will give it back to him with interest" (*G.S.*, 2:219). An almost identical passage is found among the notes on Kraus. He also belonged to those new barbarians, a combination of children and cannibals, who were the "angels," the messengers of a new era. He knows, having learned it too late,

> that there is no idealistic but only a materialistic deliverance from myth, and that at the origin of creation stands not purity but purification. . . . Only in despair did he discover in quotation the power not to preserve but to purify, to tear from context, to destroy; the only power in which hope still resides that something might survive this age—because it was wrenched from it. (*Reflections*, 270–271)

Hence, the "aura" must be destroyed inasmuch as authenticity is mingled with myth and pretense. This destructive dimension of his thinking links Karl Kraus to the other avant-garde artists of his era.

Franz Kafka: The Gesture and Its Interpretation

Instead of elaborating a doctrine, Kraus confined himself to destroying falseness and inauthenticity. Kafka's failure to illustrate doctrine is, in Benjamin's view, symptomatic of the *same* historical situation. Through his failure, Kafka reveals the distance separating the lives of his era from a life that conforms to Scripture. Benjamin wrote the essay "Franz Kafka" about four years after the essay on Kraus, and it was published in an abridged version by *Jüdische Rundschau* (Jewish review) in late 1934. The text on Franz Kafka shows little similarity to the essay on Karl Kraus—except that in both cases Benjamin is concerned with the complex forms of a secularization of Judaism. But where the text on Karl Kraus attempts to establish an internal link between theology and materialism, the essay on Kafka abandons this attempt; at almost the same time, Benjamin was writing one of his politically most radical texts, one that was also among the most distant from any theological preoccupation: the article of Brechtian inspiration entitled "The Author as Producer." What mattered for Benjamin at the time was solely the profound compatibility between the convictions of an author and historical materialism; according to Benjamin, this compatibility seemed to exist for Kafka.[20] That said, the profane level is inadequate and does not allow him to ground such a commitment. That is why the theological conception underlies Benjamin's "materialist" texts and remains implicit in them, until that relation is clearly formulated in "Theses on the Philosophy of History."

Benjamin's essay on Kafka is one of his least conceptual and most narrative texts. Of the four parts, three are introduced by a story, the fourth by the description of a photo of Kafka as a child. As a result, the interpretation is not made explicit.[21] From the point of view of method, however, two things are certain: In the name of his conception of the gap between discursive thought and literary creation in any authentic writer, Benjamin rejects both Kafka's self-interpretation, as it can be drawn from his "posthumous reflections," and the theological interpretation, as it was developed by a great number of authors. He grounds his entire reading on the often obscure "gestures" or "motifs" through which the content of what Kafka had to say is expressed. But this reading is ultimately theological. In other words, according to the conception already expressed in the essays on Goethe and tragic drama, Benjamin situates the element of contemporary thought that matters from the theological viewpoint precisely in the images, figures, and gestures that remain obscure to the authors themselves.

The gap between the discursive propositions of a great writer and his literary oeuvre is interpreted as the distance between a limited rationality and a practice guided by truth: "It is easier to draw speculative conclusions from Kafka's posthumous collection of notes than to explore even one of the motifs that appear in his stories and novels" (*Illuminations*, 128). It is when an uncomprehending Kafka confines himself to showing that Benjamin finds the keys to his vision: "Kafka could understand things only in the form of a *gestus,* and this *gestus* which he did not understand constitutes the cloudy part of the parable. Kafka's writings emanate from it" (*Illuminations,* 129).

This fact was inadmissible for Kafka; in his view, it constituted a failure that would bring on the destruction of his oeuvre:

> He did fail in his grandiose attempt to convert poetry into doctrine, to turn it into a parable and restore to it that stability and unpretentiousness which, in the face of reason, seemed to him to be the only appropriate thing for it. No other writer has obeyed the commandment "Thou shalt not make unto thee a graven image" so faithfully. (*Illuminations,* 129)

In another passage, Kafka's parables are assimilated to the relation between the Haggadah and Halakah in the talmudic tradition, in other words, the relation between interpretation (or illustration) and the law:

> This does not mean that his prose pieces belong entirely in the tradition of Western prose forms; they have, rather, a similar relationship to doctrine as the Haggadah does to the Halakah. They are not parables, and yet they do not want to be taken at their face value; they lend themselves to quotation and can be told for purposes of clarification. But do we have the doctrine which Kafka's parables interpret and which K.'s postures and the gestures of his animals clarify? It does not exist; all we can say is that here and there we have an allusion to it. (*Illuminations,* 122)

In this regard, Benjamin and Scholem disagree. For Scholem, the loss of doctrine (of "Scripture") and the incapacity to decipher are not at all the same thing; that is "the greatest error"[22] Benjamin could have committed. In contrast, for Benjamin,

> it comes down to the same thing, because, without the key that belongs to it, the Scripture is not Scripture, but life. Life as it is lived in the village at the foot of the hill on which the castle is built. It is in the attempt to metamorphose life into Scripture that I perceive the meaning of "reversal" [*Umkehr*], which so many of Kafka's parables endeavor to bring about. (*Correspondence,* 453)

In reconstituting the tradition of the Kabbala, Scholem is seeking to preserve the possibility of implementing doctrine, in spite of our current incapacity to decipher it. For Benjamin—and according to him, for Kafka— "the work of the Torah has been thwarted" (*Correspondence,* 2:125). The effort of Kafka's oeuvre consists entirely in metamorphosizing life into Scripture: According to Benjamin, that is "the meaning of 'reversal' [*Umkehr*], which so many of Kafka's parables endeavor to bring about. . . . Sancho Panza's existence is exemplary because it actually consists in rereading one's own existence—however buffoonish and quixotic" (*Correspondence*, 453). Karl Kraus's destructive practice of quotation and Benjamin's efforts to reread the tradition against the grain in order to destroy its false appearances move in the same direction.

By insisting on the *gestures* through which Kafka presents his vision, Benjamin links them to the gestural aspect of Brechtian theater. Brecht, too, was unable to limit himself to literature alone. He, too, wanted to illustrate a "doctrine"—in his case, that of Marx. He also presented gestures whose importance escaped him to a certain extent. That is undoubtedly the reason Benjamin insists on the analogies between Kafka and the eminently gestural Chinese theater that Brecht claimed as one of the precursors of epic theater. At the same time, Benjamin establishes a relation between the messianic hope of seeing the "disfigured" world put back in order and the materialist hope for a revolution, which was proper to Brecht. But what distinguishes messianism from materialism is the scope of their hopes. The theological character of the Benjaminian vision translates into the hope characteristic of fairy tales, which consists in seeing the hunchback lose his hump.[23] Once more, to differentiate himself from Scholem, Benjamin underscores a convergence between the Jewish tradition and the European—and particularly the German—tradition of the fairy tale, reactualized by romanticism: Through the figure of the hunchback, the man with the curved back bearing the weight of the ages of the world, Kafka

> touches the ground . . . the core of folk tradition, the German as well as the Jewish. Even if Kafka did not pray—and this we do not know—he still possessed in the highest degree what Malebranche called "the natural prayer of the soul": attentiveness. And in this attentiveness he included all living creatures, as saints include them in their prayers. (*Illuminations*, 344)

According to Benjamin, Kafka presented the world in a disfigured state, in the expectation of deliverance. This alteration is such that no rational action could correct it; only a messianic miracle could put it back in order. Benjamin cannot do without theology, since the reconciliation he wishes for is not within the reach of human reason; in addition, reason finds no support in this world. In this period between the two world wars, what he perceives in Kafka and Kraus is the return of prehistory: "Kafka did not consider the age in which he lived as an advance over the beginnings of time" (*Illuminations*, 130).

As in Proust's works, forgetting is central in Kafka's oeuvre and determines his narrative technique: The most important things are said in passing, as if the hero "must really have known it all along" (*Illuminations,* 131) or "as though the hero was being subtly invited to recall to mind something that he had forgotten" (*Illuminations,* 131). Memory, a central notion of Judaism, is the opposite pole: "Everything forgotten mingles with what has been forgotten of the prehistoric world" (*Illuminations,* 131). Forgetting always affects the best part. That is why all of contemporary humanity's efforts must consist in rediscovering the lost gesture, must consist in taking it up again. "It is a tempest that blows from the land of oblivion, and study is a cavalry attack against it" (*Illuminations,* 138, translation slightly modified). For Kafka, the wind often blows "from the prehistoric world," " 'from the nethermost regions of death,' " and the study to which "students" turn in Kafka's work is the reversal, the conversion "that transforms existence into writing" (*Illuminations,* 138). As for Kraus, the object of study is the relation between law and justice: "The law which is studied and not practiced any longer is the gate to justice" (*Illuminations,* 139). This is the utopia of a society in which there would be no more conflicts of interest, in which the practice of law would be pointless.

For Benjamin, the urgency of leaving behind the primitive world justifies the break with an autonomous aesthetics that does not seek to transcend the indetermination of meaning. The paradox of Benjaminian aesthetics is that, even as it rules out discursive meaning in order to set forth the particularity of modern art, in Goethe, in surrealism, and in Kafka— that of producing *images without meaning*—it also attributes to *those very images* a precise theological significance, which necessarily escapes the authors. This operation is the exact reverse of the Nietzschean approach, which consists in bringing *any* value—whether of truth or justice—back to the intensity of modern art's "images without signifieds," and thus reducing philosophy and the normative dimensions of social life to the sole value of the artistic "will to power" or to the most intense aesthetic experience. In surrealism, Benjamin does not find the normative background that would assign a redemptive finality to the "nihilist," destructive operation of the work of art; in the works of Kraus and Kafka, he observes the failure of an attempt to transcend art in the direction of a doctrinal authority inspired by the Jewish tradition. Only the interpretation of artistic signs permits him to discover a perspective that transcends the current horizon. Benjamin will apply this method of interpretation to the "art" that seems to him the most innovative, that grounded in mechanical reproduction: cinema and the mechanical "arts" that structure everyday life, from the architecture of glass and iron to advertising and urbanism.

Among the symptoms of the state of "alienation" of contemporary humanity, Benjamin cites, in his essay on Kafka, film and the record player: "Man does not recognize his own walk on the screen or his own voice on the phonograph" (*Illuminations*, 137). In 1934, the media of mechanical reproduction still appeared to Benjamin to be obstacles for persons seeking to reappropriate themselves; the next year, film would be interpreted as a means of regaining a grip on oneself.

DESTRUCTION OF THE AURA: PHOTOGRAPHY AND FILM

"A Small History of Photography," in which Benjamin formulates for the first time his definition of *aura,* one of the central concepts of his aesthetics, dates from the same year as the essay on Kraus. In this text, the discussion is linked to surrealism in particular and to "the liquidation of the aura" that it brings about in photography. Four years later, in "The Work of Art in the Age of Mechanical Reproduction," conceived as the vanishing point for the research on *Paris Arcades,* the stakes are higher. Benjamin attacks the religious foundations of art as they dominate the aesthetic experience in the traditional sense; according to him, this experience is contemplative and fetishistic. This theory draws inspiration from the Weberian theses on desacralization. But what will replace the ritual underlying any work of art is now, according to Benjamin, not an autonomous experience but rather politics: not the ideal receiver, God, but the idealized receiver, the public of the struggling class. Temporarily, then, theology seems to lose all its interest for aesthetic theory. In the earlier essays, however, destruction still had a hidden theological sense, which might very well be resonating here as well.

At the beginning of the 1930s, Benjamin granted a theoretical status to the concept of *aura* by announcing its decline in the restricted field of photography. In "The Work of Art," film seems to provoke a *crisis of art* in general. For better or for worse, however, art has survived the crisis precipitated by film, just as it survived Dadaism, which, if we are to believe Benjamin, was only the prelude to cinematic shock effects. Above all, even if we except commercial film, film itself has hardly evolved in the direction of politicization announced by Benjamin; it has not radically escaped the field of art, and that cannot be attributed solely to the fact that the political project supported by Benjamin has failed. That failure and the obsolescence of "The Work of Art" are closely related.

Benjamin traces the awareness of a crisis in the aura back to Hegel. In his speculations on "the end of art"—to which all the philosophers of art in the following decades will refer, from Heidegger to Gadamer and Adorno—Hegel "sensed a problem" (*Illuminations*, 245), according to Benjamin: "We are beyond the stage of reverence for works of art as divine and objects deserving our worship. The impression they produce is one of a more reflective kind, and the emotions they arouse require a higher test" (Hegel, quoted in *Illuminations,* 245). For Hegel, this test was philosophical science, which had sublimated art, especially since the Reformation.[24]

In spite of Nietzsche's desperate revolt, this analysis has continued to make its way through modern thought. Not only does art seem condemned to a role secondary to that of science, but it also suffers the consequences of the *desacralization* that affects all modern reality: "The fate of our times is characterized by rationalization and intellectualization and, above all, by the 'disenchantment of the world,' " writes Max Weber in 1919, adding: "Precisely the ultimate and most sublime values have retreated from public life. . . . It is not accidental that our greatest art is intimate and not monumental."[25]

For Hegel, art is not, properly speaking, desacralized; rather, it can no longer make claims to being the *supreme* expression of metaphysical truth defended by philosophy, which preserves the connotations of rational theology. In the works of Weber and Georg Simmel, modern rationalization provokes a general disenchantment of the world, so much so that art, now without effect on public life, survives only in the private sphere. It is to this decline that Benjamin is reacting, but in a different way from Nietzsche. Inasmuch as the "beautiful appearance" of art is now mere lies and artifice, it is no longer appropriate to celebrate pure and simple appearance, the vital lie that brings us intense experiences: Rather, we must sacrifice art in the traditional sense to preserve the public status and the pragmatic role of its productions. Unlike Max Weber, Benjamin is not part of the tradition of a "Protestant" and rationalist critique of the image, nor does he confine himself to observing in a general way the desacralization of art; he undertakes to precisely show the modifications that certain arts have undergone, according to their technical composition, their relation to reality, and the social context of their reception.

In 1931, when Benjamin introduced his concept of aura,[26] it was not just a general reflection on the destiny of art but, rather, one aspect of the history of *photography.* Benjamin's most famous essay, then, represents an audacious, perhaps even a reckless, generalizing and radicalizing of his early theses. A few years later, in his last essay on Baudelaire, Benjamin once more modified his theory. Such are the three stages of his reflection on this phenomenon.

In "A Small History of Photography," the concept of aura appears for the first time—and already in a context of "decline"—in reference to a photograph of Kafka as a child: "The picture in its infinite sadness forms a pendant to the early photographs in which people did not yet look out at the world in so excluded and god-forsaken a manner as this boy. There was an aura about them, an atmospheric medium, that lent fullness and security to their gaze" ("Photography," 247). The old photograph is exemplified in the portraits of David Octavius Hill. Their "aura" is due both to the technical conditions of the period and to the status of photography: Because of its low sensitivity, film required a long and concentrated exposure, producing "the absolute continuum from brightest light to darkest shadow," so that "the way light struggles out of darkness in the work of Hill is reminiscent of mezzotint" ("Photography," 248). Paradoxically, when we consider what follows, Benjamin speaks here of the "technical considerations" of the aura:

> Many group photos in particular still preserve an air of animated conviviality for a brief space on the plate, before being ruined by the print. It was this atmosphere that was sometimes captured with delicacy and depth by the now old-fashioned oval frame. That is why it would be a misreading of these incunabula of photography to make too much of their *artistic perfection* or their *taste*. The pictures were made in rooms where every client was confronted, in the photographer, with a technician of the latest school; whereas the photographer was confronted, in every client, with a member of a rising class equipped with an aura that had seeped into the very folds of the man's frock coat or floppy cravat. For that aura was by no means the mere product of a primitive camera. ("Photography," 248)

That aura was the result of a rigorous congruence between "subject and technique": it existed in the reality of the young bourgeoisie, just as it existed on the plate. During the epoch of the triumphant bourgeoisie—such is Benjamin's sociological thesis—it disappeared from both dimensions; at that point, artifice took its place:

> After 1880, though, photographers made it their business to simulate with all the arts of retouching, especially the so-called rubber print, the aura which had been banished from the picture with the rout of darkness through faster lenses, exactly as it was banished from reality by the deepening degeneration of the imperialist bourgeoisie. ("Photography," 248)

Benjamin celebrates the decline of this artificial aura, not the primitive aura. The abandoning of artifice is celebrated first by Eugène Atget, the "forerunne[r] of surrealist photography," who took shots of deserted streets, provoking a "salutary estrangement":

> He was the first to disinfect the stifling atmosphere generated by
> conventional portrait photography in the age of decline. He cleanses this
> atmosphere, indeed he dispels it altogether: he initiates the emancipation
> of object from aura which is the most signal achievement of the latest
> school of photography. ("Photography," 250)

At this point, "A Small History of Photography" formulates a definition of the aura that we find in every version of "The Work of Art in the
Age of Mechanical Reproduction": "What is aura, actually? A strange weave
of space and time: the unique appearance of semblance or distance, no matter
how close the object may be" ("Photography," 250). Two negative qualities
seem to define the aura: the uniqueness of a moment of temporal apparition
and its unapproachability, its distancing despite a possible spatial proximity.
And yet, modern society has developed needs that are incompatible with
such principles:

> To bring things *closer* to us, or rather to the masses, is just as passionate
> an inclination in our day as the overcoming of whatever is unique in
> every situation by means of its reproduction. Every day the need to
> possess the object in close-up in the form of a picture, or rather a copy,
> becomes more imperative. ("Photography," 250)

Let us note that this need to possess is a completely different criterion than
that which led Atget to liberate the photographic image from the aura. If
it were solely an empirical tendency that was anti-artistic in nature and that
conformed to the spirit of appropriation that had become widespread in the
social system, it is difficult to see why Benjamin would take it into account
in a theory of photography. He can only have in mind the *legitimate*
imperatives of the "masses" to reverse cultural privilege. And yet, Benjamin
concludes this development with an ambiguous sentence that refers to still
another aspect of the decline of the aura: "The stripping bare of the object,
the destruction of the aura, is the mark of a perception whose sense of the
sameness of things has grown to the point where even the singular, the
unique, is divested of its uniqueness—by means of its reproduction"
("Photography," 250).

It is no longer a *need*—perhaps legitimate—for proximity on a large
scale and for appropriation but, rather, a *sense* of identity, an *identity*-based
spirit, that reduces any singularity to multipliable unity and that sets aside
differences. We find both a critical judgment on a tendency toward leveling
and a comment on an anthropological transformation in the field of
cognitive perception, now dominated by the spirit of science.

There are, then, at least three reasons for the destruction of the aura:
aesthetic authenticity, which is opposed to artifice; *ethics* (or politics), the

questioning of privilege and of the exclusive character of the aura; and, finally, *anthropology,* a metamorphosis of perception, moving in the direction of a primacy of the *cognitive* attitude, which Benjamin notes here without making a value judgment. Only the third reason is linked to Hegel's or Weber's theses on the progression of the rational mind in Western culture, in the sense of a progress of cognitive rationality. In this same text, Benjamin will develop yet another theory of knowledge to which photography is supposed to contribute.

Benjamin also reinterprets aesthetic authenticity and the ethical imperative for equal access to art in the light of another form of art: cinema, and in particular, the revolutionary films of Sergey Eisenstein and Vsevolod Pudovkin. After the purification of the false aura brought about by Atget, the authenticity of the human face must be restored—this thesis will leave no trace in "The Work of Art":

> To do without people is for photography the most impossible of renunciations. And anyone who did not know it was taught by the best of the Russian films that milieu and landscape, too, reveal themselves most readily to those photographers who succeed in capturing them in anonymous faces. ("Photography," 251, translation modified)

Anonymity is an essential feature here, in that it excludes the pose, which destroys authenticity: "So the Russian feature film was the first opportunity in decades to put people before the camera who had no use for their photographs. And immediately the human face appeared on film with new and immeasurable significance. But it was no longer a portrait" ("Photography," 251).

The photographs of August Sander suggest the new meaning of these anonymous faces; they have a cognitive, even "scientific" finality. Sander's images provide a "training manual" to members of a society in which each person must orient him- or herself in relation to the physiognomies of others. In addition to restored authenticity and equal access to images, this cognitive function defines the status of photography. At the same time, photography transforms the perception of traditional art, both in granting greater equality of access and, especially, in contributing toward a progress in knowledge: "In the final analysis, mechanical reproduction is a technique of diminution that helps men to achieve a control over works of art without whose aid they would no longer be useful" ("Photography," 253, translation slightly modified).

In using the terms "control" and "useful," Benjamin is clearly defining the relation to art in terms of instrumentality. We recognize here the influence of Brecht and of his conception of the "use value" of art. As for "photography as art," Benjamin believes that a fundamental tension opposes art to photography. The primordial interest of photography is not aesthetic:

> The creative in photography is its capitulation to fashion. *The world is beautiful*—that is its watchword. Therein is unmasked the posture of a photography that can endow any soup can with cosmic significance but cannot grasp a single one of the human connexions in which it exists, even where most far-fetched subjects are more concerned with saleability than with insight. ("Photography," 255)

In this spirit, Benjamin accepts Baudelaire's critique of photography "as a violent reaction to the encroachment of artistic photography" ("Photography," 256). The task of this nonart is purely cognitive according to him: At the "scene of a crime"—the political crime of modern cities—photography's role is to "reveal guilt and point out the guilty" ("Photography," 256). "Will not the caption become the most important part of the photograph?" asks Benjamin ("Photography," 256). In fact, the image as such always remains open to several readings.[27] The caption is necessary because the cognitive function of photography as such is not assured. This is also true for the succession of filmic images, whose effect Benjamin compares to the function of the caption: "The directives which the captions give to those looking at pictures in illustrated magazines soon become even more explicit and more imperative in the film where the meaning of each single picture appears to be prescribed by the sequence of all the preceding ones" ("The Work of Art," *Illuminations,* 226). Here again, Benjamin attempts to reduce the function of cinematic images to knowledge. Nevertheless, "A Small History of Photography" is far from the radicality of the theses in "The Work of Art." It makes no general judgment on the destiny of art in the contemporary period and does not break with a humanist spirit, as evidenced by its attachment to the human face.

Four years after the article on the history of photography, right in the middle of his work on *Paris Arcades,* "The Work of Art in the Age of Mechanical Reproduction" approached the theme of the aura from a much wider angle, this time clearly attached to the Weberian thesis of the disenchantment of the world. No longer is Benjamin concerned with the halo characteristic of old photographs, artificially reproduced by industrial photography; at issue is a much less easily observable quality, attributed to *all* art and stemming from its magic and religious origins. The theoretical ambition is incomparably greater; hence the theses in the essay are much riskier.

In "A Small History of Photography," the aura was linked to the technical condition of a weak sensitivity to light and to the human condition of an absence of ostentatious externalization characteristic of the posed photograph. That "authenticity" takes on a much more generalized sense in the 1935 essay: "The presence of the original is the prerequisite to the concept of authenticity" *(Illuminations,* 220). It is thus linked in a general way to the "uniqueness" of the presence of the work of art "at the place where it happens to be" *(Illuminations,* 220). This quality is no longer linked to a precise form of art at a determined time—photography in its beginnings— but rather to a general characteristic of *plastic arts before their mechanical reproduction.* It remains to be seen whether, given such generality, the terms "aura" and "authenticity" still have any pertinent meaning: "The whole sphere of authenticity is outside technical—and, of course, not only technical—reproducibility. Confronted with its manual reproduction, which was usually branded as a forgery, the original preserved all its authority; not so *vis-à-vis* technical reproduction" *(Illuminations,* 220).

On the one hand, technical reproduction is "more independent of the original" *(Illuminations,* 220), from which it can extract certain aspects "with the aid of certain processes, such as enlargement or slow motion" *(Illuminations,* 220). On the other hand, it allows us to link the work of art to the viewer or listener, thanks to photography or phonograph records *(Illuminations,* 220–221). In opposing authenticity and reproduction—Adorno was the first to point this out—Benjamin simplifies a more complex relation he had underscored in the essay on photography: In that case, the aura was due to the *technical* conditions of photography. But that simplification is linked to a guiding idea that appears only in the next passage. The concept of authenticity refers to the notion of *tradition*: "The authenticity of a thing is the essence of all that is transmissible from its beginning, ranging from its substantive duration to its testimony to the history which it has experienced" *(Illuminations,* 221).

Through reproduction, what is disturbed

is the authority of the object. One might subsume the eliminated element in the term "aura" and go on to say: that which withers in the age of mechanical reproduction is the aura of the work of art. This is a symptomatic process whose significance points beyond the realm of art. One might generalize by saying: the technique of reproduction detaches the reproduced object from the domain of tradition. *(Illuminations,* 221)

Hence, Benjamin is convinced that the authority of tradition presupposes the uniqueness of an object that can be neither approached nor appropriated. Why is that? Why would tradition be linked to the here and now? Why would it not be maintained through diffusion? The printing press had long ago desacralized and diffused writing. Did it thereby disturb the traditions conveyed in writing? In a certain way, yes. The Lutheran disclosure of the

Bible deprived the church of its authority by permitting every reader to have access to the text, to interpret it and to feel its truth; it favored critical judgment and thus no doubt the critique of religion as a heteronomous institution. But fundamentally, it only accelerated the process of copying manuscripts. In addition, however, control over that diffusion now escaped the privileged and cloistered readers, the copyists. Before actually creating images, the technical reproduction of images was at first only an extension of that diffusion of the written text, applied this time to the pictorial, sculptural, and architectural tradition. In that case, it was a kind of "democratization of images":

> By making many reproductions, [the technique of reproduction] substi-
> tutes a plurality of copies for a unique existence. And in permitting the
> reproduction to meet the beholder or viewer in his own particular
> situation, it reactivates the object reproduced. These two processes lead
> to a tremendous shattering of tradition which is the obverse of the
> contemporary crisis and renewal of mankind. (*Illuminations,* 221)

What does this danger, this "obverse" of the contemporary crisis, this "tremendous shattering," consist in? What is revolutionary in Benjamin's view is the *exotericism* of mass culture: the fact that tradition escapes *authorized* transmission. Humanity renews itself, but at the cost of abandoning esoteric traditions. The word "tradition"—Benjamin has to have this in mind—also translates the term "Kabbala," that which, in religious tradition, deserves to be preserved.

Film elicits Benjamin's interest because it is "the most powerful agent" in this process, which hands images over to the masses: "Its social significance, particularly in its most positive form, is inconceivable without its destructive, cathartic aspect, that is, the liquidation of the traditional value of cultural heritage" (*Illuminations,* 221). Benjamin fears that the generalized actualization of cultural heritage undermines tradition. But technical reproduction is also an interpretation of traditions. It remains to be seen whether any particular interpretation stems from vulgarity, from misunderstanding, or, instead, from an authentic and fruitful rereading. It is thus not technical reproduction as such that represents a danger but the possibility that it opens of exploiting cultural heritage merely for the ends of profit or propaganda, outside the traditional mechanisms of cultural transmission. The dividing line between the preservation or renewal of tradition and its liquidation thus moves *inside* reproduction—between different ways of interpreting transmitted works—and not *between* authenticity and reproduction themselves. In spite of the aura of actors who are present "in person," theater can betray Shakespeare just as surely as can cinema, and film can renew the interpretation of Shakespearean dramas.

Having introduced the theme of the aura through the influence that technical reproduction exerts on it, Benjamin returns to the theory of "A Small History of Photography." He once more takes up the aspect of an ethical imperative and a change in human perception: The masses today tend to master the uniqueness and the distancing of images, to which they demand access; and this taste for reproduction can be compared to "the increasing importance of statistics" (*Illuminations,* 223). But this time, the ambiguity of this process falls clearly on the side of reproduction. In the field of art, Benjamin gives a positive sense to the desacralization and "disenchantment of the world." The artistic tradition appears indissociable from a notion of a *ritual* that has lost its legitimacy:

> Originally the contextual integration of art in tradition found its expression in the cult. We know that the earliest art works originated in the service of a ritual—first the magical, then the religious kind. It is significant that the existence of the work of art with reference to its aura is never entirely separated from its ritual function. In other words, the unique value of the "authentic" work of art has its basis in ritual [in theology, says the first version of the text], the location of its original use value. (*Illuminations,* 224)

This is not a thesis that appears in the 1931 essay. Beauty, according to Benjamin, is now indissociable from ritual:

> This ritualistic basis, however remote, is still recognizable as secularized ritual even in the most profane forms of the cult of beauty. The secular cult of beauty, developed during the Renaissance and prevailing for three centuries, clearly showed that ritualistic basis in its decline and the first deep crisis which befell it. (*Illuminations,* 224)

Contemporary with the invention of photography, the "negative theology" of *l'art pour l'art* seemed to prove the sacred character of beauty. According to this reasoning, the historical process of desacralization had to lead ineluctably toward decline, both of art in the technical sense and of beauty. "For the first time in world history, mechanical reproduction emancipates the work of art from its parasitical dependence on ritual" (*Illuminations,* 224).

All artistic production, from that of the Renaissance to Mallarmé's "pure" art stripped of object and social function—the Brechtian verdict is resonating in the background at this point—is stigmatized by this term "parasitic," which implicitly assimilates all traditional art to the "rubber print" and "artifice" of denatured photography. But whereas Benjamin's severe judgment on the synthetic aura that characterized posed photography was well founded, this global and hasty verdict on the metamorphoses of the ideal of beauty since the Renaissance is reductive and unfair. Of course, Benjamin seems to be linking his theory of cult value to the critical background of his essays on Goethe and tragic drama. Hence, he establishes a continuity between the aesthetic of the "inexpressive" and of allegory, his critique of the beautiful appearance, and the thesis of the decline of the aura. But at the time of the essay on Goethe, he knew that beauty cannot be reduced to the "beautiful appearance." In 1935, he sacrifices beauty and the aura to the "emancipation" that technical reproduction as such, freed from the original, is supposed to signify: "To an ever greater degree the work of art reproduced becomes the work of art designed for reproducibility" (*Illuminations*, 224). There exists no "original" or "authentic" copy of the negative of a film. Benjamin draws a radical conclusion from this fact: "But the instant the criterion of authenticity ceases to be applicable to artistic production, the total function of art is reversed. Instead of being based on ritual, it begins to be based on another practice—politics" (*Illuminations*, 224).

Politics—and, more precisely, Marxist politics—takes over for the sacred, "auratic" foundation of traditional art. It must be added that once Benjamin traced artistic autonomy back to a parasitical form of ritual, he had little choice. The distinction he introduces, based on the sacred origin of art, between the historical poles of cult value and exhibition value, would theoretically have allowed him to escape the choice between the religious and the political. But Benjamin does not interpret exhibition value in terms of a public and profane status of the work of art. Rather, he focuses on its *quantitative* aspect, access to the greatest number of works of art, *in opposition to* the exclusive character of access to cult values; in addition, he focuses on the *mechanical* aspect, the apprenticeship of perception and testing that is *analogous* to the practical functions of primitive art. Hence, through the very choice of concepts, he excludes both the specifically aesthetic content, interest, and value of works of art *and* the particular forms of exchange that govern that content, interest, and value. Benjamin does not allow himself to recognize in the aesthetic quality of works—their coherence, their force of revelation, their ability to open eyes and elicit new ways of seeing and evaluating—the desacralized heir to what he had called aura. In a peculiar manner, his sociological theory of art now leads him to be interested not in works of art, but only in the social functions that art as such fills "in the age of its mechanical reproducibility." Yet these functions are no longer linked to the significance of a unique work. In a certain way, for Benjamin—at least in this essay—the medium is already the message; the significance of art is reduced to the medium through which it addresses the public. At the beginning and the end of art history, the artistic is secondary:

In prehistoric time . . . by the absolute emphasis on its cult value, it was, first and foremost, an instrument of magic. Only later did it come to be recognized as a work of art. In the same way today, by the absolute emphasis on its exhibition value the work of art becomes a creation with entirely new functions, among which the one we are conscious of, the artistic function, later may be recognized as incidental. (*Illuminations,* 225)[28]

That is the final consequence of the founding idea of the *Paris Arcades* project in 1935—from which "The Work of Art" stemmed—the idea that, for the structuring forms of urban space, "the emancipation from the yoke of art" signified a dissipation of phantasmagorical illusions.

Independent of the aura, its theological background, and its anchoring in tradition, the question of reproducibility reveals the peculiar status of the work of art's identity in the field of the visual arts. As Nelson Goodman demonstrates in *Languages of Art,* the problem of authenticity is raised only for the arts he calls *autographic.* "There are, indeed, compositions falsely purporting to be by Haydn as there are paintings falsely purporting to be by Rembrandt: but of the *London Symphony,* unlike the *Lucretia,* there can be no forgeries. Haydn's manuscript is no more genuine an instance of the score than is a printed copy off the press this morning, and last night's performance no less genuine than the premier."[29] This is because, in literature and music, there exists an alphabet of characters and signs that assures the orthographic identity of the work:

In painting, on the contrary, with no such alphabet of characters, none of the pictorial properties—none of the properties the picture has as such—is distinguished as constitutive; no such feature can be dismissed as contingent, and no deviation as insignificant. The only way of ascertaining that the *Lucretia* before us is genuine is thus to establish the historical fact that it is the actual object made by Rembrandt. Accordingly, physical identification of the product of the artist's hand, and consequently the conception of forgery of a particular work, assume a significance in painting that they do not have in literature.[30]

This is what Benjamin calls "its presence in time and space" (*Illuminations,* 220), except that he does not explain that the problem he raises in relation to the "work of art" in general applies only to "autographic" works. But Goodman, who is concerned with symbolic classifications, is not interested in the fact that the development of technical reproduction produces *arts of the image for which the problem of authenticity does not arise.* This is a central question for Benjamin. The art of the ready-made (and Benjamin underscores Dadaism's anticipation of the later problems of reproduction) often presents an object fabricated as part of a series, with no original, as an authentic object; if only from the fact of its presentation, the object presented, whose secondary qualities the artist foregrounds, preserves a certain uniqueness. In the case of film, that uniqueness disappears; every exact copy is identical to the "original," without even needing the sort of system of notation that exists for literature and music.

Precisely in relation to the ready-made, Arthur Danto seeks to show, against Goodman, that what constitutes a work of art is not a difference in perception between an ordinary object and its artistic equivalent but the conceptual difference between any ordinary object and an object interpreted in the light of a theory: "To see something as art at all demands nothing less than this, an atmosphere of artistic theory, a knowledge of the history of art. Art is the kind of thing that depends for its existence upon theories; without theories of art, black paint *is* just black paint and nothing more."[31] What Danto calls "artistic theory"—a historically defined criterion that nevertheless disregards aesthetic value—Benjamin designates either as "tradition" (founded in a "ritual") or "politics." According to Benjamin, the only perceptions of a work of art that remain are either the decadent forms of ritual and contemplation or the lucid forms of a political reading.

It may be true that there is ultimately no politically indifferent reading of a work of art; but the fact that the reading of a work of art is politically *grounded* is not enough to produce a reading that is both *aesthetic*—attentive to the requirements of the work of art as medium of experience and thus as distinct from a cognitive communication—and aesthetically *adequate.* And if the political reading does not take the aesthetic into account, it also runs a grave risk of being inadequate from the political point of view.

Since, for Benjamin, the idea of the autonomy of art is linked to its magical and religious aura, it no longer has any raison d'être; it now appears purely illusory. At the same time, the true history of art, which considers Greek, medieval, Renaissance, and modern works of art, loses its value, as does the history of aesthetics, which, ever since the eighteenth century, has sought to establish the autonomy of its domain: "When the age of mechanical reproduction separated art from its basis in cult, the semblance of its autonomy disappeared forever" (*Illuminations,* 226). As in Nietzsche's work, the history of culture is traced back to the history of an illusion or a false sublimation. This reduction throws overboard both the ideological aspects of theology and idealism and the elements of a theory of specificity proper to aesthetic logic, which was still present in Benjamin's "theological" writings.

From this perspective, Benjamin purely and simply sets aside the debates on the artistic character of photography and cinema. "Much futile thought had been devoted to the question of whether photography is an art. The primary question—whether the very invention of photography had not transformed the entire nature of art—was not raised" (*Illuminations*, 227). But it is one thing to transform the entire nature of art, and another to set aside any aesthetic criterion in order to turn immediately to pragmatic or political criteria. Benjamin no longer even asks about the aesthetic quality of works of art. Only the general role of cinematic technique in modern society interests him:

> For contemporary man the representation of reality by the film is incomparably more significant than that of the painter, since it offers, precisely because of the thoroughgoing permeation of reality with mechanical equipment, an aspect of reality which is free of all equipment. And that is what one is entitled to ask from a work of art. (*Illuminations*, 234)

But cinematic technique as such has no more significance—artistic or nonartistic—than does the painter's technique: It all depends on what an artist makes of it. Otherwise, the industry of "popular" movies would be progress as such beyond modern painting, which is what Benjamin in fact suggests, despite his reservations about purely commercial cinema. He confuses technical progress with the progress of art, instrumental rationality with aesthetic rationality. "The Work of Art" stems from the ideology of progress denounced in Benjamin's late works: from an idea of the "wind of history" blowing toward technical development.

Because of its vagueness, the Benjaminian concept of aura is no longer even operative. It is obviously possible to change its meaning, but in so doing we would run the risk of returning to the trivial sense of an "atmospheric" value of the work of art. The *successful work of art* has the "aura" of its artistic authenticity; in contrast, a nonauratic work created by means of the most advanced technologies of reproduction may have no more than symptomatic interest. The opposition Benjamin sees between theater and cinema, between the "here and now" of the aura and reproduction, is not tenable:

> The aura which, on the stage, emanates from Macbeth, cannot be separated for the spectators from that of the actor. However, the singularity of the shot in the studio is that the camera is substituted for the public. Consequently, the aura that envelops the actor vanishes, and with it the aura of the figure he portrays. (*Illuminations*, 229)

The aura supposedly disappears because of the mere presence of the camera. But the camera is not independent of the human gaze, which, as in the theater, directs the actor; moreover, that gaze directs the camera, and thus, *that aura* does not disappear in film. In addition, whether at the theater or at the cinema, that aura is not constitutive of *art*. The "magic of presence" is not enough to confer on the work as a whole an auratic quality. Even the best actor loses his aura when he is badly directed in a badly written work.

It is just as difficult to maintain the analogy that Benjamin establishes between, on the one hand, the Dadaists' desacralization of art through "the studied degradation of their material" (*Illuminations,* 237), which prevents the viewer from adopting a contemplative attitude toward it, and, on the other, the "shock" provoked merely by the technique of cinema:

> No sooner has the eye grasped a scene than it is already changed. It cannot be arrested. . . . Like all shocks, [that of film] should be cushioned by heightened presence of mind. By means of its technical structure, the film has taken the physical shock effect out of the wrappers in which Dadism had, as it were, kept it inside the moral shock effect. (*Illuminations,* 238)

Once again, this confuses the medium and the message, the mechanical shock and the aesthetic shock. For the same reason, Benjamin will later compare the succession of cinematic images to the mechanical movement of an assembly line, thus reversing his once-positive evaluation of film. It goes without saying that this same cinematic technique can serve—and does serve in most cases—to present the most traditional plots, with no common ground with avant-garde literature or painting. However attractive Charlie Chaplin might be, it is for all the wrong reasons that Benjamin distinguishes between the masses' "progressive" attitude toward his films and the "backward"—because "contemplative"—attitude of that same audience toward Pablo Picasso's paintings and sculptures. Most of these objections were in fact made immediately by Adorno, in the name of the critical rigor of the early Benjamin himself.

Unlike the observations made in the essay on photography, the theory of the aura as it is developed in "The Work of Art" rests on an anthropological hypothesis. According to the first version of the text:

> Film's function is to train man in his apperceptions and the new reactions that the use of mechanical equipment conditions, whose role in his life is increasing almost daily. To make the immense technical apparatus of

our age the object of human innervation—that is the historical task in which the true sense of film resides. (*G.S.*, 1:444)

Benjamin reduces "the theory of perception that among the Greeks bore the name 'aesthetics' " (*G.S.*, 1:466) to an exercise relating to the forms that allow humanity to adapt to a dangerous environment, whether it consists of primitive beasts or modern wars.

What can "the politicization of art" mean from such a perspective? How is politics to be substituted for ritual? There is nothing in the text to indicate that it might be a question of something besides a pure and simple rejection of the aura, of cult value, and of the contemplative or meditative attitude before the work of art. In Benjamin's view, cinematic technique as such is political, inasmuch as it allows and calls for a "simultaneous collective reception" and incarnates the critique of "traditional conceptions of art" (*Illuminations*, 231), and inasmuch as every individual can now be found on either side of the camera: "Any man today can lay claim to being filmed" (*Illuminations*, 231). In the preface to "The Work of Art," the concepts of creativity (already manhandled in the essay on Kraus), of genius, of the value of eternity, and of mystery were ruled out (*Illuminations*, 218). This radical thesis finds its explanation here, even though Benjamin glimpses neither the dogmatic use that could be made of it nor the spasms of a generalized amateurism that could lay claim to such a disqualification. With the aura, Benjamin eliminates any particular artistic competence, just as he sets aside any specific critical competence. As in sports, everyone is supposedly an "expert" on the film representing everyday reality—whose aesthetic approaches are entirely set aside. "With regard to the screen," writes Benjamin, "the critical and the receptive attitudes of the public coincide" (*Illuminations*, 234). But what does criticism consist in if the aesthetic sphere and its own criteria are "liquidated" along with the aura? It can only be a criticism of what is represented, apart from any aesthetic mediation of images. The pretext for that liquidation is provided by the *star system*, which—like the rubber print in photography—artificially reconstitutes the aura, even *outside* works of art:

> The film responds to the shriveling of the aura with an artificial build-up of the "personality" outside the studio. The cult of the movie star, fostered by the capital of the film industry, preserves not the unique aura of the person but the "spell of the personality," the phony spell of a commodity. (*Illuminations*, 231, translation slightly modified)

From that moment on, Benjamin can no longer grant classical cinema the magic of an aura emanating from the presence of an actor or an actress, as showcased by a great film director; he ignores the aura of black-and-white photography, camera movements, and colors. In "The Work of Art," the human face has lost the central role it still had in the study on photography: "It is no accident that the portrait was the focal point of early photography. The cult of remembrance of loved ones, absent or dead, offers a last refuge for the cult value of the picture. For the last time the aura emanates from the early photographs in the fleeting expression of a human face" (*Illuminations,* 226).[32] By "refuge" he means a last escape in the face of technical progress and politics. Benjamin thus no longer insists on the return of the face in Russian cinema.

"The Work of Art in the Age of Mechanical Reproduction" may be the extreme form of Benjamin's *nihilism* in the economy of his oeuvre. The "decline" of the aura, the "liquidation" of tradition, and the disappearance of the human are the expression of a fundamentalism that expects redemption to come only out of the ruins of false and illusory reality: "Nature is Messianic by reason of its eternal and total passing away," writes Benjamin in 1920. "To strive after such passing, even for those stages of man that are nature, is the task of world politics, whose method must be called nihilism" ("Theologico-Political Fragment," *Reflections,* 313); "if necessary, to outlive culture . . . laughing" (*G.S.,* 2:219), we read in "Erfahrung und Armut" (1933). This nihilistic background combines with the desire to improve on Brecht's radicality.

Having pushed his approval of reductive and regressive tendencies to the limits of cynicism, Benjamin will change his mind in 1936 and, in a third phase of his oeuvre, will once more question the beneficent effects of the "liquidation" of the aura. We read the first indication of this shift in "The Storyteller," but the most explicit text in this respect is "On Some Motifs in Baudelaire," which is also a self-portrait.

In "On Some Motifs in Baudelaire," we find an evaluation of photography that cannot be reconciled with the earlier texts except in its observation of a crisis in perception. Benjamin interprets modernity in both Freudian and Proustian terms, seeing in the decline of the aura a specific deficiency of memory due to the shocks modern humanity has experienced. This decline is thus not simply the emancipation from an illusory appearance but, rather, a pathological phenomenon; disillusion does not compensate for the liquidation of tradition:

> If the distinctive feature of the images that rise from the *mémoire involontaire* is seen in their aura, then photography is decisively impli-

cated in the phenomenon of the "decline of the aura." What was
inevitably felt to be inhuman, one might even say deadly, in daguerreo-
typy was the (prolonged) looking into the camera, since the camera
records our likeness without returning our gaze. (*Illuminations*, 187–
188)

"Returning the gaze" is now the expression of auratic experience in
relation, more precisely, to nonhuman realities: "To perceive the aura of an
object we look at means to invest it with the ability to look at us in return"
(*Illuminations*, 188). A painting can thus possess an aura, whereas photography, according to Benjamin, excludes the exchange of gazes by placing
man in a confrontation with the camera. Estranged from involuntary
memory, photography knows nothing of the beautiful (*Illuminations*, 188).
"The Work of Art" said nothing less, but was overjoyed to see the disappearance of the phantasmagoria linked to appearance and inherited from
ritual.

In "The Work of Art," painting is seen as an art incapable of addressing
a mass public and hence obsolete in comparison to the arts of technical
reproduction. The last essay on Baudelaire returns to more traditional
conceptions. Cinema, which in 1935 was the canonical art of modernity, is
now assimilated to alienated labor (*Illuminations*, 175).

Benjamin reaches this conclusion based on the fact that photography
is entirely a function of voluntary memory. According to him, this kind of
memory is unfamiliar with the distancing of time, the aura, and the memory
of prehistory and origins that characterize involuntary memory and the
beautiful in general. Yet, just as a photograph can be "spoiled" by an
inadvertent movement or a momentary grimace, it can also "succeed"
precisely because the camera does not control its object, or at least controls
it much less than does the painter, who depends on no mechanical imprint
manifesting itself on the canvas. It is thus not for *that* reason that the
beautiful is inaccessible to photography. Furthermore, we must admit that
there exist aesthetic criteria constitutive of a photographer's *work of art*,
whose qualities are not due simply to the chance events of the shot.

To those who, like Scholem and Adorno, disapproved of "The Work of
Art," Benjamin responded that he had sacrificed the aura because that was
the only way to remain faithful to the theological issues of art, to a mode of
thinking to which art offers an essential knowledge. If that theology of
catastrophe is not enough to legitimate artistic modernity, then we must
also abandon *that* concept of aura and explain in some other way the magical
effect of certain works of art.

The essay on Baudelaire tries to show that the aura of his poetic works
is due to the fact that the artist has given up the poet's romantic aura. Under
the rubric of the "sacrifice of the aura," Benjamin formulates an aesthetics

of negativity, which Adorno will later develop. What Adorno in his *Aesthetic Theory* calls "the redemption of appearance" corresponds to what in Benjamin's late works is a "liquidation of the aura" by the culture industry, which "The Work of Art" seemed to applaud. According to Adorno, the aura belongs to objectified, successful works of art—more than successful, because true—which their dynamic as a whole fleetingly reveals. Authentic works of art, even though inhuman through their rigor, make no concessions to preserving the human they seem to deny. The magic of works of art is thus linked to an idea of humanity that is sometimes pushed to the point of a shocking inhumanity so as not to betray the *idea* of humanity: to remain faithful to utopia.

Whether naive, as in the authenticity of the old photograph, or terrible, as in the brushwork that surrounds the mutilated beings of Vincent Van Gogh or Francis Bacon, the aura is always a moving experience. It reminds us that we share a fragile humanity surrounded by a fleeting halo of light; it is a kind of appeal to solidarity. For precisely that reason, it is not certain that the aura is objectifiable in Adorno's sense. Great works of art can be without any apparent aura; minor works sometimes have that magic. The Benjaminian theory does not illuminate this phenomenon; that is not its goal. Bataille's oeuvre, an inquiry into the moral aspect of the aura—into the "sacred horror" that, for example, emerges from the work of Edouard Manet—is perhaps more instructive in this regard.

Everything indicates that the aura is not the most *artistic* aspect of a work of art. It is, rather, an affective charge received from the context or the time; it can be a sense of scandal or catastrophe—like that surrounding the *Olympia* or Duchamp's urinal, which brutally confront us with the reverse side of sublimation—or that which, in historical anticipation, emerges from Kant's writings. Just as there is in the beautiful an aspect of chance that is not at the disposition of the artist, the aura seems to be the sign of unlikely happiness or the threat of death; it is a part of the humanity that is threatened and captivated by a work of art. There is an aura of childhood, of happiness, of limitless possibilities suddenly glimpsed, and there is an aura of translucid old age, of the convict sentenced to death. The distance imposed by the aura may be linked to these inaccessible limits.

EMANCIPATION FROM THE YOKE OF ART

The primacy of the political over the aesthetic reading, clearly asserted in "The Author as Producer" in 1934, is one of the fundamental hypotheses on which *Paris Arcades* was based. Benjamin formulated this project in 1935, a few months before drafting "The Work of Art in the Age of Mechanical Reproduction," which, in fact, develops perspectives introduced in the outline of the *Arcades* project. The 1935 Exposé of *Paris Arcades* and the essay "The Work of Art" thus illuminate each other.

In writing these texts, Benjamin, as he often did, was responding to contradictory expectations. On the one hand, he was seeking to satisfy Brecht's imperatives, namely, to purge any trace of "theology" or "metaphysics" from his thinking and to develop an immediately applicable theory of cultural politics. On the other hand, the members of the Frankfurt School, in particular Adorno, were expecting from *Paris Arcades* the philosophical and aesthetic dimension that was lacking in Marx's oeuvre. To encourage him to write what would become the 1935 Exposé, Adorno wrote to Benjamin on 6 November 1934: "You know that I consider this work truly the share of original philosophy that it is incumbent upon us to write" (*G.S.* 5:1106). And again, on 20 May 1935: "I consider the *Arcades* not only the center of your philosophy but the last word that philosophy can today pronounce" (*G.S.*, 7:856). As Adorno explained to Horkheimer, "It is an effort to decipher the nineteenth century as 'style,' through the category of commodity understood as a dialectical image" (*G.S.*, 7:860). As an enthusiastic reader of the early writings of Benjamin, Adorno idealized the project and made it his own concern. That is why he continued to respond to the fragments he came to know with his own conception of a "critique of ideology."[33] Benjamin was attempting to do justice to two imperatives, all the while defending himself against Brecht's philosophical simplifications and against a tendency toward elitism that he suspected in Adorno, the student of Alban Berg.

The ambitious project changed at the beginning of the 1930s, when Benjamin abandoned his original idea of a "dialectical fairy play" in the spirit of *Einbahnstrasse* to turn, under the influence of the critiques of Horkheimer and Adorno, toward a more sociological, more "Marxist" project. The experience of the city, half Proustian and half surrealist, that had been at the origin of the project then had to find refuge in another, more literary form: *Berliner Kindheit um Neunzehnhundert* (A Berlin childhood around 1900).

In the 1935 Exposé for *Paris Arcades*, the problem of the aura appears only marginally and indirectly. But the sacrifice of art in the name of its perceptive, adaptive, and therapeutic functions, as it would be defended in "The Work of Art," was already clearly announced. In the service of the commodity (but fundamentally, by virtue of technical development or "productive forces") the nineteenth century emancipated all forms of figuration and creation—from architecture to painting to literature—from art. Benjamin even went so far as to compare this process to the way that "the sciences freed themselves from philosophy in the sixteenth [century]" (*Reflections*, 161). That comparison makes of *art* and *philosophy obstacles to the autonomous development of technology and science.* In the spirit of positivism, they are assimilated to the theological legacy that kept guard on thought and creation in an authoritarian manner and to a mystifying appearance that surrounded human productions before their liberation from tradition. We can gauge the difficulty inherent in that theory when we remember the systematic importance that Benjamin gave to art in his early works, that of anticipating doctrine. His abandonment of art can then be explained only by the fact that he is convinced of the imminence of the great historical turning point. At the slightest doubt regarding its imminence, it was inevitable that Benjamin would once more take up art's defense.

Art nouveau, then, "represents art's last attempt to escape from its ivory tower, which is besieged by technology" (*Reflections*, 154–155). Benjamin attempts to explain all modernity's forms of expression through a dual determination, which in fact he does not differentiate. According to Benjamin, architecture has passed into the hands of construction engineers; the reproduction of nature has fallen to photography, advertising, internal architecture, and urbanism; and literature is now controlled by the large presses. In the first place, this dynamic is inherent in technical development: "As architecture begins to outgrow art in the use of iron construction, so does painting in the panoramas" (*Reflections*, 149); second, it is part of the phantasmagorical context of the commodity: "All these products are on the point of going to market as commodities. But they hesitate on the brink. From this epoch stem the arcades and interiors, the exhibitions and panoramas. They are residues of a dream world" (*Reflections*, 162, translation slightly modified).

The relation between the emancipation of technology and the entry into the world of the commodity is not clearly articulated. We do not know whether these "products" are hesitating because they draw back before technology or because they refuse to become commodities. Benjamin confuses in a single historical complex a technical principle that functions only unconsciously (*Reflections*, 148)—whereas an aesthetic *consciousness* constructs factories in the form of houses, railroad stations in the shape of chalets, and metal supports designed on the model of Pompeiian columns— and a commodity principle that engenders its *own* appearances, those of fetishism, which are at the origin of the "phantasmagoria" of modern society. Any aesthetic principle intervening in the use of technology, whether it expresses the sensibility of an age or different ways of seeing—ironic, futurist, nostalgic, naive, aggressive, sophisticated, and so on—is subsumed under the single conception of an archaic aesthetic consciousness. Such a radical negation of the aesthetic mode of validity could only lead to an impasse.

The 1935 and 1939 Exposés of *Paris Arcades* can be distinguished by the relative weight they give each of these two aspects, the technological and the aesthetic. In 1935—as the final summary of the 1935 version, which was suppressed in the 1939 version, shows—the emphasis is placed on the substitution of technology for art, a substitution that is equivalent to a *suppression* of illusory appearance. But at the same time, the phantasmagoria engendered by commodity society—the arcades, the flaneur, the interior—include an aspect of utopia that shapes an aspiration to transcend the society of class, a utopia that Benjamin seeks to liberate from its ideological cocoon. In 1939, the substitution of technology for art moves to the background. Commodity society is under the influence of the phantasmagoria, associated with mythic anxiety; any utopian aspect has disappeared. In contrast, this version introduces a distinction between Baudelaire's art, his conception of the beautiful and of modernity, and the ideological ennoblement of technological necessities for "artistic pseudo-ends" (*G.S.*, 5:1257) that we find in Georges-Eugène Haussmann's urbanism: The "beauty" of views masks the political intention to control the city by the monied class, while the beauty of the Baudelairean work of art is authentically artistic and virtually critical.

The two diagnoses of the age are quite different. In the two Exposés, the social space is dominated by the phantasmagoria constitutive of nineteenth-century culture: the interpenetration of the most modern and the most ancient, of avant-garde technology and imaginary regressions; the relation of *compensation* between, on the one hand, technology and a market that are more and more anonymous and, on the other, the interiors of houses, more and more often erected as a shell for the personality itself, the receptacle for traces, accents in velvet and fur, collections that save objects from the anonymity of relations of exchange. But, in the place of the utopian aspect of phantasmagoria that the first version of the Exposé maintained, the second substitutes the truth of an authentic art—that of Baudelaire in "Les sept vieillards" (The seven old men)—and the critical force of a supreme phantasmagoria: that of the aged Blanqui, who, in *L'éternité par les astres* (Eternity by the stars), formulates the thesis of the eternal return of the same on an earth without hope, prey to that "mythic anxiety" already evoked in the essay on Goethe. In 1935, the dynamic of productive forces seems irresistibly to undermine the universe of phantasmagoria: "In the convulsions of the commodity economy we begin to recognize the monuments of the bourgeoisie as ruins even before they have crumbled" (*Reflections,* 162). In 1939, after his 1938 discovery of *L'éternité par les astres,* written by Auguste Blanqui while in prison, Benjamin is not far from adopting the point of view of the old rebel, for whom humanity is "a damned figure":

> All it can hope for that is new will prove to be nothing but a reality that
> has always been present; and this novelty will be as unable to provide it
> with a liberating solution as a new fashion is able to renew society.
> Blanqui's cosmic speculation includes this lesson: that humanity will be

prey to a mythic anxiety to the extent that the phantasmagoria occupy
a place. (*G.S.*, 5:1256)

In 1939—as in 1935—Benjamin is convinced that "the age has not
been able to find a new social order to correspond to its own technological
horizons" (*G.S.*, 5:1257). If technical development is not enough to bring
down the reign of phantasmagoria, the entire problem consists in knowing
how to bring about the awakening that will liberate us from them.
Technology has a subversive function, which society must learn to seize in
order not to be prey to myth. Technology strips the world of its illusory
dreams; in contrast, the development of the market—the perpetuation of
the "old" social order—favors phantasmagoria.

In 1935, such dreams were not entirely devoid of value. Rather than
being reduced to ideology, they bear within them utopia. What is an illusory
and deadly appearance in the technological context becomes fruitful appearance in the context of social anticipation. Regarding Charles Fourier, whom
he admired, Benjamin develops a theory of the "collective unconscious," to
which he links dialectical images and dream images. All his work in *Paris
Arcades,* as he conceived it in 1935, undertakes to decipher these images
according to their dual status, ideological and utopian. To the observation
that the new technology presents itself first in the form of the old—like the
metallic support disguised as a Greek column—Benjamin adds two theoretical ideas: first, that of "wishful fantasies" (*Reflections,* 148), which
attempt to compensate for the inadequacies of a given society; and second,
that of an anchorage of these utopias in the collective unconscious, the
depository of archaic promises that reemerge when a society breaks with the
recent past, with what has aged. He thinks that through the imaginary, from
which emerge the archaic images of the collective unconscious, the projection of a society into the future is always indebted to the origin.

He resorts to the concept of the collective unconscious, the bearer of
archaic images—Adorno immediately pointed out the similarity to the
ideas of Carl Gustav Jung (*Correspondence,* 497)—for two reasons. First, he
attempts to situate in society the operation—both messianic and surrealist—by which he himself extracts an explosive moment from the past: The
"collective unconscious" is the Benjaminian critique transformed into a
social subject aspiring, unbeknownst to itself, to actualize utopia. Second,
he has no concept of social modernity that, given the present constellation,
would allow him to explain the utopias through which certain social groups
project themselves into the future.

Regarding Baudelaire, he explains the second of these ideas:

Modernity . . . is always quoting primeval history. This happens here
through the ambiguity attending the social relationships and products

of this epoch. Ambiguity is the pictorial image of dialectics, the law of dialectics seen at a standstill. This standstill is utopia and the dialectical image therefore a dream image. Such an image is presented by the pure commodity: as fetish. Such an image are the arcades, which are both house and streets. Such an image is the prostitute, who is saleswoman and commodity in one. (*Reflections,* 157, translation slightly modified)

This idea attempts to integrate into Marxian theory Benjamin's own intuitions concerning his philosophy of the origin. The "dialectic at a standstill"—which will also be at issue in the Benjaminian theory of history—is an attempt to place in the service of political commitment the very principle of the critical approach, which consists in interpreting images as a function of their truth content. The standstill is that of the Hölderlinian "caesura" or the "inexpressive," which suspends the movement of images in order to quote them before the tribunal of truth. Placed in relation to the "ambiguity" of images, the dialectic refers to the critical and political sense of an interpretation that rests on Marxian concepts such as the dependence of the superstructure and the omnipresence of the fetishism of the commodity. The ambiguity is, in fact, that of an essence contradicted by a function: The satisfaction promised by the commodity is annulled by the systematic character of its economic mode of operation. In that way, Benjamin attempts to integrate his own intuitions into a Marxist-inspired critique of ideology. But the aesthetic experience does not allow itself to be so directly instrumentalized by social criticism.

Within the framework of the work on *Paris Arcades,* Baudelaire's literary oeuvre is difficult to integrate into the functionalist schema applied to other cultural phenomena. Through the phantasmagoria of the flaneur, the new, and the always-the-same, illustrated by such poems as "Le voyage" (The voyage), Benjamin attempts to *deduce* this poetic oeuvre from the fetishism of the commodity. The flaneur, the idle man-about-town, becomes the model for alienated humanity on the threshold of commodity society: still a romantic dreamer, already a client of the future department store, and a salesman of his "lived experiences" (*Erlebnis*) in the literary marketplace. Under his eyes, the city still presents the idyllic aspects of landscape, and his "mode of life still surrounds the approaching desolation of city life with a propitiatory luster. The *flâneur* is still on the threshold, of the city as of the bourgeois class" (*Reflections,* 156).

In conformity with a classical figure of the Marxist thinking of his time—but already inscribed within his own logic of the "disenchantment of art"—Benjamin participates in the masochistic operation of the leftist intellectual who denounces his or her own autonomy. The autonomy of art and thought is considered incompatible with political commitment; as a result, Benjamin no longer argues in terms of relations of force. Thus, he

also seeks to show that the intellectual of the bourgeois era is the complacent victim of false consciousness. This intellectual is convinced of the autonomy of his approach, even though the only way to escape the mechanisms of bourgeois society would be to renounce autonomy and indirectly aim at reconquering it through political consciousness. The flaneur's illusion is that, in his person, "the intelligentsia pays a visit to the marketplace, ostensibly to look around, yet in reality to find a buyer. In this intermediate phase, in which it still has patrons but is already beginning to familiarize itself with the market, it appears as bohemianism" (*Reflections*, 156). "Baudelaire's poetry draws its strength" (*Reflections*, 157) from the pathos of rebellion proper to this social milieu, where "professional conspirators" are also recruited—an ambiguous group to which the future Napoleon III and Blanqui are linked. But it remains fully prisoner to the ambiguity that characterizes the productions and social relations of that time.

The same is true for the notion of novelty. "*Au fond de l'inconnu pour trouver le Nouveau!*" (To the depths of the unknown to find the New!)—Benjamin laconically comments on this last line of "Le voyage":

> The last journey of the *flâneur*: death. Its destination: the new. . . . Novelty is a quality independent of the intrinsic value of the commodity. It is the origin of the illusion inseverable from the images produced by the collective unconscious. It is the quintessence of false consciousness, whose indefatigable agent is fashion. The illusion of novelty is reflected, like one mirror in another, in the illusion of perpetual sameness. . . . The art that begins to doubt its task and ceases to be "inseparable from utility" (Baudelaire) must make novelty its highest value. (*Reflections*, 157–158)

Down to the smallest details in Baudelaire's universe of images, Benjamin seeks to explain the poet's oeuvre by means of the determinism of bourgeois society, inasmuch as this poetry pushes to the extreme what is illusory and ideological in the collective unconscious.

The work on *Paris Arcades* raises the more general problem of a sociology of cultural phenomena. Benjamin embraces an undertaking that goes beyond the framework of literary criticism. His concept of the flaneur dissimulates a Marxist theory that questions the supposed autonomy of the bourgeois intellectual, just as his concept of a commodity indissociable from the advertising slogan of novelty is not revealed as such through an interpretation of poetic texts. They are in reality *applied* or *brought in* from the outside, from a preexisting theory. Benjamin is not seeking to find in Baudelaire an articulated reaction to the phenomena of commodity society; he views his poetry as one of the symptomatic manifestations of the fetishism of commodities. Art for art's sake and its extension, "the total artwork," are reduced to ideological conceptions that, even as they "abstract from the

social existence of man" (*Reflections,* 158), attempt to "isolate art from the development of technology" (*Reflections,* 158).

Hence the problematic character of the idea of a disappearance of art in favor of technology. Benjamin no longer has any concept of what constitutes the value proper to works of art, of what is inherent in their imperative for validity, independent of the ideological or utopian function they perform in a given social context. Even if the architecture of arcades is a function of the commercial ends that turn technical innovations away from their natural tendency, it is nevertheless not reducible to those ends. Furthermore and a fortiori, Baudelaire's oeuvre cannot be viewed as a mere epiphenomenon of the fetishism of commodities. Unlike architecture, advertising, bourgeois interiors, and urbanism, this oeuvre is itself a reflection on its age and does not limit itself to "expressing" the age's illusions and phantasmagorias.

Yet in the folders collected in preparation for drafting *Paris Arcades,* the folder dedicated to Baudelaire represents four times the volume of the largest of the other folders, and the book on Baudelaire—originally merely a chapter of *Paris Arcades*—tends to absorb the whole project. The work on Baudelaire undertaken in 1937–1938 reveals the impossibility of dealing in the same way with the *symptom* of the arcades, an architectural oddity without the slightest reflective content, and Baudelaire's poetic *oeuvre,* which includes critical thinking and a truth content; that is undoubtedly one of the reasons that, in the end, the book on Baudelaire absorbed the *Paris Arcades* project.

In the 1935 Exposé, as in "The Work of Art" (in which the process of rationalization leads to the magic of fetishism and to a wordless technology), aesthetic value is sacrificed to the functions of adaptation and instrumentality.[34] This reduction is due to the too broad use of the concept of *appearance.* The analysis of *reification*—an extension of the concept of the fetishism of the commodity as Lukács, for example, developed it in *History and Class Consciousness*—and the complementary notion of *phantasmagoria* (also Marxist in origin), are superposed in the theory of *aesthetic* appearance, whose critique Benjamin continued to develop beginning with his study of romanticism. This superimposition of the two concepts of appearance leads to an error, inasmuch as aesthetic appearance cannot be reduced to a false appearance: As the essay on Goethe had remarked, it is the normative form in which the work of art presents itself, a fiction that suspends certain pragmatic functions of signs. In this radical phase of his oeuvre, Benjamin extends the concept of phantasmagoria to aesthetic appearance itself. For him, the philosopher's task seems to be to wrench humanity away from the dream state into which the phantasmagoria of commodity society has plunged it.

In seeking to place his thinking in the service of social transformation, Benjamin interprets the confusion of categories constitutive of fetishism as the dream of a social subject who needs to be reawakened. From antiquity, the relation between dream (sleep) and awakening has been a constant theme of philosophy: Dream is considered the deceptive and illusory state of subjectivity, and awakening the state of rational lucidity and the absence of illusion. In the context of the philosophy of the subject, the emancipation from illusion and dream is a duty and a rigorous asceticism. Benjamin had always interpreted works of art as both bearing a truth content and as masked by a veil that required a destructive task, in which historical time and critical intervention converged. Here he attempts to apply that critical method to society as a whole, which, in its state of dream and phantasmagoria, is in some sense a work of art that has to be submitted to a process of "mortification." The destructive work of historical time has been transformed into a dynamic of productive forces, of technology that, for its side, tends to efface the mystifying aspect of art in architecture, in urbanism, in utilitarian objects, and in interiors. The conception of the "dialectical image" is in this sense the sociological transposition of a method of literary criticism. In bringing out the truth content of images, Benjamin attempts to provoke society's awakening. But he does not realize that such a therapeutic approach toward a society in its entirety presumes too much of the forces of a critical subject.

Benjamin did not maintain the program formulated in 1935. *Paris, capitale du XIXe siècle*[35]—that collection of disparate texts grouped by "folder" as it is read today—is in fact the construction site of three successive projects, all of which failed: (1) a "dialectical fairy play" that would have resembled *Einbahnstrasse* and certain surrealist books such as Louis Aragon's *Le paysan de Paris* (The Parisian peasant); (2) a revolutionary theory of the end of autonomous art and the decline of the aura, a theory illustrated by the 1935 Exposé and "The Work of Art"; and (3) beginning in 1936, a philosophical rehabilitation of the aura and the beautiful as conditions for a life and an art worthy of the name, where mass art is not up to the task of compensating for its disappearance. This last conception is illustrated in "The Storyteller" and "On Some Motifs in Baudelaire." We find elements of these three approaches in almost every one of the folders that make up the *Paris Arcades* project.

There is, therefore, no single perspective in this labyrinth. The work probably could not have been finished except in the literary form of the first project, which would have dealt with the surrealist discoveries related to the shock provoked by obsolete objects, the pathologies of space for the flaneur and of time for the gambler, the nineteenth century as a hell of immanence comparable to the baroque universe. The other two projects are problematic for complementary reasons. The second abstracts away from the intrinsic value of artistic (or philosophical) phenomena by subordinating them to two types of more powerful interests: economic interests linked to collective phantasmagoria and revolutionary interests emancipated from aesthetic appearance and phantasmagoria. The third project, which reintroduces aesthetic logic, nevertheless attempts to reconcile it with the functionalism of the second project. During this phase, *Paris Arcades* was in fact transformed into a book on Baudelaire. The decline of the aura became the explicit theme of Baudelaire's poetry, which, as an oeuvre, preserves an element of aura, the element of aesthetic value, through the poetic authenticity of negation.

It is primarily in the second project that the emancipation of technology in relation to art is the central theme. At that time, Benjamin was seeking to improve on Brecht by requiring a change of function for the artist. "The Work of Art" assigns to cinema the task of abolishing the gulf between creators and receivers: Both can demand to be filmed and can judge, as experts, the quality of a film. Hence, "The Author as Producer" redefines the task of the writer: It is not to tame but, rather, to transform the "productive apparatus" (*Reflections*, 230). To transform it is to "overthrow another of the barriers, to transcend another of the antitheses that fetter the production of intellectuals" (*Reflections*, 230). Hence, "what we require of the photographer is the ability to give his picture the caption that wrenches it from modish commerce and gives it a revolutionary use value" (*Reflections*, 230, translation slightly modified). Among the barriers that need to be overthrown, the most important is that of exclusive competence: "The conventional distinction between author and public, which is upheld in the bourgeois press, begins in the Soviet press to disappear. For the reader is at all times ready to become a writer, that is, a describer, but also a prescriber. As an expert—even if not on a subject but only on the post he occupies—he gains access to authorship" (*Reflections*, 225).

To transform the apparatus of production is to devote all one's attention to the technology of the media used. According to Benjamin, who here becomes the spokesperson for Brecht, the writer must become an "engineer" (*Reflections*, 237). Not to transform the means of production is to "tame" them and maintain their routine. To transform them is to teach something to the public and to other technicians: "An author who teaches writers nothing teaches no one" (*Reflections*, 233). The contemporary writer, who cannot compete with film or radio, must attempt to use them and to learn from them. "This debate," writes Benjamin, "the epic theater has made its own affair" (*Reflections*, 235). It has done so by adopting the montage procedure characteristic of film. The songs that interrupt the action of the play "constantly counterac[t] an illusion in the audience. For such illusion is a hindrance to a theater that proposes to make use of elements of reality in experimental rearrangements" (*Reflections*, 235). The audience is called upon to adopt vis-à-vis real society the distanced and critical attitude that the actors and playwright adopt vis-à-vis the play.

Benjamin deals with literary techniques as an equivalent of labor within the framework of relations of production:

> Rather than ask, "What is the *attitude* of a work to the relations of production of its time?" I should like to ask, "What is its *position* in them?" This question directly concerns the function the work has within the literary relations of production of its time. It is concerned, in other words, directly with the literary *technique* of works. (*Reflections*, 222)

Although literature is invited to draw inspiration from cinematic techniques, which, however, it can never rival, it is manifestly cinema that, for contemporary production, has the canonical aesthetic value. In Benjamin's view, film is the form of art that best corresponds to the role of technology in modern society. He is convinced that the status of technology has been reversed over the course of history. Another innovative aspect of cinema is that it escapes the traditional criterion of *eternity,* inasmuch as it possesses a quality opposed to the definitive character of sculpture, namely, perfectibility: "A completed film is nothing less than a creation in a single spurt; it is composed of a succession of images which the editor must choose among—images that from the first to the last shot have been retouched at will" (*G.S.,* 1:446).

This choice on the part of the editor establishes the different shots in a hierarchy that makes the selected version that which has best passed the test of the apparatus. Once more, Benjamin thinks he can eliminate any aesthetic criterion in the traditional sense, as if the editor's choice is a purely technical performance: "The camera director . . . occupies a place identical with that of the examiner during aptitude tests" (*Illuminations,* 246). Benjamin forgets that the writer and the composer—and even the painter who chooses among his sketches for some element of the painting, or who paints "pentimenti"—have long worked toward "montage" based on aesthetic criteria, whose importance in the case of film he misunderstands.

In making film the distinguishing art form for the aesthetics of modernity, Benjamin inaugurates a type of reasoning that makes a fetish of the most advanced technology, independent of the significance of works of art. According to that reasoning, we would today have to give priority, a priori as it were, to computer art or electronic images, whatever the importance of the productions realized through these technologies. Such a valorization is not justified, since the "forces of production" are not aesthetically revolutionary except inasmuch as they set in place a potential for experience, criticism, and revelation. It is true that the use of the most advanced technologies has always been a determining factor for artists, but it has never sufficed in itself to guarantee the quality of a work of art.

Finally, just as Brecht's epic theater goes against the audience's illusion,

Benjamin thinks that cinematic technique manhandles the category of aesthetic *appearance*, this time within the artistic performance itself. In the second version of the German text of "The Work of Art," Benjamin defines appearance as the *magical* aspect of mimesis, to which he opposes the *ludic* aspect, which is linked to the second phase of technology.

> What goes hand in hand with the destruction of appearance, with the decline of the aura in works of art, is a formidable gain in the possibilities of play. The broadest possibility of play has been opened in film. In it, the element of appearance has been totally effaced in favor of the element of play. (*G.S.*, 7:369 n. 10)

He does not see that, independent of the genesis of cinematic images—in which artifice, tricks, and manipulation play an important role—the completed film presents a more convincing illusion of reality than does any other art form. That is a conclusion he should have drawn from his own observations:

> Its illusionary nature is that of the second degree, the result of cutting. That is to say, in the studio the mechanical equipment has penetrated so deeply into reality that its pure aspect freed from the foreign substance of equipment is the result of a special procedure, namely, the shooting by the specially adjusted camera and the mounting of the shot together with other similar ones. The equipment-free aspect of reality has become the height of artifice; the sight of immediate reality has become an orchid in the land of technology. (*Illuminations*, 233)

Benjamin attempts to show that, contrary to what happens at the theater, where, on principle, one "is well aware of the place from which the play cannot immediately be detected as illusionary" (*Illuminations*, 233), "[t]here is no such place for the movie scene that is being shot" (*Illuminations*, 322). But, unlike what happens in classical theater, where lighting and setting mask the stage as much as possible, film does not need to hide from the absent audience the equipment that surrounds the sound stage as the film is being made; the result of the final editing merely offers a more complete illusion, which in no way breaks with the tradition of the "beautiful appearance." The fact that this result is obtained in a situation in which "the mechanical equipment has penetrated so deeply into reality" (*Illuminations*, 233) changes nothing. In fact, painting, contrary to what Benjamin thinks, is just as capable as film of setting out the genesis of the illusion by exposing the process of production. In a very traditional manner, Benjamin again asserts that "one is entitled to ask from a work of art" a reality whose aspect is "free of all equipment" (*Illuminations*, 234). Unlike the cinema of the time, painting had long since begun to break with this dogma and was, in fact, ahead of cinema.

In a minor text of 1936, "Pariser Brief II. Malerei und Photographie," (Parisian letter II: Painting and photography; *G.S.*, 3:495–507), Benjamin rehabilitates painting, for which "The Work of Art" had left little future, by discovering in it a "usefulness," a political function. On the one hand, painting seems to be parasitical on photography, whose value as witness appeared most important to Benjamin at the time. In fact, if painters such as John Heartfield became photographers for political reasons, "the same generation has produced painters such as George Grosz or Otto Dix, whose work moves in the same direction." And Benjamin adds, "Painting has not lost its function" (*G.S.*, 3:506). He is speaking of caricature or of painting used to the same ends of denunciation as Heartfield's photomontage. Among the great caricaturists, such as Hieronymus Bosch, William Hogarth, Francisco Goya, and Honoré Daumier, Benjamin writes, "political knowledge" has profoundly permeated "physiognomic perception" (*G.S.*, 3:506). From this same point of view, he defends not only painting with a political subject but also nonrealist painting, whose effect is "destructive, purifying" in a Europe threatened by fascism, where there are countries that forbid these painters from painting. "What led to this prohibition," explains Benjamin, "was rarely the subject, but most often their manner of painting" (*G.S.*, 3:507). These painters paint at night with their windows covered.

> They rarely experience any temptation to paint "after nature." In fact, the pallid landscapes of their paintings, peopled with shadows or monsters, are not borrowed from nature but from the class State. . . . [These painters] know what is useful in an image today: any sign, public or secret, showing that fascism has encountered in man limits as insurmountable as those it encountered on the earthly globe. (*G.S.*, 3:507)

This text, though less dogmatic than "The Work of Art," does not move away from it in any fundamental way but submits all judgment on art to political criteria. The Manichaean situation, in a context in which Benjamin—true to the Marxist doctrine of the era—judges that liberalism is only an inconsistent fascism (*G.S.*, 3:496, 507), seems to justify a theory of art that places any consideration of aesthetic value to the account of the phantasmagoria of bourgeois society.

In 1936, a few months after he had drafted the first version of "The Work of Art," he thus reached a second turning point, relatively less brutal than the one that had led him from his first aesthetics to that of political commitment but that would nevertheless lead him to defend theses dialectically opposed to those that made up the radicality of "The Work of Art." The sacrifice of the aura—of that traditional substance of works of art in whose name he had conceived his philosophy of language—was meaningless unless politics, allied with the most innovative technology, saved the essence of the "theological" *intention.* Several factors seem to have convinced Benjamin in 1936 to abandon the radical idea of the "liquidation of the aura." It was not a change in political attitude—he continued to write texts that were just as committed. What changed was his confidence both in the dynamic of technology and in the solidity of the political forces whose cause he had defended. In fact, the reservations and objections formulated both by Scholem and by Adorno regarding the 1935 essays seem this time to have left their mark. We might argue that it was not a real change in his thinking, inasmuch as he wrote, practically at the same time, his essay on Kafka and "The Author as Producer." But the essay on Kafka contains nothing that contradicts the radical theses of "The Work of Art." In contrast, the texts written as of 1936 frequently present ideas that are no longer compatible with the critique of the aura as it was developed in "The Work of Art." We must therefore admit that a change had intervened in Benjamin's thinking at the beginning of 1936.

Among the arguments that could be opposed to this thesis, at first glance the most difficult to refute is the argument that underscores the fact that Benjamin continued until 1938 to elaborate different versions of "The Work of Art." But we can interpret this as simply an effort to have the essay published in *German*; in fact, during Benjamin's lifetime, only a French translation was published, in the review for the Institut de Recherche Sociale (Institute of social research). Moreover, the modifications Benjamin made in the essay, just before he drafted "The Storyteller" in March–April 1936, concern in particular two central concepts of the essay: that of the masses and that of technology. Although the revisions do not entail any critical inquiry into the value of technical reproduction, a differentiation is made that indicates a certain embarrassment. Benjamin had justified the liquidation of the aura through the legitimate imperative of the modern *masses.* Yet a note to the second version of "The Work of Art" relativizes this concept by asserting that the proletariat, whose cohesion is grounded in an explicit solidarity, tends to suppress the existence of the masses (*G.S.,* 7:370). As for *technology,* the second German version, like the French version, differentiates between a first and a second phase of technology:

> [T]he first engages man as much as possible, the second as little as possible. The exploit of the first, if we dare say so, is human sacrifice, that of the second would be announced in the pilotless airplane guided from a distance by Hertzian waves. . . . Art is in solidarity with the first and with the second technology. [The first technology] truly aimed at the subjugation of nature—the second much more at a harmony of nature and humanity. The decisive social function of current art consists in

initiating humanity into this *"harmonian"* game. That is especially the
case for film. (*G.S.,* 1:716–717)

These reflections subvert the first version of the essay; in fact, they virtually
invert its values. They tend to change the relation between the aura, which
is in solidarity with the "first technology" through its magical character,
and technical reproduction, which is in solidarity with the "second." With
this hypothesis, it could no longer be a question either of an alienating effect
of cinematic technique as such—and thus of a "productive force of alienated
man"—or of a destructive effect on a tradition thus placed in peril. In an
experimental and speculative manner, Benjamin is led to give to the
concepts of the masses and of technology a more differentiated meaning,
before retracting them altogether in "The Storyteller" and in the essays on
Baudelaire, in which the masses and technical reproduction appear only in
a negative and destructive light.

3. The Price of Modernity

In Benjamin's "third aesthetic," art is no longer an immediate instrument
of the revolution. But Benjamin also does not return to an aesthetics of the
sublime. What appeared only by way of contrast in the first chapters of "The
Work of Art," the decline of the aura that traditionally surrounded artistic
phenomena, now becomes the object of a reevaluation. Benjamin inquires
into the price to be paid for arriving at modernity. In the 1935 essay, the
loss of traditional experience could be compensated for by a new collective
experience symbolized by cinema. In what was to be the last period of his
oeuvre, Benjamin doubts this possibility, seeing no analogous compensation
in the fields of storytelling or lyric poetry.

Nothing has fundamentally changed in Benjamin's orientation toward
an aesthetic of "truth." Faithful to a philosophy of art in the Kantian
tradition developed by the romantics—Friedrich Schelling and Hegel—he
remains opposed to the "subjective" tendency issuing from a Kantian
aesthetics. Such an aesthetics of taste, appropriate for the analysis of the
pleasure experienced in seeing a flower or ornamentation, does not allow for
the realization of the significance and importance of a work of art—its
historical stakes and its depth, dimensions that are not a matter of indifference for aesthetic judgment. Benjamin embraces the other side of the

Kantian aesthetics, which sees in beauty part of the thing in itself, inaccessible to discursive knowledge.

In a mystical definition, the last essay on Baudelaire defines the beautiful as the representation of the object of experience in the state of "resemblance." Such an objectivism, which neutralizes aesthetic judgment, cannot be said to be any more defensible. Nonetheless, Benjamin's analyses remain instructive in their penetration into what is *at stake* in art. When we discuss works of art, we do not limit ourselves to observations about "purely aesthetic" qualities. The artistic form has existential, cognitive, ethical, and political dimensions, all the more so since they stem from the formal coherence of the work of art itself and not from its explicit "message." Even though he confuses the levels of aesthetics and criticism, Benjamin shows in an exemplary fashion how a work of art can determine the interpretations of our individual lives and our era.

CHILDHOOD AND MEMORY

From just before his departure from Germany and for almost the entire duration of his exile, until 1938—beginning with his first stay on the island of Ibiza in 1932, a period of his life that was marked by personal and economic difficulties that led him to seriously contemplate suicide, then in Berlin and in the different sites of his exile—Benjamin was working on numerous versions of *Berliner Kindheit* (A Berlin childhood). He published fragments of it in different journals and magazines. Written for the most part in the interval between the essays on Kraus and Kafka, *Berliner Kindheit* initiates the preponderance of memory in the last period of his oeuvre, a shift from the political strategy that dominated his second period. This collection of exemplary memories is constructed in the gap between the dream of the nineteenth century—which did not end in 1900—and the awakening represented by the entry into the twentieth. With an irony marked by nostalgia, Benjamin undertakes this work of memory, more Proustian than surrealist, regarding his experience of Berlin.

As he writes in the foreword to the last version, recently rediscovered in Paris, "I hope these images at least make readers feel how much this writer has been deprived of the security that surrounded him in childhood" (*G.S.,* 7:385). In 1932, he began to write his "Berlin Chronicle" to "vaccinate" himself in advance against the homesickness that exiles experience: "Just as the vaccine should not overtake the healthy body, the feeling of homesickness was not about to overtake my mind. I attempted to limit it by becoming conscious of the irremediable loss of the past, due not to biographical contingencies but to social necessities" (*G.S.,* 7:385). Benjamin undertakes to seize "*images* by means of which the experience of the big city is imprinted in a child of the bourgeoisie" (*G.S.*, 7:385). He thus attempts to found a genre of the big city to correspond to one that had long existed for the experience of nature.

Berliner Kindheit has yet to render up its secrets.[1] It is clear, in any case, that we learn little from it—or that we learn only indirectly—about Berlin and much about the experience of the child who lived there during a historic epoch that had already become antiquated for the adult. The irony in the text signals the distance between the mind, a prisoner of the past, and the consciousness that reconstructs that vision of the past. It is a vision of objects and places that are too grand, around which mythologies of childhood and of an age that is itself childish—like a fairy tale—are crystallized.

Under the original title "A Berlin Chronicle," Benjamin assembled what is, first of all, a series of autobiographical texts. The final form, *Berliner Kindheit*, retains only the exemplary topography of a childhood spent in a city such as Berlin: "A kind of tête-à-tête between a child and the city of Berlin around 1900" (*G.S.*, 4:964). Having abandoned the task of composing a "dialectical fairy tale" on the arcades—a project that "permitted no direct figuration—unless it be an inadmissable 'poetic' one" (*Correspondence*, 506–507, letter of 16 August 1935), Benjamin felt free to give to the mythological aspect of the modern city the form of a series of childhood memories.

Two fragments from *Paris Arcades* suggest its philosophical background. Benjamin's desire for a disenchanted and lucid vision is always contradicted by his fear of seeing the world reduced to abstract signs. He cannot do without either myth or disenchantment, the archaic "dream" of a child's awareness or the awakening of the adult's acute memory. *Berliner Kindheit* is a subtle play on illusion, forgetting, faltering awareness, and involuntary memory, the occasion for a lucid deciphering of accumulated images. Benjamin underscores the importance of childhood for the symbolic appropriation of technical innovations: "Every childhood achieves something great, irreplaceable for mankind. Through its interest in technical phenomena, its curiosity about all kinds of discoveries and machinery, every childhood ties technological achievement to the old symbol-worlds" ("N" 2a, 1, p. 49). A complementary fragment indicates, in contrast, that the mythic aspect of the recent past is linked to a particular lack in modern society: "The prehistoric impulse to the past—this, too, at once a consequence and a precondition of technology—is no longer hidden, as it once was, by the tradition of church and family. The old prehistoric dread already envelops the world of our parents, because we are no longer bound to it by tradition" ("N" 2a, 2, p. 49).

Among the texts of *Berliner Kindheit*, "Das Telephon" (The telephone) illustrates this relation to technology. A mythical object as in Proust, the recently introduced telephone sows terror in the apartment by disturbing not only the parents' nap "but also the era of the history of the world in the middle of which they were taking that nap" (*G.S.*, 4:243). "The voice talking there" has the omnipotence of myth:

> There was nothing to attenuate the strange and troubling violence with which it gripped me. I suffered, powerless, as it wrenched from me the respect for time, duty, and resolutions, negated my own reflection, and, just as the medium obeys the voice of the beyond that seizes her, I gave in to the first proposal that came to me over the telephone. (*G.S.*, 4:243)

"For the first time" is one of the most common expressions in *Berliner Kindheit*. In "Tiergarten," the first of his "prose poems,"[2] Benjamin calls the writer Franz Hessel "one acquainted with the land," the "Berlin peasant" who had initiated him into the secrets of the city: "The little stairways, the vestibules supported by columns, the friezes, the architraves of the villas near the Tiergarten—for the first time, we took them at their word" (*G.S.*, 4:238). This "first time" is that of adults who have gone off to discover the past. It hides a more distant origin: the inaccessible origin of repeated gestures that are buried in our bodies. Hence, most of the "first times" designate primitive experiences: I can "dream as I once learned to walk. But it is of no use to me. Now I know how to walk; I can no longer learn how" (*G.S.*, 4:267). "The first closet that opened when I wanted it to" (*G.S.*, 4:283) was one of the primitive victories over the malice of things, from which we draw all our self-assurance; the "first telephone calls" are archaic memories that go back to the mythical eras of childhood, an unprecedented reality irrupting in the space of humanity's experience. In the face of such a break with tradition, reason falters, and an actual apprenticeship is required to reintegrate that myth into the symbolic space.

"The first time" is also one of Benjamin's constant questions in his writings in *Paris Arcades*. Whether in the life of the individual or that of humanity, Benjamin is always watching for the inaugural moment of a form that will define the age: "The construction of the arcades is the advent of building in iron" (*Reflections*, 147); "in iron, an artificial building material makes its appearance for the first time in the history of architecture [since Rome]" (*Reflections*, 147, bracketed words not in English edition); Edgar Allan Poe is "the first physiognomist of the interior" (*Reflections*, 156). These questions of "origin" are linked to Benjamin's philosophy of language and his philosophy of history.[3] As the "unavoidable encounter between the sign and its referent as attested to even now in poetic language,"[4] the origin represents for him the moment just before the imprint of creation is forever dissociated from its object and the sign becomes arbitrary. It is the crucial moment toward which Benjamin's thought is continually attracted, as by a magnet.

Benjamin's writing is an incessant effort to restore the power of these origins through translation, criticism, and historical memory. Without such efforts, vital resources for humanity are in danger of being lost forever. But the "origin," "although an entirely historical category" (*Origin,* 45), is not to be confused with genesis. The origin, always incomplete and, because of this, always in quest of its completion, is reproduced throughout history: "There takes place in every original phenomenon a determination of the form in which an idea will constantly confront the historical world, until it is revealed fulfilled, in the totality of its history" (*Origin,* 45–46). This was also true during Benjamin's "materialist" period. Technology and inventions have their precursors: The arcade, heir to the archway and the heated pavilion, anticipates the department store just as, before cinema, there existed "photo booklets with pictures which flitted by the looker upon pressure of the thumb, thus portraying a boxing bout or a tennis match" (*Illuminations,* 249 n. 17; cf. *G.S.,* 4:304). It is always an authentic aspiration that is reproduced as an origin, an aspiration to happiness associated with knowledge but deflected from its finality by particular social interests that transform it into a phantasmagoria. Rediscovered childhood, the inaugural moment when an authentic experience is formed, is a source of happiness: "With the joy of remembering . . . another is fused: that of possession in memory. Today I can no longer distinguish them" (*Reflections,* 57). *Berliner Kindheit* proposes an archetypal image of that renewed origin, the image in which childhood, the fairy tale, and the philosophy of history intersect. Hence the image of the child in the pantry:

> Grateful and wild as a girl taken from her parents' house, the strawberry jam allowed itself to be taken without bread and by starlight as it were. . . . The hand, a youthful Don Juan, had soon penetrated into all the nooks and crannies, behind the collapsing piles and the falling heaps of things; a virginity renewed without complaint. (*G.S.,* 4:250)

The return to the origin, as Proust experienced it, is barred by all kinds of impediments that make of Berlin around 1900 a well-guarded safe. The obsessive force of places, of topographies, lies precisely in the fact that the past is closed off. One night, Benjamin's father came to his son's bedside to tell him of the death of a distant relative.

> My father gave the news with details, took the opportunity to explain, in answer to my question, what a heart attack was, and was communicative. I did not take in much of the explanation. But that evening I must have memorized my room and my bed, as one observes exactly a place where one feels dimly that one will later have to search for something one has forgotten there. (*Reflections,* 60)

Years later, Benjamin would learn what his father had hidden from him: His cousin had died of syphilis. This may be one explanation for the numerous descriptions of places. Benjamin retained their image because he later had to look for something forgotten or deformed there, like the names from childhood that are enriched by misunderstandings: "Mummerehlen," "Mark-Thalle," "Blume-zoof," "Brauhausberg," the "Anhalter" station, etc., whose prosaic sense escaped the child. Like the objects whose use escapes him and the incomprehensible stories told him to conceal the truth, these names stand out for the powerless child and confer a mythological reality on what they designate. But that obscurity due to powerlessness deforms prosaic reality, renders it poetic, and at the same time, reveals a truth. The eyes and ears of the child, in making reality strange for him, also reveal what is truly strange about reality. Benjamin turns the romantic theme of childhood into an instrument of poetic knowledge.

The Benjaminian child adds a subversive, transgressive quality to the romantic myth of childhood, foregrounded by the near nonexistence of the parents. He continually tries to escape the bourgeois apartment or the despised school in order to discover forbidden worlds. In "A Berlin Chronicle," Benjamin writes, "I never slept on the street in Berlin. I saw sunset and dawn, but between the two I found myself a shelter. Only those for whom poverty or vice turns the city into a landscape in which they stray from dark till sunrise know it in a way denied to me" (*Reflections*, 27). In his childhood in Berlin, Benjamin was a "prisoner" to the new and old "West End." "At that time, my clan lived in those two neighborhoods with an attitude where stubbornness and pride were combined and which made of them a ghetto, which they considered a fief. I remained enclosed in that neighborhood of the propertied classes without knowing any other" (*G.S.*, 4:287). Misery and vice, poverty and sexuality, such are the two cursed regions—in Berlin perhaps more than elsewhere, because of their threatening proximity. Sexuality is here associated with savage animality, to such an extent that the young Benjamin—who encounters his own *passante*—refuses to see what he most desires (*Reflections*, 4). Running errands with his mother, he remains obstinately a half-step behind "in the stubborn refusal . . . to form a united front, be it even with my own mother" (*Reflections*, 11). When his mother chastises him for his "dreamy recalcitrance" (*Reflections*, 4), he obscurely glimpses

[the possibility of one day escaping her custody through the complicity of these streets in which I could not find my way.] There is no doubt, at any rate, that a feeling of crossing the threshold of one's class for the first time had a part in the almost unequaled fascination of publicly accosting a whore in the street. [But things could go on for hours before I reached that point.] (*Reflections*, 11; *G.S.*, 4:288; bracketed passages not in English version)

In the same spirit, the young Benjamin fled the constraints of religious ceremonies. A passage (which Scholem, shocked no doubt, advised him to suppress, and which he did suppress in the later versions) evokes the "first stirring of my sexual urge" (*Reflections*, 52) one day of the Jewish New Year, when he went to find a distant relative to accompany him to the synagogue. Benjamin got lost and, on a sudden, transgressive impulse, sensed for the first time the services the street could render to adult desires (*Reflections*, 52–53).

The limit of the bourgeois apartment in Berlin is the loggia that overlooks the courtyard. With the loggia "the home of the Berliner has its border. Berlin—the god of the city itself—begins there" (*G.S.*, 4:295). In the courtyard, the convalescent child listens to

the ebb of the carpet beating that came in at the window with the moist air on rainy days and engraved itself more indelibly in the child's memory than the voice of the beloved in that of the man, the carpet beating that was the language of the nether world, of servant girls, the real grownups. (*Reflections*, 44)

Benjamin is convinced that the caryatids of the loggia, on which the loggia of the floor above is supported, had sung to him in his cradle. It is in the air of the courtyards, he thinks, in this text he considers a self-portrait, "where bathe the images and allegories that reign in my thoughts like the caryatids of the loggias in the courtyards of Berlin's West End" (*G.S.*, 4:294). Here, he is applying a concept from his mimetic theory of language to his childhood. It is within this framework of the city of Berlin that he begins both to read the signs of the world and to be read by an environment that he has begun to resemble and to which he is obliged to give the greater part of his being and his gifts. Discovering colors, he is "metamorphosed" (*G.S.*, 4:262–263): He becomes a soap bubble, a wet cloud in a watercolor painting, the silvery paper around a piece of chocolate. His "superior sense" of images is nourished on that source.

If he failed in his life, it was, he believed, not only because of the circumstances but also because he had forgotten an essential part of his experience, which is then picked up by the mythic figure of the "little hunchback." In the essay on Kafka, written a few months after the fragment in *Berliner Kindheit* entitled "The Little Hunchback," this invisible being is evoked as a character from a fairy tale, "the core of folk tradition, the German as well as the Jewish" (*Illuminations*, 134), two peoples whom Benjamin, in 1934, refuses to grant a definitive divorce. Scholem sees in this nothing less than an immense historical error; the years that followed proved him right, at least for their generation, which tragically paid the price for it. "The little man," writes Benjamin regarding the little hunchback, "is at home in distorted life" (*Illuminations*, 134). The burden he bears is that of forgetting; it will be lifted only at the messianic end of history. But this end cannot be reached without human efforts of memory, the rescuing of the stifled virtualities of the past. The work of memory undertaken by Benjamin goes against the automatic movement of history, which, through the force of forgetting and repression, accumulates catastrophes in the lives of individuals and capital cities and in the life of humanity as a whole. Forgetful of its origins, humanity loses its presence of mind and initiative, submitting to the events from that time on. Such was also the case for Benjamin, as he depicts himself in *Berliner Kindheit*. When he sees the little hunchback appear, the harbinger of forgetting, he has "only to consider the damage" (*G.S.*, 4:303).

This metaphor of "bad luck" (*poisse*), of the individual "curse" (*guigne*), refers to the destiny of an entire generation, whose only surviving image "is that of a vanquished generation" ("Theses on the Philosophy of History," *E.F.*, 345; not in English edition). What had to be excluded from the sociological project of *Paris Arcades*, the "inadmissible poetic" aspect (*Correspondence*, 506–507) or the evocation of experience, was thus reserved for *Berliner Kindheit*: "The Ur-history of the nineteenth century reflected in the vision of the child playing on its doorstep has a totally different countenance than that of the signs, that they engrave on the map of history" (*Correspondence*, 507). This literary preserve is one sign that Benjamin was never able to commit himself totally to the radicality of the theoretical project that defined the second period of his thinking: the "emancipation from the yoke of art."

THE END OF THE ART OF STORYTELLING

A few months after finishing "The Work of Art," Benjamin formulated a clear relation not only of complementarity but of contradictory tension between that essay and "The Storyteller." On 3 May 1936, in a letter to Scholem in which he speaks of "The Work of Art," he suggests that this text has not exhausted his ideas on mechanical reproduction: "I will attempt a companion piece to it as soon as I return to this subject" (*Correspondence*, 528). The term "companion piece" might lead us to think that Benjamin was free from the beginning to adopt one or the other position. And indeed, with the two poles of the conceptual duality remaining constant, the scales tipped now to one side, now to the other, according to the state of his reflection. In June 1936, when he sent Scholem the French text of "The

Work of Art," Benjamin announced that he had just finished "another, not quite so voluminous manuscript . . . which you would probably find far more agreeable."[5] This was "The Storyteller." The fact that Scholem would find it "more agreeable" indicates a shift in Benjamin's thinking. In a letter to Adorno of 4 June 1936, Benjamin explains: "I recently wrote a piece on Nicolas Leskov which, without in any way claiming to have the scope of the piece on art theory, presents a few parallels with the 'decline of the aura,' through the fact that the art of storytelling is reaching its end" (*G.S.*, 2:1277).

The parallels in question involve the conceptual couple aura/mechanical reproduction. But this time, Benjamin finds no advantage in the decline of the aura. Of course, he had written notes for the drafting of "The Storyteller" that leaned in the direction of "The Work of Art"; these notes rejected any nostalgic lament regarding the loss of the art of storytelling and asserted the legitimacy of the most modern forms of narrative literature—the "new inexactitude" and the slang that had appeared in James Joyce's *Ulysses* (*G.S.*, 2:1282–1286).[6] But these notes found no place in the essay itself; Benjamin thus deliberately excluded them from the published text.

"The Storyteller" opens a new period in Benjamin's thinking: With the acquisition of a sociological interpretation of art, it both links itself to the apocalyptic vision of history proper to *The Origin of German Tragic Drama* and revises the verdict on the aura and beauty. We find elements of this new mode of thinking in the essays on Kraus and Kafka, but in those essays the perspective of carefree destruction remains dominant. In its completed form, the new version of Benjaminian thought appears in the 1939 Exposé of *Paris Arcades,* in the essay "On Some Motifs in Baudelaire" of the same year, and in the "Theses on the Philosophy of History" (1939–1940). Several of the theses already figure in the 1937 essay "Eduard Fuchs, Collector and Historian." But even the apparently more "committed" texts, such as the Fuchs essay or "The Paris of the Second Empire in Baudelaire," are distinguished from "The Work of Art" inasmuch as they abandon the task of finding any compensation in the decline of art, the aura, and tradition. Benjamin insists on the price of modernity and the absence of compensation for the losses it brings. The masses and technology no longer have any promising potential; hence the considerable importance that Benjamin's thought now grants to the *memory* of irremediably destroyed traditions. Such a cult of memory is missing from "The Work of Art" and from the sociological *Paris Arcades* project.

On the basis of the distinction between aura and mechanical reproduction, between cult value and exhibition value, between a traditional experience and an impoverished experience, and fundamentally, according to the old sociological duality established by Ferdinand Tönnies, between "community" and "society," Benjamin tries in 1935 to confer an emancipatory value on both the innovative and the destructive elements of the technology of reproduction, public exhibition, and the reduction of experience. He sees in them a promise of social transformation; aesthetic desacralization seems to open the way both to profane illumination and to a presence of mind favorable to political action. The public status of the new forms of communication, the fact that they place themselves within the reach of the masses and satisfy their legitimate imperatives, seems to counterbalance the loss of traditional substance. In "The Work of Art," the mourning for the riches of the lost past seemed to be at an end. "The Storyteller" reveals that this mourning is continuing because the compensation does not meet expectations. The technically reproducible work of art, as Benjamin had described it, no longer has any properly artistic value; desacralization has left in its wake only instrumental and therapeutic functions. Until "The Work of Art," Benjamin had not succeeded in conceiving of aesthetic value independent of theological categories. In general, he had not accepted the order of *society* in its opposition to the traditional *community*. In pursuing avantgarde art and political revolution, Benjamin masked his desire to preserve the traditional character of community life; in fact, he was explicitly running toward "redemption."

In his assertion that "the art of storytelling is coming to an end" (*Illuminations,* 83), Benjamin found support in a mundane experience: the loss of our ability to tell stories, to exchange our experiences (*Illuminations,* 83).[7] According to him, two complementary phenomena account for this incapacity: the boundless development of technology and the privatization of life that it brings. The mutism of soldiers who returned from the 1914–1918 war, overwhelmed by the hardware used for massive destruction, was coupled with an overextension of the private sphere of existence, revealed especially in the growing place of bawdy stories, by means of which private life invades the public communication of experience.

Traditional storytelling is linked to the conditions of an artisanal, preindustrial society: first, the oral transmission of experience, the bearer of ancestral wisdom; second, a spatial or temporal distance that confers on the story the aura of faraway places; and third, the authority of death, of a "natural history" where the destiny of creatures is written. These conditions are under attack in modern life, which is dominated by the need for proximity and immediate interest, communication through technical or literary media, and the hygienic dissimulation of death.

The artisan class represents the fusion of the two great traditional schools of oral storytelling, the trading seaman and the resident tiller of the soil. One transmits the experience of distant voyages, the other that of distant times. The storyteller remains faithful to the age of "naive poetry" (*Illuminations,* 97), "in which man could believe himself to be in harmony with nature" (*Illuminations*, 97). In the artisan class, the two ancient types interpenetrated. In several ways, the time of the artisan class created conditions favorable for the transmission of stories. In the first place, it was still acquainted with boredom, which was dissipated in the telling of tales. It allowed the audience to devote itself to manual activities as it listened: "The more self-forgetful the listener is, the more deeply is what he listens to impressed upon his memory. When the rhythm of work has seized him, he listens to the tales in such a way that the gift of retelling them comes to him all by itself" (*Illuminations*, 91). In addition, the artisanal context favored individual and collective memory. And finally, storytelling is itself an artisanal form. "It does not aim to convey the pure essence of the thing, like information or a report. It sinks the thing into the life of the storyteller, in order to bring it out of him again. Thus traces of the storyteller cling to the story the way the handprints of the potter cling to the clay vessel" (*Illuminations*, 91–92). Paul Valéry linked the soul, the eye, and the hand in every artisanal activity, including oral storytelling, where the gesture accompanies speech. "The role of the hand in production," adds Benjamin, "has become more modest, and the place it filled in storytelling lies waste" (*Illuminations*, 108).

Benjamin is not alone in according a high value to the artisan in the art of storytelling. We find similar ideas in the work of Ernst Bloch and Heidegger, regarding Johann Peter Hebel, a storyteller held in esteem—for different reasons—by all three philosophers. In any case, they are all convinced that they are witnessing the decline in modern society of a precious and irreplaceable art. This attachment to the artisanal era is accompanied by a reserved and hostile attitude toward industrial modernity. As soon as experience is no longer transmitted orally but, rather, through writing, storytelling, according to Benjamin, is "confined within literature" (*G.S.*, 2:1293; not in English version); the storyteller and his public are then separated, each plunged into a solitude unfavorable to the transmission of experience. At its origin, storytelling was oriented toward practical life. It

> contains, openly or covertly, something useful. The usefulness may, in one case, consist in a moral; in another, of some practical advice; in a third, in a proverb or maxim. In every case the storyteller is a man who has counsel for his audience. But if today "having counsel" is beginning to have an old-fashioned ring, this is because the communicability of experience is decreasing. In consequence we have no counsel either for ourselves or for others. (*Illuminations*, 86)

The form that confirms the decline of storytelling is the novel. "The dissemination of the novel became possible only with the invention of printing" (*Illuminations*, 87). Therefore, it is a technology of reproduction that contributes essentially to the decline of storytelling and its traditional character by depriving it of its "aura" or original authenticity. In that sense, the novel presents a few analogies with film, except that film is addressed to a collective audience while the novel is transmitted in solitude. Unlike Lukács, the author of *Theory of the Novel,* Benjamin is not sensitive to the richness of the novel as literature. A central element of traditional storytelling is lacking, wisdom and good counsel. "To write a novel means to carry the incommensurable to extremes in the representation of human life" (*Illuminations,* 87). The incommensurable is the irreducibly individual aspect of an experience torn from the framework within which it could be exchanged. The loss of wisdom is also, according to Benjamin's last interpretation of Kafka, what constituted his failure. He had sought to teach the true doctrine through parables and, in the end, he wrote novels; he had succumbed to the demon of literature:

> Kafka's work represents tradition falling ill. Wisdom has sometimes been defined as the epic side of truth. Such a definition marks wisdom off as a property of tradition; it is truth in its haggadic consistency. It is this consistency of truth that has been lost. . . . Kafka's real genius was that he tried something entirely new: he sacrificed truth for the sake of clinging to transmissibility, to its haggadic element. Kafka's writings are by their nature parables. But that is their misery and their beauty, that they had to become more than parables. They do not modestly lie at the feet of doctrine, as Haggadah lies at the feet of Halakah. (*Correspondence,* 565, letter of 12 June 1938)

According to Benjamin, the loss of wisdom made Kafka move from ancient storytelling, to which he had aspired, to the modern world of "rumor" and of slight "madness," characteristic of "literature" in the pejorative sense.

Next to the novel, the second form of modern communication to put an end to storytelling was the press, or *information.* This was already Karl Kraus's target. In showcasing the news story, in mixing in the private lives of individuals, and in clinging to the idea of satisfying the most immediate interests of readers, the press attacks both the public status of experience and the authority of tradition. Information strips traditional storytelling of its sobriety by introducing psychological explanations. At the same time, the story can no longer be repeated and reinterpreted forever. It loses its properly narrative character, constitutive of its life across the ages. From "aesthetic truth," it falls to the level of discursive truth.

Paul Valéry also observed that the idea of eternity, too, was tending to disappear. Benjamin deduces from this that the correlative experience of *death* was being transformed, particularly because of efforts to dissimulate the spectacle of death from us:

> Not only a man's knowledge or wisdom, but above all his real life—and this is the stuff that stories are made of—first assumes transmissible form at the moment of his death. Just as a sequence of images is set in motion inside a man as his life comes to an end—unfolding the views of himself under which he has encountered himself without being aware of it— suddenly in his expressions and looks the unforgettable emerges and imparts to everyone that concerned him that authority which even the poorest wretch in dying possesses for the living around him. (*Illuminations*, 94)

With the dissimulation of the act of dying, therefore, a part of humanity disappears, the part, precisely, that distinguishes storytelling from information void of all experience.

The transformation of death and the development of the press are two commonplaces frequently found in the criticism of modern culture. But how many dying men actually transmitted tellable stories on their deathbeds? Must we abandon the services of modern medicine to preserve the art of storytelling? Is not the differentiation between storytelling and information also a good thing? Whatever the faults of the press, does it not perform functions that the storyteller by the fireside cannot satisfy in a modern civilization? Benjamin refrains from asking such questions. What matters to him is the price of modernity, the fact that it forgets the part of natural history that human life entails, the part that associates tradition with death and elicits a need that is more than aesthetic: a religious need, satisfied by storytelling.

Death is "the sanction of everything that the storyteller can tell. He has borrowed his authority from death. In other words, it is natural history to which his stories refer back" (*Illuminations*, 94). This notion of natural history, which had disappeared in "The Work of Art," recalls *The Origin of German Tragic Drama* and "The Task of the Translator"; it refers to the theological horizon of Benjaminian thought that reappears here with the "creature." In the same spirit, Benjamin opposes the chronicler, the "history-teller," to the historian (*Illuminations*, 95). He insists that the question of whether the "inscrutable course of the world" is "eschatologically determined or is a natural one makes no difference" (*Illuminations*, 6). From the implicitly theological point of view peculiar to him, he approaches a problematic that had occupied several generations of thinkers—from Wilhelm Dilthey and the neo-Kantians around Heinrich Rickert and Max Weber, through Heidegger, Gadamer and his school, and, finally, Paul Ricoeur—who were anxious to distinguish historical, narrative, or hermeneutic knowledge from that of nature. The distinction between explanation and interpretation refers directly to that debate. The same is true for the valorization of the concepts of authority and tradition, which Benjamin associates with storytelling: "There is one form of authority," Gadamer would write twenty-five years later in *Truth and Method,*

> particularly defended by romanticism, namely tradition. That which has been sanctioned by tradition and custom has an authority that is nameless, and our finite historical being is marked by the fact that the authority of what has been handed down to us—and not just what is clearly grounded—always has power over our attitudes and behavior. All education depends on this.[8]

As in the hermeneutic tradition, Benjamin rightly refuses to dissociate historiography and narration. He makes explicit the hermeneutic theme of the irreducible horizon within which any questioning on the part of a historian is contained. But he sets aside any discussion of the conditions of communicable objectivity to which his work is subject. In the face of the hold exercised by actuality, through which Benjaminian historiography evokes a past capable of overturning the perception of the present, the question of historical truth pales to the point of insignificance.

The concept of tradition, as it is associated with that of storytelling, leads Benjamin to modify the theory of memory that he had sketched in relation to Proust and that he would later develop, also in relation to Proust, in "On Some Motifs in Baudelaire." In "The Image of Proust," memory appeared as the *organon* of an integral presence of mind, indispensable to political action. Benjamin now links it to preserving ancestral traditions: "*Memory* creates the chain of tradition which passes a happening on from generation to generation" (*Illuminations,* 98). Here again, the epic genre is the matrix from which the forms of memory were differentiated at the time of the decline of the epic. Benjamin opposes "the perpetuating remembrance of the novelist" to "the short-lived reminiscences of the storyteller" (*Illuminations,* 98). One results from a breathless struggle against time, illustrated by the solitary reader devouring the novel like "fire devours logs in the fireplace" (*Illuminations,* 100); the other is the instructive and entertaining memory of a storyteller "who could let the wick of his life be consumed completely by the gentle flame of his story" (*Illuminations,* 109). In giving preference to storytelling, Benjamin does not do justice to the richness of the novel as literature; he depreciates the novel as a modern form—and more precisely, as a form that, in a certain way, *accepts* the conditions of modernity. His thinking finds profound affinity only with premodern forms or with expressions of a radical rejection of modernity. Nevertheless, he is not simply a romantic turned toward the past, who would seek to oppose myth to the Enlightenment. He defends the authority of the religious tradition, but still for rational ends. In that, he is also distinguished from the conservative tendencies of German romanticism and from postmodern antirationalism.

He has some affinities with Heinrich Heine, who also sought to reconcile the critical spirit of the Enlightenment with a romantic imperative for happiness. That is what Benjamin's interpretation of the fairy tale reveals (*Illuminations,* 102ff.). When Benjamin opposes storytelling to scientific history or the novel, it is in the name of an *imperative for happiness* apparently unknown to modern society and ascetic rationality. Only the resources of a "theological" mode of thought, the story, and poetry still seem to offer the possibility of acceding to it. At least in memory, modern man must keep alive the old storytelling, so as not to lose an irreplaceable part of his experience.

LYRIC POETRY AT THE APOGEE OF CAPITALISM

Despite their different tones, the essays written in 1937–1938, "Eduard Fuchs, Collector and Historian" and "The Paris of the Second Empire in Baudelaire," do not seem to contradict the change observed in his 1936 essay "The Storyteller." The *revision* of the thesis that had asserted, in the name of the revolutionary character of the technologies of reproduction, the need to liquidate the aura and the end of aesthetic autonomy—a revision that would be more explicitly confirmed by "On Some Motifs in Baudelaire"—is not called into question. It is true, however, that the discussion of this central theme is discussed only parenthetically in these essays. Despite his doubts regarding the emancipatory character of the technologies of reproduction, despite his growing skepticism regarding the "masses," Benjamin wants to maintain the essentials of the *political* positions he defended in "The Work of Art," in which the imperatives of the "masses" still justified abandoning the esoteric aura. That was undoubtedly one of the aspects of "The Paris of the Second Empire in Baudelaire" that disturbed Adorno and Scholem. A coherent position would be found only in "On Some Motifs in Baudelaire" and in the "Theses on the Philosophy of History."

"The Paris of the Second Empire in Baudelaire" was the fruit of an enormous effort, yet Adorno suggested that Benjamin give up the idea of publishing it (*Correspondence,* 583–584, Adorno's letter of 10 November 1938). It became the grounds of a quarrel between two Benjaminian "schools": the school that took Adorno's side and the school that, on the contrary, leaned toward a defense of Benjamin's view. Although this quarrel continues to divide Benjamin's readers, it has little contemporary interest. On the one hand, Benjamin agreed to modify his text when he drafted a more explicitly theoretical essay; on the other, neither of the respective views—Benjamin's rather elementary sociological approach or Adorno's theory of the commodity, which claimed to be more rigorous and more critical—is current any more. Today, both these positions are historical, and they no longer carry authority as verdicts on contemporary culture.

Baudelaire—this is what constitutes his "unique importance" for Benjamin (*Correspondence*, 557)—"apprehended, in both senses of the word, the productive energy of the individual alienated from himself" (*Correspondence*, 557). This sentence recalls certain formulations of the first two versions of "The Work of Art": "In the representation of the image of man by the apparatus, the alienation of man by his own hand finds a highly productive use" (*G.S.*, 1:451). Such is the experience of a film actor confronted not with the public but with the apparatus, an experience that Baudelaire seems to anticipate in his poetry. But in applying that formula to Baudelaire's poetry, Benjamin revises the theses of "The Work of Art," in which such an approach was reserved for cinema and its *technical* liquidation of the aura. Introduced into the heart of poetry, the productive force of alienated man is no longer foregrounded by the technology of reproduction but is inscribed in the poet's approach—a conclusion Benjamin will not draw explicitly until "On Some Motifs in Baudelaire."

In reference to "The Paris of the Second Empire in Baudelaire," Benjamin predicts, in a letter accompanying his manuscript, that it will not be possible to grasp from this single part (the only one to be written) "the philosophical bases of the *whole* book" (*Correspondence*, 573). This part (which was intended to be the second part) "undertakes the sociocritical interpretation of the poet" but gives neither "the Marxist interpretation" foreseen for the third part (which was to deal with the central theme of "novelty") nor Baudelaire's "aesthetic theory," which was to figure in the first part (*Correspondence*, 574).

When Adorno criticized Benjamin for having avoided "theory" by limiting himself to "the wide-eyed presentation of the bare facts" (*Correspondence*, 582), he was familiar with Benjamin's letter. Nevertheless, he disputed the approach adopted. In his response, Benjamin called his own approach "philological": "Philology is the examination of a text, which, proceeding on the basis of details, magically fixates the reader on the text" (*Correspondence*, 587); according to Benjamin, there was inevitably a "magical" element "which is reserved for philosophy to exorcise, reserved here for the concluding part" (*Correspondence*, 588). It is nonetheless true that the second part was published alone, without the philosophical complement that was to exorcise it, and that, therefore, there was at the very least a risk of misunderstanding. In the absence of theory, the facts and quotations presented by Benjamin seem "deceptively epic" (*Correspondence*, 582, Adorno's letter of 10 November 1938).

"The Paris of the Second Empire in Baudelaire" is tied together in a purely narrative way. Benjamin deals with a great number of concepts and notions that had appeared in the Exposé for *Paris Arcades*, but without making explicit their theoretical status, as if he were seeking to familiarize the reader with a historical universe—the Paris of the Second Empire in fact—rather than to present a theoretical analysis. It is a presentation of the "subject matter" of Baudelaire's oeuvre, linked to the lessons provided by documents from the era. This text is a "commentary" in the sense given this term in the essay on Goethe's *Elective Affinities,* "the exegesis of what is astonishing and bewildering in the work" (*G.S.,* 1:125), and not a critique, an examination of the work's truth content. Isolated from the critical part, the completed fragment retains a certain ambiguity: The writings of Baudelaire appear as *documents* of the era, not in the sense of a surrealist subversion of art but in a purely sociological sense, analogous to the quotations from numerous other authors, and not as *works of art* whose life lies in their "truth."

This essay represented a partial realization of the original *Paris Arcades* project, in which Baudelaire figured as a symptom, among the architectural witnesses and phantasmagoria of the nineteenth century. A number of themes were already included in the program of the 1935 Exposé: the bohemian and the flaneur; Baudelaire's ambiguous fascination for Blanqui and Napoleon III; and his pursuit of literary strategies in a market handed over to the popular press. The poet seems to be a prisoner of the myths of his age. "The Paris of the Second Empire in Baudelaire" is one of Benjamin's texts that is closest to a "critique of ideology" and furthest from the "rescue operation" characteristic of his approach. And yet, even though Baudelaire shares the ambivalent feelings of the rebels—the bohemian and the flaneur—especially "the social illusion that crystallizes in the crowd" (*G.S.,* 1:569), he cannot be reduced to a symptom of his age. Unlike Victor Hugo, who saw in the crowd "the masses of his readers and his voters" (*G.S.,* 1:568), he was the guardian of the gate "that separates the individual from the crowd" (*G.S.,* 1:569). That individual is the "hero" through whom modernity is linked to antiquity: "Baudelaire," writes Benjamin at the beginning of his chapter "Modernity," "modeled his image of the artist on an image of the hero" (*G.S.,* 1:570). Here, the poet forges an image to impose his own aesthetic logic: "The hero," writes Benjamin, "is the true subject of *modernity.* This means that, to live modernity, one must be heroic in nature" (*G.S.,* 1:577). This sentence reiterates and makes explicit what Benjamin had written about Kafka, namely, that "to make a decent table nowadays, a man must have the architectural genius of a Michelangelo" (*Illuminations,* 113). In the same way, Baudelaire "rediscovers [in "L'âme du vin (The soul of wine)] the gladiator in the proletarian. . . . What the salaried worker brings about each day in his work is nothing less than the exploit that brought glory and applause to the gladiator in Antiquity. This image is the stuff of Baudelaire's best intuitions; it is born of the reflection on his own condition" (*G.S.,* 1:577).

This passage is revealing for the text as a whole: Written in Brecht's house in Denmark, it is characterized both by a manifest desire to submit Baudelaire to Marxist analysis and by an identification coupled with self-criticism. This identification is even more obvious in another aspect of modern heroism that Benjamin takes up immediately after these remarks. The difficulties that modernity opposes to "man's natural productive élan" (*G.S.*, 1:578) lead him to find refuge in death: "Modernity must remain under the sign of suicide. Suicide places its seal below the heroic will, which cedes nothing to the spirit that is hostile to it. This suicide is not renunciation but a heroic passion. It is *the* conquest of modernity in the field of passions" (*G.S.*, 1:578). Benjamin had been tempted by suicide on several occasions, and he turned to it a few years later rather than be handed over to his persecutors. This was, then, a form of "heroism" familiar to him. Through Baudelaire, he continually spoke of himself.

He reviewed a whole series of incarnations of the modern hero: the *apache* (thug), the ragpicker, the lesbian, the dandy—all physiognomies to which were attached, of course (in the view of the "critique of ideology") the "illusions" of the age[9] but through which an identification and thus a form of "rescue" were made manifest. Such was the case in particular for the ragpicker. The *Paris Arcades* project constantly sets out to decipher an epoch through its castoffs, just as the psychoanalyst interprets a subject's desire based on the detritus of his language—dreams, slips of the tongue, unconscious acts. "Method of this project: literary montage," we read in one of the epistemological reflections of *Paris Arcades*:

I need say nothing. Only exhibit [*zeigen*]. I won't filch anything of value or appropriate any ingenious turns of phrase. Only the trivia, the trash—which I don't want to inventory, but simply allow it to come into its own in the only way possible: by putting it to use. ("N" 1a, 8, p. 47)

This method accounts for the absence of interpretation for which Adorno criticizes "The Paris of the Second Empire." It is modeled on the method of the modern poet:

The poet finds society's castoffs in the street, and in them his heroic subject. In that way, the poet's distinguished image seems to replicate a more vulgar image where the features of the ragpicker—who so often occupied Baudelaire—show through. . . . Ragpicker or poet—castoffs matter to both of them. (*G.S.*, 1:582)

In linking his own approach to the poet's, Benjamin casts an ambiguous light on his work as a philosopher and a theorist. The method that—as the last avatar of Benjamin's "theology" of language—consists in calling things by their names, citing them by convoking them before the supreme tribunal, runs the risk of falling into a pretentious impressionism or, in Adorno's expression, a "magical positivism." The facts selected do not speak for themselves but only refer to the interests that the essayist attaches to them and that the reader familiar with his oeuvre guesses. At the limit, any *concept* disappears in this evocative approach; through this approach, Benjamin became, in spite of himself, one of the precursors of a defeatist philosophy that is afraid of conceptual rigor.

Later on, however, he proposes a more explicit interpretation. Beginning with the relation in Baudelaire between modernity and antiquity, Benjamin introduces again, in narrative and almost anecdotal fashion, the allegorical form that he considers central for the comprehension of the work. It is here, as well, that the poet fleetingly appears within the perspective of his aesthetic value and not simply as a historical and social symptom, only to be immediately brought back to the limits of his illusions. It had seemed at first that the hero of the big city might be the *apache* as well as the poet who made him his subject. But "the aging Baudelaire," to whom Benjamin accords the greatest value, no longer recognizes himself in "that race of men where, in his youth, he sought heroes" (*G.S.*, 1:583–584). From then on, heroism consists in arranging things so that, through poetry, modernity can one day become antiquity. In the way he presents this imperative of Baudelaire's, Benjamin suggests a link with Nietzsche's thought: "Modernity characterizes an epoch; it characterizes at the same time the energy that is at work in that epoch and links it to Antiquity. . . . Wagner appeared to him as an unlimited and authentic expression of that energy" (*G.S.*, 1:584). From an analogous point of view, *The Birth of Tragedy* links Wagner to the most authentic aspirations of antiquity. But we shall see that Benjamin does not take the notion of antiquity literally.

As always, he does not find the authentic link between modernity and antiquity in Baudelaire's *theory*. He considers it weak even in its famous formulations, where the beautiful is designated as an amalgam of the absolute and the relative, of the eternal and the fleeting, of the age, fashion, morality, and passion (*G.S.*, 1:585). "The aesthetic reflections of Baudelaire," he writes, "never succeeded in presenting modernity in its interpenetration with the ancient as clearly as certain poems from *The Flowers of Evil*" (*G.S.*, 1:585). That is particularly the case for the "Tableaux parisiens," in which Paris appears in its fragility: "It is precisely through that precariousness that modernity, finally and at the deepest level, is espoused and wed to the ancient" (*G.S.*, 1:586). For, in its precariousness, the modern city already appears as an ancient *ruin*. Through the faculty of perceiving or anticipating such ruins, Baudelaire becomes part of a tradition that, for Benjamin, stretches from the decline of antiquity through the beginning of the Middle

Ages and on to surrealism, including in its sweep the baroque and Baudelaire, the tradition of ruin and of allegory. Unlike antiquity as it appears in Victor Hugo's work—"chthonian" (*G.S.*, 1:586), a perception of immutable, eternally human realities from High Antiquity—in Baudelaire's work it is a "mimesis of death" (*G.S.*, 1:587), which, through the detour of allegory, transforms modernity into antiquity. Pursuing his approach through sociological associations, Benjamin recalls the work of Haussmann, whose "great urban cleanup" (*G.S.*, 1:589), in the view of contemporaries, illustrated the fragility of the big city: "When we know something will soon have to disappear from our view, it becomes an image. That is probably what had to happen to the streets of Paris at that time" (*G.S.*, 1:590).

One of the rare interpretive passages links the modern aspiration for antiquity to a process of rapid aging, according to that sense for the antiquated and the obsolete that the surrealists saw with such acuity:

> Baudelaire wanted to be read as a writer of Antiquity. This requirement was satisfied extraordinarily quickly. For the distant ages the sonnet ["Je te donne ces vers" (I give you these lines)] speaks of arrived in as many decades after his death as Baudelaire would have imagined centuries. Of course, Paris is still standing; and the great tendencies of social development are still the same. But it is the very fact that they have remained that makes any contact with what was born under the sign of the "truly new" even more fragile. Modernity has remained largely the same, and Antiquity, which was to find itself in its bosom, in reality presents the image of the obsolete. (*G.S.*, 1:593)

Benjamin brings out a surrealist aspect in Baudelaire. From a sociological point of view, he underscores the limits of the poet's lucidity. Next to the *apache* and the ragpicker, two other figures with "ancient" resonances characterize modern heroism in Baudelaire's view: the *lesbian* and the *dandy*. In describing them, Benjamin—in a Brechtian style—attempts to show that Baudelaire creates a phenomenological abstraction of these figures, whose economic genesis he refuses to see: "A heroine of modernity" (*G.S.*, 1:594), the lesbian emerges from the context of Saint-Simonism and its cult of the androgyne, linked, according to Benjamin, to the masculinization of woman, who had been integrated into factory work. Yet Baudelaire moves away from that aspect: "It was important for him to detach it from economic dependence. He succeeded therefore in giving to that developmental trend a strictly sexual emphasis" (*G.S.*, 1:597). That allowed him to write both a hymn to Sapphic love ("Lesbos") and a condemnation of lesbian passion ("Delphine et Hippolyte"), since damnation was indissociable from "the heroic nature of that passion" (*G.S.*, 1:597).[10] Similarly, when Benjamin evokes the dandy, "the hero in [his] last incarnation" (*G.S.*, 1:599), he confronts Baudelairean stylization at its historical origins (*G.S.*, 1:599–600). In once more disregarding the social and economic backdrop, Baudelaire reduces the dandy's social "tic" to a Satanic grimace, thus losing the dandy's charm, his "gift for pleasing" (*G.S.*, 1:600). The dandy adopts an attitude of idleness and contained energy without having the means to support it. According to Benjamin, all these incarnations of the hero are only "roles": "Heroic modernity proves to be a tragic drama [*Trauerspiel*] where the role of the hero is still to be cast" (*G.S.*, 1:600). Fundamentally, to use Jules Vallès's malicious expression (*G.S.*, 1:601), Baudelairean heroism is only that of a mime, a "ham."

To these illusory aspects Benjamin opposes Baudelaire's poetic achievements, of which allegory is the linchpin: "Under the masks he used, the poet in Baudelaire preserved his incognito. . . . Incognito was the law of his poetry" (*G.S.*, 1:601). He knowingly calculated its effects, introducing into his lines "vulgar" comparisons ("*la nuit s'épaississait ainsi qu'une cloison*" [the night was growing thick, like a membrane]) or using words borrowed from the language of the city: *quinquet, wagon, bilan, voirie* (oil lamp, train car, balance sheet, dump). "Thus," writes Benjamin, "the lyric vocabulary was created in which, abruptly, an allegory emerged that nothing had prepared for. If we can somehow grasp Baudelaire's linguistic spirit, in it we find that abrupt coincidence, according to Claudel, of the Racinian style and the journalistic style of the Second Empire" (*G.S.*, 1:603).

These outlines of formal analyses are immediately linked to the sociological thesis that is the essay's starting point. Allegory appears as the characteristic gesture of the bohemian conspirator:

> He places his trust in allegories for this surprise attack that poetry is for him. They are the only ones in on the secret. Where Death, or Memory, or Repentance, or Evil appear, they are the centers of the poetic strategy. The sudden appearance of these soldiers, recognizable by the capital letters that irrupt right in the middle of a text, which does not reject the most banal of vocabularies, betrays Baudelaire's hand. His technique is putschist. (*G.S.*, 1:603)

In this way, Baudelaire's poetry, his "dream," joins hands with Blanqui's "action," which Marx, using an implicitly critical term, called "putschist." In adopting this term for his own use, Benjamin introduces into it a pathos of desperate solidarity with the vanquished: Blanqui's acts and Baudelaire's dream "are the hands joined on a stone under which Napoleon III had buried the hopes of the June fighters" (*G.S.*, 1:604). This ambiguity characterizes the text as a whole: It is a critique of ideology linking poetry to a socially situated gesture, but a critique that reveals the identification of an author full of pathos, who sees no alternative to these desperate gestures that are endowed with a certain dignity. On the pretext of denouncing putschist behavior from a Marxist perspective, Benjamin implicitly rehabilitates its hopeless grandeur. Because these gestures do not reveal a "just politics" in the Marxist sense, they interest Benjamin as experiments. However problematic these gestures might be, they save the "victims" that history would have liked to condemn, if not to oblivion, then at least to misunderstanding. Restoring the political meaning of the Baudelairean gesture amounts to rescuing an aspiration for revolt, condemned to failure but containing a germ of that "weak Messianic power" discussed in Thesis 2 of the "Theses on the Philosophy of History."

Under the contrary pressures of Brechtian objections and the imperatives of his own philosophy of history, Benjamin accords little space to an analysis that would have underscored the aesthetic interest of Baudelaire's poems. But the analytic perspective of symptoms and documents cannot be applied to the *Paris Arcades* project as a whole. In his last essay on Baudelaire, responding this time to Adorno's imperatives, Benjamin proceeds to a comprehensive interpretation that reveals the aesthetic value of the work. Sociological categories, such as that of commodity, have no direct influence on the position taken by the artist; they directly influence only the themes he encounters in the historical context. The early texts on Baudelaire explain the poet's attitude in terms of the place he occupies within the ambiguous bohemian milieu and in terms of the social role of the flaneur, in which the relation between client and commodity is anticipated in the desperate heroism of those excluded from modernity: rebels, lesbians, and dandies. The last essay tries above all to show the aesthetic appropriateness of Baudelaire's choices.

"The Paris of the Second Empire in Baudelaire" represents the sociological viewpoint of *Paris Arcades,* which moves away from the value of the poetic work itself and sees in it only one symptom among others of the submission of art to the market. The essay written the following year, "On Some Motifs in Baudelaire," addresses, at least in part, the point of view of the writer who, to save the authenticity of his work, sacrifices the poet's traditional aura. What moves to the foreground is no longer the "relation of expression" between a technological and sociological infrastructure and a cultural phenomenon but the coherence of the work of art. Nevertheless, the force of this essay cannot be dissociated from historical and sociological inquiries. It is only by reconstituting the context that Benjamin succeeds in comprehending the internal coherence of the work and articulates possible meanings. The text's weakness rests on its failure to devote much attention to the form of poetry and to the quality of the texts as such. Benjamin was no doubt convinced that a more precise reading would not have revealed anything fundamentally new to him, nothing that could call into question the results of his analogical reading of expressive values.

The *Correspondence,* a few posthumous notes, and a series of fragments
brought together under the title "Central Park" suggest what the other parts
of the planned book on Baudelaire might have looked like. Outside the
sociological section, which was the only part drafted, there was to have been
an introduction dedicated to the opposition between a critical "rescue
operation" and the traditional "homage" given an author, a first part dealing
with allegory from the perspective of art theory, and a final section whose
object would have been the commodity as "fulfillment" of the allegorical
vision in Baudelaire (*Correspondence,* 557). Benjamin would have once more
attempted to reconcile a philological presentation of the thinking of the age
and an underlying theoretical hypothesis that was explanatory in nature.
Poetry seems to be confined to reproducing the different aspects of the
commodity as it was analyzed in Marx's *Capital.* All these reflections suffer
from the fact that Benjamin does not define the status of the work of art
independent of phantasmagoria, a status it shares with speeches, everyday
phenomena, and ideologies pure and simple.

   Unlike apologetic approaches, the issue is to not neglect "those
points at which tradition breaks down and thus misses those jags and
crags that offer a handhold to someone who wishes to move beyond them"
("N" 9a, 5, p. 65, translation slightly modified). Such an approach leads
Benjamin to distinguish between the themes explicitly targeted by
Baudelaire—"Satanism, *spleen,* and deviant eroticism" ("Central Park,"
39)—and the poet's "true subjects," those "decisive new subjects"—"the
big city, the masses—[that] were not visualized by him as such" ("Central
Park," 39). Whether looking at the works of Kafka or Knut Hamsun,
Benjamin always distinguishes between the theoretical intention of an
authentic writer and his poetic work, which obeys a different logic,
inaccessible to his theoretical consciousness. This distinction is justified
by the fact that theoretical modes of thought and artistic practice obey
different logics and do not necessarily communicate within the author's
mind. Art is a technique whose workings the artist can understand no
better than can the receiver. For Benjamin, precisely from the point of
view of "reception," it is a matter of breaking with the conformism of
transmitted visions, with the false continuity of traditions. That is what
he sees as the true task of philosophy, which he develops in the "Theses
on the Philosophy of History." For Benjamin, the destructive, critical
element is constitutive of any study of a historical object, not—as for
Heidegger—in order to be rid of a "metaphysics" that would dissimulate
the authentic but, rather, to avoid the hold of established "culture," always
suspect of complicity with the socially dominant forces.

   Allegory is the aspect of Baudelaire's oeuvre that had in fact escaped critical attention before Benjamin. He had translated "Tableaux parisiens" in his youth and had become interested in Baudelaire when he began to reflect on German baroque drama. The first part of the book on Baudelaire would have thus dealt with the "prehistory" of Baudelairean poetry: from baroque allegory and the new function of the allegorical vision, to the nineteenth century (*G.S.*, 1:1084, letter of 3 August 1938). A few elements of such a comparison are found among the fragments of "Central Park." Through allegory, Baudelaire was setting modernity at a distance. *Spleen* transforms any present moment into Antiquity ("Central Park," 35), into a fragile reality of which, the next instant, only ruins remain.

From the point of view of literary history, Baudelairean allegory emerges in a precise context: "The introduction of allegory answers in a far more meaningful way the same crisis of art which, around 1852, the theory of *l'art pour l'art* was intended to counter" ("Central Park," 34). As in the seventeenth century, allegory is an inquiry into art in general. Baudelaire "could hardly have written his essay on Dupont if Dupont's radical critique of the concept of art did not correspond to an equally radical one of his own" ("Central Park," 52). This fragment is indicative of the modification that the essays on Baudelaire bring to the perspective on the "end of art" as it had appeared in "The Work of Art." The questioning of aesthetic appearance is now situated *within* art and not in an externality, as in the case of film.

The first part of the book was to respond to a difficulty that Benjamin experienced before the "fundamental paradox" of Baudelairean aesthetics: "the contradiction between the theory of natural correspondences and the rejection of nature" (*Correspondence*, 556, letter of 16 April 1938). In "Central Park," this paradox remains an insoluble problem (33), but, among the notes for *Paris Arcades*, we find an attempt to solve it:

> There is between the theory of natural correspondences and the rejection of nature a contradiction that is resolved when impressions become detached in the recollection of lived experience [*Erlebnis*]. Thus, the experience contained in these impressions is freed and can be joined to the allegorical heritage. (*G.S.*, 5:436)

Correspondences do not contradict the rejection of nature, inasmuch as they keep only its sublimation in memory, the place for authentic experience. In a more narrow sense, the "*souvenir*"—in the sense that Baudelaire writes, "*J'ai plus de souvenirs que si j'avais mille ans*"—is the means by which Benjamin differentiates between baroque allegory and modern allegory. The "*souvenir*" is the opposite of authentic experience; it is its alienated form through the "lived experience," which one collects like a souvenir photo:

> The *souvenir* is the complement of lived experience [*des Erlebnisses*]. In it
> the increasing self-alienation of the person who inventories his past as
> dead possessions is instilled. In the 19th century allegory left the
> surrounding world, in order to settle in the inner world. The relic derives
> from the corpse, the souvenir from deceased experience [*Erfahrung*]
> which calls itself euphemistically "*Erlebnis.*" ("Central Park," 49, trans-
> lation slightly modified)

Here the move from the first part of the book to the third is announced;
this last part was to be devoted to the commodity as poetic object. According
to another fragment:

> Melancholy bears in the 19th century a different character, however, to
> that which it bore in the 17th. The key figure of the early allegory is the
> corpse. The key figure of the later allegory is the "*souvenir.*" The "*souvenir*"
> is the schema of the transformation of the commodity into a collector's
> object. The *correspondances* are the endlessly multiple resonances of each
> *souvenir* with all the others. ("Central Park," 54–55)

At issue, then, is a sort of internalization or sublimation of death.
Internalized death is more difficult to grasp than that represented by the corpse
displayed on the baroque stage; hence the status of violence and destruction
in Baudelaire, which has to display itself with particular relentlessness:
"Baudelaire's allegory bears, in contradistinction to that of the Baroque, traces
of a wrath which was at such a pitch as to break into this world and to leave
its harmonious structures in ruins" ("Central Park," 42).
    But that violence does not seek to annihilate what it breaks; it clings
to it:

> That which is touched by the allegorical intention is torn from the
> context of life's interconnections: it is simultaneously shattered and
> conserved. Allegory attaches itself to the rubble. It offers the image of
> transfixed unrest. The destructive impulse of Baudelaire is nowhere
> interested in the abolition of that which falls to it. ("Central Park," 38)

Allegorical destruction is an ostentatious destruction; it wants to reveal to
the reader the significance of the annihilation unfolding before his or her
eyes, and of which the poet makes an experience staged on *his own* initiative.
    Several fragments underscore the link between allegory and the com-
modity, which was to be explained in the concluding part.

> Ever more callously the object world of man assumes the expression of
> the commodity. At the same time advertising seeks to veil the commod-

ity character of things. In the allegorical the deceptive transfiguration of the world of the commodity resists its distortion. The commodity attempts to look itself in the face. It celebrates its becoming human in the whole. ("Central Park," 42)

Benjamin would have wished to give Baudelairean allegory a sociological explanation of the Marxist type; he thought he had found in modern allegory a response to commodity *reification*[11]:

> The refunctioning of allegory in the commodity economy must be presented. It was Baudelaire's endeavour to make the aura which is peculiar to the commodity appear. In a heroic way he sought to humanize the commodity. His attempt had its equivalent in the simultaneous attempt of the bourgeoisie to personify the commodity: to give the commodity, like a person, housing. This then was the promise of the *etui* [small box], the covers, the sheaths with which the bourgeois household effects of the time were being covered. ("Central Park," 42)

The central idea is thus that classical allegory devalorizes the phenomenal world by reducing it to meaning. Yet, "the devaluation of the world of objects in allegory is outdone within the world of objects itself by the commodity" ("Central Park," 34). But this devaluation is not immediately visible. Baudelaire seizes hold of this world to destroy its appearances. He undertakes to set forth commodity devaluation through allegorical destruction. For him, allegory represents the poet as someone who heroically prostitutes himself by making of poetry a commodity. That is what Benjamin calls revealing "the productive force of alienated man." Appearance or illusion cannot be destroyed by such cynicism: "The lack of appearances and the decline of the aura are identical phenomena. Baudelaire puts the artistic means of allegory at their disposal" ("Central Park," 41).

These ideas are not always coherent. Visibly, and at the expense of any other explanation, Benjamin undertakes to reintegrate the critical aspects of the Baudelairean oeuvre into the schema of the fetishism of the commodity. But if commodity devaluation surpasses that effected by allegory, the poetic technique chosen by Baudelaire is of little interest. In a comment on the poem "Une martyre," written no doubt toward the beginning of 1938, we find an insight into the whole book on Baudelaire:

> The allegorical vision is always founded on a devalued phenomenal world. The specific devaluation of the world of things that one encounters in the commodity is the foundation for the allegorical intention in Baudelaire. As an incarnation of the commodity, the prostitute occupies

a central place in Baudelaire's poetry. On the other hand, the prostitute is allegory made flesh. The accessories with which fashion bedecks her are the emblems with which she bedecks herself. The fetish is the sign guaranteeing the authenticity of the commodity, just as the emblem is the sign guaranteeing the authenticity of allegory. The inanimate body, still offered up to pleasure, unites allegory and the commodity. (*G.S.*, 1:1151)

"On Some Motifs in Baudelaire" abandons any attempt to link Baudelaire's poetry to an illustration of fetishism and the commodity, in favor of a conceptuality of experience that takes up some of Benjamin's old ideas. Therefore, the collection "Central Park" does not allow us to complete "The Paris of the Second Empire in Baudelaire" by making of the whole a homogeneous conception.

As foreseen in the 1935 Exposé of *Paris Arcades*, the last part of the book on Baudelaire was to deal with the new and the always-the-same as two complementary aspects of the commodity, aspects that Baudelaire fallaciously opposed to each other:

The third part treats the commodity as the fulfillment of Baudelaire's allegorical vision. It turns out that what is new, which explodes the experience of the immutable under whose spell the poet was placed by spleen, is nothing other than the halo of the commodity. (*Correspondence*, 557, letter of 16 April 1938)

That duality, which leads Baudelaire—in his ignorance of the nature of the commodity—to oppose the new to the eternal return of the same, was to bring about two digressions, dedicated to the two aspects of the commodity: its illusory aspect, represented by what in Baudelaire anticipates *Jugendstil*, and its true aspect, incarnated in a demystifying manner by the prostitute (*Correspondence*, 557). The fragments brought together under the title "Central Park" further explain these points. Within the framework of his reflection on the impact of the technologies of reproduction, Benjamin considers *Jugendstil* an attempt to repress the rivalry between art and mechanical reproduction; it is, according to him, "the second attempt of art to come to terms with technology. The first was Realism. There the problem was more or less conscious for the artists who were unsettled by the new processes of technological reproduction. . . . For *Jugendstil* the problem as such had already succumbed to repression" ("Central Park," 34). *Jugendstil* worships the virgin body and, in that spirit, develops a "regressive interpretation of technology" ("Central Park," 43). *The Flowers of Evil* anticipates *Jugendstil* in its floral motif and in the theme of the "new." It was through his illusions that Baudelaire was the precursor of *Jugendstil*, whereas he was its antagonist in his allegorical technique and the destruction of the "halo," whether that of the prostitute or of the poet.[12]

But the cult of the new was not just an illusion. In it, Benjamin discovers an undertaking whose historical significance was close to the ideas of Nietzsche and Blanqui; he reads it as a response to the mythical phenomenon of the always-the-same, the frightening repetition of the same that the poem "Les sept vieillards" illustrates:

> The idea of the eternal return is here the "new" that breaks through the circle of eternal return even as it confirms it. Through the conjunction with Nietzsche—and especially with Blanqui, who developed, ten years before him, the doctrine of the eternal return—Baudelaire's work appears in a new light. . . . Blanqui thought that the eternity of the world and of man—the always-the-same—was guaranteed by the order of the stars. Yet Baudelaire's abyss is deprived of stars. In fact, Baudelaire's poetry is the first in which stars are absent. The line "dont la lumière parle un langage connu" [whose light speaks a familiar language] is the key to this poetry. In its destructive energy—through the allegorical conception—it breaks not only with the pastoral nature of the idyll, but, through the heroic resolution with which it introduces lyric poetry into the heart of reification, it also breaks with the nature of things. It is situated at the point where the nature of things is dominated and re-created by the nature of man. History has since shown he was right not to expect that re-creation from technological progress. (*G.S.*, 1:1152)

Benjamin attempts to draw from the Baudelairean oeuvre a theoretical position comparable to Nietzsche's and Blanqui's ideas, which he had just discovered in Blanqui's *L'Éternité par les astres* (Eternity by the stars). Here again, he hesitates between an explanatory position that reduces thought to an expression of the antinomies of the commodity and a process that makes a hero of the poet who has grasped the reification of nature.

MODERN ART
AND THE SACRIFICE OF THE AURA

Catchphrases such as "the decline of the aura" or the "end of the art of storytelling" are linked to the Hegelian idea of the "end of art." Before Heidegger, Adorno, or Danto, Benjamin evoked such a perspective, in a tone that alternated between manifest satisfaction, despair, and nostalgia. In the 1935 Exposé and in "The Work of Art," he is convinced that art will be replaced by technology and that other functions will replace those of the magical domination of nature and sacred ritual, functions that will help us adapt to a perilous environment, that will offer us a form of therapy to heal collective psychoses through laughter and a knowledge that allows us to get our bearings in the social space. Whatever the case, the imperatives either to liquidate the aura or to preserve its memory are dictated by a concern for a form of *public* communication: In "The Work of Art," that seems to be the function of cinema, compared to the privatization of the aura in other arts and in bourgeois culture generally.

According to the essays of the last period, in which the distance imposed by the work of art of the past goes hand in hand with a public communication that keeps tradition alive, the arts of storytelling and of painting seem to have had that function. The arts of mechanical reproduction are now interpreted as degraded forms of confrontation between an isolated *individual* and a *mechanism*. In the first theory of cinema, this new art was celebrated in the name of an interpretation of the technology of reproduction guaranteeing a public status to the forms of representation; in the second, that art, which is no longer an art, seems to disappoint such an expectation: Technology appears as a privatizing force, as it will in fact be in the automobile and television.

"On Some Motifs in Baudelaire," which formulates the second theory, is one of Benjamin's most complex texts. He once more takes up the themes of experience and memory as they were introduced in "The Storyteller." He underscores the changes they have undergone in the modern big city, the fact of the crowd, and the experiences of shock. He returns to the status of mechanical reproduction and, above all, delves deeper into the theory of the beautiful and of modern art in a way that both explains and modifies the sacrifice of the aura in "The Work of Art." This essay by Benjamin, the final formulation of his aesthetic thought, is linked to the formulation in the essay on Goethe's *Elective Affinities.* But he is no longer concerned either with the symptoms of urban life under the hold of the fetishism of the commodity or with the false consciousness of bohemia; he is now concerned with the truth of a work of art, whose gesture contains a historical knowledge offered for philosophical interpretation.

The themes of experience and memory are developed through their formulation in late-nineteenth-century philosophies, from Baudelaire's to Bergson's to Proust's. According to Benjamin, the introductory poem of *Flowers of Evil* is addressed to a reader who does not favor lyric poetry. Poetry has lost contact with the reader's experience. Benjamin explains that break through his early theory of a change affecting the very structure of experience (*Illuminations,* 156). As if to supply the proof, the "philosophy of life"—Dilthey, Klages, and Bergson—attempted, beginning at the end of the nineteenth century, to define "true" experience in opposition to the experience encountered "in the standardized, denatured life of the civilized masses" (*Illuminations,* 156). These are the masses of modern readers who take no interest in poetry, to the point that Apollinaire could imagine a pogrom directed against poets. Among the vitalist thinkers, Benjamin gives preference to Bergson, who "preserves links with empirical research" (*Illuminations*, 157). But, in the style of Critical Theory, he criticizes philosophers as a whole for not beginning with "man's life in society" (*Illuminations*, 156). He wishes to deal with the themes of that philosophy from a point of view that integrates the results obtained by the social sciences, and especially by Marxism and psychoanalysis.

Bergson's *Matière et mémoire* (Matter and memory) links experience to memory, in other words, to the transmission of tradition. "Experience is indeed a matter of existence," writes Benjamin, "in collective existence as well as private life" (*Illuminations*, 157). Experience "is less the product of facts firmly anchored in memory than of a convergence in memory of accumulated and frequently unconscious data" (*Illuminations*, 157). This unconscious part of experience escapes Bergson, as does the historical character of experience, the "inhospitable, blinding" experience that belongs to the age of "big-scale industrialization" (*Illuminations*, 157). Bergson fixes his attention only on the reverse of that experience, that of duration, which he describes in such a way, according to Benjamin, that "the reader is bound to conclude that only a poet can be the adequate subject of such an experience" (*Illuminations*, 157).

In fact, it was a writer who tested the Bergsonian theory of experience. Proust's *Remembrance of Things Past* is for Benjamin an attempt to reconstitute the experience of duration under current social conditions. Proust is led to distance himself from the Bergsonian conception of pure memory, which "leads us to believe that turning to a contemplative actualization of the stream of life is a matter of free choice" (*Illuminations*, 157–158). In insisting on the powerlessness of "voluntary memory" and on the fortuitous character of the advent of "involuntary memory," Proust underscores the difficulty in the modern age of having an experience in the full sense of the term. Experience—as the essay "The Storyteller" had already underscored—has become "issueless [and] private" and, in that way, is both inaccessible and incommunicable. This evolution, according to Benjamin, is due to the fact that modern man is "increasingly unable to assimilate the data of the world around him by way of experience" (*Illuminations*, 158). Benjamin is summarizing the argument of his earlier essays by making of the modern press both a cause and a symptom of the growing cleavage between information and experience. Information no longer provides readers with stories to "pass . . . on as experience to those listening" (*Illuminations*, 159), and thus it contributes to the privatization of experience. Condemned to the Herculean and heroic task of modernity, literature is obliged to *compensate* for that gap: "Proust's eight-volume work conveys an idea of the efforts it took to restore the figure of the storyteller to the present generation" (*Illuminations*, 159).

The tendency toward the privatization of existence seems to be linked to the development of technologies of reproduction that bring the individual face to face with the mechanism while cutting him off from the community. This vision of the modern world allows Benjamin to give a definition—one incompatible with the theses in "The Work of Art"—of experience and ritual in their nonpathological form:

> Where there is experience in the strict sense of the word, certain contents of the individual past combine with material of the collective past. The rituals with their ceremonies, their festivals (quite probably nowhere recalled in Proust's work) kept producing the amalgamation of these two elements of memory over and over again. They triggered recollection at certain times and remained handles of memory for a lifetime. In this way, voluntary and involuntary recollection lose their mutual exclusiveness. (*Illuminations,* 160)

Between the first and the second sentence of this passage, Benjamin moves from the present tense to the imperfect: He is not unaware that his model of intact experience belongs to an age that has passed. Between this model and the contemporary era, no mediation is possible. Only a messianic perspective—a confirmation of the gap existing between the present and a reconciled future—allows us to imagine a restoration of integral experience. Without ritual and its ceremonies, experience can present itself only in the degraded form of "lived experience" (*Erlebnis*) which art alone, through a heroic effort, can transform into a true experience (*Erfahrung*), now confined to literature. Contrary to the theses in "The Work of Art," it is in ritual form that art is placed in the service of social life. "The Work of Art" showed the powerlessness of any attempt aimed at restoring ritual within the framework of modern society, but, at the same time, it opened the perspective of a society reconciled with technology. As soon as such a reconciliation has been ruled out by virtue of the profound nature of technology—the source of a relation between the isolated individual and the mechanism— Benjamin can no longer abandon the idea of a reactualization of ritual. He does not imagine a type of social relation, resolutely profane, in which individuals would invent nonreligious forms of exchange and transmission of experiences, forms with which literature and modern art have long since begun to experiment.

Benjamin draws on certain hypotheses from psychoanalysis to determine the relation between voluntary memory (identified with consciousness) and involuntary memory (identified with the unconscious). According to Freud's *Beyond the Pleasure Principle,* consciousness and the memory trace are mutually exclusive, since the function of consciousness is to protect the psychic system against excessive excitation:

"Becoming conscious and leaving behind a memory trace are processes incompatible with each other within one and the same system." Rather, memory fragments are "often most powerful and most enduring when the incident which left them behind was one that never entered consciousness." Put in Proustian terms, this means that only what has not been experienced explicitly and consciously, what has not happened to the subject of an experience, can become a component of the *mémoire involontaire*. (*Illuminations*, 159–160)

The function of consciousness would thus be to parry the *shocks* provoked not by "experience" in the full sense of the term but by traumatic "lived experiences," which are more and more frequent in modern life. That is what leads the reflection back to its starting point, the relation between experience and poetry: "That the shock is thus cushioned, parried by consciousness, would lend the incident that occasions it the character of having been lived in the strict sense. If it were incorporated directly in the registry of conscious memory, it would sterilize this incident for poetic experience" (*Illuminations*, 162). Under these conditions, "the question suggests itself how lyric poetry can have as its basis an experience for which the shock experience has become the norm" (*Illuminations*, 162). In all likelihood, this would resemble the literature, from Poe's through Baudelaire's to Valéry's, that is distinguished by its high degree of consciousness and calculation.

Benjamin first proposes to illuminate the ways that this modern poetry, exposed to the sterilizing shock of poetic experience, nevertheless succeeds in restoring experience. A first explanation is suggested in the way that Baudelaire portrays himself, presenting the poetic labor as a kind of "fencing." A second seems to be provided by "Spleen de Paris," which associates the ideal of poetic prose with "the frequenting of enormous cities." The shock to be parried now seems to emanate from the amorphous crowd of passersby, which is only implicitly present in Baudelaire's poetry but whose obsessive omnipresence Benjamin thinks he can demonstrate. The example of a shock experience is provided in the sonnet "A une passante," a fleeting encounter in the crowd of the big city; very unlike the love poem, this sonnet evokes only the "lived experience" of "the kind of sexual shock that can beset a lonely man" (*Illuminations*, 169). These verses "reveal the stigmata which life in a metropolis inflicts upon love" (*Illuminations*, 169). Nevertheless, the crowd is not only "an opposed, antagonistic element, this very crowd [also] brings to the city dweller the figure that fascinates. The delight of the urban poet is love—not at first sight, but at last sight" (*Illuminations*, 169). This sonnet is the very model for the transformation of a "lived experience" into an experience in the full sense of the term. From the pathology of experience in modernity, Baudelaire fashions a literary experience of great intensity. That was only possible, according to Benjamin, because Baudelaire, through the idea of *correspondances,* had a notion of true experience that was linked to ritual.

The essay then examines the perception of the crowd in the nineteenth century, the crowd of the popular classes and the vast public for Victor Hugo, the frightening crowd in the work of the young Friedrich Engels in London, the disturbing crowd in Edgar Allan Poe's "The Man of the Crowd," which Baudelaire translated. Benjamin shows that civilized people in large cities have returned to a savage state; in other words, they have lost the sense of what links individuals within the community. Benjamin attributes the return to barbarism to modern technology and, among other things, to those techniques of reproduction such as photography and film that he had earlier celebrated as factors favoring the secularization of the aura and as the means allowing for the satisfaction of the legitimate aspirations of the masses:

> Comfort isolates; on the other hand, it brings those enjoying it closer to mechanization. The invention of the match around the middle of the nineteenth century brought forth a number of innovations which have one thing in common: one abrupt movement of the hand triggers a process of many steps. . . . Of the countless movements of switching, inserting, pressing, and the like, the "snapping" of the photographer has had the greatest consequences. A touch of the finger now sufficed to fix an event for an unlimited period of time. The camera gave the moment a posthumous shock, as it were. (*Illuminations,* 174–175)

In the first chapter of "The Work of Art," this same process of accelerating reproduction was presented under more promising auspices. The following passage, dealing with cinema, from "On Some Motifs in Baudelaire," completes the reversal of the 1935 text:

> Thus technology has subjected the human sensorium to a complex kind of training. There came a day when a new and urgent need for stimuli was met by the film. In a film, perception in the form of shocks was established as a formal principle. That which determines the rhythm of production of a conveyor belt is the basis of the rhythm of reception in the film. (*Illuminations,* 175)

In "The Work of Art," this same acceleration due to the development of reproduction techniques appears as a salutary exercise allowing modern humanity to adapt to a dangerous environment (*G.S.,* 1:717). Benjamin's new evaluation of technology leads him to underscore only the aspect that is destructive, deadly, to experience in general. The model is provided in the relation between the worker and the machine. Supported by a series of quotations from Marx, Benjamin contrasts this relation, defined as a succession of shocks, to the fluidity that characterizes artisanal work (*Illuminations,* 176). In spite of the difference of the spheres of activity, he then establishes an analogy between the worker at his machine and the gambler, between the "jolt" in the movement of the machine and the "throw" (*coup*) in the game of chance (*Illuminations,* 177).

But what matters most in this analogy is once more the idea of the loss of experience. If, in "Le jeu" (The game), Baudelaire—without being himself a gambler—identifies with gamblers' empty passion, it is because "he too has been cheated out of his experience—a modern man" (*Illuminations,* 180). The concept of experience once more reveals its theological backdrop. The allusions to Goethe, then the comparison between the ivory marble on the roulette wheel and the falling star, refer to the essay on Goethes's *Elective Affinities.* According to Benjamin, the gambler's greed is opposed to "a wish in the strict sense of the word" which "is a kind of experience" (*Illuminations,* 178–179):

> "What one wishes for in one's youth, one has in abundance in old age," said Goethe. The earlier in life one makes a wish, the greater one's chances that it will be fulfilled. The further a wish reaches out in time, the greater the hopes for its fulfillment. But it is experience that accompanies one to the far reaches of time, that fills and divides time. Thus a wish fulfilled is the crowning of experience. In folk symbolism, distance in space can take the place of distance in time; that is why the shooting star, which plunges into the infinite distance of space, has become the symbol of a fulfilled wish. The ivory ball which rolls into the *next* compartment, the *next* card which lies on top are the very antithesis of a falling star. (*Illuminations,* 179)

Gambling time is an *infernal* time, in the theological sense of the term, because it represents a loss of patience in waiting for the wish and because it knows nothing of the fulfillment of experience, the salvation that is granted only to the one who earns it, not to the one who forces it: The gambler himself "has a hand in it" (*Illuminations,* 179). Yet the necessary distance of experience is that which, according to the essay on photography and film, is inherent in the aura. There is thus no authentic experience without the aura, without ritual and tradition, without at least a memory of these realities.

The essay then returns to the initial reflection on duration and memory, in order to comprehend, beginning from what has just been said, the sense of *The Flowers of Evil.* Proust had observed that "time is peculiarly chopped up in Baudelaire; only a very few days open up, they are significant ones" (quoted in *Illuminations,* 181). According to Benjamin, these are the days of authentic experience. It is these days of remembrance that Baudelaire associates with *correspondances*. These *correspondances*, writes Benjamin,

> record a concept of experience which includes ritual elements. Only by appropriating these elements was Baudelaire able to fathom the full meaning of the breakdown which he, a modern man, was witnessing. Only in this way was he able to recognize in it the challenge meant for him alone, the challenge which he incorporated in the *Fleurs du mal.* (*Illuminations,* 181)

This passage announces the final reversal of the essay, the reversal that distinguishes it from "The Storyteller." What Benjamin could not admit regarding epic literature—the profound modification that would make it accede to modernity—he conceives in lyric poetry. This evolution is differentiated both from the evolution that substituted photography and film for painting, and from the irremediable loss without compensation that characterized the end of storytelling. To be a modern within a traditional form that no longer has any hold on contemporary reality, one must have a notion, a memory of that aura and that experience that are broken down by modern reality. According to Benjamin the experience of Baudelairean *correspondances* "attempts to establish itself in crisis-proof form. This is possible only within the realm of the ritual. If it transcends this realm, it presents itself as the beautiful. In the beautiful the ritual value of art appears" (*Illuminations,* 182).

This ambiguous definition continues to give precedence to the type of community in which ritual has remained intact, one that knows nothing of the artistic beautiful in the grandiloquent sense. The beautiful, and in particular the artistic beautiful, appears only when experience can no longer represent itself within ritual. The ambiguity of the beautiful resides in the fact that it is the only receptacle of experience when ritual is under attack from social secularization, but it is still only an experience of substitution and is thus susceptible to crises. In a long note, Benjamin insists on the "aporetic" character of the beautiful, which is manifested through the "appearance" linked to it.

This appearance is manifested from the *historical* perspective, through the fact, observed by Goethe, that "everything that has had a great effect can really no longer be evaluated" (*Illuminations,* 199); in other words, the identity of the object escapes us by virtue of the fact that admiring gazes, in the end, veil the work of art. "Beauty," writes Benjamin, "is an appeal to join those who admired it at an earlier time" (*Illuminations,* 198). Admiration harvests only "what earlier generations have admired in it" (*Illuminations,* 198–199). It is nonetheless true that the criticism of every age discovers a beauty that is proper to it, and, in doing so, destroys a part of the beauty transmitted. In illustrating his thesis of the aporetic character of the beautiful and of art, Benjamin seems to identify the beautiful with what persists and is fixed in the historical chain of admiration.

In a more essential way, appearance comes into being in the relation between the beautiful and *nature*. According to a formulation in the essay on Goethe's *Elective Affinities,* the beautiful is what "remains true to its essential nature only when veiled" (*Illuminations,* 199). For aesthetic criticism, then, the goal is to respect this veil and not strip the work of art of what conferred consistency on it. But in attempting to explain his idea at this point, Benjamin may merely have complicated it:

> The *correspondances* tell us what is meant by such a veil. We may call it, in a somewhat daring abbreviation, the "reproducing aspect" of the work of art. The *correspondances* constitute the court of judgment before which the object of art is found to be a faithful reproduction—which, to be sure, makes it entirely problematic. If one attempted to reproduce this *aporia* through language, one would define beauty as the object of experience in the state of resemblance. This definition would probably coincide with Valéry's formulation: "Beauty may require the servile imitation of what is indefinable in objects." (*Illuminations,* 199)

What is aporetic in the case of appearance would thus be tied to the notion of a faithful reproduction of the "object of experience" or a resemblance to that object. Reproduction and resemblance are concepts that refer to the type of symbolic relation between the work of art and what it refers to. In "On the Mimetic Faculty," Benjamin speaks of a "nonsensuous similarity" that is a determining factor in the origin of human language. This paradoxical expression might rest on a mystical interpretation of the symbolic relation to the object of experience. As he has always done, Benjamin rejects the idea of the arbitrary or conventional character of symbols. In *The Origin of German Tragic Drama,* he undertook to show that even allegory, far from being an abstract and purely conventional meaning, is a form of original *expression.* The process of naming or of symbolizing in general preoccupies Benjamin in all his reflections. The central concept of origin and the notion of the prehistoric refer back to the emergence of the symbol from an authentic experience. Benjamin refuses to see the symbol cleanly severed from the symbolized and from experience. "The origin is the goal" because one must always reconnect with the point of emergence. Above all, the enigmatic character of that emergence is tied to the fact that Benjamin deciphers in it both a symbolic process and a historical event of ontological and theological scope: The fact that a symbol comes into being constitutes a caesura in the messianic process of history. If we wish to discern the rational foundation of Benjamin's conception, we have to dissociate it from its roots in the theory of language and in the mystical relation to the object of experience. The work of art is situated at the juncture of these fields, inasmuch as it constitutes a form of symbol that, before being publicly readable, presupposes a *break* with communication, the installation of a new "origin" of language, a "private" symbol, irreducibly unique and new, seeking to have its eloquence acknowledged. The artistic symbol, which might have been madness pure and simple, is rational only through the anticipation of an exemplarity that makes it intelligible, that makes it the object of an experience that can be shared: Its eloquence cannot in fact be acknowledged except inasmuch as the new symbol has the ability to reveal to us a new object of experience and to evoke a new reality that we were not capable of naming. The artistic symbol never fully accedes to the status of abstract and conventional meaning but—in an ever renewed disturbance of codified language—remains linked to its origin in a singular experience to which it bears witness, an individual but historically situated experience, exemplary in the issues it addresses and intelligible for all.

Benjamin, along with Baudelaire, links this experience that is "prior to" the artistic symbol (which refers back to its irreducibly unique origin) to the "Rousseauist" theme of Paradise lost[13]: "The *correspondances* are the data of remembrance—not historical data, but data of prehistory. What makes festive days great and significant is the encounter with an earlier life" (*Illuminations,* 182). Hence the kinship between festive days and works of art; both bring together a singular origin and an actualizing repetition. But, by reason of the historical process of secularization, the "ritual" experience is only the idyllic backdrop against which the contemporary reality of *spleen* or the destruction of the aura stands out: "*Le Printemps adorable a perdu son odeur!*" (Spring, the Beloved, has lost its scent); Benjamin interprets this line using a Proustian vocabulary:

> The scent is the inaccessible refuge of the *mémoire involontaire*. . . . If the recognition of a scent is more privileged to provide consolation than any other recollection, this may be so because it deeply drugs the sense of time. A scent may drown years in the odor it recalls. This gives a sense of measureless desolation to Baudelaire's verse. For someone who is past experiencing, there is no consolation. (*Illuminations,* 184)

Spleen results from the reification of time through the domination of voluntary memory and clock time; for experience, it substitutes the lived experience provoked by the shocks of modern life. According to Benjamin, "Spleen" and "Vie antérieure" are "the scattered fragments of genuine historical experience" (*Illuminations,* 185). True experience is an amalgam of "prehistory" and clock time.

Benjamin applies the results of his examination of experience to the status of the arts of technical reproduction. Photography, the medium of the "optical unconscious" in "The Work of Art," is here an instrument in the service of voluntary memory:

> If we designate as aura the associations which, at home in the *mémoire involontaire,* tend to cluster around the object of a perception, then its analogue in the case of a utilitarian object is the experience which has left traces of the practiced hand. The techniques based on the use of the camera and of subsequent analogous mechanical devices extend the range of the *mémoire volontaire*; by means of these devices they make it possible for an event at any time to be permanently recorded in terms of sound and sight. Thus they represent important achievements of a society in which practice is in decline. (*Illuminations,* 186)

Technology is a stopgap measure allowing us to satisfy a need but not to preserve that vital resource of involuntary memory, the source of the aura. In "The Work of Art," film prevailed over painting, both owing to its ability to penetrate reality like a surgeon and its capacity for satisfying the demand for simultaneous perception by a large audience. Here, painting is rehabilitated; it alone is capable of offering to the gaze that of which our eyes "will never have their fill": "What distinguishes photography from painting is therefore clear, and why there can be no encompassing principle of 'creation' applicable to both: to the eyes that will never have their fill of a painting, photography is rather like food for the hungry or drink for the thirsty" (*Illuminations,* 187).

Painting satisfies infinite desire, whereas photography, according to this text, confines itself to satisfying a need that nothing can further transfigure. As in "The Storyteller," technical reproduction brings only losses:

> The crisis of artistic reproduction which manifests itself in this way can be seen as an integral part of a crisis in perception itself. What prevents our delight in the beautiful from ever being satisfied is the image of the past, which Baudelaire regards as veiled by the tears of nostalgia. . . . Insofar as art aims at the beautiful and, on however modest a scale, "reproduces" it, it conjures it up . . . out of the womb of time. This no longer happens in the case of technical reproduction. (The beautiful has no place in it.) (*Illuminations,* 187)

In "The Work of Art," Benjamin saw this as one of the *contributions* of the arts of technical reproduction, which were emancipated from an appearance linked to cult value. Here, he sees the absence of beauty and of involuntary memory as an insurmountable deficiency of photography. In

"The Work of Art," the anxiety and alienation of the movie actor in front of the lens were compensated for by the reversibility of roles: The difference between author and audience, actor and producer tended to become blurred. Here, Benjamin retains only the inhumanity of photographic equipment: "The camera records our likeness without returning our gaze." This alienation complements that which wrenches the photographic image away from the resources of involuntary memory:

> But looking at someone carries the implicit expectation that our look will be returned by the object of our gaze. Where this expectation is met (which, in the case of thought processes, can apply equally to the look of the eye of the mind and to a glance pure and simple), there is an experience of the aura to the fullest extent. . . . [It] thus rests on the transposition of a response common in human relationships to the relationship between the inanimate or natural object and man. The person we look at, or who feels he is being looked at, looks at us in turn. To perceive the aura of an object we look at means to invest it with the ability to look at us in return. This experience corresponds to the data of the *mémoire involontaire*. (*Illuminations,* 188)

This transposition of intersubjectivity to inanimate nature, adds Benjamin, is "one of the sources of poetry" (*Illuminations,* 189, translation modified). Intersubjectivity and involuntary memory are thus linked through traditional activities. Tradition is transmitted through language or, in a general way, through symbols. Benjamin makes this process enigmatic by attempting to conceive of it in terms of perception and the gaze. The intersubjectivity of the gaze without speech can only be "the observation of an observation." It is thus impossible to enter "into the views" of others and understand them. Revealingly, Benjamin discovers intersubjectivity, which has very little place in his thinking, only through the detour of the mystical or poetic relation to nature; such a relation takes the place of the break in the tie between persons whose gazes no longer respond to one another: Baudelaire "describes eyes of which one is inclined to say that they have lost their ability to look" (*Illuminations,* 189).

Finally, Benjamin once more takes up the theme of the "decline of the aura," this time through Baudelaire and in a manner that differs from his treatment of it in "The Work of Art" and that retrospectively makes it intelligible. In fact, one of the intentions of this last essay on Baudelaire is no doubt to make comprehensible—and perhaps to excuse—the experimental radicality of "The Work of Art." Through the example of Baudelaire, Benjamin attempts to show that the sacrifice of the aura corresponds to a profound necessity of artistic modernity. But this sacrifice must now be inscribed within the very *tradition* of art, instead of moving with weapons and gear into the camp of that barbarous enemy, technical reproduction.

Benjamin thus rediscovers the "decline of the aura" in *The Flowers of Evil* through this theme of "eyes of which one is inclined to say that they have lost their ability to look." These are the eyes of nymphs, which replace the erotic magic of the returned gaze with the simple power of sexual attraction. As in the case of the *passante*, the passerby, Baudelaire has transformed a degraded lived experience into an experience in the full sense of the term. Moreover, like Benjamin, he seems "to feel something like pleasure in the degradation" of the dream (*Illuminations*, 191). Referring to the landscape painting of his day, Baudelaire says he prefers "the backdrop paintings of the stage": "Those things, so completely false, are for that very reason much closer to the truth, whereas the majority of our landscape painters are liars, precisely because they fail to lie" (quoted in *Illuminations*, 191). Benjamin does not attempt to analyze this passage; he simply suggests that Baudelaire "judge[s] landscapes by the standard of paintings in the booths at fairs." In some sense, the poet makes the practical demonstration of the Benjaminian theory of the disenchantment of art. The "magic of distances"—the aura—must be destroyed *in the name of truth*. Landscape paintings are a lie as soon as their supposed aura is a pure fiction. Baudelaire is opposed to an art of nostalgic compensation that would provide a substitute aura in the place of that which was disappearing from reality. For Baudelaire, "the lyric poet with a halo" is "antiquated." In "Perte d'auréole" (Loss of halo), one of the *Petits poèmes en prose* (Short prose poems), he anticipates the degradation to which Dadaism subjects the image of the artist with a halo. In Benjamin's view, this Baudelairean sacrifice corresponds to a profound logic of modern art. In a world in which, according to Apollinaire's title, the poet is "murdered" in the name of the most trivial interests, abandoned and "prodded" by the crowds, that is, by the very people in whose name he rebelled in abandoning the task of leading a life worthy of the name, he refuses to be the provider of a consolatory beauty. He is himself without a halo, and produces an art that sacrifices the halo to truth.

> This is the nature of lived experience to which Baudelaire has given the weight of true experience. He indicated the price for which the sensation of the modern age may be had: the disintegration of the aura in the experience of shock. He paid dearly for consenting to this disintegration—but it is the law of his poetry. (*Illuminations*, 194, translation slightly modified)

Benjamin does not distinguish between auratic beauty and aesthetic value. What matters here is the justification of an aesthetic quality in

Baudelaire's work that no longer has the status of a symptom. The foundation of that poetry is neither "ritual" nor "politics," the choice formulated in "The Work of Art." It resides in an aesthetic authenticity that has vanquished an experience void of substance.

ALLEGORY, AVANT-GARDE, MODERNITY

Even before postmodern thinkers joined the fray, art theory had asked which philosophy best allowed it to account for the artistic avant-garde. Without a doubt, Adorno's ambition in *Aesthetic Theory* was to elaborate the avant-garde's conceptual bases after the fact; his borrowings (at times critical) from Benjamin's thought are considerable. In particular, his focus on the dialectic is more Hegelian. In response, Peter Bürger, drawing support from Benjamin in particular, disputes the pertinence of that philosophy of the avant-garde.[14] Adorno reestablishes the logic of aesthetic autonomy without taking into account the avant-garde critique of the "institution of art" and the project to reintegrate art into everyday life. Albrecht Wellmer might object, to Bürger, that the elimination of autonomy and of aesthetic appearance and the generalized practice of art, required in the mind of the avant-garde, runs the risk of leading to a false egalitarianism; according to Wellmer, it is only at the level of an aesthetics of reception that one can envision a "transformation of the *constellations* in which art and everyday life are found each time."[15]

In German aesthetics, avant-garde movements have been interpreted primarily in the light of the concepts elaborated by Benjamin and Adorno. In France, in contrast, whether or not a particular critic favors the avant-garde, he attempts to understand it through Nietzsche.[16] A philosophical opposition to Nietzsche may bring with it an aesthetics-based hostility to avant-garde art; conversely, "to be avant-garde" amounts to considering Nietzsche's thinking indisputable.

Independent of any particular analysis of an avant-garde moment and its possible presuppositions—Nietzschean, Benjaminian, or Adornian—we must first set aside any confusion due to an inadequate differentiation between the normative bases of philosophy and attempts to account for the most radical artistic movements. Nietzsche makes the sovereignty of modern art the foundation of his philosophical discourse. Inasmuch as that art tends to set aside any criterion *brought in from* the logical or moral order, letting stand only the criteria of force and lived intensity,[17] "truth" is only a vital illusion and the truth of art a tonic lie.[18] For Benjamin and Adorno, in contrast, the "truth content" of the work of art has not lost its logical and ethical stakes. Unlike Nietzsche, these thinkers have a tendency to make the opposite mistake: They refuse to allow for a modern or avant-garde art that would obey a purely aesthetic logic. Where Nietzsche brings philosophy down to the level of a radically differentiated art, in relation both to discursive knowledge and to moral imperatives, Benjamin and Adorno invest art with their own imperatives, truth and justice, which are ultimately *theological.*

It remains to be seen whether the real avant-garde is more of a "Nietzschean" orientation, in the sense of embracing amoralism and throwing out a challenge to discursive knowledge, or of a Benjaminian or Adornian orientation, in the sense of possessing a strong imperative for truth and justice. Along with Kafka, Arnold Schönberg may be among the most enlightening examples of Benjaminian or Adornian orientation[19]—if these artists can really be considered representatives of the avant-garde. There is no doubt that the rejection of traditional harmony has strong ethical resonances for these artists. For them, theology functions as a barrier against a unilateral logic of art. It is not certain, however, that this is true of the other masters of the avant-garde, such as Picasso or Duchamp, Wassily Kandinsky, or Joyce. Each of them had interpreters who were convinced that they had before them the *true* avant-garde art. In any case, all modern art is the field of a polar tension: between a sovereignty of aesthetic logic that no cognitive or moral criterion can arrest, and a totality that would reintegrate these criteria.[20] Benjamin himself knew the temptation of the first of these paths, through romanticism and then surrealism and the cinema. But each time, he rejected this subversion in the name of a *theological* subversion that seeks to be more radical, by postulating, from the disorder it creates, the restoration of an ethical order.

In Benjamin's work, the second tendency takes on successively the forms of an aesthetics of the sublime, a "politicization" of avant-garde art, and a "sacrifice of the aura" in the modern work of art. In every case, art moves away from the trajectory that the spontaneous movement of modernization would impose on it. In situating the break with the aura *within* the work of art and no longer in the move to a postartistic practice that favors only an apprenticeship of perception, the late Benjamin defined the framework within which Adorno's *Aesthetic Theory* would unfold. We do not find a univocal model of what modern art, avant-garde art, or contemporary art should be. The lesson of Benjamin's writings is, rather, that one must be wary of any general model and must adjust theory to phenomena. From *Einbahnstrasse* to "The Work of Art," from surrealism to revolutionary cinema, Benjamin attempts to conceptualize certain avant-garde movements. Beginning with "The Storyteller," he interests himself only in "modern" works of art: In the late reflections on idleness in bourgeois society and its religious counterpart, "study," he links Baudelaire to Kafka (*G.S.,* 1:1175–1180). "On Some Motifs in Baudelaire" abandons any allegorical interpretation of *The Flowers of Evil.* Certain critics have deduced from this that Benjamin, having underscored the difference between baroque allegory and modern allegory in the fragments of "Central Park," had finally abandoned the concept of allegory in relation to Baudelaire.[21] He nevertheless maintained until the end the project of complementing "On Some Motifs in Baudelaire" with other "chapters" of the book, of which the first was to deal with "Baudelaire as allegorist." Allegory, which links revolt to the authoritarian gesture, remains in his view a pertinent response to abstract meaning as it characterizes modernity; through it, a theological promise irrupts in homogeneous and empty time.

More critics, however, have made of allegory the very model for an art that is no longer "organic," that is, for the avant-garde work of art in general.[22] This is hardly defensible. And finally, the method projected for *Paris Arcades*—in particular the "montage" of quotations—has often been considered "allegorical."[23] Certain formal analogies invite such extrapolations: the fragmentary character of allegory; the abstractly superimposed meaning; the melancholic relation to an apocalyptic history; the doubt in relation to the value of art. In addition, allegory, as well as the avant-garde work of art, breaks with the principles of classical art: "Artists who produce an organic work," writes Peter Bürger,

> treat their material as something living. They respect its significance as something that has grown from concrete life situations. For avant-gardistes, on the other hand, material is just that, material. Their activity initially consists in nothing other than in killing the "life" of the material, that is, in tearing it out of its functional context that gives it meaning. Whereas the classicist recognizes and respects in the material the carrier of a meaning, the avant-gardistes see only the empty sign, to which only they can impart significance. The classicist correspondingly treats the material as a whole, whereas the avant-gardiste tears it out of the life totality, isolates it, and turns it into a fragment.[24]

Even if such a distinction between the "classicist" and the contemporary artist can be allowed, it would still be difficult to recognize in the avant-garde artist thus defined a baroque playwright or a Baudelaire. In contrast to baroque art, whose fragmentation is opposed to the harmonious totalities of the Renaissance—and in which the discovery of nonsense threatening an immanence that had become profane was reversed when this empty world was reflected in abstract transcendence—we need to distinguish modern art, which is more internalized, more subjective, more emancipated from representation, and more conscious of its paradoxical social role. Finally, we need to distinguish such modern art, still respectful of the forms transmitted, from an avant-garde art that sovereignly makes use of its material to translate "a derangement of all the senses," an experience radically foreign to everyday perception. Benjamin never pretended to present a theory of allegory in general, or, above all, a theory of modernity or of the avant-garde that would be in the first place a theory of the allegorical form.[25] At the very most, he attempted to explain the resurgence of an undeniably allegorical technique and spirit in Baudelaire's poetry.

In Benjamin's oeuvre, the interest in allegory grows out of an *antimodern* impulse; it is nevertheless inscribed within a movement characteristic of aesthetic modernity. To elucidate the complex relation it entertains with "modernity," we need to recall the overlapping itinerary of his oeuvre. Benjamin begins, first, from a philosophy of language that is biblical in inspiration and opposed to any modern linguistics of the "arbitrariness of the sign," but that refers to the modern poetry of Mallarmé; he begins, second, from the *modern* aesthetics of German romanticism, one of Mallarmé's sources, which had already opposed the vital sources of poetry—which was reestablishing its links to ancestral traditions—to social and scientific modernity. This *aesthetic* modernity seeks precisely to conquer, in the medium of language, the empty abstraction that results from the historical process constitutive of *social* modernity, of desacralization and rationalization. But, at the same time, it is in solidarity with this movement through its tendency toward *disenchantment,* that is, inasmuch as it is opposed to the myth of the harmonious beautiful appearance that conceals the true nature of historical life. The essay on Goethe deploys this double orientation both in its opposition to myth—through the sublime caesura of the work of art—and in the rescue operation of messianic hope in artistic beauty. *Elective Affinities* attempts to undo the myth of the Enlightenment, of modern morality and law, which it denounces as a fabric of illusions and finally as the source of a renewed fall into archaic destiny. Never, then, does Benjamin succeed in perceiving the *modern* complementarity between the radicality of subversive art and that of profane reason.

In his book on tragic drama—which also takes up the polemic among modern, romantic, and idealist aesthetics, which are accused of having misunderstood the theological dimension of allegory and the symbol—allegory crystallizes this double movement. In the end, the destruction of the beautiful appearance and the revelation of the deathly face of history change into a messianic promise: Evil *is only* allegorical, a reflection of the empty world in the plenitude of God. The most disenchanted art, deprived of all the charms of beauty, comes to provide support for a promise of happiness as it is constituted in the profound nature of art. But the theological horizon of the baroque forbids any assimilation between that art and modernity. What is missing from German tragic drama, what keeps it from being modern, is first, the principle of aesthetic autonomy and, second, radical independence from the social powers of the court and the church.

Avant-garde milieux led Benjamin to understand this; he then entered a *second* period in his aesthetic thought. From baroque allegory, he moves not to modernity but to the avant-garde, and especially Dadaism, surrealism, and Brecht's political theater. From a hidden, theological, heteronomy, he turns toward a subversion of aesthetic autonomy in the name of an attempt to integrate art and life. He then sets aside aesthetic value and becomes interested in art's contribution to the apprenticeship of perception among members of a society rich in dangers of every kind. The disenchantment in this case reaches the point of a *destruction* of art. But such a horizon presupposes the promise of a radical change in life itself. Art is sacrificed in the name of exotericism and the social utility of techniques of reproduction.

In the end, overcome by doubt regarding the consequences of a liquidation of tradition, Benjamin turned away from the avant-garde to defend a certain modernity. The avant-garde's rejection of the theological foundations of art could be justified only insofar as it gave birth to a social solidarity that honored theological imperatives. In the absence of such a solidarity, the beautiful remains the essential mediator of a memory of ritual solidarity, in the expectation of secularization. In "The Storyteller," Benjamin underscores the *beauty* of an art condemned to disappear; Baudelaire's oeuvre reveals to him a disenchantment that *preserves* the autonomy of aesthetic form. In this modern work of art, allegory no longer has the sense merely of an irruption of transcendence in the profane world. It fulfills a twofold function, both bursting the harmonious beautiful appearance that a highly pathogenic modern society seeks to bestow on itself, and safeguarding, in the autonomy of the work of art, the promise of happiness constitutive of art.

The promise of happiness is inherent in the heroic effort through which artistic modernity, particularly in allegory, is related to the greatness of ancient art. This effort consists in transforming into "true experience" the vulgar and humiliating sensations that make up the daily life of modernity. When Baudelaire addressed the *"hypocrite lecteur,"* his *"semblable,"* his *"frère,"* the intimate enemy of poetry and nonetheless his accomplice whom he cannot do without, he "indicated the price for which the sensation of the modern age may be had: the disintegration of the aura in the experience of shock" (*Illuminations,* 194). In opening the abyss between daily experience and the autonomous law of the work of art that no longer represents it, the aesthetic shock of the modern work of art also denounces any reconciliation with a social world that is itself unreconciled.[26] Aesthetic autonomy and the shocking break with a trivial world are only two faces of a single logic that, unable to pursue the escalation of shocks, at every moment risks making modern art veer toward its self-dissolution. "What guarantees the authentic quality of modern works of art?" asks Adorno. "It is the scars of damage and disruption inflicted by them on the smooth surface of the immutable. Explosion is one of the invariable traits of art, whose anti-traditional energy becomes a voracious eddy that consumes everything. To that extent modernism is myth turned against itself."[27] To a great extent, this process is due to a confusion between the medium of experience proper to art, and the imperative for truth that is traditionally associated with it; the destruction of harmony, of appearance, of totality is a subversion only of a traditional form of the medium of artistic experience, not of the medium itself.

Like Benjamin, Adorno shrinks from the radicality of contemporary art because he is seeking in it the guarantees of a concept of truth that transcends the limits of reason. Yet, inasmuch as philosophy has managed to establish the autonomy of the debate on truth, independent of the criteria provided by the most significant works of art, contemporary art has also liberated itself from the constraints that the avant-garde imperative for truth imposed upon it.

✳

History, Politics, Ethics

THE EPISTEMOLOGY OF PARIS ARCADES

Benjamin consigned his ideas on history to a folder entitled "Re the Theory of Knowledge, Theory of Progress": He published a few elements of them—excluding, however, the "theological" aspects—in his 1937 essay "Eduard Fuchs, Collector and Historian."[1] In January 1939, while reworking his essay on Baudelaire into "On Some Motifs in Baudelaire," he announced to Horkheimer that he was beginning a new overall plan for *Charles Baudelaire*

> from the viewpoint of the theory of knowledge. At the same time, what is becoming important is the concept of history and the role progress plays in it. The act of destroying the representation of a continuum of culture, a destruction postulated in the essay on Fuchs, must have consequences for the theory of knowledge. One of the most important of these seems to be to determine the limits within which the concept of progress can be used in history. (*G.S.*, 1:1225, letter of January 1939)

A year later, another letter announced the provisional completion of the "Theses on the Philosophy of History":

> I have just completed a certain number of theses on the concept of History. They are linked to views outlined in chapter 1 of "Fuchs" but should also serve as a theoretical armature for the second essay on Baudelaire. They represent a first attempt to set down an aspect of history that can establish an irremediable scission between our way of seeing things and the relics of positivism which, in my view, so profoundly mark even those concepts of History that in themselves are the closest and most

familiar to us. (*G.S.*, 1:1225, letter in French to Horkheimer, 22 February 1940)

Benjamin adds that these texts not only represent the already announced introduction to the *Paris Arcades* project—or to *Charles Baudelaire*, which was excerpted from it—but also attest to the fact that he felt moved "by the theoretical problems that the world situation unavoidably presents us with" (*G.S.*, 1:1226).[2] In April 1940, he explained to Gretel Adorno that the theses would reveal the long-standing foundations of his thought. Thesis 17 seemed particularly important to him, since it "ought to make the hidden but conclusive tie appear between these reflections and my earlier work, whose method it succinctly announces." And he added: "The war and the constellation from which it developed have led me to put on paper a few thoughts, which I can say I have kept to myself, even kept before me, for nearly twenty years" (*G.S.*, 1:1226). Benjamin was no doubt alluding to the theological ideas whose open expression he had set aside when he began to place his thinking within a materialist framework—not for twenty years, but for about fifteen; what went back twenty years was the apocalyptic perspective of the "Theologico-Political Fragment."

His first theological writings had represented a break with university neo-Kantianism. In a sense, the return to those themes was provoked by the analogy—through the idea of progress—between that neo-Kantianism and a certain Marxist and social democratic tradition. Numerous neo-Kantians—in the drafts of the "Theses" we find the names "Schmidt and Stadler, Natorp and Vorländer" (*G.S.*, 1:1231)—were in fact eminent social democrats. As in his youth, then, Benjamin felt the need to mark a radical break, not this time with neo-Kantianism but with an ossified Marxism; and once more, theology seemed to him to offer the means for such a break.

However, he ruled out the possibility of publication, which, he felt, could not fail to elicit "enthusiastic misunderstandings" (*G.S.*, 1:1227, letter to Gretel Adorno, n.d. [April 1940]). He probably feared such misunderstandings above all from those of his friends who had established their solidarity with the U.S.S.R. and who, it seemed to him, would have had a hard time accepting his return to theological themes and categories. In fact, however, Bertolt Brecht, whose reaction he seemed to fear, received this text very favorably, though with some reservations (*G.S.*, 1:1227, excerpt from Brecht). It is true, however, that Brecht read it only after learning of Benjamin's death. Another reason for Benjamin's reluctance to publish the "Theses" may have been his awareness that he had not reached a definitive formulation. The theses are presented in no set order, with no sequential argument. Certain of them intersect; others have an elaborately literary form and can be read in various ways. They are more like formulas and formulations to which he had become attached, even though they were redundant from the theoretical point of view. He wrote them down so as to see clearly into his own thinking, but they did not yet allow him to explain his thoughts to others. Nor can they serve as a basis for a theoretical elaboration. Hence we can give only hypothetical interpretations of them.

It was just before the *Paris Arcades* project in its "materialist" form that, for the first time, Benjamin called himself a "historian" rather than a "critic." *Paris Arcades* was an attempt to provoke a "historical awakening" through a criticism of the nineteenth century, whose impact was still being felt. Benjamin seemed to realize that his philosophy of language did not in itself allow him to ground the sociological and historical research he had undertaken. In 1935, he felt the need to elaborate, as a function of the *Paris Arcades* project, something equivalent to the "epistemo-critical prologue" that had served as an introduction to *The Origin of German Tragic Drama*. "Whereas the baroque book mobilized its own theory of knowledge, this will be the case for *Arcades* at least to the same extent" (*Correspondence,* 482).

The figure of the historian took shape with "The Storyteller" when Benjamin, revising the notion of "liquidation" proclaimed in "The Work of Art," reintroduced the concepts of tradition and memory. The historian thus emerged bearing the "theological" features of the "chronicler," who, according to Benjamin, is the precursor of modern historiography:

> The historian is bound to explain in one way or another the happenings with which he deals; under no circumstances can he content himself with displaying them as models of the course of the world. But this is precisely what the chronicler does, especially in his classical representatives, the chroniclers of the Middle Ages, the precursors of the historians of today. By basing their historical tales on a divine plan of salvation—an inscrutable one—they have from the very start lifted the burden of demonstrable explanation from their own shoulders. Its place is taken by interpretation, which is not concerned with an accurate concatenation of definite events, but with the way these are embedded in the great inscrutable course of the world. (*Illuminations,* 96)

Just as he had little appreciation for the modern novelist, Benjamin was suspicious of the rational historian who "explained" events in terms of causality and motivation instead of presenting them as significant illustrations of the "history of nature." Far from converting to an explanatory approach, the "historian" of the "Theses on the Philosophy of History" inherited certain qualities from the chronicler:

> A chronicler who recites events without distinguishing between major and minor ones acts in accordance with the following truth: nothing that

has ever happened should be regarded as lost for history. To be sure, only a redeemed mankind receives the fullness of its past—which is to say, only for a redeemed mankind has its past become citable in all its moments. Each moment it has lived becomes a *citation à l'ordre du jour*—and that day is Judgment Day. (*Illuminations,* 254; E.F., 340)[3]

For Benjamin, the chronicler remains the model for the historian: Both theological and materialist history considers events from the point of view of a decisive deliverance. In giving narrative history precedence over explanatory history, Benjamin emancipates historiography from any scientific character, since he suspects the "science" of history of having empathy for and systematic complacency with regard to the victor. Between historicism and a history written from a messianic perspective, he sees little place for a critical historiography.

History is always both an act of narration in relation to a determined horizon of interest into which the past is reappropriated and an orientation in relation to theoretical imperatives, without which the selection of material to be transmitted could only be arbitrary.[4] Benjamin pushes the break with historicism to the point of a break with scientific history. He cites Nietzsche's *The Use and Abuse of History*: "We need history, but not the way a spoiled loafer in the garden of knowledge needs it" (quoted in *Illuminations,* 260; E.F., 345). Benjamin is not simply aiming for a history that has been reappropriated from a "living" perspective. He thinks that the vital interest of history is linked to the point of view of the social class that, in each instance, carries the torch of emancipation. The problem, then, is to ascertain whether it is possible to write history from the point of view of the "struggling class" by gaining access in a single stroke to the "truly universal" viewpoint of the chronicle or of messianic history. It is only in this case that the difference between historiography and the narrative prose of the chronicler would disappear.[5] In contrast, if the "virtually universal class" is only a theoretical construct, then that difference is insurmountable and the tension between historical objectivity and narrative identity remains. If the history of the oppressed can no more gain access to the perspective of the ideal chronicler than can a history that adopts the point of view of the bourgeoisie, then scientific explanation, the confrontation of arguments, is the only method capable of settling once and for all the divergent interests of different identities.

THEOLOGY AND MATERIALISM

In Benjamin's later works the theory of history occupies the place that, in his earlier writings, fell to the philosophy of language. Certain structural analogies are evident. The theory of the name as absolute expression or revelation, as it was developed in "On Language as Such," is opposed to a "bourgeois" linguistics of "abstract meaning," of the word considered as an arbitrary sign (*Reflections*, 318); in the same way, the mimetic and "materialist" theory of language as the "onomatopoeia" of a "nonsensuous similarity" between language and world is opposed to a conception of language as "a conventional system of signs" (*Reflections*, 334). In the "Theses," this corresponds to a theory of the present as "the 'time of the now' which is shot through with chips of Messianic time" (*Illuminations*, 263) as opposed to a conception of history as a "homogeneous, empty time" (*Illuminations*, 261; see discussion 261–264). In each case, a substance is substituted for a function, a living presence for an abstraction, a false homogeneity, or a void. What characterizes both the power of the name in the philosophy of language and the power of seizing the now, of apprehending the constellation between the present era and "a definite earlier one" (*Illuminations*, 263), is the break with a process of degradation, falsifying abstraction, and banalization—a true original sin affecting the authenticity, the "origin" of language or of history—and the will to reconquer the "intensive totality" (*Reflections*, 318) of a practical and immediate relation to the natural and human world. Benjamin is linked to a tradition of thought that suspects Western rationalism of impoverishing and devitalizing the original substances of culture. Unlike Hegel, he does not think that reason possesses within itself the resources that would allow it to correct its defects; what distinguishes him from Nietzsche is that, to find a corrective for disastrous abstraction, he attempts to return not to an irrational "pre-Socratic" foundation but to one of the *sources* of this rationalism, namely, biblical thought.

At both the beginning and the end of his career, Benjamin seeks to reappropriate an alienated part of redemptive forces. Certain fragments among the drafts of the "Theses" attempt to show that the concept of history could, so to speak, substitute for that of language in its foundational role:

> The messianic world is the world of universal and full actuality. It is only in it that there will be a universal history. What today bears that name can only be a kind of Esperanto. Nothing can correspond to it as long as the confusion brought on by the Tower of Babel is not eliminated. [That universal history] presupposes the language in which one could fully translate any text of a language, living or dead. Or better, it is that language itself. But not as written language: rather as a language celebrated as a holiday. Such a holiday is purified of any solemnity; it knows nothing of song. Its language is the idea of prose itself and is understood by all men, just as babies born on Sunday understand the language of birds. (*G.S.*, 1:1239)[6]

The ideas of "The Task of the Translator," taken up again in "The Story-teller," form the link between the theory of language and the theory of a universal, messianic history. The hermeneutics of translation must allow one to reach an integral actuality both of transmitted meaning and of the forgotten past, that of oppressed and vanquished humanity.

Just as the philosophy of art was in Benjamin's early works linked to a theological critique of myth and violence, the philosophy of history is, in Benjamin's late works, placed under the sign of "theology." The famous apologue that opens the "Theses on the Philosophy of History" confines itself to affirming theology's secret and indispensable role: historical mate-rialism, compared to a chess-playing automaton, cannot "win" without the help of a "theological" philosophy whose services it enlists. This means that "materialism" is in the end a mechanistic philosophy. As such, it is indispensable, of course: "Seek for food and clothing first," says Benjamin with Hegel, "then the Kingdom of God shall be added to you" (Quoted in *Illuminations*, 254). But it has no living soul.

Must *theology* breathe life into it? In other words, is theology the only means to correct mechanistic materialism? To that question, Benjamin responds with a reflection borrowed from a syncretist philosopher from the nineteenth century, Hermann Lotze: " 'One of the most remarkable charac-teristics of human nature,' writes Lotze, 'is, alongside so much selfishness in specific instances, the freedom from envy which the present displays toward the future' " (*Illuminations*, 253; *E.F.*, 339ff.).[7] For Benjamin, this self-sufficiency of the present is the starting point for a consideration of history. He deduces from it the need to turn to theology to conceive history and, to that end, introduces the notion of *happiness* to complement that of *envy* introduced by Lotze:

> Reflection shows us that our image of happiness is thoroughly colored by the time to which the course of our own existence has assigned us. The kind of happiness that could arouse envy in us exists only in the air we have breathed, among people we could have talked to, women who could have given themselves to us. In other words, our image of happiness is indissolubly bound up with the image of redemption. The same applies to our view of the past, which is the concern of history. The past carries with it a temporal index by which it is referred to redemption. [The image of salvation is its key. Does not the air breathed by the deceased of earlier times still hang about us somewhat? Do not the voices of our friends sometimes hauntingly echo the voices of those who walked upon the earth before us? And is the beauty of women of another age so unlike that of our lady friends? It thus falls to us to realize that the past calls for redemption, the tiniest part of which may be within our power.] (*Illuminations*, 253–254; *E.F.*, 340; the bracketed section does not appear in the English edition)

Not only does Lotze speak only implicitly of happiness, but he speaks neither of salvation nor of theology. Another fragment of his book, cited among the fragments of *Paris Arcades,* indicates the sense of his reflection: "Whatever its various movements," Lotze writes, "history cannot reach a destination that does not lie within its own plane, and we will save ourselves the trouble of searching for progress in the duration of history, since history is not fated to make such progress longitudinally, but rather in an upward direction at every single one of its points" ("N" 13a, 2, p. 72). Fundamentally, Lotze is speaking of the rather trivial and widespread idea that true "progress" belongs not to humanity as a whole but only to the fulfilled individual, whatever his era. According to Lotze, such "spiritual" fulfillment does not stem from a linear progress of history but from a "vertical" progression that everyone should seek to realize by his or her own means. What Benjamin means is quite different. Like Lotze, he is convinced that fulfillment, the happiness of each individual in every age, is independent of progress. But unlike Lotze, he thinks that fulfillment is the object of a messianic expectation for *redemption* that each generation transmits to the following one, without its progressive realization being possible: "There is a secret agreement between past generations and the present one. Our coming was expected on earth. Like every generation that preceded us, we have been endowed with a *weak* Messianic power, a power to which the past has a claim" (*Illuminations,* 254; *E.F.,* 340). If we were expected by our ancestors, according to Benjamin, it is to redeem a part of the happiness they could not achieve. Every human generation is confronted with the *same* quest for fulfillment. The preceding generation does not envy us because it cannot imagine what happiness would be in a different context, but it expects something from us; it even has a *right* to our redemptive power, according to Benjamin. How so? Benjamin does not say. He simply evokes a profound *kinship* among the air, the timbre of voices, the beauty of the past, and those whom we know. The happiness we seek is of the same nature as the happiness that earlier generations dreamed of. They expected it and sought it *in the same way* we do and transmitted that quest to us, by virtue of what was granted or refused them. Such would be our debt.

This passage is a good indication of the modifications Benjamin's thought has undergone. The critique of the ideology of progress is by no means a new element (it was already in his earliest writings), and texts such as "The Work of Art" stem in a certain way from that ideology by granting to *technical* progress a key role in the history of humanity. In "Central Park," we find a fragment that tells the dialectician to "have the wind of world-history in [his] sails. Thinking means for him: setting the sails" ("Central Park," 44). The "Theses" represent a break in that confidence in the wind of history—the "wind of the absolute," according to another fragment ("N" 9, 3, p. 63). The *"weak* Messianic power" of which the "Theses" speak is linked more to an *ethics* of solidarity than to a *philosophy of history* in the sense usually given that term (which is the sense of Marxism as well); this sense accords a determinate, precise meaning to the "wind," the general dynamic of history. When the "Theses" evoke the wind, it is a "storm" identified with progress, which is only an accumulation of ruins and catastrophes; nonetheless, that storm blows "from Paradise." This evil wind prevents the historian—or "the angel of history"—from being able to "stay, awaken the dead, and make whole what has been smashed" (*Illuminations*, 257), in other words, to do the work of redemption. It is no longer a question here of setting sail. To follow the ethical impulse of rescue and reparation, the historian must be emancipated from the hold of that catastrophic push, which seems to be due to the very dynamic of Creation. Humanity must go against the historical movement, and perhaps, in a gnostic sense, against God. The weak messianic power on which humanity counts is the force of *individuals* who seek to satisfy the expectation for happiness, which, until now, has been betrayed throughout the course of history and on which the past has a claim.

Benjamin cannot imagine—and this is precisely what his rejection of the notion of progress consists in—a gradual modification. He does not conceive of historical transformations under the sign, for example, of a fragile "democratization" such as has taken shape in certain parts of the world since World War II—without, obviously, bringing about universal happiness. He would have assimilated this type of change, encumbered by compromise and half-measures, to the compromises of "social democracies" that certain of the "Theses" place on the pillory of history. This is because, on the one hand, he identifies *true* progress—which has not yet begun—with the advent of a happiness without compromise, though it is not certain whether it is historically realizable; on the other, he situates continuous "progress" in a purely empirical dimension. These two options are complementary: Both oppose a conception that would confine itself to aspiring toward a maximum of *conditions* for happiness and would situate "progress" in the dimension of a *normative apprenticeship* for humanity. Whatever the historical underside to democracy, its gains, once realized, can never be forgotten. Anything beyond objectives of this type can only stem from a "theological" aspiration or, perhaps, from an imaginary and artistic quest.

BENJAMIN'S POLITICS

The notion of *justice*, which could have legitimately appeared alongside happiness as the object of human desire, appears in the "Theses" only as a general *vengeance* of the oppressed classes. Benjamin turns to Marx to contrast materialism to a political idealism concerned for the happiness of "liberated grandchildren." This materialism serves as the mouthpiece for the "last of the enslaved classes," "the avenger that completes the task of liberation in the name of generations of the downtrodden" (*Illuminations,* 260; *E.F.,* 345). Such would ultimately be the sense of "law" that the vanquished generations of the past would set up for us. Their accumulated desire for vengeance would be translated into "hatred" and the "spirit of sacrifice" (*Illuminations,* 260):

> Both are nourished by the image of enslaved ancestors rather than that of liberated grandchildren. [Our generation has learned it the hard way, since the only image it will leave behind is that of a vanquished generation. That will be its only legacy to those who are to come.] (*Illuminations,* 260; *E.F.,* 345)[8]

These ideas of vengeance and hatred, which are among the most unpleasant and embarrassing aspects of the text, can be explained by Benjamin's refusal to make the struggle for justice and happiness a lasting one. Marx could still reject hatred as the driving power for revolution.[9] To the extent that Benjamin denounces confidence in the "process of natural history" (another name for progress), he reintroduces not the imperative for justice and legitimacy (needless to say, this would have been easier to do in a more peaceful context) but hatred and the desire for vengeance as the driving force of social revolution. Among the notes for the "Theses," we find this: "Critique of the theory of progress in Marx. Progress is defined there as the development of productive forces. Man—in other words, the proletariat—is part of it. But the question of criterion is merely displaced thereby" (*G.S.,* 1:1239).[10] The rights of past generations—vanquished generations like Benjamin's own—would thus extend to vengeance for past suffering.

We can easily imagine what a revolution of this kind would look like: It would be a massacre, as certain revolutions have in fact brought. Rather disagreeably, Benjamin's position here recalls the Nietzschean verdict on a socialism founded on resentment; this was *not* in Marx's theory. In any case, it cannot be a question of opposing to Benjamin's position a Marxian version of the theory of progress; he criticized the theory of progress for the good reason that he was deprived of the resources needed to have confidence in the march of history. Everything indicates, however, that *this form* of revenge for past suffering can only prolong the list of injustices committed and thus reproduce once more the desire for vengeance, ad infinitum.[11] Beyond the imperative for justice, Benjamin mobilizes passions for dispensing justice that have no rationale outside certain extreme situations of legitimate defense. To be precise—and in this Benjamin is consistent—he formulates his idea of vengeance within the perspective of a "permanent state of emergency":

> The tradition of the oppressed teaches us that the "state of emergency" in which we live is not the exception but the rule. We must attain to a conception of history that is in keeping with this insight. Then we shall clearly realize that it is our task to bring about a real state of emergency, and this will improve our position in the struggle against Fascism. (*Illuminations*, 257)

The recourse to an authoritarian policy, indissociable from the concept of the state of emergency forged by Carl Schmitt, is understandable within the desperate context of triumphant Nazism in Europe; but, contrary to what Benjamin's formulation implies, it cannot be generalized beyond that situation. If the state of emergency is the rule, then the only sensible policy is the worst-case policy. In the 1970s, the ethics of certain terrorist groups grew out of this despair; they described Western capitalist societies as fascist regimes, against which they attempted to "bring about a real state of emergency." When Benjamin's oeuvre was enjoying its greatest political influence, it was in the name of a *false* actualization. Whatever the ambiguities of postwar European regimes, their constitutions are those of states of law and do not rest on naked violence and oppression. We must be able to differentiate between fascist regimes and democratic regimes that include certain class privileges: Benjamin's thinking does not allow us to do so. The terrorist violence that has struck those regimes has mistaken its target, and, far from redeeming the suffering undergone by the victims of the preceding generation, has only created new injustices.

As a complement to the voluntarism of the state of emergency "brought about" through an instrumental conception of politics, the "Theses," in negating the possibility of gradual change, formulate a reduction of historical time to a scientist representation. Benjamin defends this way of thinking, which shrinks from participation in lived time by adopting the point of view of Sirius, in the name of theological messianism:

> "In relation to the history of organic life on earth," writes a modern biologist, "the paltry fifty millennia of *homo sapiens* constitute something like two seconds at the close of a twenty-four-hour day. On this scale, the history of civilized man would fill one-fifth of the last second of the last hour." The present, which, as a model of Messianic time, comprises the entire history of mankind in an enormous abridgement, coincides exactly with the stature which the history of mankind has in the universe. (*Illuminations*, 263; *E.F.*, 347)

This analogy between two abridgements is fallacious. The historian's "present" does not entail any objectification as in physics; it is intrinsically linked by a thousand ties to the particular moments of a history in which its perspective is always partial, indissociable from the problems of its era. Benjamin suggests here that the messianic point of view, which brings about the true state of emergency, would succeed in embracing in a single glance the totality of history and in settling once and for all the problem of historical objectivity. Such a pretension is just as fallacious as that which he criticizes in the "universal history" of historicism.

A thesis added as Appendix B also deals with the notion of the instant, this time explaining messianic time in terms of the Jewish tradition. In opposition to the mythical time of seers who claim to predict the future, there stands a future in which "every second of time was the strait gate through which the Messiah might enter" (*Illuminations*, 264). Benjamin defends this Jewish tradition as a theory of history turned primarily toward the past. To be precise, "the Torah and prayers" teach the Jews "remembrance" (*Illuminations*, 264), interpreted in this case as the memory of an "oppressed past." Judaism thus symbolizes a mode of thought that is not prisoner to the fetishism of the future characteristic of the modern cult of progress, which is a secularization of Christian millennialism. Judaism's expectation of the Messiah, which fills all future time, is converted into a presence of mind grasping the "revolutionary chance" (*Illuminations*, 263; *E.F.*, 347). Whatever the legitimacy of such an interpretation, which makes the historian's vigilant intervention the key to the present and to the future, it characterizes through and through the short-circuit between theology and revolutionary politics that is the mark of the "Theses."

Four theses (10–13) are devoted to the "fundamental vices of leftist politics" (*E.F.*, 344; this expression is not in the English version). They interrupt the philosophical series of passages dedicated to the critique of historicism and the exposition of the historian's method. As in 1914, when neo-Kantianism transformed itself into German nationalism, Benjamin again turned to theology following a betrayal:

> At a moment when the politicians in whom the opponents of Fascism had placed their hopes are prostrate and confirm their defeat by betraying their own cause, these observations are intended to disentangle the political worldlings from the snares in which the traitors have entrapped them. (*Illuminations*, 258)

These remarks have often been read as a reaction to the German–Soviet pact.[12] In fact, at the end of the 1930s, they could hardly have applied to anything but the U.S.S.R. and Western Communist parties; at the time, the social democrats no longer existed as a political force.[13] According to other interpreters, these reflections are general. In his letters, Benjamin had already expressed the same idea regarding the Front Populaire.[14] The "leftist politics" of his age appeared to him as the continuation of a confidence in progress that went back to nineteenth-century historicism. In particular, it was founded on the conviction that "moving with the current" (*Illuminations*, 258) by virtue of technological development would automatically bring about social progress owing to a boundless exploitation of nature, and, as a result, it allowed the hope of a better future for one's grandchildren. It is to this conception of history that Benjamin opposes his ideas—which are just as problematic—of combative hatred and vengeance for past suffering (Thesis 12). He plausibly proposes to distinguish between the progress of humanity and that of its aptitudes and knowledge; at the same time, he disputes the boundless and irresistible character of progress. These remarks are compatible with a nonempirical conception of history that sets the real dynamic against a logic of evolution.[15]

But what Benjamin criticizes above all is the notion of *time* that underlies the social democratic ideology and that leads him to the heart of his reflection: "The concept of the historical progress of mankind cannot be sundered from the concept of its progression through a homogeneous, empty time. A critique of the concept of such a progression must be the basis of any criticism of the concept of progress itself" (*Illuminations*, 261). The concept of time characteristic of historicism would be identical to that of the social democrats: Benjamin's essential thesis is that the concept of "homogeneous, empty time," the linear time of immanence, is opposite to the idea of "fulfilled time," which historical materialism itself must borrow from "theology," lest it fall into the ideology of progress. At the level of history, this is the equivalent of the language of the name opposed to abstract meaning.

Inasmuch as the "task of liberation" was far from taking shape at the time of the "Theses," there remained, as the concrete element of deliverance, only the act of the historian who redeems a past threatened with forgetting or misunderstanding. Benjamin identifies that act—fundamentally, the act of the critic establishing a correspondence with a revealing past—with revolutionary action itself. Among the different versions of the theses, we find this:

> In reality, there exists not a single instant that does not entail *its* revolutionary chance—we must simply define it as a specific chance, in other words, the chance for a completely new solution in the face of a completely new task. For the revolutionary thinker, the political situation reinforces the revolutionary chance of every historical instant. But this chance is also reinforced for him through the power of the keys that allow him at that instant to enter an entirely determinate room of the past that has been closed until now. Entering that room is rigorously

identical to political action; and it reveals that action—however destructive it might be—as a messianic action. (*G.S.,* 1:1231)

What is unfulfilled in human lives, "everything about history that,
from the very beginning, has been untimely, sorrowful, unsuccessful"
(*Origin,* 166), cannot be redeemed by the progress of future generations, but
only—in the absence of a decisive revenge of the oppressed—by a recollection, which it is the historian's task to elicit. Benjamin considers all his work
just such a "theological" recollection, which saves certain essential fragments of the past from the "oppression" of forgetting or deformation. When
no other action is possible—such as, for example, the positive formulation
of a criticism addressing the overestimation of the impact the historian can
hope for—there remains the force of thought: "Every line we succeed in
publishing today—no matter how uncertain the future to which we entrust
it—is a victory wrenched from the powers of darkness." (*Correspondence,* 623,
letter of 11 January 1940).

THE HISTORIAN'S METHOD

For Benjamin, the issue is to save *certain* concealed meanings capable of
revealing the present to itself and of guiding decisive action, which will put
an end to all oppression. It is uncertain whether we can confer on such an
undertaking the *systematic* place of conserving the semantic potentials
necessary for the hermeneutic renewal of meaning.[16] Benjamin's project
abandons, without regret, entire vistas of transmitted meanings. Each time
he seeks to rediscover the authentic meaning of the romantic criticism of
Elective Affinities, for example, or of baroque allegory, or Baudelaire's poetry,
he undertakes to save some *threatened* meaning that forms a precise constellation with a critical experience of the present. In his last period, he attempts
to erect *that* operation of the critic into revolutionary action par excellence.
Now the critic's task is a matter not of simply transferring into the world
of Ideas fragments of a literary heritage that have been excluded from it but,
rather, of intervening in history by discovering certain concealed meanings
that appear highly illuminating to the critic and vital for the era. It entails
conferring an immediate *political* function on the critic's activity.

Like Karl Kraus, who is in fact cited in an epigraph to Thesis 14,
Benjamin's historian wants to *cite* the past from the viewpoint of the Last
Judgment; he wants to "call the past by its name." To write history from
this perspective is an exercise in view of the final "chronicle" that, according
to Thesis 3, can cite the past "in all its moments." He wants to write history
from the inaccessible point of view of the last historian, from the point of
view of the "end of history." Hence his claim to an objectification that is at

once scientistic and messianic. But the interest of the Benjaminian theory
of history resides primarily in his effort to formulate his own critical
approach. The exposition of this approach is distributed throughout a
number of aphorisms in the "Theses" themselves, in the draft notes, and in
the series of posthumous fragments dealing with the theory of knowledge
in *Paris Arcades*. We can distinguish three moments in these writings, each
with a different commentary attached: first, the analysis of the conditions
of the instant, "the now," when *historical knowledge is possible,* conditions that
stem from a (Freudian or Proustian) theory of memory and a (Marxian)
theory of class consciousness; second, the analysis of the nature of the
dialectical image, as it is presented to the historian who fulfills these
conditions; and third, the construction of the historical object as *monad*. Of
these central concepts, the first two do not figure in the "Theses" as such
but are implicitly present and can be reconstituted from variants.

The Sociopsychological Conditions of Historical Knowledge

Regarding the "refined and spiritual" things that intervene in the social
struggles for "crude and material" things, Thesis 4 evokes courage, humor,
cunning, and fortitude. These qualities, according to Benjamin, are not
exhausted in the present: "They have retroactive force and will constantly
call in question every victory, past and present, of the rulers. As flowers turn
toward the sun, by dint of a secret heliotropism the past strives to turn
toward that sun which is rising in the sky of history" (*Illuminations,* 255;
E.F., 341).

In addition to the transmission of the *"weak* Messianic power," this
"heliotropism" is another indication of a link existing between past and
present experiences. In the first case, an expectation for deliverance was
transmitted to us; here, it is rather a questioning of the past by the present.
But in both cases, the present is the place for redemptions, the imperative
for which traverses history. More precisely—such is the meaning of "heliotropism"—each present is challenged by a determined past that it echoes
and whose knowledge is reserved for it. That is what Benjamin calls the
"now of its possible knowledge":

> According to its broader determination, the image of the past that flashes
> up for a fleeting moment in the now of its possible knowledge is a
> memory image. It resembles images from a man's own past that appear
> to him at the moment of danger. We know that these images arise
> unbidden. History in the strict sense is thus an image from involuntary
> memory, an image that suddenly presents itself to the subject of history
> at the moment of danger. The historian's legitimacy depends on his keen

consciousness of the crisis that the subject of history is encountering each time. This subject is far from being a transcendental subject; it is the struggling class, the oppressed class in the most exposed situation. There is historical knowledge only for it and for it only in the historical instant. (*G.S.*, 1:1243)

This brief synthesis establishes a link between the aspects of Proustian memory (applied to the collectives of history), the instant (that is, the temporality of knowledge), the danger (which both legitimates and motivates the interest in knowing), and the historical subject. Can the Proustian (and Freudian, according to the Benjaminian interpretation) concept of *involuntary memory,* which was one of the theoretical foundations of "On Some Motifs in Baudelaire," be extended beyond individual biography to the social groups engaged in historical processes? Can what the historian remembers at the critical moment be taken for such a memory? For that to be the case, there would have to be, as Benjamin had supposed in his 1935 Exposé of *Paris Arcades*, a "collective unconscious." Yet, although collective acts of forgetting may exist, inasmuch as the members of a group—individually—have an interest in not remembering certain facts, is it plausible to speak of an "involuntary memory" at the social level?

Such is in any case Benjamin's wager. His historical reflection is founded on the idea of a *reawakening*, a form of disenchantment that converts the dream, the nightmare, or the myth of the past into a knowledge allowing one to lucidly confront the present and the future. That ambitious operation is designated "the *Copernican revolution in the vision of history*" (*G.S.*, 5:490, my emphasis) and thus, according to the sense of the Kantian expression, as the recentering of history around the subjective conditions of knowledge:

> We considered the "Then" a fixed point and we thought the present was tiptoeing toward the knowledge of that fixed element. Now this relation must reverse itself and the Then become a dialectical reversal and an irruption of awakened consciousness. Politics now takes precedence over history. Facts become something that have only just struck us this very instant, and establishing them is the stuff of remembrance. (*G.S.*, 5:490–491)

That Copernican revolution in the vision of history thus frees us from the requirement of establishing a chimerical "truth" about past events; what matters is the vital significance of these events for our present and for the interest that such a rediscovered past represents under different auspices.

According to other fragments, the contemporary age seems to have a particularly good chance of experiencing such a Copernican revolution. For the knowledge of the past to necessarily have the character of a reawakening, the continuity between past and present must be pathologically broken. That seems to be the case for the current era. For Benjamin, as we have seen, the current era is hardly distinguishable from the "state of emergency" that the historical process has always been, but it may offer a new chance for knowledge. When "the prehistorical impulse to the past . . . is no longer hidden, as it once was, by the tradition of church and family" ("N" 2a, 2, p. 49), the past takes on a prematurely obsolete, archaic aspect and elicits a "surrealist" gaze (*G.S.*, 5:493). At the same time, the historian is transformed into a "ragpicker" who collects castoffs the way the psychoanalyst gathers the "residue" of the phenomenal world that has been deposited in dreams:

> Method of this project: literary montage. I need say nothing. Only exhibit [*zeigen*]. I won't filch anything of value or appropriate any ingenious turns of phrase. Only the trivia, the trash—which I don't want to inventory, but simply allow it to come into its own in the only way possible: by putting it to use. ("N" 1a, 8, p. 47)

For Benjamin, this means fanning the spark of hope, saving what has been forgotten or set aside in the name of the new. But it also means bringing about an awakening. In that spirit, the actualization of the obsolete past "lights a fuse of the explosive that is buried in the Then (and whose authentic figure is *fashion*). To thus approach the Then means to study, not as in the past historically, but politically, with political categories" (*G.S.*, 5:495). The "Copernican revolution in the vision of history" is once more placed under the double sign of *messianic* remembrance of the expectations of the past and a *surrealist* gaze on a past that has prematurely fallen into ruins through the decline of tradition. That double inspiration, linked to the rejection of the idea of progress, determines the *instantaneous* nature of remembrance. According to Thesis 5,

> The true picture of the past flits by. The past can only be seized as an image which flashes up at the instant when it can be recognized and is never seen again. . . . For every image of the past that is not recognized by the present as one of its own concerns threatens to disappear irretrievably. (*Illuminations*, 255)

This conception is linked to that of involuntary memory. It presupposes that the *instant* of possible knowledge is extremely fleeting, both because of the continuity of forgetting and oppression and because of the modern discontinuity with tradition. It is hardly possible to verify such an assertion. The knowledge of the past can be made easier through the analogy between certain past and present experiences; we must nevertheless suppose that a sufficiently sensitive hermeneutic method is capable of surmounting the absence of such analogies and of emancipating itself from the projection of the historian's immediate interests.

We should also note that Benjamin links the truth of knowledge to the form of the fleeting *image,* not to the concept: "That in which the past and the present join to form a constellation is an image" (*G.S.,* 1:1242). The privilege of the image lies in its capacity to enter into correspondence with other images. Furthermore, the image—according to an old theme of romanticism and German idealism—possesses the power to speak to everyone, while the concept is addressed only to the educated classes. Knowledge through images is more accessible, more universal, but it is also more ambiguous. An image can be interpreted in more ways than a concept.

What primarily legitimates and motivates the interest in knowledge is the *danger* that makes the image of the past flash up. That is the theme of Thesis 6:

> To articulate the past historically does not mean to recognize it "the way it really was" (Ranke). It means to seize hold of a memory as it flashes up in a moment of danger. Historical materialism wishes to retain that image of the past which unexpectedly appears to man singled out by history at a moment of danger. The danger affects both the content of the tradition and its receivers. The same threat hangs over both: that of becoming a tool of the ruling classes. In every era the attempt must be made anew to wrest tradition away from a conformism that is about to overpower it. The Messiah comes not only as the redeemer, he comes as the subduer of Antichrist. Only that historian will have the gift of fanning the spark of hope in the past who is firmly convinced that *even the dead* will not be safe from the enemy if he wins. And this enemy has not ceased to be victorious. (*Illuminations,* 255; *E.F.,* 342)

In his work as a critic, Benjamin's task was always to wrest an unjustly "oppressed" and forgotten past from a conformism that was threatening it. In doing so, he obeyed an ethical imperative that he never formulated as such. But, in applying his idea to the tradition of Marxism threatened from the outside and from the inside (by its social democratic deformation), he attempts here to give an *immediately* political significance to his criticism, when such a significance can no doubt only be mediated. The political effect that consists in reestablishing authenticity in the interpretation of a tradition can stem only from a public questioning and a patient and long-term transmission.

The danger that Benjamin perceives in nineteenth-century historiography resides in the fact that it had become complicitous with the under-lying barbarism of all earlier culture:

> Whoever has emerged victorious participates to this day in the triumphal procession in which the present rulers step over those who are lying prostrate. According to traditional practice, the spoils are carried along in the procession. They are called cultural treasures, and a historical materialist views them with cautious detachment. For without exception the cultural treasures he surveys have an origin which he cannot contem-plate without horror. They owe their existence not only to the efforts of the great minds and talents who created them, but also to the anonymous toil of their contemporaries. There is no document of civilization which is not at the same time a document of barbarism. (*Illuminations,* 256; E.F., 343)

This radicalization of skepticism with regard to culture—which Adorno will improve on—would come close to attacking Benjamin himself if he did not make an exception for a single authentic and nonbarbaric culture, which transmits the expectations of redemption, happiness, and justice, and is addressed to us by the vanquished past. We must, then, always "brush history against the grain" (*Illuminations,* 257; E.F., 343), especially since Benjamin is intimately acquainted with the mechanisms that lead to the grandiloquent attitude toward the victors who write official history:

> It is a process of empathy whose origin is the indolence of the heart, *acedia,* which despairs of grasping and holding the genuine historical images as it flares up briefly. Among medieval theologians it was regarded as [one of the seven deadly sins,] the root cause of sadness. (*Illuminations,* 256; E.F., 342ff., bracketed section not in English edition)

This indolence of the heart called *acedia,* or mortal sadness, had been analyzed in Benjamin's earliest writings, especially in *The Origin of German Tragic Drama* (*Origin,* 155), in a way that attested to his familiarity with melancholy. It was partly to escape from it that he turned away from his initial metaphysics in order to place his thinking in the service of social transformation. Benjamin considers his critical work to be that of a historian in solidarity with the oppressed. It is owing to an identification with their battle that the access to the knowledge of a past acquires the value of political action in the fullest sense.

According to Benjamin, the subject of history is the struggling class, the oppressed class, but as a historian, he willingly forgets that he is only its advocate and that his arguments are open to dispute. Nothing guarantees that such a legitimation is adequate. Every struggling class interprets history in conformity with its own interests. For there to be no other interest but the truth, it would have to have, according to Marx's expression, nothing to lose but its chains; it would have to be universal in power, to a point that cannot even apply to the proletariat. It would also have to assume the legitimate interests of all humanity, including the issue of individual rights. Yet the "truths" formulated by those who have claimed to represent the struggling class remain just as disputable as those of authors who aspire for a scientific objectivity without relying on a universal "class interest." There is no privileged class that allows the historian to accede in its name to an indubitable historical objectivity; the historian's arguments must be solid. Benjamin senses this when he opposes the "theoretical armature" (*Illuminations,* 262) of historical materialism to the additive approach of universal history. But, believing with Brecht that he holds the elements of a "doctrine" that is beyond dispute, he does not draw all the consequences.

Such is, then, the psychosociological constellation that conditions the method of historical thought for Benjamin: involuntary memory; the instantaneous seizing of a fleeting image; a rescue operation called for by an imminent danger; the oppressed class as the subject of history. In the spirit of the philosophy of the subject, Benjamin's own political project consists in bringing humanity to accede in a single leap to a transparent knowledge of self and to rediscover the origin from which it has been alienated. The antinomies within which the philosophy of consciousness evolved from Hegel to Husserl to Freud, as Foucault distinguishes them in *The Order of Things*—"the empirical and the transcendental," "the cogito and the unthought," and "the withdrawal and the return of the origin"[17]— are also found in Benjamin's philosophy of history: a finite subject that is seeking to transcend itself; an empirical continuity of oppression to which is opposed a transcendental subject of history, in this case, a struggling class that inherits all the aborted revolts of the past; the tension between the mythic opacity of history and the transparence of reawakening; and, finally, the opposition between an alienated origin and a final reconquest of the past.[18] These antinomies, associated with the ambition for a radical reappropriation, whether instantaneous (through a "reawakening" or coming to consciousness) or progressive (through the historical process of an "odyssey of the mind") are due to the uncrossable gulf between a subject and an object that can never come together. The thinker who proposes to bring forth the unconscious of society both overestimates his or her own strength and underestimates that of the subjects who are prisoners to myth and ideology.

At this collective level, consciousness can progress only through public debate, which presupposes the existence of a democratic context, of which Benjamin knew only the premises. He was limited by the fact that he did not recognize normative values. His strength is to have sensed the disaster of 1939–1940, but the radical absence of free and critical debate in Europe was a situation to which his catastrophic thinking was always drawn. That mode of thinking offers no solution to such a crisis, but some of his discoveries deserve to survive the decline of the philosophy of the subject. This is particularly true for the critique of the concept of "timeless truth." Truth, writes Benjamin, is linked to "a time-kernel [*Zeitkern*] that is planted in both the knower and the known" ("N" 3, 2, p. 51). The historical "object" and the knowing subject are tied precisely by the force of truth that calls for their correspondence: to reveal one through the other. Benjamin is opposed to the idea that truth, as a stable and immobile object, "will not run off and leave us" ("N" 3a, 1, p. 51; cf. *Illuminations*, 255). He does not wish to relativize the idea of truth in that way; rather, he wishes to link it to the *current imperative* for truth that must always again be proved, that cannot be stabilized in the form of a proposition that would be truly independent of its assertion. This idea can be taken up again by a pragmatic theory of truth.

The Nature of the Dialectical Image

The historical image, writes Benjamin, is opposed to any representation of a historical *process*. We have already seen one reason for this discontinuity: the continuity of history is that of oppression. Revolt and freedom are only instants in a mythical and catastrophic continuum, immediately stifled and forgotten. Thus, deliverance can intervene, according to Benjamin, only if the historical process comes to a *standstill*. To the dynamic of history, Benjamin opposes a constellation. He speaks of the "dialectic at a standstill" and of a "dialectical image," concepts whose precise explanation he was unable to complete and that therefore remain rather difficult to grasp.

The 1935 Exposé is the first of Benjamin's writings[19] to introduce these concepts:

> Ambiguity is the pictorial image of dialectics, the law of dialectics seen at a standstill. This standstill is utopia and the dialectical image therefore a dream image. Such an image is presented by the pure commodity: as fetish. Such an image are the arcades, which are both house and street. Such an image is the prostitute, who is saleswoman and commodity in one. (*Reflections*, 157, translation modified)

The dialectical image would move from a "dream image" to an "involuntary memory of humanity delivered" (*G.S.*, 1:1233). This involves only a slight displacement, inasmuch as the image in *Paris Arcades* must also appear to us at the moment of awakening or of deliverance, as anticipated by the historian. The dialectic at a standstill slices across the historical process, in order to extract from it an image of revealing ambiguities: both dream of happiness and mythic phantasmagoria. It is incumbent upon us to recover the utopian expectation of the past and to deliver it from the phantasmagoria that have condemned it to failure. There is every indication that Benjamin considered the Marxian analysis of the commodity as the model for such an evocation of a dialectical image ("N" 4a, 5, p. 54). But it also seems that this concept did not reach a definitive clarification. An impressive number of aphorisms attempt to focus on it, from different angles, without ever succeeding in elucidating it fully.

In certain texts, the dialectical image is linked—as one image is linked to another—to the philosophy of language that Benjamin had developed around "the mimetic faculty." The most developed form of that mimetic faculty is reading:

> If we are to consider history as a text, then what is true for literary texts, as a recent author has explained it, is also true for history: the past has left images comparable to those that light leaves on a photosensitive plate. "Only the future possesses chemicals active enough to perfectly develop such negatives" (Monglond). The historical method is philological; its foundation is the book of life. In Hofmannsthal we find: "Read what has never been written." The reader we must imagine in this case is the true historian. (*E.F.*, 354)

The classical theme of reading in the Book of Life or in the Book of Nature is modified by this philology of Benjamin's, which consists in reading "what has never been written." Such a reading resembles the displacements that a theory such as Freud's brings about in classical tragedy. Another fragment explicitly establishes the link between the dialectical image and language as a medium of transmission:

> It isn't that the past casts its light on the present or the present casts its light on the past: rather, an image is that in which the Then [*das Gewesene*] and the Now [*das Jetzt*] come into a constellation like a flash of lightning. In other words: image is dialectics at a standstill. For . . . the relation of the Then to the Now is dialectical—not development but image[,] leaping forth [*sprunghaft*].—Only dialectical images are genuine (i.e., not archaic) images; and the place one happens upon them is language. ("N" 2a, 3, p. 49)

Discontinuity is essential to the dialectical image. Benjamin links it to the moment of standstill, the caesura, which, according to the essay on Goethe's *Elective Affinities*, suspends the movement of tragedy and introduces an "inexpressive" moment of reflection:

> Thinking involves both thoughts in motion and thoughts at rest. When thinking reaches a standstill in a constellation saturated with tensions,

the dialectical image appears. This image is the caesura in the movement of thought. Its locus is of course not arbitrary. In short, it is to be found wherever the tension between dialectical oppositions is greatest. The dialectical image is, accordingly, the very object constructed in the materialist presentation of history. It is identical with the historical object; it justified its being blasted out of the continuum of the historical process. ("N" 10a, 3, p. 67)

Thesis 16 underscores the unique and nonreiterable character of the moment when the historian discovers that the dialectical image is destined for *him* and for the historical moment when he can save such a constellation of memory:

A historical materialist cannot do without the notion of a present which is not a transition, but in which time stands still and has come to a stop. For this notion defines the present in which he himself is writing history. Historicism gives the "eternal" image of the past; historical materialism supplies a unique experience with the past. The historical materialist leaves it to others to be drained by the whore called "Once upon a time" in historicism's bordello. He remains in control of his powers, man enough to blast open the continuum of history. (*Illuminations*, 262)

Against historicism, Benjamin seeks to safeguard the originality of an unprecedented relation to the past.[20] In claiming the historical materialist is "man enough," he is referring to Nietzsche's notion of virility, which denounces historicism in the name of a certain vitalism:

Here we see clearly how necessary a third way of looking at the past is to man, beside the other two [monumental and traditionalist]. This is the "critical" way, which is also in the service of life. Man must have the strength to break up the past, and apply it, too, in order to live. He must bring the past to the bar of judgment, interrogate it remorselessly, and finally condemn it. Every past is worth condemning. . . . *You can explain the past only by what is most powerful in the present.*[21]

To that, Benjamin adds a notion of the present's weight of *responsibility* not only for the future but also for the past, inasmuch as, through suffering and unfulfilled expectations, we owe it to the past to remember.

The Construction of the Historical Object as Monad

In addition to the psychosocial conditions of historical knowledge and the fleeting nature of the dialectical image—a constellation formed between a past and a present—Benjamin includes the work of the historian properly speaking, which consists, according to him, in "liquidating the epic element in the representation of history" (*G.S.,* 1:1243). That entails a constructive aspect and a destructive aspect. The destructive aspect obeys a critical impulse; it is directed against the false continuities of history.

In that way, the historian knows he is in solidarity with revolutionary movements:

> The awareness that they are about to make the continuum of history explode is characteristic of the revolutionary classes at the moment of their action. The great revolution introduced a new calendar. The initial day of a calendar serves as a historical time-lapse camera. And, basically, it is the same day that keeps recurring in the guise of holidays, which are days of remembrance. Thus the calendars do not measure time as clocks do; they are monuments of a historical consciousness of which not the slightest trace has been apparent in Europe in the past hundred years. (*Illuminations,* 261–262; *E.F.,* 345)

Here, Benjamin establishes a direct relation between the aesthetic reflections on time that he developed in "On Some Motifs in Baudelaire" and the time of history, especially the time of revolutions. The days that matter for Benjamin "are days of completing time, to paraphrase Joubert. They are days of recollection" (*Illuminations,* 181). They are linked to the "rituals with their ceremonies" and to festivals (*Illuminations,* 159). In a manner we again find in Hannah Arendt, Benjamin confers an implicitly aesthetic quality on these inaugural moments of history, that is, on revolutions. Revolutions have that density of a full and fulfilled time that characterizes works of art and celebrations. In them, an origin is renewed, without any dissociation between signifier, signified, and referent, and without "homogeneous, empty time." History, art, and religion come together to illustrate fulfilled time, for which, here as in Rousseau, celebration provides the model. In this case, however, the celebration is not the instantaneous suppression of all mediations but, rather, the reassertion of an origin and the reinforcement of a memory.

The calendar, the reiterated memory of an inaugural moment, points to a problem that risks annulling the break in continuity. Benjamin formulates it as a "fundamental aporia": "The history of the oppressed is a discontinuum." "The task of history consists in seizing hold of the tradition of the oppressed" (*E.F.,* 352). He seeks to solve this problem by asserting that "the representation of the continuum ends with a leveling and the representation of the discontinuous is at the foundation of any authentic tradition" (*E.F.,* 352). The *authenticity* of tradition thus lies in the fact that a representation is *wrenched from* a historical continuity placed under the sign of oppression, conformism, and falsification: continuity levels out both suffering and revolt. The French Revolution is the example of this:

> History is the subject of a structure whose site is not homogeneous, empty time, but time filled by the presence of the now [*Jetztzeit*]. Thus, to Robespierre ancient Rome was a past charged with the time of the now which he blasted out of the continuum of history. The French Revolution viewed itself as Rome reincarnate. It evoked ancient Rome the way fashion evokes costumes of the past. Fashion has a flair for the topical, no matter where it stirs in the thickets of long ago; it is a tiger's leap into the past. (*Illuminations*, 261)[22]

What interests Benjamin about the French Revolution is not its institutional innovations and their consequences in the field of values, but the very *experience* of revolutionary discontinuity, which, on principle, cannot last. Benjamin is also not bothered by the fact that the revolutionaries' desire, to give new life to the Roman republic, was illusory and was no doubt partly responsible for the failures that the "ideas of 1789" encountered in the early days; he is not embarrassed by the fact that historical action is placed on the same level as fashion, which, according to the first Exposé of *Paris Arcades*, was allied with the fetishism of the commodity. What counts for him in these examples is the fact that a present can abruptly recognize itself in a past and, through that dazzling discovery, can create the new. Here again, artistic innovation provides the model for historical action.

This analysis is confirmed by the last concept that Benjamin introduces in presenting his theory of history, that of the *monad,* which had already figured in *The Origin of German Tragic Drama* (*Origin,* 47) and in the essay on Fuchs:

> Thinking involves not only the flow of thoughts, but their arrest as well. Where thinking suddenly stops in a configuration pregnant with tensions, it gives that configuration a shock, by which it crystallizes into a monad. A historical materialist approaches a historical subject only where he encounters it as a monad. In this structure he recognizes the sign of a Messianic cessation of happening, or, put differently, a revolutionary chance in the fight for the oppressed past. (*Illuminations*, 262–263; *E.F.,* 346)

It is striking that this same concept of monad could have figured in the preface to *The Origin of German Tragic Drama* without being linked to a revolutionary historical methodology. Benjamin at the time was concerned with extracting from the empirical succession of history certain privileged forms that had the quality of "origin" or of *authenticity.* Baroque tragedy as such was not a revolutionary form but, rather, the expression of the most profound melancholy elicited by a disabused contemplation of the course of history. It was, however, a form that had been the victim of a forgetting characteristic of the official history of German literature: the forgetting of a radical lament concerning the vanity of all things and a subversion of art through the consciousness of death. Such forms, which are blasted out of the continuum of history, nevertheless contain historical time. According to Benjamin, suspended time returns within the moment wrenched away from continuity:

> [The historian] takes cognizance of it in order to blast a specific era out of the homogeneous course of history—blasting a specific life out of the era or a specific work out of the lifework. As a result of this method the lifework is preserved in this work and at the same time cancelled [*aufgehoben*, in the Hegelian sense]; in the lifework, the era; and in the era, the entire course of history. (*Illuminations,* 362; *E.F.,* 347)

To judge from this passage, Benjaminian "monadology" is in fact a kind of "genetic structuralism" that seeks the sense of historical acts and works in coherent signifying structures.[23] The "monad" is such a structure, constitutive of a "vision of the world." The number of these visions is limited, as is the number of Benjamin's "Ideas," and each monad possesses a "prehistory" and a "posthistory," through the repeated themes and variations of these Ideas over the course of history. The particularity of the Benjaminian monad—due to his original vision of history—resides in the fact that on each occasion it incarnates the "revolutionary chance" to redeem a part of the forgotten past and (this is the principal justification for its name) in the fact that the monad in itself sums up the whole of history: the conflict between an awakening and the forgetting of a messianic chance.

The aesthetic element of this philosophy of history is not simply a confusion of categories. Benjamin insists unilaterally on an aspect neglected by objectivist historiography. He emphasizes the fact that the historian is never indifferent to his or her objects, that they belong to the historian's own irreplaceable experience and that he or she is responsible for a past always threatened by the interests of the present. Beginning with World War II, the history of the victims has earned its rightful place in the discipline, even though history as "giver of meaning" and "affirmation of national identities" is far from dead.[24] But an orientation that thus "brushes history against the grain" is also not without risk. It can serve as a pretext for a conception of history that simply opposes the victors' history. Such an inversion would change nothing in the underlying error. If we believe that no essential progress has ever come about and that, under its appearance of commitment and with its rational thought, morality, and profane law, democratic society is only a new disguise for ancestral domination, *more totalitarian than antiquity perhaps,*[25] we establish a false continuity. Through Horkheimer's and Adorno's *Dialectic of Enlightenment,* on which Benjamin's "Theses" have left their mark, such a vision of history has become canonical for a contemporary mode of thought that can no longer point to the despair of the years 1940–1944. There is a very good chance that Benjamin would have broken with such a reformed conformism.

ETHICS AND MEMORY

It would be vain to try to make Benjamin into a good democrat. He had known the empire of William II, World War I, Nazism, exile, the German refugee camps in France, and persecution, and he was unable to consider the babbling of the Weimar Republic and the half-measures of a leftist politics—that of the Front Populaire—"with which the rightists would provoke revolts" (*Correspondence,* 542) as models for a credible politics. In his view, the "state of emergency" was the rule, and democracy was dupery or, at most, a vain effort to forestall the decisive rescue operation. In addition, there is no way to fully share Benjamin's skepticism in the context of Western democracies, where the state of emergency has, in any case, not been the rule for more than half a century and where the problem of injustice, though far from disappearing, is not posed in the same terms as during the age of Nazism. The idea of a "redemptive" working class operating in the name of the tradition of the oppressed seems to have been definitively set aside (*G.S.,* 1:1246, ms. 486).

A third error—along with styling Benjamin as a democrat or sharing his skepticism—would be to believe that a *radical* demand for justice and the realization of democratic principles no longer has any rightful place, given the gains of our Western societies. An ocean of misery and oppression surrounds these islets of democracy and prosperity. And these democracies are and have been, in the past and in the present, largely responsible for that state of affairs, which they favored through colonization and the often advantageous exchange of technological expertise for raw materials; linked to humanitarian aid to ease our consciences, fueled by ancestral traditions, the cynicism about inequality and injustice inhabits our societies.

Benjamin never heard of Auschwitz, but having experienced the Nazi era and forced exile, the prospect of a Europe without Jews hardly astonished him; he discussed it with Scholem. In reaction, he adopted an extreme position that effaced the distinction between might and right. But if the state of *emergency*—fascism—is the *rule* in history, in the name of what idea can we criticize such a state? Not in the name of any right or law, in any case. In fact, Benjamin always considered law a mythic reality. The historical "fact" of genocide is of an enormity such that the imperative for "law"—even emancipated from myth—no longer has any hold on it. Thus Benjamin wrote: "The current amazement that the things we are experiencing are "still" possible in the twentieth century is *not* philosophical. This amazement is not the beginning of knowledge—unless it is the knowledge that the view of history which gives rise to it is untenable" (*Illuminations,* 257).

Benjamin is speaking ironically of a *naive* conception of progress that supposes that this century *ought to* be safe from barbarism. But at the same time, he excludes any notion of a *regression* in history. As a result, there is no longer any criterion allowing us to distinguish degrees of inhumanity. For most of those who have reflected on it, Auschwitz crossed a threshold. What constitutes the horror of the death camps is not that there existed oppression and massacres, which had always existed throughout history: In its scope, the inhumanity was not simply regressive but went beyond anything that had ever been perpetrated. In that sense, Benjamin might have found confirmation for his thesis; Adorno, in fact, interpreted all the history of the West, from the massacre committed by Ulysses to Auschwitz, as a continuous escalation. But this was also a case of barbarism surging up from within a *civilized* society whose constitution, that of the Weimar Republic, was founded on humanist, universalist, and democratic values. Not to admit that there was regression is to fail to take seriously the age-old struggle for the realization of democracy and the generalization of universalist principles. Progress in this sense does not mean, as Benjamin supposes, that humanity has definitively acceded to a "messianic" stage that henceforth excludes barbarism but, rather, that certain normative gains can be repressed but not forgotten. Just as there will probably never be a society without violence and individual murders, no society will ever be able to exclude barbaric regressions on a larger scale. We must nevertheless maintain the notion of regression, and thus also of a "progression" in the apprenticeship and the institutionalization of legal and moral norms. Despite the naiveté of expression, what is right in the astonishment about the fact that such things "are 'still' possible" is the revolt against such a regression. Without such a revolt against regressive violence and injustice—a revolt that appeals to an *acquired* level of institutionalized norms—there is no notion of law; there is only hatred, thirst for vengeance, and a messianic hope that is not of this world. Benjamin does not place himself in the domain of law, because he is convinced of the powerlessness of any norm before the massive empirical *fact* of continual oppression. He faces no opponent in the guise of normative expectations; he speaks of victors and vanquished in the third person; he resigns himself to merely observing relations of force.

✳

In Benjamin's work, the contemporary debate on ethics is confronted with a mode of thought situated to one side of what seems to have become its immutable framework, the opposition between Kantians and Aristotelians or Hegelians. Here again, Benjamin occupies a peculiar place: He is claimed both by thinkers who, like Ricoeur, lean toward a neo-Aristotelian philosophy and an anchoring of ethics in narration,[26] and by those who, like Habermas, defend a procedural ethics of discussion.[27] How are such contradictory claims possible? We find very little moral theory in Benjamin; thus the two sides can draw support only from his intuitions and implicit presuppositions.

Benjamin's thought is both traditionalist and critical. It is even *critical* precisely to the extent that it lays claim to a *tradition* of the forgotten and the oppressed. It seeks to give voice to what in history has been condemned to mutism. The essay on Carl Gustave Jochmann and his *Rückschritte der Poesie* (Regression of poetry) provides an example. Benjamin exhumes a nearly forgotten Baltic author who wrote in German and who emigrated to France, and exhumes with him an entire culture of Baltic liberation movements of which almost every trace has disappeared. Jochmann's mode of thinking went against the current. At a time dominated by romanticism, he was its intransigent adversary: He was opposed to the nostalgic hunt for false riches, the insatiable thirst for and assimilation of the past, "not through a progressive emancipation of humanity by virtue of which it considers its own history with increased vigilance, but through the imitation and relentless acquisition of all the works of disappeared peoples and eras" (*G.S.*, 2:581). Before Adolf Loos, Jochmann was one of the first opponents of nineteenth-century historicism, which Benjamin targets in his *Paris Arcades* project. "Of what belongs to the past," he writes, "all is not lost; of what has been lost, all has not been lost irremediably; of what has not been replaced, all is not irreplaceable" (*G.S.*, 2:582). What counts for Jochmann, as for Vico, from whom he draws inspiration, are the heights of a very old heroic humanity and of its poetry. When he comes in contact with it, "his prophetic gaze catches fire" (*G.S.*, 2:578). In that poetry, humanity for the first time discovered its own nature and drew strength for the long voyage that awaited it (*G.S.*, 2:585). Like Benjamin midway between the *Aufklärung* and romanticism, Jochmann turned toward this distant past to gather hope and a promise of emancipation.

Friedrich Schlegel said that the historian was a "prophet turned toward the past." Benjamin translates this into a method whereby the historian sees "his own era through the medium of past destinies" (*G.S.*, 1:1250). The ethical dimension is introduced through the notion of a "rescue operation": It is a matter of saving an image from the past that *legitimately expects* to be delivered because we have a *debt* toward it. For it transmits to us that "weak Messianic power" that will redeem history from being that of the victors alone. The rescue operation confers on the past its "incompletion." We pursue its insurrectional initiative because we owe it that much.

Among the fragments from *Paris Arcades,* we find on this subject the excerpt from an exchange of letters between Benjamin and Horkheimer. According to his essay on Eduard Fuchs, Benjamin had spoken of the "incompleteness of the past" in the case of a historian who considered culture not a transmitted good but, rather, a set of meanings whose sense later history reveals and modifies. Horkheimer then makes this observation: "The assertion of incompleteness is idealistic, if completeness isn't included in it. Past injustice has occurred and is done with. The murdered are really murdered. [In the last instance, your claim is theological.] If one takes incompleteness completely seriously, one has to believe in the Last Judgment" (Horkheimer's letter of 16 March 1937, quoted in "N" 8, 1, p. 61; bracketed section not in English version).[28]

In responding to Horkheimer's letter, Benjamin avoids taking on the criticism that he remains prisoner to idealism and theology. In a note for *Paris Arcades,* in contrast, he calls for theology. After the passage from Horkheimer, he writes:

> The corrective to this line of thought lies in the reflection that history is not just a science but also a form of memoration [*eine Form des Eingedenkens*]. What science has "established," memoration can modify. Memoration can make the incomplete (happiness) into something complete, and the complete (suffering) into something incomplete. That is theology; but in memoration we discover the experience [*Erfahrung*] that forbids us to conceive of history as thoroughly atheological, even though we barely dare not attempt to write it according to literally theological concepts. ("N" 8, 1, p. 61)

What is "theological" in Benjamin's mind is the profane faculty of memory to make death and past suffering incomplete. Remembrance is theological through its function of transmitting a "messianic" power. Without that function of memory, the narcissistic present forgets its debt toward all aspirations for freedom that have been vanquished in the past. Yet the injustices of the past that have not been redeemed haunt us and poison us all the more when they are forgotten: They can then be reproduced with impunity.

Art is a privileged manifestation of such a memory. Even if that is not its first goal, it saves from mutism and forgetting certain irreplaceable experiences to which society assigns no other rightful place. Its works make public and conserve through time the possibilities of humanity, the hope they elicit, the defeats they have undergone. Art is the symbolic crystallization par excellence of those of humanity's aborted dreams that cannot or could not be translated into action or institutions, that could leave no trace in history. In that sense, criticism has an ethical task before any consideration of the ethical implications of works of art. It must gather together and amplify, by wrenching away from oblivion, the exemplary experiences that question those that are accepted and defused. That is how it contributes to writing "the history of the vanquished."

But such a "history of the vanquished" or "tradition of the oppressed" is itself an ambiguous reality. Like any tradition, it submits its norms to the laws of empirical transmission: The fact of being transmitted counts more for the tradition than the legitimacy of what is thereby transmitted. The tradition of the oppressed conserves the memory of injustices committed and suffering undergone, but it also transmits the *deformations* and pathologies of oppression: accumulated hatred, the desire for vengeance and revenge, the thirst to dominate those by whom one has been dominated. In his solidarity with every revolt against power, Foucault came to realize the perversity of such a reversal, when the domination of the formerly oppressed proved to be just as appalling, or even more atrocious, than the domination against which they had arisen. Such reversals are always possible, and even probable, within the framework of a revolt animated by hatred and vengeance and this risk even exists in the Benjaminian model for a decisive vengeance of *all* the oppressed of history by a redemptive class. Instead of considering hatred and the desire for vengeance—which is not to be confused with indignation and the imperative for justice—as precious driving forces in the struggle for emancipation, he would have had to see in them the pathological symptoms of resentment.

The Benjaminian history of the vanquished rests on an ethics of solidarity but not of reconciliation. "What Benjamin has in mind," writes Habermas,

> is the supremely profane insight that ethical universalism also has to take seriously the injustice that has already happened and that is seemingly irreversible; that there exists a solidarity of those born later with those who have preceded them, with all those whose bodily or personal integrity has been violated at the hands of other human beings; and that this solidarity can only be engendered and made effective by remembering.[29]

That presupposes that everyone, including the heirs of the oppressors, participate in such a remembrance, to which Habermas, referring to Benjamin, relentlessly calls the Germans of today:

> The universalist content of a form of patriotism that is crystallizing
> around the constitutional democratic state must no longer be linked to
> a history of victories; it is incompatible with that crude state of nature—
> but to the second degree—that characterizes a historical consciousness
> remaining obtuse regarding the profound ambivalence of all tradition,
> the chain of irreparable damage—the dark side of all cultural conquests
> up to the present.[30]

Adapting the Benjaminian idea to his own ends, Habermas sets aside what
in Benjamin *limits* ethical universalism: the hatred and thirst for vengeance
that, for the author of the "Theses" in his despair of 1940, enables the
oppressed class to find the way to decisive deliverance. The Benjaminian
ethic of solidarity is deficient because it thinks it can rise above the
abstraction of a formal principle of justice, which the oppressed themselves
would be obligated to respect. That is, Benjamin confuses the categories of
historical narration and ethics, in the name of a tradition of injustice, which
he wrenches away from mutism and forgeting.

On the one hand, in "The Storyteller," Benjamin evokes with nostalgia
the figure of the *just man,* the man of counsel, who disappears at the same
time as the art of storytelling. Benjamin cannot conceive of a kind of justice
that would no longer be incarnated in substantial virtues such as those of
the exemplary man of antiquity. Yet the validity of modern morality does
not depend on its exemplary incarnation in a just man. In that sense,
Benjamin is not a modern: He cannot dissociate ethics from narration,
justice from the just man. If literature and the arts—tragedy, the novel, and
film—despite their autonomy of structure, are never indifferent to ethical
issues, this is not true of literature's—or, in general, narration's—importance for ethics. Ethical action or discourse can *draw support from* narrative
givens, but their structure is not narrative. They are guided by reasons that
can justify the acceptability of an action or the norm that inspires it.

On the other hand, Benjamin brings out an important aspect of ethical
universalism. He formulates the intransigent imperative for *social justice,*
without which a supposed reconciliation between oppressors and oppressed
will always be worthless. However indispensable the *symbolic* recognition of
sins committed against the oppressed and the exploited, it cannot replace
reparation in the form of a modification of the structures of power and of
economic relations. As long as the good things in life belong for the most
part and with rare exceptions to an immutable circle of social groups who
assure the transmission of cultural privilege, social relations, and material
advantages to their posterity, nothing will prevent the reproduction of
hatred and violence in those who, as a general rule, remain excluded.
Equality of opportunities remains a promise that has not been kept, and
recreation centers in poor neighborhoods will not change a thing about that.

The statistics on the social origin of the delinquents and criminals who people our prisons speak volumes.[31]

John Rawls's *A Theory of Justice* formulates "two principles of justice." According to the first, "each person is to have an equal right to the most extensive basic liberties compatible with a similar liberty for others." This principle is limited by the economic realism of the second: "Social and economic inequalities are to be arranged so that they are both a) reasonably expected to be to everyone's advantage, and b) attached to positions and offices open to all."[32] At the level of universal principles excluded a priori from the discussion, Rawls introduces a justification for inequalities, in the name of "the advantage of everyone." Thus, the imperative to redistribute freedoms and goods must take into account the risk of inefficiency, which would produce disadvantages for all—which means that the leaders of the economic system should fix limits on redistribution in the interest of everyone or guarantee the balance of dissatisfaction in the way it has been maintained since the Keynesian rebalancing of the liberal economy. On the other hand, everyone must have an equal chance to accede to positions and functions that society cannot do without. This means that *everyone* must have the "chance" to become a garbage man or warehouse worker, unless society extends unemployment through automation and robotization.

This important theory's historical merit is to have served as a starting point for the contemporary debate on ethics, political theory, and subjects such as civil disobedience; it is, in fact, presented here only in the form of an almost caricatured reduction. Hillary Putnam has added to it a third principle that moves toward the Benjaminian imperative: "Do not make the underprivileged wait forever." We could add: Do not abandon the defense of this principle to the political organizations of resentment. Whatever the practical reality that could be given to such a principle, the *theory* of justice cannot, without ideological deformation, anticipate the principles in whose name a just *action* would or should be directed. It can at the most define—or, rather, reconstruct—the conditions under which justice has the chance to come into being and of which we have an intuitive notion.

In such a theory of justice, ethics would not be founded solely on memory. In a general way, memory—or tradition—could not be a *criterion* for justice. It goes without saying that there would be no justice *without* memory, but there would also not be no justice without living beings, without the possibility and the reality of injustice, and so on. In actuality, justice is always practiced as a function of traditions. But as soon as different traditions confront one another, they are obliged to move toward more universal principles. It is a strike against Benjamin that the act of founding ethics on memory, even the universal memory of injustice, stems from a particularist attitude. It does not accede to the principles and procedures of a universalist ethics. Yet *without* such a conceptual horizon, the act of decentering ethical universalism in order to include in it redemption for past injustices leads to a regression that is manifested in the tendency toward hatred.

Ethics is not the strong point of Benjamin's thought. In 1940, he found himself in an apocalyptic situation, facing opponents who flouted the most elementary bonds among human beings; although they may excuse Benjamin, such considerations cannot be erected into a valid principle beyond that situation. In relation to ethical universalism, the history of the vanquished stems from moral skepticism and reasoning in terms of relations of forces.

Benjamin remains one of the most remarkable thinkers of his century, through the force he was able to give to the reading of works of art and historical documents and, in particular, through his ability to make aesthetic criticism the field for a highly political practice of memory, the exercise of the most intense presence of mind and one most favorable for consciousness-raising. The examples he provided make the history of Western ideas before him seem like a tradition truncated from some of its most subversive artistic intuitions. That tradition does not survive—and does not deserve to survive—except as it is questioned from within.

✳

Conclusion

To seize the unity of Benjamin's thought is no easy task; its very identity seems to escape at times, to amount to no more than a style. The systematization and periodization of Benjamin's thinking in this book should allow readers to understand and reduce to a minimal coherence the multiplicity of facets this thinker presents to posterity. But this systematic character is not *proper* to Benjamin's thought. It is a construction, a schematization introduced for purposes of clarification. For the most part, the unity of Benjamin's philosophical thought is assured only by the reflections he devotes to it in his *Correspondence,* under pressure from the questions raised by his baffled friends; he admits at times that he has not succeeded in reconciling the extremes that constitute the poles of his mode of thinking. Without these letters, it would hardly be possible to get our bearings in his multiform oeuvre; hence the considerable place they legitimately occupy in the German edition of his works. The fact that the *Correspondence* constitutes the principal link in a mode of thought that is in fact splintered indicates that the coherence is less conceptual than, if not biographical, then at least tied to the hermeneutic effort to constitute an intellectual, literary, and political biography that presents a minimum of continuity.

If every reader has managed to appropriate a different Benjamin in privileging either the "theological" approach, the "materialist" approach, or a purely aesthetic approach and, within these overall visions, one "moment" rather than others—a baroque Benjamin; a modern close to Baudelaire; a critic committed to the avant-garde, Kafka, Proust, surrealism, or Brecht; a theorist of the media; a literary writer, author of *Einbahnstrasse* and *Berliner Kindheit*—if such an atomization has been possible, it is also because of a peculiarity in this aesthetic *criticism* that has been erected into a full-blown philosophy. In approaching a work of art or an artistic or literary current, it deals each time with a "way of seeing the world" whose coherence is irreducible.

The *suggestion* of Benjamin's writings is that each of these "moments" of his criticism, each of the "visions" considered significant, is related to a virtual philosophical unity that was never formulated as such. The writers and artists seem to be linked by an intellectual solidarity, defined above all by their shared *rejection* of an order of the world symbolized by totalitarianism. In fact, however, there is little conceptual synthesis possible between the profane approach of surrealism, the modern versions of Judaism in Kraus and Kafka, the political theater of Brecht, and the poetry of Baudelaire. Through the schemata of his interpretations, Benjamin makes us believe that such an ideal unity exists. He did not adequately distinguish between the principles of an aesthetics and the considerations of a criticism that, in each case, is indebted to a particular work of art and its context of reception. He did not do so because his concept of *truth* obliged him to decipher individual works of art and their context as unforeseeable indexes of a doctrinal unity to come. The fragility of that undertaking lies in a theory that places truth in a dependent role in relation to historical events; the chance events of literary and art history and of political upheavals make Benjamin the plaything of contexts, to the point that his identity seems at times to escape us. Independent of real history, there is no imperious necessity in the succession of periods and moments that compose his oeuvre; no internal logic that would lead from theology to materialism and from materialism to an indelible residue of theology; no teleology leading from a philosophy of language founded on the idea of a communication with God to a conception of history founded on the principle of the memory of the vanquished and forgotten. Benjamin would not be a thinker worthy of the name if his incessant changes were merely opportunistic and incoherent. They always obey the same fundamental quest for salvation in the search, first, for the power of lost naming; second, for presence of mind and political effectiveness; and finally, for the memory of the vanquished and the oppressed through a broadening solidarity with the dead and forgotten.

From a systematic point of view, the center of all this work of reflection is the question of the work of art. The work of art constitutes the strategic place where the theological situation of the contemporary age, the source of tradition and of memory, manifests itself; but the modern work of art is also the stakes in multiple subversions that target the deceptiveness of art's appearance, its illusory beauty, myth, and ideology. The fundamental aporia of Benjaminian thought forms around a philosophical need for art, formulated in the name of truth, and a need to reduce the ambiguity and illusions that are linked to art in the name of that same truth. Hence the process of disenchantment combined with the recurrent image of a rescue operation. But this process is also close to that of modern art itself and its self-destructive adventure, of which Benjamin has become, for that very reason, one of the exemplary theorists.

*
Notes

NOTES TO INTRODUCTION

1. For works on Benjamin's life, see the Bibliography.

2. See especially N. Bolz and W. van Reijen, *Walter Benjamin* (Frankfurt & New York: Campus, 1991), 117–126.

3. See J. Bouveresse, *Le mythe de l'intériorité: Expérience, signification, et langage privé chez Wittgenstein* (Paris: Minuit, 1976).

4. References to Walter Benjamin's works will be cited in the text; full publication information appears in the Bibliography.

5. The set of works by P. Ricoeur constituted by *La métaphore vive* and *Temps et récit* provides another example of this.

6. "My concept of origin [*Ursprung*] in the *Trauerspiel* book is a strict and compelling transfer of this fundamental principle of Goethe's from the realm of nature to that of history. Origins—the concept of the primal phenomenon, carried over from the pagan context of nature into the Jewish contexts of history" ("N" 2a, 4, pp. 49–50); "I will let my Christian Baudelaire be taken into heaven by nothing but Jewish angels. But arrangements have already been made to let him fall as if by chance in the last third of the ascension, shortly before his entrance into glory" (*Correspondence*, 612, letter of 21 September 1939). This indicates that Baudelaire's complete rescue seems impossible to Benjamin.

7. See G. Scholem, "Walter Benjamin," in *On Jews and Judaism in Crisis* (New York: Schocken Books, 1976), 172–197.

8. See G. Scholem, *Walter Benjamin: The Story of a Friendship,* trans. H. Zohn (New York: Schocken Books, 1981): "Benjamin knew next to nothing about Jewish affairs. . . . About details of Jewish history he was totally uninformed" (72).

9. See Scholem's letter to Benjamin, 26 August 1933, in W. Benjamin and G. Scholem, *Briefwechsel 1933–1940* (Frankfurt: Suhrkamp, 1980), 87ff.

10. According to Scholem ("Walter Benjamin and His Angel," in *On Jews and*

Judaism in Crisis, 233–234n.), Benjamin was acquainted with the notion of *tiqoun,* messianic redemption, through the book by F. J. Molitor, *Philosophie der Geschichte oder über die Tradition* (1827–1853), which he had owned since 1916 (*Correspondence,* 82, letter of 11 November 1916), and through an article by Scholem himself that appeared in the *Encyclopoedia Judaica,* but only in 1932.

11. F. Rosenzweig, *The Star of Redemption,* trans. W. W. Hallo (New York: Holt, Rinehart, & Winston, 1971). See also S. Mosès, *Système et révélation: La philosophie de Franz Rosenzweig* (Paris: Seuil, 1982).

12. See D. Janicaud's critique, *Le tournant théologique de la phénoménologie française* (Combas, France: Eclat, 1991).

13. See J. Habermas, "Zu Max Horkheimers Satz: 'Einen unbedingten Sinn zu retten ohne Gott, ist eitel,' " in *Texte und Kontexte* (Frankfurt: Suhrkamp, 1991), 121ff.

14. M. Foucault, course on Kant's *Was ist Aufklärung?* (What is Enlightenment?), *Magazine littéraire* 207 (May 1984): 39.

15. See G. Deleuze and F. Guattari, *Qu'est-ce que la philosophie?* (Paris: Minuit, 1991).

16. T. W. Adorno, *Prisms,* trans. S. Weber and S. Weber (Cambridge, Mass.: MIT Press, 1981), 229–241.

17. Scholem sees in Benjamin a metaphysician of language and "the legitimate heir of the most productive and most genuine traditions of Hamann and Humboldt" (*Correspondence,* 374).

NOTES TO CHAPTER I

1. See, for example, *Correspondence*: "my particular place as a philosopher of language" (372, translation modified); and "Curriculum vitae" (6), p. 41.

2. An exegetical exercise often undertaken by the mystics of language; see Jakob Böhme, *Mysterium magnum* (1623) and Johann Georg Hamann, *Aesthetica in nuce* (1762).

3. [In French, this distinction is grammatical: *Le verbe,* in addition to signifying the word of God (the logos), also means "verb." *Le nom* is the word both for "noun" and for "name."—J. M. T.]

4. L. Wittgenstein, *Philosophical Investigations,* trans. G. E. M. Anscombe (New York: Macmillan, 1958), 19e (aphorism 38).

5. R. Jakobson, "Linguistique et poétique," in *Essais de linguistique générale,* trans. N. Ruwet (Paris: Minuit, 1963), 218 [J. M. T.'s translation from the French].

6. L. Wittgenstein, *Tractatus logico-philosophicus,* in *The Wittgenstein Reader,* ed. A. Kenny (Oxford & Cambridge: Blackwell, 1994): "Whereof one cannot speak, thereof one must be silent" (#7, p. 31). But Wittgenstein further explains: "There is indeed the inexpressible. This *shows* itself; it is the mystical. The right method

of philosophy would be this. To say nothing except what can be said, i.e. the propositions of natural science, i.e. something that has nothing to do with philosophy: and then always, when someone else wished to say something metaphysical, to demonstrate to him that he has given no meaning to certain signs in his propositions" (#6.522, 6.53, p. 31). Thus, Wittgenstein would have used this method against Benjamin.

7. H.-G. Gadamer, *Truth and Method,* trans. J. Weinsheimer and D. G. Marshall, 2nd rev. ed. (New York: Continuum, 1994): "Hence the critique of the correctness of names in the *Cratylus* is the first step toward modern instrumental theory of language and the ideal of a sign system of reason" (418).

8. Ibid., 384.

9. Ibid., 474.

10. Ibid., 490–491.

11. See the detailed study by W. Menninghaus, *Walter Benjamins Theorie der Sprachmagie* (Frankfurt: Suhrkamp, 1980).

12. D. Diderot, *Correspondance* 4, ed. Georges Roth and Jean Varloot (Paris, 1955–1970), 57; quoted in Michael Fried, *Absorption and Theatricality: Painting and Beholder in the Age of Diderot* (Berkeley, Los Angeles, and London: University of California Press, 1980), 147.

13. Gadamer, *Truth and Method,* 383–389, 395–396.

14. J.-J. Rousseau, *Essai sur l'origine des langues,* ed. J. Starobinski (Paris: Gallimard, 1990), 68 [J. M. T.'s translation].

15. J. G. Hamann, *Aesthetica in nuce,* preceded by *Sokratische Denkwürdigkeiten* (1759–1762) (Stuttgart: Reclam, 1986), 87, and 81 [J. M. T.'s translation].

16. Cf. M. Heidegger, *Being and Time,* trans. J. Macquarrie and E. Robinson (London: SCM Press, 1962): "If, however, *truth* rightfully has a primordial connection with *Being,* then the phenomenon of truth comes within the range of the problematic of fundamental ontology" (256, para. 44). He here clearly contrasts this conception of truth as "disclosedness" and "Being-uncovering" (263–264) to the "traditional concept of truth" according to which "the 'locus' of truth is assertion (judgment)" (257).

17. Cf. E. Tugendhat, *Der Wahrheitsbegriff bei Husserl und Heidegger* (Berlin: Walter de Gruyter, 1967).

18. Ibid.

19. T. W. Adorno, *Über Walter Benjamin,* rev. ed. (Frankfurt: Suhrkamp, 1990), 35ff.

20. Cf. my article, "De la philosophie comme critique littéraire: Walter Benjamin et le jeune Lukács," *Revue d'Esthétique* 1 (1981), repr. 1990. In *The Origin of German Tragic Drama,* Benjamin often cites *Soul and Form,* but only the essay on tragedy.

21. G. Lukács, *Soul and Form,* trans. A. Bostock (Cambridge, Mass.: MIT Press, 1978), 16.

22. There is a very similar definition of philosophical activity as a "creation of concepts," compared to science and art, in G. Deleuze and F. Guattari, *Qu'est-ce que la philosophie?* (Paris: Minuit, 1991).

23. Cf. Gadamer, *Truth and Method*: "Plato was the first to show that the essential element in the beautiful was aletheia . . . . The beautiful, the way in which goodness appears, reveals itself in its being: it presents itself" (487).

24. Benjamin is alluding here to "The Task of the Translator."

25. Cf. K. Bühler, "L'onomatopée et la fonction représentative du langage" (1932), in J.-C. Pariente, ed., *Essais sur le langage* (Paris: Minuit, 1969), 111–132.

26. Regarding the difference between similarity and denotation, cf. N. Goodman, *Languages of Art: An Approach to a Theory of Symbols* (Indianapolis & New York: Bobbs-Merrill, 1968): "A picture, to represent an object, must be a symbol for it, stand for it, refer to it; and . . . no degree of resemblance is sufficient to establish the requisite relationship of reference. Nor is resemblance *necessary* for reference; almost anything may stand for almost anything else. A picture that represents—like a passage that describes—an object refers to, and, more particularly, *denotes* it. Denotation is the core of representation and is independent of resemblance" (5).

27. Cf. Thesis 5 in "Theses on the Philosophy of History": "The past can be seized only as an image which flashes up at the instant when it can be recognized and is never seen again" (*Illuminations,* 255).

28. Benjamin will refer to this in 1935 in "Probleme der Sprachsoziologie," his essay written for the Frankfurt School's *Zeitschrift für Sozialforschung,* but this late discovery did not have any influence on his own thinking.

NOTES TO CHAPTER II
1. Aesthetics of the Sublime

1. "Dichtermut" (1800) and "Blödigkeit" (1803), two versions of the same poem.

2. A concept borrowed from Hölderlin's essay on Sophocles.

3. Benjamin is citing a passage from a book by C. Pingoud, *Grundlinien der ästhetischen Doktrin Fr. Schlegels* (Stuttgart, 1914).

4. I. Kant, *Critique of Judgment,* trans. J. H. Bernard (New York & London: Hafner, 1968), 17.

5. J. G. Fichte, *The System of Ethics Based on the Science of Knowledge* (London: Kegan Paul, 1897) [J. M. T.'s translation].

6. See E. Tugendhat, *Selbstbewusstsein und Selbstbestimmung: Sprachanalytische Interpretationen* (Frankfurt: Suhrkamp, 1979), 62; see also D. Henrich, "La découverte de Fichte," *Revue de métaphysique et de morale* (1967): 154–169.

7. See C. Menke, *Die Souveränität der Kunst* (Frankfurt: Athenäum, 1988; Suhrkamp, 1991).

8. G. Lukács, *Theory of the Novel*, trans. A. Bostock (Cambridge, Mass.: MIT Press, 1971), 57. See also R. Rochlitz, *Le jeune Lukács* (Paris: Payot, 1983).

9. This is the origin of Benjamin's concept of resemblance, which he will still be using in 1939 in reference to Baudelaire, when he defines the beautiful as "the object of experience in the state of resemblance" (*Illuminations,* 199).

10. This text and *The Origin of German Tragic Drama,* "The Work of Art in the Age of Mechanical Reproduction," "On Some Motifs in Baudelaire," and "Theses on the Philosophy of History" must be considered among Benjamin's key works.

11. In fact, the journal never appeared: The publisher who had requested it went bankrupt.

12. As an example of the mythic ambiguity of the law, Benjamin cites the well-known claim by Anatole France that "poor and rich are equally forbidden to spend the night under the bridges" (*Reflections,* 296). Inasmuch as Benjamin links the normative dimension of the law to the factual dimension of injustice that results from its application, he can situate justice only in the transcendent and ungroundable sphere of "divine violence."

13. For an analogous and equally problematic ethical model in the work of the young Lukács (*On Poorness of Spirit*), see my book *Le jeune Lukács,* 125–139.

14. J. Habermas, "Consciousness-Raising or Redemptive Criticism: Walter Benjamin's Contemporaneity," *New German Critique* 17 (Spring 1979): 40.

15. See A. Danto, *The Transfiguration of the Commonplace: A Philosophy of Art* (Cambridge, Mass.: Harvard University Press, 1981).

16. See R. Bubner, "De quelques conditions devant être remplies par une esthétique contemporaine," trans. R. Rochlitz, in R. Rochlitz, ed., *Théories esthétiques après Adorno* (Arles: Actes Sud, 1990), 83ff.

17. I. Kant, *Verkündigung des nahen Abschlusses eines Traktats zum ewigen Frieden in der Philosophie.* In *Werke.* (Frankfurt: Suhrkamp, 1968), 408–409 [J. M. T.'s translation].

18. See Bubner, "Quelques conditions," 87.

19. In 1937, Benjamin published a French translation of a fragment of his essay on Goethe under the title "L'angoisse mythique chez Goethe" (Mythic anxiety in Goethe), trans. P. Klossowski, *Cahiers du Sud* (1937): 194.

20. "Clear the land where only madness has until now grown in abundance. Advance with the sharpened ax of reason, looking neither right nor left, so as not to succumb to the horror that, deep in the virgin forest, seeks to seduce you. All the earth must one day be cleared by reason, stripped of the brush of delirium and myth. That is we what we wish to do here for the fallow land of the nineteenth century" (*G.S.,* 5:579). It is nevertheless *reason*—an incorruptible lucidity, a sobriety that resists all seduction—that he invokes, raising the question of beauty in relation to *Elective Affinities:* "To confront it, we need a courage which, from the safety of indestructible reason, can abandon itself to its prodigious, magical beauty" (*G.S.,* 1:180).

21. For theological reasons: "For it is not a work made by the hand of man but the work of the Creator himself" (*G.S.*, 5:60).

22. When T. W. Adorno affirms in his *Aesthetic Theory,* trans. C. Lehnhardt (London and New York: Routledge & Kegan Paul, 1984), that the "redemption of appearance" is "central to aesthetics" (157, translation modified), he starts from the same theological idea as does Benjamin, whose intuitions he is translating.

23. G. W. F. Hegel, *Aesthetics: Lectures on Fine Art,* trans. T. M. Knox (Oxford: Clarendon Press, 1975).

24. "Tragic poetry is opposed to epic poetry as a tendentious re-shaping of tradition" (*Origin,* 106).

25. D. Diderot, *De la poésie dramatique,* in *Oeuvres esthétiques,* ed. P. Vernière (Paris: Garnier, 1968), 252 [J. M. T.'s translation].

26. See F. C. Rang, *Historische Psychologie des Karnevals* (Berlin: Brinkmann & Bose, 1983).

27. Cf. C. Schmitt, *Political Theology: Four Chapters on the Concept of Sovereignty,* trans. G. Schwab (Cambridge, Mass.: MIT Press, 1985).

28. Max Weber is not cited in *The Origin of German Tragic Drama,* but a text that its publishers date from 1921, entitled "Capitalism as Religion" (*G.S.*, 6:100ff.), shows that Benjamin had read Weber's writings on the sociology of religion. According to Benjamin, capitalism is not simply, "as Weber thinks," a structure conditioned by religion (i.e., Protestantism) but "an essentially religious phenomenon." It is a religion without dogma, reduced to ritual pure and simple, which universalizes guilt by extending it to God, thus plunging the world into despair. Benjamin cites Nietzsche (and his theory of the overman), Freud (and the "capitalization" of the repressed), and Marx (and the capitalization of debt) as thinkers of capitalist religion, a religion from which any idea of conversion and purification has been eliminated; hence the idea of vanquishing capitalism through a critique of its mythic religion, which is compared to "primitive paganism" (6:103) and is characterized as being of a purely "practical" orientation and devoid of all "moral," "higher" interest.

29. M. Weber, *The Protestant Ethic and the Spirit of Capitalism,* trans. T. Parsons (New York: Charles Scribner's Sons; London: Georg Allen & Unwin, 1952), 181.

30. Ibid., 85.

31. Ibid., 80.

32. See H. Lausberg, *Elemente der literarischen Rhetorik* (Munich: Max Hueber, 1963), 139.

33. Ibid., 140–141 [J. M. T.'s translation].

34. D. Diderot, *Essais sur la peinture,* in *Oeuvres esthétiques,* 712 [J. M. T.'s translation].

35. Nietzsche, however, links the Dionysian to a particular "intoxication" that is foreign to Benjaminian allegory but that will return in the "intoxication" and

"profane illumination" that are the watchwords of Benjamin's second aesthetics; see F. Nietzsche, *The Birth of Tragedy*, trans. W. Kaufmann (New York: Vintage Books, 1967), 40.

36. See A. Wellmer, "Dialectique de la modernité et de la postmodernité," trans. M. Lhomme and A. Lhomme, *Les Cahiers de Philosophie* 5 (Spring 1988): 120.

37. These themes are developed by J. Derrida in *De la grammatologie* (Paris: Minuit, 1967), but from a perspective that claims to be atheological.

38. Two references were probably seminal for Benjamin as he was drafting *The Origin of German Tragic Drama*: Rosenzweig's *The Star of Redemption* and Lukács's *Theory of the Novel* (which he does not cite, although he does quote *Soul and Form*); in his correspondence, he also invokes *History and Class Consciousness,* which he discovered as he was completing *The Origin of German Tragic Drama.* Benjamin's "theological" perspective is so close to that of the *Theory of the Novel* that the work on tragic drama could be read as a development of the theory of Shakespearean drama that is merely outlined in Lukács's book.

39. As Scholem has shown, Benjamin attributed Satanic qualities to himself (see G. Scholem, "Walter Benjamin and His Angel," in *On Jews and Judaism in Crisis* [New York: Schocken Books, 1976] 213ff.); Benjamin's critique of Goethe's demonism can be understood as a self-criticism.

40. "Irony, the self-surmounting of a subjectivity that has gone as far as it was possible to go, is the highest freedom that can be achieved in a world without God" (Lukács, *Theory of the Novel,* 93).

41. In a letter to Scholem (16 September 1924), written before the completion of the book, Benjamin goes so far as to suppose that the Marxist theory of the primacy of praxis over theory in Lukács's *History and Class Consciousness* approaches epistemological "principles [that] resonate for me or validate my own thinking" (*Correspondence,* 248).

42. See J. Habermas, *Moral Consciousness and Communicative Action* (Cambridge, Mass.: MIT Press, 1990), 198.

43. See Lausberg, *Elemente,* 139.

2. Art in the Service of Politics

1. See his remarks in *Origin* (53–55), where he calls the twenty years of expressionist literature a period of "decadence" (55).

2. In another text, "Traumkitsch" (Dream kitsch; probably from 1925), where we also find the first sign of Benjamin's interest in surrealism, we read the following: "What we used to call art only begins two meters from the body" (*G.S.,* 2:622).

3. This aphorism appears under the advertising rubric "For Men," which suggests a play on the word *überzeugen* (to convince). *Zeugen* means "to procreate," an activity that would thus be more "fruitful" than that of trying to convince other people.

"Procreation" is also the last word in *Einbahnstrasse,* a magic formula for a kind of Nietzschean Marxism: "The living being conquers the frenzy of destruction only in the intoxication of procreation" (*Reflections,* 94, translation modified).

4. "Mallarmé's [typographical experiments] . . . grew out of the inner nature of his style. . . . [Hence] the topicality of what Mallarmé, monadically, in his hermetic room, had discovered through a pre-established harmony with all the decisive events of our times in economics, technology, and public life" (*Reflections.* 77).

5. "If the elimination of the bourgeoisie is not accomplished before an almost calculable moment of technical and scientific evolution (indicated by inflation and chemical warfare), all is lost" (*G.S.,* 4:122).

6. Telepathy is also the center of the theory of language that Benjamin develops in 1933 under the name "mimetic faculty," which he links to Freud's essay on "Telepathie und Psychoanalyse" (Telepathy and psychoanalysis). See *Correspondence,* 521, letter of 30 January 1936.

7. In a 1926 essay entitled "Carl Albrecht Bernouilli, Johann Jacob Bachofen, und das Natursymbol" (*G.S.,* 3:43–45), Benjamin refers to the "great philosopher and anthropologist" Ludwig Klages, who like Benjamin was a graphologist and who was the author of *Geist als Widersacher der Seele* (Mind as the adversary of the soul). "Among the realities of 'natural mythology,' which Klages, in his research, attempts to restore to human memory, by wrenching them from a millennial oblivion, we find in the first place what he calls 'images,' real and active elements, by virtue of which a deeper world, which is discovered only in ecstasy, exerts its power through the intermediary of man, in the world of the mechanical senses. But images are souls, whether the souls of things or human souls; they are the souls of a distant past that constitutes the world, where the consciousness of primitive men, comparable to the dream consciousness of modern man, receives its perceptions" (*G.S.,* 3:44).

8. "For in the joke, too, in invective, in misunderstanding, in all cases where an action puts forth in its own image and exists, absorbing and consuming it, where nearness looks with its own eyes, the long-sought image sphere is opened, the world of universal and integral actualities, where the 'best room' is missing—the sphere, in a word, in which political materialism and physical nature share the inner man, the psyche, the individual, or whatever else we wish to throw to them, with dialectical justice, so that no limb remains unrent. Nevertheless, indeed, precisely after such dialectical annihilation—this will be a sphere of images and, more concretely, of bodies" (*Reflections,* 191–192).

9. See G. Bataille, *La littérature et le mal,* in *Oeuvres complètes,* vol. 9 (Paris: Gallimard, 1979), 271–286.

10. This metaphor will later be found in Heidegger, in the notion of a "retreat" of Being, present in its absence.

11. See the letters of 20–25 May 1925 (*Correspondence,* 266–270) and 7 May 1940 (*Correspondence,* 628–635).

12. This interest seems to have been elicited by Werner Kraft.

13. "Karl Kraus liest Offenbach" (Karl Kraus reads Offenbach), published in *Die*

literarische Welt (20 April 1928), *G.S.*, 4:515–517; "Karl Kraus," published in the Dutch journal *i 10* (20 December 1938), *G.S.*, 2:624ff.; and "Wedekind und Kraus in der Volksbühne" (Wedekind and Kraus in the people's theater), published in *Die literarische Welt* (1 November 1929), *G.S.*, 4:551–554).

14. All Benjamin's writings and notes on Kafka can be found in the *Gesammelte Schriften*. In addition to the long 1934 essay (*G.S.*, 2:409–438), see also the 1931 essay "Franz Kafka: Beim Bau der Chinesischen Mauer" (Franz Kafka: On the construction of the wall of China; *G.S.*, 2:675–683) and the notes and reflections (*G.S.*, 2:1190–1264). The majority of these texts, as well as excerpts from the correspondence with Scholem, W. Kraft, and Adorno, have been brought together in H. Schweppenhauser, ed., *Benjamin über Kafka: Texte, Briefzeugnisse, Aufzeichungen* (Frankfurt: Suhrkamp, 1981).

15. "It was therefore Loos's first concern to separate the work of art from the article of use, as it was that of Kraus to keep apart information and the work of art. The hack journalist is in his heart at one with the ornamentalist" (*Reflections*, 241).

16. See, in addition to *The Origin of German Tragic Drama*, "Karl Kraus," "the origin is the goal" (*Reflections*, 265, translation modified), a quotation from Kraus that is also used as an epigraph for the fourteenth thesis of "Theses on the Philosophy of History," and " 'origin'—the phenomenon's seal of authenticity" (*Reflections*, 266, translation modified).

17. See T. W. Adorno, *Jargon der Eigentlichkeit* (Frankfurt: Suhrkamp, 1964), 8.

18. Yet Kraus does disappoint Benjamin in 1934 in his "capitulation to Austro-fascism" (*Correspondence*, 458, letter of 27 September 1934), a fall that Benjamin attributes to the triumph in Kraus of the demon over the inhuman angel, and which signifies the loss of his authority. That is not the only explanation possible for this lapse. Inasmuch as no judgment is infallible, the distinction between opinion and judgment is problematic. It is the claim to infallibility that links thinkers as diverse as Kraus, Benjamin, and Heidegger in the cult of authenticity.

19. That "the age has not been able to find a new social order to correspond to its own technological horizons" (*G.S.*, 5:1257) will be one of the guiding ideas for the work on *Paris Arcades*.

20. "The not insubstantial importance to me of Kafka's work resides not least in the fact that he doesn't take up *any* of the positions communism is right to be fighting" (*Correspondence*. 440, letter of 6 May 1934).

21. See the letter from Scholem to Benjamin on 14 August 1934: "Too many quotations and too little interpretation," in W. Benjamin and G. Scholem, *Briefwechsel 1933–1940* (Frankfurt: Suhrkamp, 1980), 169.

22. Ibid., 175.

23. The figure of the "little hunchback" also appears at the end of *Berliner Kindheit*.

24. "Art in its beginnings still leaves over something mysterious, a secret foreboding and a kind of longing, because its creations have not completely set forth their full content for imaginative vision. But if the perfect content has been perfectly

revealed in artistic shapes, then the more far-seeing spirit rejects this objective manifestation and turns back into its inner self. This is the case in our own time. We may well hope that art will always rise higher and come to perfection, but the form of art has ceased to be the supreme need of the spirit. No matter how excellent we find the statues of the Greek gods, no matter how we see God the Father, Christ, and Mary so estimably and perfectly portrayed: it is no help; we bow the knee no longer" (G. W. F. Hegel, *Aesthetics: Lectures on Fine Art,* trans. T. M. Knox [Oxford: Clarendon Press, 1975], 1:103).

25. M. Weber, "Science as a Vocation," in *From Max Weber: Essays in Sociology,* ed. and trans. H. H. Gerth and C. Wright Mills (New York: Oxford University Press, 1946), 155.

26. Although it did not play a comparable theoretical role, the term had already appeared in 1930, especially in texts involving experiments with hashish. Opposing the theosophical conception of the aura in particular, Benjamin wrote: "1) The authentic aura is manifested in every thing, and not only in determinate things as people imagine; 2) the aura absolutely changes altogether with every movement of the object of which it is the aura; 3) the authentic aura cannot be imagined in any way as the magic of spiritualist light rays that the books on vulgar mysticism describe. What characterizes the authentic aura is rather: the ornament, an orna-mental circle in which the thing or being is solidly enclosed as in a container. Nothing, perhaps, gives such an accurate idea of the true aura as the late paintings of Van Gogh where—this is how one could describe these paintings—the aura of every thing is painted along with the things" (*G.S.,* 6:588). This conception of the "authentic aura" could be linked to observations about the halo and the oval form of old photographic portraits. See M. Stoessel, *Aura: Das vergessene Menschliche* (Munich: Hanser, 1983).

27. See J.-M. Schaeffer, *L'image précaire: Du dispositif photographique* (Paris: Seuil, 1987), 81.

28. In the early versions of the text, this analogy between primitive society and modern society is explained through the different stages of the confrontation between technology and nature: technology blending with ritual in the first phase to dominate primitive nature, and emancipated technology confronting a second nature, society, that escapes human control; see *G.S.,* 1:444.

29. N. Goodman, *Languages of Art: An Approach to a Theory of Symbols* (Indianapolis & New York: Bobbs-Merrill, 1968), 112.

30. Ibid., 116.

31. A. Danto, *The Transfiguration of the Commonplace: A Philosophy of Art* (Cam-bridge, Mass.: Harvard University Press, 1981), 135.

32. In *La chambre claire* (Gallimard, 1980), Roland Barthes formulates an idea similar to this conception of the aura: Between the general features drawn from semiology and the idiosyncratic pleasure that I take, he too abandons the notion of an art that can be evaluated according to *shared* criteria. For him, the aura is the *punctum* of an image that touches me for reasons that are mine alone.

33. See J. Habermas, "Consciousness-Raising or Redemptive Criticism: Walter Benjamin's Contemporaneity," *New German Critique* 17 (Spring 1979): 52–54.

34. That is why Adorno—who also has no concept of the "autonomy" of aesthetic validity in relation to cognitive, instrumental, utilitarian, or ethical functions (the autonomy of art in relation to society is virtually meaningless)—attempts in his *Aesthetic Theory* to redeem aesthetic "appearance," a project that for him is the *central* problem of contemporary aesthetics itself.

35. [This French edition brings together all Benjamin's writings relating to the *Paris Arcades* project. It has no exact equivalent in English.—J. M. T.]

3. The Price of Modernity

1. See the contributions of B. Lindner, B. Witte, and H. T. Lehmann in H. Wismann, ed., *Walter Benjamin et Paris* (Paris: Cerf, 1986).

2. For certain of these texts, there are in fact versions in verse; see *G.S.*, 7:705–714.

3. See S. Mosès, "L'idée d'origine chez Walter Benjamin," in Wismann, ed., *Walter Benjamin et Paris,* 809–826.

4. Ibid., 812 [J. M. T.'s translation].

5. G. Scholem, *Walter Benjamin: The Story of a Friendship,* trans. H. Zohn (New York: Schocken Books, 1981), 201–202.

6. "Television, the record player, etc., make all these things problematic. Quintessence: we didn't ask for so many precisions. Why is that? Because we have fears founded on the discovery that it is all going to be disavowed: description by television, the words of the hero by the phonograph, the morality of the story by the next statistic, the person of the storyteller by everything we learn about him.—The idiocy of death. Well, then, storytelling is also idiocy. Thus, *to begin with,* will the whole aura of consolation, wisdom, and solemnity that we have placed around death disappear? *So much the better.* Don't cry. The absurdity of any critical prognosis. Film in the place of storytelling. Nuance, the source of eternal life (*G.S.,* 2:1281).

7. The 1933 essay "Erfahrung und Armut" (Experience and Poverty) celebrated the loss of this same experience in the name of a new "positive barbarism."

8. H. G. Gadamer, *Truth and Method,* trans. J. Weinsheimer and D. G. Marshall, 2nd rev. ed. (New York: Continuum, 1994), "The Rehabilitation of Authority and Tradition," 281.

9. "The *apache* abandons all virtues and all laws. He voids once and for all the social contract. He believes that in so doing a world separates him from the bourgeois, and does not see on the face of that bourgeois the features of his accomplice" (*G.S.*, 1:582).

10. Similarly, we might suggest that Georges Bataille defends the condemnable

character of "modern passions," which he does not wish the public at large to accept in any way.

11. In a letter to Scholem on 20 May 1935, Benjamin defines the *Paris Arcades* project as a whole as the "unfolding of a handed-down concept . . . the fetish character of commodities" (*Correspondence,* 482).

12. "The motif of the *perte d'aureole* (loss of the aura or halo) is to be brought out as a decisive contrast to the motifs of *Jugendstil*" ("Central Park," 34).

13. The conceptual couple aura/reproduction obeys the logic of the "supplement," substitution of a deficiency, whose principle Derrida deduced from Rousseau. But this logic is not ineluctable except inasmuch as one confuses rationalization with a pathological process entailing the destruction of traditional substance. But rationalized "society" is not unavoidably more pathogenic than is traditional society, inasmuch as it succeeds in replacing the "vertical" principle of authority with a "horizontal" principle that preserves the transmission of experience.

14. P. Bürger, *Theory of the Avant-Garde,* trans. Michael Shaw (Minneapolis: University of Minnesota Press, 1984).

15. A. Wellmer, "Vérité—apparence—réconciliation: Adorno et le sauvetage esthétique de la modernité," in R. Rochlitz, ed., *Théories esthétiques après Adorno* (Arles: Actes Sud, 1990), 283. In his book *Prosa der Moderne* (Frankfurt: Suhrkamp, 1988), Bürger moves closer to Adornian aesthetics and recent French aesthetics.

16. See, in particular, the work of G. Deleuze; in J.-F. Lyotard's works, the influence of Adorno and Benjamin can be felt, though it gives way to a nonrationalist interpretation of the Kantian aesthetics of the sublime. In contrast, L. Ferry, like Deleuze (to whom he pays tribute), understands the avant-garde as essentially Nietzschean; see his *Homo Aestheticus: L'invention du goût à l'âge démocratique* (Paris: Grasset, 1990) "Nietzsche can be considered the true thinker of avant-gardism," 212.

17. See F. Nietzsche, *Beyond Good and Evil,* in *Basic Writings of Nietzsche,* trans. W. Kaufmann (New York: Modern Library, 1968).

18. See Ferry, *Homo Aestheticus,* 243ff.

19. Ibid., 304, where the author refers to Adorno to interpret Schoenbergian "dissonance" along Nietzschean lines.

20. See J. Habermas, *Moral Consciousness and Communicative Action* (Cambridge, Mass.: MIT Press, 1990) 18.

21. Such is the idea defended by C. Imbert, for example, in his important essay, "Le Présent et l'histoire," in Wismann, ed., *Walter Benjamin et Paris,* 743–792, esp. 776–779. It is hardly probable, however, that the concept of allegory was *replaced* by that of dialectical image; in fact, according to Benjamin, the commodity and the prostitute are dialectical images as such, independent of any allegorical *figuration,* by virtue of the ambiguity inherent to them.

22. As does, for example, Bürger in *Theory of the Avant-Garde,* who links "montage," the formal principle of the avant-garde, to the technique of allegory.

23. See, for example, H. Meschonnic, "L'Allégorie chez Walter Benjamin, une aventure juive," in Wismann, ed., *Walter Benjamin et Paris*, 707ff., esp. 716.

24. Bürger, *Theory of the Avant-Garde*, 70.

25. W. Menninghaus underscores this point in *Walter Benjamins Theorie der Sprach-magie* (Frankfurt: Suhrkamp, 1986), 142.

26. See J. Habermas, "Modernity—an Incomplete Project," in H. Foster, ed., *The Anti-Aesthetic: Essays on Postmodern Culture* (Port Townsend, Wash.: Bay Press, 1983), 3–15.

27. T. W. Adorno, *Aesthetic Theory*, trans. C. Lehnhardt (London & New York: Routledge & Kegan Paul, 1984), 34.

NOTES TO CHAPTER III

1. We find, for example, elements of Theses 6, 14, 16, and 17 in "Eduard Fuchs, Collector and Historian."

2. Benjamin is thinking in particular of the German–Soviet pact of 28 September 1939, which deeply disturbed him.

3. [The author cites the uncompleted French version of Benjamin's essay whenever possible. I have retained his reference to the French edition and have translated sections from it (including variants) that do not appear in the English edition—J. M. T.]

4. Cf. A. Danto, *Analytic Philosophy of History* (New York: Cambridge University Press, 1965). Danto also evokes (critically) the figure of the "ideal chronicler."

5. For the tension between a narrative history constitutive of identities and the imperative for objectivity, see P. Ricoeur, *Temps et récit* (Paris: Seuil, 1985), vols. 2 and 3.

6. Cf. *E.F.*, 350: "The idea of prose intersects the messianic idea of universal history. Cf. in 'The Storyteller': the different kinds of artistic prose form something like the ghost of historical prose."

7. The passage from Lotze is taken from his book *Mikrokosmos* (Leipzig: Hirzel, 1864), vol. 3.

8. Benjamin's observation concerning his own generation appears only in the French version.

9. "I paint the capitalist and the landlord in no sense *couleur de rose*. But here individuals are dealt with only in so far as they are the personifications of economic categories, embodiments of particular class-relations and class-inter-ests. My standpoint, from which the evolution of the economic formation of society is viewed as a process of natural history, can less than any other make the individual responsible for relations whose creature he socially remains, however much he may subjectively raise himself above them." K. Marx, *Capital*, preface

to the first German edition, in *The Marx–Engels Reader,* 2d ed., ed. R. C. Tucker (New York: Norton, 1978), 297.

10. Cf. *G.S.,* 1:1231, ms. 1100: "Marx says that revolutions are the locomotive of universal history. But perhaps they are something completely different. Perhaps revolutions are humanity's effort, as it takes a train trip, to pull the emergency brake." See also *G.S.,* 1:1232, ms. 1103.

11. Cf. R. Tiedemann, "Historischer Materialismus oder politischer Messianismus? Politische Gehalte in der Geschichtsphilosophie Walter Benjamins," in P. Bulthaup, ed., *Materialien zu Benjamins Thesen "Über den Begriff der Geschichte": Beiträge und Interpretationen* (Frankfurt: Suhrkamp, 1975), 108.

12. Cf. the prudent reflections of C. Kambas, "Actualité politique: Le concept d'histoire chez Benjamin et l'échec du Front populaire," in H. Wismann, ed., *Walter Benjamin et Paris* (Paris: Cerf, 1986), 249–272.

13. See Tiedemann, "Historischer materialismus," 102.

14. See P. Ivernel, "Paris capitale du Front populaire ou la vie posthume du XIXe siècle," in H. Wismann, ed., *Walter Benjamin et Paris,* 249–272.

15. See J. Habermas, "Geschichte und Evolution," in *Zur Rekonstruktion des Historischen materialismus* (Frankfurt: Suhrkamp, 1976).

16. See J. Habermas, "Consciousness-Raising or Redemptive Criticism: Walter Benjamin's Contemporaneity," *New German Critique* 17 (Spring 1979).

17. M. Foucault, *Les mots et les choses* (Paris: Gallimard, 1966), 329–346 [J. M. T.'s translation].

18. See J. Habermas, *The Philosophical Discourse of Modernity: Twelve Lectures,* trans. F. Lawrence (Cambridge, Mass.: MIT Press, 1987).

19. In his book on Kierkegaard, Adorno had already used the concept of dialectical image, referring to Benjamin's thought and particularly to his concept of allegory; see also "N" 2, 7, pp. 48–49.

20. Habermas, *Philosophical Discourse of Modernity,* 11–16.

21. F. Nietzsche, *The Use and Abuse of History* (Indianapolis & New York: Bobbs-Merrill, 1957), 20–21, 40.

22. The first line of this quotation repeats a sentence in the essay on Eduard Fuchs.

23. Basing his work on Jean Piaget and on certain texts in the dialectical tradition, L. Goldmann in particular has elaborated a method of this kind. See, for example, "Le tout et les parties," in *Le dieu caché* (Paris: Gallimard, 1959), 13–31.

24. See *Devant l'histoire: Les documents de la controverse sur la singularité de l'extermination des Juifs par le régime nazi* (Paris: Cerf, 1988).

25. Many thinkers inspired by Nietzsche and Heidegger defend such an "an-archistic" theory. In fact, in the case of both Foucault and Adorno, it is not incompatible with reformist political interventions.

26. See P. Ricoeur, *Soi-même comme un autre* (Paris: Seuil, 1990), 193ff.

27. See Habermas, *Philosophical Discourse of Modernity,* 11–16.

28. See Tiedemann, "Historischer Materialismus," 87.

29. Habermas, *Philosophical Discourse of Modernity,* 14–15; cf. J.-M. Ferry, *Les puissances de l'expérience,* vol. 2, *Les ordres de la reconnaissance* (Paris: Cerf, 1991), 217ff.

30. J. Habermas, "Geschichtsbewufstsein und posttraditionale Identität," in *Eine Arts/Schadensabwicklung,* (Frankfurt: Suhrkamp, 1987), 168f.

31. On this point, M. Foucault's analyses in *Surveiller et punir* (Paris: Gallimard, 1975) remain valuable.

32. J. Rawls, *A Theory of Justice* (Cambridge, Mass.: Belknap Press of the Harvard University Press, 1971), 60.

✳

Bibliography

1. CHRONOLOGICAL LIST
OF WALTER BENJAMIN'S PRINCIPAL WORKS

The texts are listed in order by the year of completion. The original title, date of original publication if during Benjamin's lifetime, volume of the *Gesammelte Schriften* (Frankfurt: Suhrkamp, 1972–1989; 2nd ed. 1991), and the location of the English translation are given in square brackets.

Abbreviations

Begriff: Der Begriff der Kunstkritik in der deutschen Romantik. In *Gesammelte Schriften,* Vol. 1.

"Central Park": "Central Park," *New German Critique* 34 (Winter 1985): 32–58.

Correspondence: The Correspondence of Walter Benjamin, 1910–1940. Ed. G. Scholem and T. Adorno. Trans. M. R. Jacobson and E. M. Jacobson. Chicago and London: University of Chicago Press, 1994.

"Curriculum vitae": "Curriculum vitae." In *Ecrits autobiographiques,* trans. C. Jouanlanne and J.-F. Poirier. Paris: Christian Bourgois, 1990.

E.F.: Ecrits Français. Ed. J.-M. Monnoyer. Paris: Gallimard, 1991.

"Goethe": "Goethes *Wahlverwandtschaften.*" In *Gesammelte Schriften,* Vol. 1.

G.S.: Gesammelte Schriften. Frankfurt: Suhrkamp, 1972–1989; 2nd ed. 1991.

Illuminations: Illuminations. Ed. Hannah Arendt. Trans. Harry Zohn. New York: Schocken Books, 1968.

"N": "N [Re the Theory of Knowledge, Theory of Progress]." In *Benjamin: Philosophy, Aesthetics, History,* ed. G. Smith. Chicago and London: University of Chicago Press, 1989, 43–83.

Origin: The Origin of German Tragic Drama. Trans. John Osborne. London: New Left Books, 1977.

"Photography": "A Small History of Photography." In *One-Way Street and Other Writings,* trans. Edmund Jephcott and Kingsley Shorter. London: New Left Books, 1979, 240–257.

"Program": "On the Program of the Coming Philosophy." Trans. Mark Ritter. In *Benjamin: Philosophy, Aesthetics, History*, ed. G. Smith. Chicago and London: University of Chicago Press, 1989, 1–12.

Reflections: Reflections: Essays, Aphorisms, Autobiographical Writings. Ed. Peter Demetz. Trans. Edmund Jephcott. New York and London: Harcourt Brace Jovanovich, 1978.

1915

["Zwei Gedichte von Friedrich Hölderlin," 2:105].

1916

["Trauerspiel und Tragödie," 2:133].

["Die Bedeutung der Sprache in Trauerspiel und Tragödie," 2:137].

"On Language as Such and on the Language of Man" ["Über Sprache überhaupt und über die Sprache des Menschen," 2:140; *Reflections*, 314–332].

1917

["*Der Idiot* von Dostojewskij," 2:237].

1918

"On the Program of the Coming Philosophy" ["Über das Programm der kommenden Philosophie," 2:157; *Benjamin: Philosophy, Aesthetics, History*, ed. G. Smith. Chicago and London: University of Chicago Press, 1989, 1–12].

1919

[*Der Begriff der Kunstkritik in der deutschen Romantik*, 1920, 1:7].

"Fate and Character" ["Schicksal und Charakter," 1921, 2:171; *Reflections*, 304–311].

1921

"Critique of Violence" ["Zur Kritik der Gewalt," 1921, 2:179; *Reflections*, 277–300].

"The Task of the Translator" ["Die Aufgabe des Übersetzers," 1923, 4:9; *Illuminations*, 69–82].

"Theologico-Political Fragment" ["Theologisch-politisches Fragment," 2:203; *Reflections*, 312–313].

1922

["Goethes *Wahlverwandtschaften*," 1924–1925, 1:123].

1925

The Origin of German Tragic Drama [*Ursprung des deutschen Trauerspiels*, 1928, 1:203; *Origin*].

1926
[*Einbahnstrasse,* 1928, 4:83; partial translation as "One-Way Street" in *Reflections,* 61–94].

1927
Moscow Diary [*Moskauer Tagebuch,* 6:292; ed. G. Smith, trans. Richard Sieburth, Cambridge, Mass.: Harvard University Press, 1986].
[*Passagen,* 5:1041].

1929
"Surrealism" ["Der Sürrealismus," 1929, 2:295; *Reflections,* 177–192].
"The Image of Proust" ["Zum Bilde Prousts," 1929, 2:310; *Illuminations,* 201–215].
["Die Wiederkehr des Flaneurs," 1929, 3:194].

1930
[*Pariser Passagen I,* 5:991].

1931
"Karl Kraus" ["Karl Kraus," 1931, 2:334; *Reflections,* 239–273].
"A Small History of Photography" ["Kleine Geschichte der Photographie," 1931, 2:368; *One-Way Street and Other Writings,* trans. Edmund Jephcott and Kingsley Shorter, London: New Left Books, 1979, 240–257].
"The Destructive Character" ["Der destruktive Charakter," 1931, 4:396; *Reflections,* 301–303].

1932
"Hashish in Marseilles" ["Haschisch in Marseille," 1932, 4:409; *Reflections,* 137–145].
"A Berlin Chronicle" ["Berliner Chronik," 6:465; *Reflections,* 3–60].

1933
["Lehre vom Ähnlichen," 2:204].
"On the Mimetic Faculty" ["Über das mimetische Vermögen," 2:210; *Reflections,* 333–336].
["Erfahrung und Armut," 2:213].

1934
["Zum gegenwärtigen gesellschaftlichen Standort des französischen Schriftstellers," 1934, 2:776].
"The Author as Producer" ["Der Autor als Produzent," 2:683; *Reflections,* 220–238].
[*Berliner Kindheit um Neunzehnhundert* (fragments), 1932–1938, 4:235; 7:385 (final version of 1938)].

"Franz Kafka" ["Franz Kafka," 1934 (partial text), 2:409 (complete text); *Illumina-tions*, 111–140].

1935

["Probleme der Sprachsoziologie," 1935, 3:452].

["Johann Jakob Bachofen," 2:219].

"Paris, Capital of the Nineteenth Century" ["Paris, die Hauptstadt des XIX. Jahrhunderts" (Exposé 1), 5:45; *Reflections*, 146–162].

"The Work of Art in the Age of Mechanical Reproduction" (first version) ["Das Kunstwerk im Zeitalter seiner technischen Reproduzierbarkeit," 1936 (French version by Pierre Klossowski and the author); 1:431; 7:350 (second German version); 1:709 (French version); 1:471 (third German version of 1939); *Illuminations*, 217–251].

1936

"The Storyteller" ["Der Erzähler," 1936, 2:709 (German text); 3:1290 (Benjamin's French translation); *Illuminations*, 83–109].

["Pariser Brief II. Malerei und Photographie," 3:495].

["Deutsche Menschen," 1936, 4:149].

1937

"Eduard Fuchs, Collector and Historian" ["Eduard Fuchs, der Sammler und der Historiker," 1937, 2:465; *One-Way Street and Other Writings*, trans. Edmund Jephcott and Kingsley Shorter, London: New Left Books, 1979, 349–386].

1938

"The Paris of the Second Empire in Baudelaire" ["Das Paris des Second Empire bei Baudelaire," 2:511; *Charles Baudelaire: A Lyric Poet in the Era of High Capitalism*, trans. Harry Zohn, London: New Left Books, 1973].

1939

"Central Park" ["Zentralpark," 1:655, trans. Lloyd Spencer, with Mark Harrington, *New German Critique* 34 (Winter 1985: 32–58)].

["Paris, die Hauptstadt des XIX. Jahrhunderts" (Exposé 2), 6:60].

"On Some Motifs in Baudelaire" ["Über einige Motive bei Baudelaire," 1940 (dated 1939), 1:605; *Illuminations*, 155–200].

[" 'Die Rückschritte der Poesie' von Carl Gustav Jochmann," 1939, 2:572].

1940

"Theses on the Philosophy of History" ["Über den Begriff der Geschichte," 1:691; *Illuminations*, 254–264].

[*Passagen-Werk 1928–1940*, 5:79; partial translation as "N [Re the Theory of Progress, Theory of Knowledge]," in *Benjamin: Philosophy, Aesthetics, History*, ed. G. Smith, Chicago and London: University of Chicago Press, 1989, 43–83].

2. CORRESPONDENCE, BIOGRAPHY, BIBLIOGRAPHY

Adorno, T. W. "Erinnerungen." In *Über Walter Benjamin,* ed. R. Tiedemann. Frankfurt: Suhrkamp, 1979; rev. ed. 1990.

Benjamin, W. *Briefe an Siegfried Kracauer.* Ed. R. Tiedemann and H. Lonitz. Marbach am Neckar: T. W. Adorno Archive, 1987.

———. *The Correspondence of Walter Benjamin, 1910–1940.* Ed. Gershom Scholem and Theodor Adorno. Trans. Manfred R. Jacobson and Evelyn M. Jacobson. Chicago and London: University of Chicago Press, 1994.

Benjamin, W., and G. Scholem. *Briefwechsel 1933–1940.* Frankfurt: Suhrkamp, 1980.

Brodersen, M. *Spinne im eigenen Netz: Walter Benjamin, Leben und Werk.* Bühl-Moos: Elster Verlag, 1990.

———. *Walter Benjamin. Bibliografia critica generale (1913–1983).* Palermo: Centro internazionale studi di estetica, 1984.

Fuld, W. *Walter Benjamin: Zwischen den Stühlen. Eine Biographie.* Munich and Vienna: Hanser, 1979; Frankfurt: Fischer, 1981.

Scholem, G. *Walter Benjamin: The History of a Friendship.* London: Faber & Faber, 1982.

Tiedemann, R., C. Godde, and H. Lonitz. "Walter Benjamin, 1892–1940." *Marbacher Magazin* 55 (1990).

Witte, B. *Walter Benjamin.* Reinbeck: Rowohlt, 1985 [*Walter Benjamin: Une biographie,* trans. A. Bernold. Paris: Cerf, 1988 (Expanded French translation)].

3. SELECTED CRITICAL STUDIES

For a complete list of French publications on Benjamin, see especially the bibliographies established by M. B. de Launay in *Revue d'Esthéthique,* the issue entitled *Walter Benjamin* (1981, repr. 1990), 201; and M. Sagnol, in H. Wismann, ed., *Walter Benjamin et Paris* (Paris: Cerf, 1936), 991–997. For a general bibliography see M. Brodersen, cited above.

Adorno, T. W. *Über Walter Benjamin.* Frankfurt: Suhrkamp, 1979; rev. ed. 1990.

———. Afterword to "Deutsche Menschen. Eine Folge von Briefen," in T. Adorno, *Über Walter Benjamin.* Frankfurt: Suhrkamp, 1979; rev. ed. 1990.

———. "Introduction to Benjamin's *Schriften.*" In G. Smith, ed., *On Walter Benjamin: Critical Essays and Recollections.* Cambridge, Mass.: MIT Press, 1988.

———. "Benjamin the Letter Writer." In G. Scholem and T. W. Adorno, eds., *The Correspondence of Walter Benjamin,* trans. M. R. Jacobson and E. M. Jacobson. Chicago and London: University of Chicago Press, 1994.

———. "A Portrait of Walter Benjamin." *Prisms,* trans. S. Weber and S. Weber. Cambridge, Mass.: MIT Press, 1992.

———. *Prisms,* trans. S. Weber and S. Weber. Cambridge, Mass.: MIT Press, 1981.

Agamben, G. *Infancy and History: The Destruction of Experience.* Trans. L. Heron. New York: Verso, 1993.

Arendt, H. "Walter Benjamin: 1892–1940." In Walter Benjamin, *Illuminations,* ed. H. Arendt, trans. H. Zohn. New York: Schocken Books, 1968.

Bensaïd, D. *Walter Benjamin: Sentinelle messianique.* Paris: Plon, 1990.

Bolz, N., and W. van Reijen. *Walter Benjamin.* Frankfurt & New York: Campus, 1991.

Bouchindhomme, C. "Walter Benjamin philosophe." *Critique* 487 (December 1987): 1064–1068.

Buci-Glucksmann, C. *La raison baroque: De Baudelaire à Benjamin.* Paris: Galilée, 1984.

Buck-Morss, S. *The Origin of Negative Dialectics: Theodor W. Adorno, Walter Benjamin, and the Frankfurt Institute.* New York: Free Press, 1977.

————. *The Dialectics of Seeing: Walter Benjamin and the Arcades Project.* Cambridge, Mass.: MIT Press, 1989.

Bulthaup, P., ed. *Materialien zu Benjamins Thesen "Über den Begriff der Geschichte": Beiträge und Interpretationen.* Frankfurt: Suhrkamp, 1975.

Bürger, P. "Der Allegoriebegriff Benjamins." In *Theorie der Avantgarde.* Frankfurt: Suhrkamp, 1974, 1980.

————. "Walter Benjamin: Contribution à une théorie de la culture contemporaine." *Revue d'Esthétique* 1 (1981; repr. 1990).

Derrida, J. "+ R (par-dessus le marché)." In *La vérité en peinture.* Paris: Flammarion, 1978, 169–209.

————. "Des tours de Babel." In J. Graham, ed., *Difference in Translation.* Ithaca & London: Cornell University Press, 1985.

Dufour-El Maleh, M.-C. *Angelus Novus: Essai sur l'oeuvre de Walter Benjamin.* Brussels: Ousia, 1990.

Garber, K. *Rezeption und Rettung: Drei Studien zu Walter Benjamin.* Tübingen: Max Niemeyer, 1987.

Habermas, J. *The Philosophical Discourse of Modernity.* Trans. F. Lawrence. Cambridge, Mass.: MIT Press, 1987.

————. "Consciousness-Raising or Redemptive Criticism: Walter Benjamin's Contemporaneity." *New German Critique* 17 (Spring 1979): 30–59.

Imbert, C. "Le présent et l'histoire." In H. Wismann, ed., *Walter Benjamin et Paris.* Paris: Cerf, 1986.

————. "Les années parisiennes de Walter Benjamin." *Esprit* 11 (1987).

Ivernel, P. "Paris capitale du Front populaire ou la vie posthume du XIXe siècle." In H. Wismann, ed., *Walter Benjamin et Paris.* Paris: Cerf, 1986.

————. "Benjamin et Brecht, ou le tournant politique de l'esthétique." In G. Raulet and J. Fürnkäs, eds., *Weimar: Le tournant esthétique.* Paris: Anthropos, 1988.

Lacoste, J. Preface to Walter Benjamin, *Sens unique.* Paris: Les Lettres Nouvelles, 1978.

————. Preface to Walter Benjamin, *Charles Baudelaire.* Paris: Payot, 1982.

Launay, M. B. de, and M. Jimenez, eds. *Walter Benjamin.* Issue of *Revue d'Esthétique* 1 (1981; repr. 1990).

Lindner, B., ed. *Walter Benjamin im Kontext.* Frankfurt: Syndikat, 1978; Königstein and Taunus: Athenäum, 1985.

———. *Walter Benjamin.* Issues of *Text und Kritik* 31–32 (1971; 1979).

Löwy, M. "L'anarchisme messianique de Walter Benjamin." *Les Temps Modernes* 447 (1983).

Menninghaus, W. *Walter Benjamins Theorie der Sprachmagie.* Frankfurt: Suhrkamp, 1980.

———. *Schwellenkunde: Walter Benjamins Passage des Mythos.* Frankfurt: Suhrkamp, 1986.

Missac, P. "L'éclat et le secret: Walter Benjamin." *Critique* 231–232 (Aug.–Sept. 1966).

———. "Walter Benjamin et l'exigence brechtienne." *Les Lettres Françaises,* 29 Oct. 1969.

———. "Walter Benjamin en France." *Allemagne aujourd'hui* (1969).

———. "Stéphane Mallarmé et Walter Benjamin." *Revue de Littérature Comparée* 43, no. 2 (1969).

———. "Du nouveau sur Walter Benjamin?" *Critique* 267–268 (Aug.–Sept. 1969).

———. "Eloge de la citation." *Change* 22 (Feb. 1975).

———. "Ce sont des thèses! Sont-ce des thèses?" *Revue d'Esthétique* (1985). Issue entitled *Adorno.*

———. "L'ange et l'automate." *Les Nouveaux Cahiers* (1975).

———. "Walter Benjamin, de la rupture au naufrage." *Critique* 395 (April 1980).

———. "Walter Benjamin à la Bibliothèque nationale." *Bulletin de la Bibliothèque Nationale* 1 (1984).

———. "Sur un nouvel avatar du flâneur." *Le Promeneur* 30 (June 1984).

———. *Passage de Walter Benjamin.* Paris: Seuil, 1987.

Mosès, S. "Walter Benjamin und Franz Rosenzweig." *Deutsche Vierteljahrsschrift für Literaturwissenschaft und Geistesgeschichte* 56 (Dec. 1982): 622–640. ("Walter Benjamin and Franz Rosenzweig." In G. Smith, ed., *Benjamin: Philosophy, Aesthetics, History* [Chicago and London: University of Chicago Press, 1989.])

———. "L'idée d'origine chez Walter Benjamin." In H. Wismann, ed., *Walter Benjamin et Paris.* Paris: Cerf, 1986.

———. "Le paradigme esthétique de l'histoire chez Walter Benjamin." In G. Raulet and J. Fürnkäs, eds., *Weimar: Le tournant esthétique.* Paris: Anthropos, 1988.

———. *L'Ange de l'Histoire: Rozenzweig, Benjamin, Scholem.* Paris: Seuil, 1992.

Perret, C. *Walter Benjamin sans destin.* Paris: La Différence, 1992.

Petitdemange, G. "Treize facettes de Walter Benjamin au fil de ses lettres." Afterword to W. Benjamin, *Correspondance.* Paris: Aubier-Montaigne, 1979.

———. "Le seuil du présent: Défi d'une pratique de l'histoire chez Walter Benjamin." *Recherches de Science Religieuse* 3 (July–Sept. 1985).

Rochlitz, R. "De la philosophie comme critique littéraire: Walter Benjamin et le jeune Lukács." *Revue d'Esthétique* 1 (1981; repr. 1990). Issue entitled *Walter Benjamin.*

———. "Walter Benjamin: Une dialectique de l'image." *Critique* 431 (April 1983).

————. "Expérience et reproductibilité technique: Walter Benjamin et la photographie." *Critique* 459 (Sept. 1985).

————. "Walter Benjamin: Esthétique de l'allégorie." *Critique* 463 (Dec. 1985).

————. "Walter Benjamin et la critique." *Critique* 475 (Dec. 1986).

————. "Benjamin écrivain: La fidélité de Pierre Missac." *Critique* 480 (May 1987).

————. "Walter Benjamin: Poétique de la traduction." *Critique* 497 (Oct. 1988).

————. "W. Benjamin: Paradoxes d'une consécration." *Critique* 515 (April 1990).

————. "Le Berlin de Benjamin." *Critique* 531–532 (Aug.–Sept. 1991). Issue entitled *Berlin n'est plus une île.*

Sagnol, M. "La méthode archéologique de Walter Benjamin." *Les Temps Modernes* 444 (July 1983).

————. "Walter Benjamin entre une théorie de l'avant-garde et une archéologie de la modernité." In G. Raulet, ed., *Weimar ou l'explosion de la modernité.* Paris: Anthropos, 1984.

————. "Théorie de l'histoire et théorie de la modernité chez Benjamin." *L'Homme et la Société* 69–70 (1983).

Scholem, G. *Walter Benjamin: The Story of a Friendship,* trans. Harry Zohn. New York: Schocken Books, 1976.

————. *On Jews and Judaism in Crisis.* Ed. W. J. Dannhauser. New York: Schocken Books, 1976.

Smith, G., ed. *Benjamin: Philosophy, Aesthetics, History.* Chicago and London: University of Chicago Press, 1989.

Stoessel, M. *Aura: Das vergessene Menschliche.* Munich: Hanser, 1983.

Szondi, P. "Hope in the Past: On Walter Benjamin." *Critical Inquiry* 4 (Spring 1978): 491–506.

————. "Die Städtebilder Walter Benjamins." *Die Monat* 14 (July 1962): 55–62.

Tiedemann, R. *Studien zur Philosophie Walter Benjamins.* Frankfurt: Suhrkamp, 1973.

————. *Dialektik im Stillstand.* Frankfurt: Suhrkamp, 1983.

Wismann, H., ed. *Walter Benjamin et Paris.* Cerf, 1986.

Wohlfarth, I. "Sur quelques motifs juifs chez Benjamin." *Revue d'Esthétique* 1 (1981; repr. 1990).

————. "Hors d'oeuvre." Preface to W. Benjamin, *Origine du drame baroque allemand.* Paris: Flammarion, 1985.

————. "L'esthétique comme préfiguration du matérialisme historique: *La théorie du roman* et *L'origine du drame baroque allemand.*" In G. Raulet and J. Fürnkäs, eds., *Weimar: Le tournant esthétique.* Paris: Anthropos, 1988.

Index

Note: The abbreviation "WB" refers to Walter Benjamin. References to notes are identified by "n." or "nn." Titles of works in French or German are alphabetized under initial articles (e.g., "Das Telephon" is under "D" and not under "T").